AF530972

AUTHENTIC VOICES
ARKANSAS CULTURE
1541–1860

AUTHENTIC VOICES

ARKANSAS CULTURE 1541–1860

Edited by

Sarah Fountain

University of Central Arkansas Press

Manufactured in the United States of America

Designer: Robert E. Lowrey
Typeface: Times Roman

LIBRARY OF CONGRESS CATALOGING IN PUBLICATION DATA
Main entry under title:

Authentic Voices: Arkansas Culture, 1541–1860
Includes Index
I. American literature-Arkansas-

I. Fountain, Sarah Jane, 1927-

ISBN-0-9615-1431-0

Table of Contents

MAPS AND ILLUSTRATIONS

FOREWORD

The colorful pageant of early Arkansas is nowhere better illuminated than in the travel accounts, letters, reminiscences and other sources which have survived from those remote times. This book brings together a representative selection of such materials beginning with the saga of the unfortunate conquistador DeSoto and extending to the threshold of the American Civil War.

Since the year 1986 marks both the tricentennial of the first permanent settlement made in Arkansas by Europeans and the sesquicentennial of our statehood, such a book could hardly be more timely. Since many of the sources used in the volume are difficult of access, being guarded as rarities in archives and libraries, much of it will have the impact of new material for many of us.

Students will find this work especially helpful, particularly in view of the perpetual dearth of good published materials on Arkansas history which are suitable for school use. The growing public awareness of our history should insure a favorable reception among a much wider circle of readers as well.

John L. Ferguson
Arkansas History Commission

INTRODUCTION

Arkansans in 1986 are holding a statewide birthday party; one hundred and fifty years ago this June, Arkansas joined the Union and became the 27th state in the United States of America. Such a birthday cannot go unnoticed and indeed it will not. There will be parades, festivals of all kinds, special programs for people of all ages, and reenactments of events which contributed so much to bringing Arkansas to this occasion. I hope that this volume will be considered a worthwhile gift at the birthday party.

States do not emerge full grown as members of the Union. Even those thirteen original states had to grow from a few seeds planted and cultivated by sturdy and courageous souls who ventured into a wilderness. Arkansas had her share of those souls whose experiences tell us a great deal about the earliest days of our state. Their letters, journals, and diaries offer a rich and vital form of literature through which we learn the feelings and thoughts, as well as the actions, of those who built the foundations upon which we reside. We will in the following pages unfold the early history of Arkansas as it is revealed in the AUTHENTIC VOICES of the people who lived that history.

The development of Arkansas did not begin in 1836 when she became a part of the Union. It began with those "natives" who first occupied this region: the Quapaws, the Caddoes, and the Osages. It was propelled by such men as DeSoto, Major William Lovely, and William Dunbar. It was examined and recorded by Timothy Flint, Thomas Nuttal, and Henry Schoolcraft. Unfortunately there is little original matter from the "natives," since they had no need for written language. However, we learn of their lives and customs in DeSoto's journal. Major Lovely, one of three Indian agents west of the Mississippi River in 1813, provides us with a glimpse of the problems they encountered as the white man moved into their territory. Dunbar's letters to Thomas Jefferson lend insight into the value of the Louisiana Purchase and Arkansas's place in that purchase. From Flint, Nuttal, and Schoolcraft we gain valuable pictures of the flora, the fauna, and the inhabitants of Arkansas County in the Missouri Territory, just before the County became the Arkansas Territory. Without these voices our early heritage would be lost to us.

When Arkansas was made a Territory in 1819, white settlers began to make the trek into the region and Arkansas culture began to develop. Travel was difficult and rewards were few. Ellen Stetson, a young woman from Massachusettes, traveled this way in 1820 with two fellow missionaries. She became lost from her companions for a period of several hours, and we can relive her frightening experiences from her journal entries. When Cephas Washburn traveled up the Arkansas River in 1819 searching for a mission location, he encountered mosquitoes, chills and fever, high water, and heavy rains. In his letters to the Foreign Mission Board, he writes graphic descriptions of these hazards and informative reports on the Cherokee Indians. The story of the Territory is also told by Hiram Whittington, who comments on the living conditions and the people he found in the Territory when he arrived here in 1827. His letters to his brother are delightful and entertaining, as well as informative. These voices, and numerous others, make life in the Territory come alive for Arkansans in the twentieth century.

The voice of Ambrose Sevier, as he writes to his friend William Woodruff, places Arkansans at the scene in Washington, D.C. where the struggle for statehood was being enacted in 1836. An account of the unprecedented session of the United States Senate, taken from the *Arlington Gazette* of June 14, 1836, gives a verbatim debate on Arkansas's admission. The molding of an infant state into a mature sovereignty lives in the voices of James Conway and John S. Roane as they address the State Legislatures.

The development of Arkansas was not just a matter for governors and other public figures. The thousands of ordinary people who lived through these early days contributed equally to the making of a state; for while important issues were decided by those in the public forum, the equally important issues of daily living were decided and executed by those tilling the soil, making the bread, educating the young, and healing the sick. The vagaries of farming are detailed as men write to family and acquaintances back East of droughts and floods and the prices of corn and cotton and livestock. The difficulties of shopping are revealed by Matilda Fulton as she sends a shopping list to her husband, Senator William S. Fulton, before he leaves Washington to return to Little Rock in 1840. From James Scull we have an eyewitness account of the fatal knife fight which occurred on the floor of the Arkansas House of Representatives in 1837. Miss Sophia Sawyer, in letters to David Green in Boston, discusses problems of education as she writes of her Female Seminary in Fayetteville in 1841. Who is better qualified to narrate these stories than the ones who lived them? Because they speak for themselves in their own unique styles and from their own points of view, we share their joys, their pains, their disappointments, and their hopes. Indeed we share the experiences of daily life in these long ago days.

Compiling the materials for this volume has been exciting and has done much for our pride in Arkansas. To learn that Stephen F. Austin ran for the first Territorial Legislature and that Sam Houston met with some of his friends in Washington, Arkansas, to plan the Texas Revolution gave us a sense of smugness for contributing to Texas history before there WAS a Texas. And to learn that Sir Henry Morton Stanley resided for a time in Arkansas long before he found Dr. Livingston in Africa gave us a sense of being of the world while savouring our sense of provincialism. The greatest excitement, however, came with reading the personal accounts of the many people who were Arkansas.

Materials for such a volume as this abound in our state. Arkansas Collections at nearly every institution of higher learning contain valuable archives. Historical societies in nearly every county are active in the collecting and publishing of interesting articles. There is a veritable gold mine housed in the Arkansas History Commission collections, and the attics of many homes surely have packed away in trunks and boxes materials of interest. Indeed, the problem lies not in availability, but in accessibility. The materials are widely scattered and are frequently locked in cases in the interest of preservation. The purpose of this volume is to gather only a portion of these materials within one cover so that Arkansans might have an opportunity to enjoy some of their heritage.

We have examined hundreds of documents in several different locales; When the files became so full that they defied lifting, we curtailed our searching and began the process of editing, which was most frustrating. Everything had an appeal which cried out to be included; however, space made it necessary to eliminate some items. In making the final selections, we tried to include items of varied interest for what we hope will be a wide and varied audience. We have attempted to include things which can be enjoyed by all Arkansans and which can be read at random as interest dictates. Once the selections were made, another frustration occurred when we attempted to edit each selection. Some items were of such length that they had to be cut, and the cutting process was often painful. Certainly the most difficult procedure of all was in the arrangement of the materials. Because the selections are so varied, continuity was a monumental problem. There is no distinct category into which an item can be conveniently "plugged"; each item has its own unique design. Therefore, the selections are grouped first according to historical period, of which there are three: Pre-territorial, Territorial, and Early Statehood. Subdivisions within the three periods are arranged loosely according to the major thrust of topics: travel, lifestyles, Indians, politics, education, etc. Since most people when writing letters or when keeping journals and diaries include several topics of interest in the same entry, a clear distinction of subject matter is impossible; therefore, the subdivisions are not clear cut. The continuity of this volume must rely upon one single thread: early Arkansans relating their own experiences, concerns, hopes, and dreams.

Achieving our purpose in this collection entailed many hours of reading raw material, much of it written in the spidery longhand of long ago. While the task was rewarding, it was also wearing. Without the dedicated assistance of Della Curran, the job of collecting would have been impossible. We are indebted to the library staff of Torreyson Library at the University of Central Arkansas for their patience and cooperation as we began our search in their Arkansas Collection. From there we moved to the Arkansas History Commission where we spent six delightful weeks of "mining." To Dr. John Ferguson, Russell Baker, Lynn Ewbank and other members of the fine staff at the History Commission, we can only say a most inadequate "thank you." They not only extended a courteous welcome to us, but they also granted us "squatter's rights" to a large work table, carried dozens of boxes of files to our table, allowed us to monopolize a microfilm reader and the copying machine, and pointed us to numerous items which we would have overlooked. After working the UCA Arkansas Collection and the History Commission, we were inundated with materials. Our search from that point focused on locating specific items at the University of Arkansas at Fayetteville and Little Rock, the Library of Congress in Washington, and the University of Oklahoma.

As is the case in most instances of research, we eventually reached the point at which our looking had to stop. The editing task had to begin. All of the copy had to be transcribed to disks and printed for closer readings. We not only had to type all the copy into the word processor, but we had to exercise utmost discipline in maintaining the spelling. For an English teacher and an English major in her last year, leaving words misspelled was particularly difficult. Being faithful to the voices, however, made it necessary to print what they wrote. The assistance of Susan Eller was invaluable during this process and is most appreciated.

Once the copy was printed, the editing began with the capable assistance of Susan and Della. Many conferences were held to make final decisions before arranging the text. As our criterion for making decisions, we tried always to consider our audience and to select those items of general interest.

To E. E. Eller fell the task of moving items from one place to another on the disks and often moving them several times as first decisions were changed. He must have felt much like the man who moves furniture while the women rearrange a room. Frequently, like that man, the items eventually returned to their original positions. His patience with the editors and his expertise in computer use deserve far more appreciation than we are capable of giving.

Without the assistance and cooperation of the administration and my colleagues at the University of Central Arkansas, this project could never have reached completion. Two committees of my peers approved my application for a research grant and the administration generously awarded me the grant to help defray expenses. They also granted me a Sabbatical Leave in the spring of 1985 to allow me time to do this work. Dr. Carl Jameson of the UCA Geography Department has offered much needed assistance in locating place names on our modern map; Dr. Ed Settgast of the UCA Department of Languages assisted in translating some of the archaic Spanish terms used by DeSoto, and Tom Dillard, UCA's Archivist, offered assistance and advice whenever it was sought. Dr. Robert Wright and the biology department of UCA helped to identify plants and fish when the names used by the writer were unfamiliar. I shall be ever grateful for their encouragement and generous assistance.

Finally, appreciation must be given to Drs. Robert Lowrey and Jeff Henderson, editors of the UCA Press, for printing this volume. All of the previous work would have been to no avail had we not gone to press eventually. They have been encouraging from the start and have offered much needed guidance in printing decisions and in marketing. And Blaize Stewart spent hours at the computer console turning the manuscript into a book.

To everyone involved, and they certainly include my family which has kept me going when the task mushroomed to impossible levels, I am deeply grateful. I hope the final product will justify all the help received along the way.

Part One
Preterritorial Arkansas
1541—1819

The region of North America from which the state of Arkansas comes has an interesting and sometimes perplexing background. The flags of both France and Spain have flown over the vast territory eventually known as Louisiana. Explorers from both nations were probing into the area as early as the 16th century: the Spanish from the South and the French coming from the North down the Mississippi River. The Spaniards laid claim to all the lands from the Atlantic Ocean to the "setting sun." The French claimed all of the lands known as the Valley of the Mississippi to the West. The Spanish called the territory "Florida" and the French called it "Louisiana." DeSoto's expedition claimed the territory for Spain in 1541, but made no effort to colonize it since they had discovered no gold or silver during their explorations.

In 1682 La Salle, coming from the French settlements in Canada, claimed the territory for France. In 1762 the secret treaty of Fontainebleau transferred the territory from France to Spain. In 1800 Napoleon, through coercion, persuaded Spain to cede the territory back to France. By this time, the United States of America had come into being and its President, Thomas Jefferson, became concerned for the many American citizens who had migrated to the vast area. The French threatened to close the port of New Orleans to free trade and to control traffic on the Mississippi River. In what was surely the greatest and cheapest real estate transaction in history, Jefferson, through his agents Livingston and Monroe in Paris, bought the territory for $27,267,622 from France, although there was some question whether France legally owned it. When the boundaries of the Louisiana Purchase were finally fixed, the United States had secured 828,000 square miles for the price of less than three cents per acre! Out of this vast territory would emerge the states of Louisiana, Missouri, Arkansas, Iowa, North Dakota, South Dakota, Nebraska and Oklahoma. In addition, the area included most of the land in Kansas, Colorado, Wyoming, Montana and Minnesota. To be sure, Arkansas was a part of one of the most enterprising, exciting, and amazing transactions ever completed in the history of this country.

The portion of that purchase which is now Arkansas was indeed a wilderness. The Caddo Indians, the Quapaw, the Chickasaw, and the Osages roamed the land; there is no record of any white men residing here. Unfortunately, there is no written record of the Indian civilization except what was passed down from explorers who ventured into the land, took what they wanted, and retreated. That the area was blessed with water, rich soil, and wild life is confirmed in these records.

With these natural resources in abundance, it was inevitable that white men would push westward from the Mississippi River and lay claim to the lands. In 1813 when the Missouri Territory changed what had been the District of Arkansas into Arkansas County, the influx of white settlers, mostly male, began. Indians, too, moved into the area, especially those of the Cherokee Nation, which was forced to give up its land east of the Mississippi. With these migrants, both red and white, civilization penetrated the wilderness and the State of Arkansas was conceived, if not born.

The journals and letters which follow recount the earliest conditions of what would become the 25th state in the Union. The holdings in this section are few and span quite broad periods of time. While there are few selections, they are valuable as reflections of what Arkansas was in those days. The topics of interest are virtually the same for all correspondents: travel, descriptions of flora and fauna, and the Indians. Certainly at the time the selections were written there was nothing more to take an interest in. Because the interests were the same, the selections have a somewhat repetitive nature; however because they come from different minds and pens, each has its own unique character. We offer them for what they are: revelations of our earliest heritage.

CHAPTER

1

Early Exploration of Arkansas

DeSoto in Arkansas

That Hernando DeSoto traveled into Arkansas in 1541 is a well-established historical fact. The exact route of his journey, however, has been a controversial subject among historians and archeologists for many years. After reading the following extract from the Elvas Narrative of the journey, the controversy is understandable. Place names bear no resemblance to a modern map. The general proximity of the expedition's route is rather accurate due to the efforts of the DeSoto Expedition Commission which issued its Final Report in 1939 as a preparation for the 400th Anniversary of the Expedition. Directed by Dr. John R. Swanton of the Smithsonian Institution, this commission studied the four narratives that detail the expedition: Elvas, Garcilaso, Biedma, and Rangel. The Final Report proves to be interesting reading for those who enjoy controversy and close study. It can be found in most large libraries under the heading: U. S. Documents; 76th Congress, 1st Session, House Document No. 71.

Having read Cabeza de Vaca's report on a vast undefined territory known as Florida in North America, DeSoto convinced Charles V of Spain to support an expedition to explore and claim that territory for Spain. DeSoto landed at Tampa Bay on May 25, 1539, where he remained until the spring of 1540. After exploring the southeast for a year, the expedition discovered the Mississippi River on June 18, 1541, at some point in south Tunica County, Mississippi. From there the Spaniards crossed into Arkansas. It is at this point we pick up the Elvas Narrative.

Elvas refers to Desoto as the Governor throughout his narrative, as he had been appointed Governor of the Florida Territory by King Charles.

And because in the town where the Governor lodged, there was a small store of maize, he removed to another half a league from the Rio Grande, where they found plenty of maize. And he went to see the river, and found, that

Rio Grande or Rio de Espiritu Santo, called by Indians Meschacebe, Mississippi.

near unto it was a store of timber to make barges, and good situation of ground to encamp in. Presently he removed himself thither. They made houses and pitched their camp in a plain field a cross-bow shot from the river. And thither was gathered all the maize of the towns which they had lately passed. They began presently to cut and hew down timber, and to saw planks for barges. The Indians came presently down the river; they leaped on shore, and declared to the Governor, "that they were subjects of a great lord, whose name was Aquixo, who was lord of many towns, and governed many people on the other side of the river, and came to tell him on his behalf, that the next day he with all his men would come to see what it *Chief.* would please him to command him." The next day, with speed, the cacique came with 200 canoes full of Indians with their bows and arrows, painted, and with great plumes of white feathers, and many other colors, with shields in their hands, wherewith they defended the rowers on both sides, and the men of war stood from the head to the stern, with their bows and *Covering.* arrows in their hands. The canoe wherein the cacique was, had a tilt over the stern, and he sat under the tilt; and so were the canoes of the principal Indians. And from under the tilt where the chief man sat, he governed and commanded the other people. All joined together, and came within a stone's cast of the shore. From thence the cacique said to the Governor, which walked along the river's side with others that waited on him, that he was come thither to visit, to honor and to obey him; because he knew he was the greatest and mightiest lord on the earth; therefore he would see what he would command him to do. The Governor yielded him thanks, and requested him to come on shore, that they might the better communicate together. And without any answer to that point, he sent him three canoes, wherein was great store of fish and loaves, made of the substance of prunes like unto bricks. After he had received all, he thanked him, and prayed him again to come on shore. And because the cacique's purpose was, to see if what dissimulation he might do some hurt, when they saw that the Governor and his men were in readiness, they began to go from the shore; and with a great cry the crossbow men, which were ready, shot at them, and slew five or six of them. They retired with great order: none did leave his oar, though the next to him were slain, and shielding themselves, they went further off. Afterward they come many times and landed: and when any of us came toward them, they fled into their canoes, which were very pleasant to behold: for they were very great and well made, and had their *Shields.* tilts, plumes, paueses, and flags, and with the multitude of people that were in them, they seemed to be a fair army of galleys. In thirty days' space, while the Governor remained there, they made four barges, in three of which he commanded twelve horsemen to enter, in each of them four. In a morning, three hours before day, men which he trusted would land in despite of the Indians, and make sure the passage, or die, and some footmen, being cross-bow men, went with them, and rowers to set them on the other side. And in the other barge he commanded John de Guzman to pass with the footmen, which was made captain instead of Francisco Maldonado. And because the stream was swift, they went a quarter of a league up the river along the bank, and crossing over, fell down with the stream, and landed right over against the camp. . . .

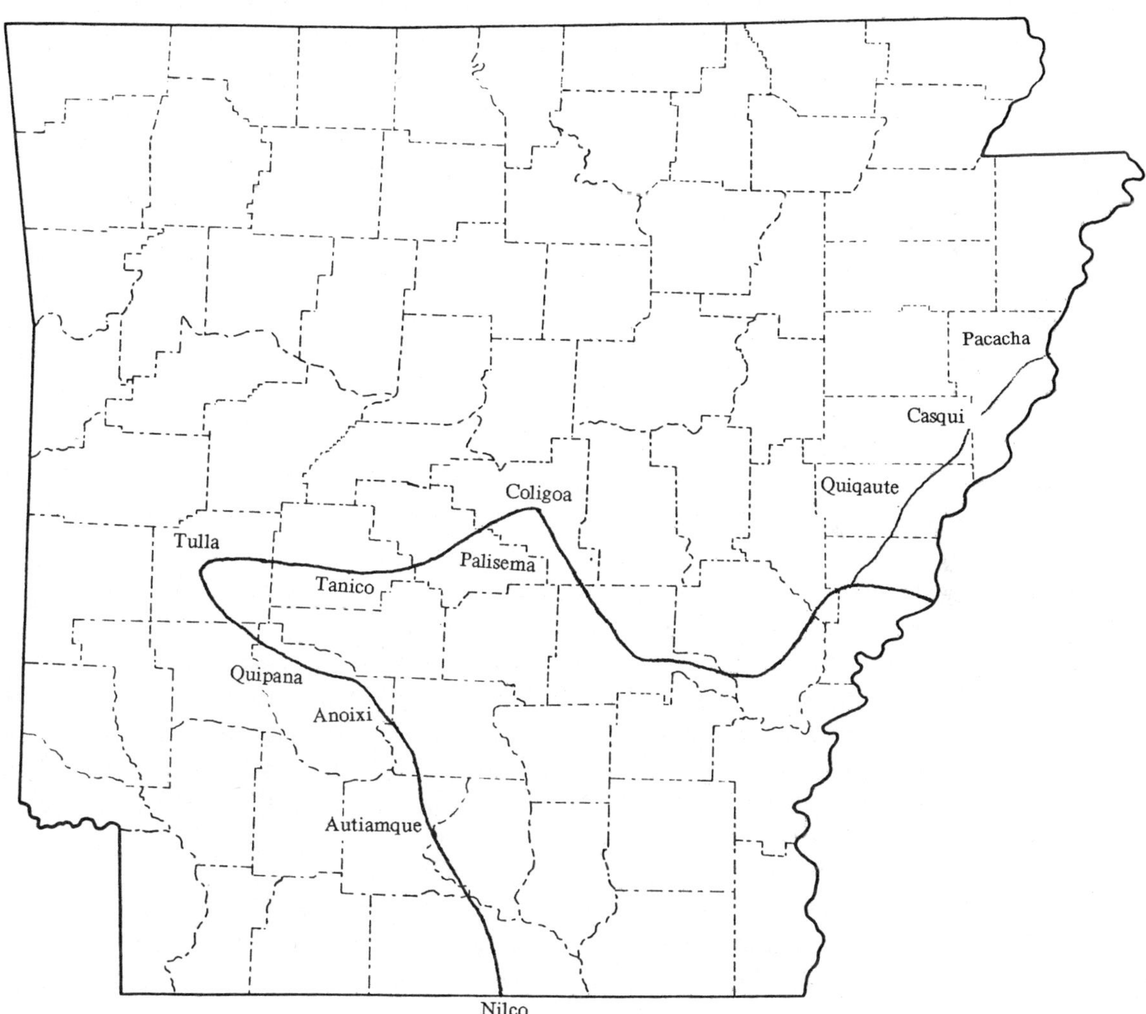

DeSoto's Route Through Arkansas

The river was of great depth, and of a strong current: the water was always muddy: there came down the river continually many trees and timber, which the force of the water and stream brought down. There was a great store of fish in it of sundry sorts, and the most of it differing from the fresh water fish of Spain, as hereafter shall be showed.

Avenue, Arkansas.

Having passed Rio Grande, the Governor traveled a league and a half, and come to a great town of Aquixo, which was dispeopled before he came thither. They espied thirty Indians coming over the plain, which the cacique sent to discover the Christian's determination; and as soon as they had sought of them, they took themselves to flight. The horsemen pursued them, and slew ten, and took fifteen. And because the town, whither the Governor went, was near unto the river, he sent a captain with as many men as he thought sufficient, to carry the barges up the river. And because in his traveling by land many times he went far from the river to compass the creeks that came from it, the Indians took occasion to set upon them of the barges, and put them in great danger, because that by reason of the great current, they durst not leave the shore, and from the bank they shot at them. As soon as the Governor was come to the town, he presently sent crossbow men down the river, which came to rescue them; and upon the coming of the barges to the town, he commanded them to be broken and save the iron for others, when it should be needful.

Province near the mouth of the St. Francis River.

Province South of Pacacha on the southern flank of Crowley's Ridge near Helena.

He lay there one night, and the day following he set forward to seek a province, called *Pacacha*, which he was informed to be near to *Chisca*, where the Indians told him there was gold. He passed through great towns of Aquixo, which were all abandoned for fear of the Christians. He understood by certain Indians that were taken that three days' journey from thence dwelt a great cacique, whose name was *Casqui*. He came to a small river, where a bridge was made, by which they passed; that day till sunset, they went all in water, which in some places came to the waist, and in some to the knees. When they saw themselves on dry land, they were very glad, because they feared they should wander up and down as forlorn men all night in the water. At noon they came to the first town of Casque: they found the Indians careless, because they had no knowledge of them. There were many men and women taken, and store of goods, as mantles and skins, as well in the forest town, as in an other, which stood in a field half a league from thence in sight of it; whither the horsemen ran. The country is higher, drier, and more champaign than any part bordering near the river that until then they had seen. There were in the fields many walnut trees, bearing soft-shelled walnuts in the fashion like bullets, and in the houses they found many of them, which the Indians had laid up in store. The trees

Pecan trees.

differed in nothing else from those of Spain, nor from those which we had seen before, but only that they had a smaller leaf. There were many mulberry trees and plum trees, which bear red plums like those of Spain, and others gray, somewhat differing, but far better. And all the trees are all the years so fruitful, as if they were planted in orchards; and the woods were very thin. The Governor traveled two days through the country of Casqui, before he came to the town where the cacique was; and the most of the way was always by champaign ground, which was full of great towns, so that from one town, you might see two or three.

Open, level country.

He sent an Indian to certify the cacique that he was coming to the place where he was, with intent to procure his friendship, and to hold him as his brother. Whereunto he answered, that he should be welcome, and that he would receive him with special good-will, and accomplish all that his lordship would command him. He sent him a present upon the way, to wit: skins, mantles and fish, and after these compliments, the Governor found all the towns as he passed, inhabited with people, which peaceably attended his coming, and offered him skins, mantles and fish. The cacique, accompanied with many Indians, came out of the town, and stayed half a league on the way to receive the Governor, and when he came to him he spake these words following:

"Right high, right mighty, and renowned lord, your lordship, is most heartily welcome. As soon as I had notice of your lordship, of your power, and your perfections, although you came into my country killing and taking captive the inhabitants thereof and my subjects, yet I determined to confirm my will unto yours, and as your own to interpret in good part all that your lordship did: believing that it was convenient it should be so for some just respects, to prevent some future matter revealed unto your lordship, and concealed from me. For well may a mischief be permitted to avoid a greater, and that good may come thereof: which I believe will so fall out. For it is no reason to presume of so excellent a prince, that the nobleness of his heart, and the effect of his will would permit him to suffer any unjust thing. My ability is so small to serve you as your lordship diserveth, that if you respect not mine abundant good-will, which humbly offereth all kind of service, I deserve but little in your presence. But if it be reason that his be esteemed, receive the same, myself, my country, and subjects for yours, and dispose of me and them at your pleasure. For if I were lord of all the world, with the same good-will would your lordship by me be received, served and obeyed."

The Governor answered him to the purpose and satisfied him in few words. Within a while after both of them used words of great offers and courtesy the one to the other, and the cacique requested him to lodge in his houses. The Governor, to preserve the peace the better, excused himself, saying that he would lodge in the fields. . . . The cacique went to his town, and came again with many Indians singing. As soon as they came to the Governor, all of them prostrated themselves upon the ground. Among these came two Indians that were blind. The cacique made a speech; to avoid tediousness, I will only tell in a few words the substance of the matter. He said, that seeing the Governor was the son of the Sun, and a great lord, he besought him to do him the favor to give sight to those two blind men. The blind men rose up presently, and very earnestly requested the same of the Governor. He answered, that in the high heavens was he that had power to give them health, and whatsoever they could ask of him; whose servant he was: and that this Lord made the heavens and the earth, and man after his own likeness, and that he suffered upon the cross to save mankind, and rose again the third day, and that he died as he was man, and as touching his divinity, he was, and is immortal; and that he ascended into heaven, where he standeth with his arms open to receive all such as turn unto him; and straightaway he commanded him to make a very high cross of wood, which was set up in the highest place of the town; declaring unto him, that the Christians worshipped the same in resemblance and memory of that whereon Christ suffered. The Governor and his men kneeled down before it, and the Indians did the like. The Governor willed him, that from thenceforth he would worship the same, and should ask whatsoever they stood in need of, of that lord that he told them was in heaven. . . .

The same day that the Governor departed thence, he lodged at a town belonging to Casqui; and the next day he passed in sight of other towns, and came to the lake, which was half crossbow shot over, of a great depth and current. At the time of his coming, the Indians had made an end of the bridge, which was made of timber, laid one tree after another: and on one side it had a course of stakes higher than the bridge, for them that passed to take hold on. . . . The Governor sent word by an Indian to the Cacique of Casqui, and though he were there, yet he would do him no disgrace nor hurt, if he would attend him peaceably, and embrace his friendship; but rather would intreat him as a brother. . . . [T]he cacique made no account of that which he told him but fled with all his men out at the other side of the town. Presently the Governor entered, and ran before with the horsemen, that way by which the Indians fled; and at another town, distant a quarter of a league from thence, they took many Indians; and as soon as the horsemen had taken them, they delivered them to the Indians of Casque, whom, because they were their enemies, with much circumspection and rejoicing, they brought to the town where the Christians were; and the greatest relief they had was this, that they could not get leave to kill them. There were found in the town many mantles and deer skins, lion skins, and bear skins, and many cat skins. Many came so far poorly appareled, and there they clothed themselves: of the mantles, they made them coats and cassocks, and some made gowns, and lined them with cat skins; and likewise their cassocks. Of the deer skins some made them also Jerkins, shirts, hose and shoes: and of the bear skins, they made them very good cloaks: for no water could pierce them. There were targets of raw ox hides found there: with which hides they armed their horses.

Upon Wednesday, the 19th of June, 1541, the Governor entered into Pacacha. He lodged in the town, where the cacique used to reside, which was very great, walled and beset with towers, and many loopholes were in the towers and wall. And in the town was great store of old maize, and great quantity of new in the fields. Within a league and a half a league were great towns all walled. Where the Governor was lodged was a great lake, that came near unto the wall; and it entered into a ditch, that went round about the town, wanting but a little to environ it around. From the lake to the great river was made a wear by which the fish come into it, which the cacique kept for his recreation and sport. . . . There was a fish which they called bagres; the third part of it was head, and it had on both sides the gills, and along the sides great pricks like very sharp awls. Those of the kind that were in the lakes were as big as pikes; and in the river there were some of an hundred and of a hundred and fifty pounds weight and many of them were taken with the hook.

Catfish.

There was another fish like barbilles, and another like breams, headed like the delicate fish, called in Spain besugo, between red and gray. This was there of most esteem. There was another fish called peel fish; it had a snout of a cubit long, and at the end of the upper lip it was made like a peel. . . . There was another fish which sometimes the Indians brought us, of the bigness of a hog; they called it the pereo fish; it had rows of teeth beneath and above. The Cacique of Casqui sent many times great presents of fish, mantles, and skins. He told the Governor that he would deliver the Cacique of Pacacha into his hands. He went to Casqui, and sent many canoes up the river, and came himself by land with many of his people. The Governor with forty horsemen and sixty footmen, took him along with him up the river. And his Indians which were in the canoes, discovered where the Cacique of Pacacha was, in a little island, situated between two arms of the river. And five Christians entered into a canoe, wherein Don Antonio Osorrio went before, to see what people the Cacique had with him. There

Paddlefish.

Buffalo.

were in the isle five or six thousand souls. And as soon as they saw them, supposing that the Indians which were in the other canoes were also Christians, the cacique, and certain which were in three canoes, which they had there with them, fled in great haste to the other side of the river. The rest, with great fear and danger, leapt into the river, where many people were drowned, especially women and little children. Presently the Governor, who was on land, not knowing what had happened to Don Antonio and those that went with him, commanded the Christians with all speed to enter with the Indians of Casqui in the canoes, which were quickly with Don Antonio in the little island, where they took many men and women, and much goods. Great store of goods, which the Indians had laid upon hurdles of canes and rifts rafts timber to carry over to the other side, drove down the river, wherewith the Indians of Casqui filled their canoes, and for fear lest the Christians would take it from them, the casique went home with them down the river, without taking his leave of the Governor, whereupon the Governor was highly offended with him, and presently returning to Pacacha, he overran the country of Casqui the space of two leagues, where he took twenty or thirty of his men. And because his horses were weary, and wanted time that day to go farther, he returned to Pacacha, with the determination within three of four days after to invade Casqui. And presently he let loose one of the Indians of Pacacha, and sent word by him to the cacique, that if he would have his friendship, he should repair unto him, and that both of them would make war upon Casqui. And presently came many Indians that belonged to Pacacha, and brought an Indian instead of the cacique, which was discovered by the cacique's brother, which was taken prisoner. The Governor wished the Indians that their master himself should come; for he knew very well that that was not he, and told them that they could do nothing which he knew not before they thought it. The next day the cacique came, accompanied with many Indians, and with a present of much fish, skins and mantles. He made a speech that all were glad to hear, and concluded, saying that though his lordship, without his giving occasion of offense had done him hurt in his country and subjects, yet he would not therefore refuse to be his, and that he would always be at his command. The Governor commanded his brother to be loosed, and other principal Indians that were taken prisoners. That day came an Indian from the Cacique of Casqui, and said that his lord would come the next day to excuse himself of the error which he had committed, in going away without license of the Governor. The Governor willed the messenger to signify unto him, that if he came not in his own person, he would seek him himself, and give him such punishment as he deserved. The next day with all speed came the Cacique of Casqui, and brought a present to the Governor of many mantles, skins, and fish, and gave him a daughter of his, saying that he greatly desired to match his blood with the blood of so great a lord as he was, and therefore he brought him his daughter, and desired him to take her to be his wife. He made a long and discreet oration, giving him great commendations and concluded saying, that he should pardon his going away without license, for that cross's sake which he had left with him; protesting that he went away for shame of that which his men had done without his consent. The Governor answered him that he had chosen a good patron; and that if he had not come to excuse himself, he had determined to seek him, to burn his towns, to kill him and his people, and to destroy his country. To which he replied, saying:

"My lord, I and mine are yours, and my country likewise is yours; therefore if you had done so, you would have destroyed your own country, and have killed your own people; whatsoever shall come unto me from your hand, I will receive as from my lord, as well punishment as reward; and know you, that the favor that you did me in leaving me the cross, I do acknowledge the same to be a very great one, and greater than I have deserved. For you shall understand, that with great droughts the fields of maize of my country were withered; and as soon as I and my people kneeled before the cross, and prayed for rain, presently our necessities were relieved."

The Governor made him and the Cacique of Pacacha friends; and set them at his table to dine with him; and the Caciques fell at variance about the seats, which of them should sit on his right hand. The Governor pacified them; telling them that among the Christians all was one to set on the one side, or on the other, willing them so to behave themselves, seeing they were with him, that nobody might hear them, and that every one should sit in the place that first he lighted on. . . .

The Governor rested in Pacacha forty days; in all which time the two caciques served him with great store of fish, mantles, and skins, and strove who should do him greatest service. At the time of his departure the Cacique of Pacacha gave him two of his sisters, saying that in sign of love that he might remember him, he should take them for his wives: the one's name was Nacanoche, and the other's Mochila: they were well proportioned tall of body, and well fleshed. Macanoche was of good countenance, and in her shape and physiognomy looked like a lady; the other was strongly made. The Cacique of Casqui commanded the bridge to be repaired, and the Governor returned through his country, and lodged in the field near his town whither he came with great store of fish, and two women, which he exchanged with

Province between the St. Francis and Arkansas Rivers.

Florida was the name given all the lands explored by Desoto.

Close to Little Rock.

Possibly the Tallahatchie River in Mississippi.

two Christians for two shirts. He gave us a guide and men for carriages. The Governor lodged at a town of his, and the next day at another near a river, whither he caused canoes to be brought for him to pass over, and with his leave returned. The Governor took his journey toward Quigaute. . . . The fourth day of August he came to the town where the cacique used to keep his residence: on the way he sent him a present . . . and not daring to stay for him in the town, he absented himself. The town was the greatest that was seen in Florida. The Governor and his people lodged in the one half of it; and within a few days, seeing the Indians became liars, he commanded the other half to be burned, because it could not be a shelter for them, if they came to assault him by night, nor a hinderance to his horsemen for the resisting of them. . . . The Governor came again to Quigaute, and willed him to cause his men to come and serve the Christians and staying some days for their coming, and seeing they came not, he sent two captains, every one his way on both sides of the river with horsemen and footmen. They took many men and women. Now seeing the hurt which they sustained for their rebellion, they came to see what the Governor would command them, and passed to and fro many times, and brought presents of cloth and fish. The cacique and his two wives were in the lodging of the Governor loose, ad the handberdiers of his guard did keep them. The Governor asked them which way the country was most inhabited? They said that toward the south down the river, were great towns and caciques, which commanded great countries, and much people. And that towards the northwest, there was a province near to certain mountains, that was called Coligoa. The Governor and all the rest thought good to go first to Coligoa: saying, that peradventure the mountains would make some difference of soil, and that beyond them there might be some gold or silver. . . . From Tascaluca to Rio Grande, or the Great River, is about three hundred leagues: it is a very low country, and has many lakes. From Pacacha to Quigaute may be a hundred leagues. The Governor left the Cacique of Quigaute in his own town. And an Indian, which was his guide, led him through woods without any way, seven days' journey through a desert, where, at every lodging, they lodged in lakes and pools in very shoal water; there was such store of fish, that they killed them with cudgels; and the Indians which they carried in chains, with the mud trouble the waters and the fish being therewith, as it were, astonished, came to the top of the water, and they took as much as they listed. The Indians of Coligoa had knowledge of the Christians, and when they came so near the town that the Indians saw them, they fled up the river which passed near the town, and some leaped into it; but the Christians went on both sides of the river, and to them. There were many men and women taken, and the cacique with them. And by his commandment within three days came many Indians with a present of mantles and deers skins, and two ox hides: and they reported that five or six leagues towards the north, there were many of these oxen, and that because the country was cold, it was evil inhabited; that the best country which they knew, the most plentiful, and most inhabited, was province called Cayes, lying toward the south. From Quigaurte to Coligoa may be forty leagues. This town of Coligoa stood at the foot of a hill, on the bank of a mean river, of the bigness of Cayas, the river that passeth by Estremadurra. It was a fat soil and so plentiful of maize, that they cast out the old, to bring in the new. There was also a great beauty of French beans and pompions. The French beans were greater, and better than those of Spain, and likewise the pompions, and being roasted, they have almost the taste of chestnuts. . . . We traveled five days and came to the province of Palisema. The house of the cacique was found covered with deers' skins, of divers colors and works drawn in them, and with the same in manner of carpets was the ground of the house covered. The cacique left it so, that the Governor might lodge in it, in token that he sought peace and his friendship. But he durst not tarry his coming. The Governor, seeing he had absented himself, sent a captain with horsemen and footmen to seek him.

Possibly buffalo.

Pumpkin.

Province South and West of Little Rock, possibly around Benton.

He found much people, but by reason of the roughness of the country, he took none save a few women and children. The town was little and scattering, and had very little maize. For which cause the Governor speedily departed from thence. He came to another town called Tatalicoya; he carried with him the cacique thereof, which guided him to Cayas. From Tatalicaya are four days' journey to Cayas. When he came to Cayas, and saw the town scattered, he thought they had told him a lie, and that it was not the province of Cayas, because they had informed him that it was well inhabited. He threatened the cacique, charging him to tell him where he was: and he and the other Indians that were taken near the place, affirmed that this was the town of Cayas, and the best that was in that country, and that though the houses were distant one from the other, yet the ground that was inhabited was great, and that there was great store of people, and many fields of maize. This town was called Tanico; he pitched his camp in the best part of it, near unto a river. . . .

Possibly on the Saline River.

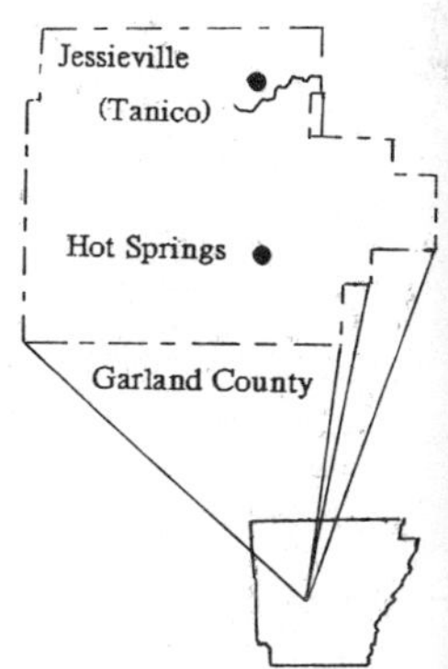

The Governor rested a month on the province of Cayas. . . . Until that time the Christians wanted salt, and there they made good store, which they carried along with them. The Indians do carry it to other places to exchange it for skins and mantles. They make it along the river, which when it ebbeth, leaveth it upon the upper part of the sand. And because they can

Possibly on the Middle Fork in Jessieville.

not make it, without much sand mingled with it, they throw it into certain baskets which they have for that purpose, broad at the mouth and narrow at the bottom, and set it in the air upon a bar, and throw water into it, and set a small vessel under it, wherein it falleth: being strained and set to boil upon the fire, when the water is sodden away, the salt remaineth in the bottom of the pan. On both sides of the river the country was full of sown fields, and there was a store of maize. The Indians durst not come over where we were; and when some of them showed themselves, the soldiers that saw them called unto them; then the Indians passed the river, and came with them where the Governor was. He asked them for the cacique. They said that he remained quiet, but that he durst not show himself. The Governor presently sent him word, that he should come unto him, and bring him a guide and an interpreter for his journey, if he made account of his friendship; and if he did not do so, he would come himself to seek him, and that it would be the worse for him. He waited three days, and seeing he came not, he went to seek him, and brought him prisoner with 150 of his men. He asked him whether he had notice of any great cacique, and which way the country was best inhabited. He answered that the best country thereabouts was a province toward the south, a day and a half's journey, which was called Tulla; and that he could give him a guide, but no interpreter, because the speech of that country was different from his, and because he and his ancestors had always wars with the lords of that province; therefore they had no commerce, nor understood one another's language. Immediately the Governor with certain horsemen, and fifty footmen departed toward Tulla, to see if the country were such, as he might pass through it with all his company: and as soon as he was arrived there, and was espied of the Indians, the country gathered together, and as soon as fifteen and twenty Indians could assemble themselves, they set upon the Christians; and seeing that they did handle them shrewdly, and that the horsemen overtook them when they fled, they got up in the tops of their houses, and sought to defend themselves with their arrows; and being beaten down from one, they got upon another. And while our men pursued some, others set upon them another way. Thus the skirmish lasted so long, that the horses were tired, and they could not make them run. The Indians killed there one horse, and some were hurt. There were fifteen Indians slain there, and forty women and boys were taken prisoners. . . . The Governor determined to return to Cayas, before the Indians had time to gather ahead; and presently that evening, going part of the night to leave Tulla, he lodged by the way, and the next day came to Cayas; and within three days after he departed thence towards Tulla with all his company. . . . He stayed three days by the way,

Caddo Gap.

and the day that he came thither, he found the town abandoned; for the Indians durst not tarry his coming. But as soon as they knew that the Governor was in Tulla, the first night about the morning watch, they came in two squadrons two several ways, with their bows and arrows, and long staves like pikes. As soon as they were descried both horse and foot sallied out upon them, where many of the Indians were slain; and come Christians and horses were hurt. Some of the Indians were taken prisoners, whereof the Governor sent six to the cacique, with their right hands and noses cut off; and sent him word, that if he came not to him to excuse and submit himself, that he would come to seek him, and that he would do the like to him, and as many of his as he could find, as he had done to those he had sent him; and gave him three days' respite for to come. And this he gave them to understand by signs, as well as he could for there was no interpreter. At the three days' end there came an Indian laden with ox hides. He came weeping with great sobs, and coming to the governor cast himself down at his feet. He took him up and he made a speech, but there was none that understood him. The Governor by signs commanded him to return to the cacique, and to will him to send an interpreter, which could understand the men of Cayas. . . . [W]ithin three days after came 20 Indians, and among them one that understood them of Cayas; who after a long oration of excuses of the cacique, and praises of the Governor, concluded with this, that he and the others were come thither on the cacique's behalf, to see what his lordship would command him to do. . . . The Governor and all his company were very glad. For in nowise could they travel without an interpreter. The Governor commanded him to be kept safe, and bade him tell the men that came with him that they could return to the cacique, and signify unto him, that he pardoned him for that which was past, and thanked him much for his presents and interpreter, which he had sent him, and that he would be glad to see him, and that he should come the next day to talk with him. After three days the cacique came, and eighty Indians with him. . . .

The Governor informed himself of all the country round about; and understood, that toward the west was a scattered dwelling, that toward the southeast were great towns, especially in a province called Autiamque, ten days' journey from Tulla; which might be about eighty leagues; and that it was a plentiful country of maize. And because winter came on . . . and fearing, that if they should stay so long in the scattered dwelling, they could not be sustained; and also because the Indians said that near to Autiamque was a great water, and according to their relation, the Governor thought it was some arm of the sea; and because he now desired to send news of himself to Cuba, that some supply of men and horses might be sent unto him (for it was about three years since Donna Isabella, which was in Havana, or any other person in Christendom had heard of him, and by this time he had lost 250 men and 150 horses), he determined to winter in Autiamque, and the next spring to go to the sea coast and make two brigantines, and send one of them to Cuba, and the other to Nueva Espanna, that that which went in safety might give news of him. . . . thus having sent away the caciques of Cayas and Tulla, he took his journey towards Autiamque; he traveled five days over rough mountains, and came to a town called Quipana, where no Indians could be taken for the roughness of the country; and the town being between hills, there was an ambush laid, wherewith they took two Indians, which told them that Autiamque was six days' journey from thence, and that there was another province towards the south, eight days' journey off, plentiful of maize, and very well peopled, which was called Guahate. But because Autiamque was nearer, and the most of the Indians agreed of it, the Governor made his journey that way. In three days he came to a town called Anoixi. . . . Within two days after, the Governor came to another town called Catamaya, and lodged in the fields of the town. Two Indians came with a false message from the cacique to know his determination. He bade them tell their lord that he should come and speak with him. The Indians returned and came no more, nor any other message from the cacique. The next day the Christians went to the town, which was without people: they took as much maize as they needed. That day they lodged in the wood, and the next day they came to Autiamque. They found much maize laid up in store, and French beans, and walnuts and prunes, great stores of all sorts. They took some Indians which were gathering together the stuff which their wives had hidden. . . . The Governor lodged in the best part of the town, and commanded presently to make a fence of timber about the camp distant from the houses, that the Indians might not hurt them from without by fire. . . . [I]n three days there was an inclosure made of very high and thick posts thrust into the ground, and many rails laid across. . . . thither came Indians on the cacique's behalf with a present of mantles and skins; and an hauling cacique, subject to the lord of Autiammque lord of a town called Tietiquaquo, came many times to visit the Governor, and to bring him presents of such as he had. The Cacique of Autiamque sent to know of the Governor, how long time he meant to stay in his country: And understanding that he meant to stay about three days, he never sent any more Indians, nor any other message, but conspired with the lame cacique to rebel. Divers inroads were made, wherein there were many men and women taken, and the lame

Possibly around Arkadelphia on the Ouachita River.

Possibly Sparkman.

Province around Camden where Desoto wintered.

cacique among the rest. . . . The Cacique of Autiamque, desiring to thrust the Governor out of the country, set spies over him. And an Indian coming one night to the gate of the inclosure, a soldier that watched espied him, and stepping behind the gate, as he came in, he gave him such a thrust that he fell down; and so he came to the Governor; and as he asked him wherefore he came, not being able to speak, he fell down dead. The night following the Governor commanded a soldier to give the alarm, and to say that he had seen Indians, to see how ready they would be to answer the alarm. And he did so sometime as well there, as in other places when he thought his men were careless, and reprehended such as were slack. And as well for this cause, as in regard of doing their duty, when the alarm was given, every one sought to be the first that could answer. They staid in Autiamque three months with great plenty of maize, French beans, walnuts, prunes and conies, which until that time they knew not how to catch. And in Autiamque the Indians taught them how to take them, which was with great springs which lifted up their feet from the ground, and the snare was made with a strong string, whereunto was fastened a knot of a cane, which ran close about the neck of the cony, because they should not gnaw the string. They took many in the fields of maize, especially when it froze or snowed. The Christians staid there one whole month so inclosed with snow that they went not out of the town; and when they wanted firewood the Governor with his horsemen going and coming many times to the wood, which was two crossbow shots from the town, made a pathway whereby the footmen went for wood. In this mean space, some Indians which went loose killed many conies with their knives and with arrows. There conies were of two sorts; some were like those of Spain, and the other of the same color and fashion and as big as great hares, longer and having greater loins.

Rabbits.

Upon Monday, the 6th of March, 1542, the Governor departed from Autiamque to seek Nilco, which the Indians said was near the great river, with the determination to come to the sea, and procure some succor of men and horses; for he had but three hundred men of war, and forty horses, and some of them lame, which did nothing but help to make up the number; and for want of iron they had gone a year unshod, and because they were used to it in the plain country, it did them no great harm. John Ortiz died in Autiamque, which grieved the Governor very much; because without an interpreter he feared to enter far into the land, where he might be lost. From thenceforward a youth that was taken in Cutifachiqui did serve for an interpreter, which had by that time learned somewhat of the Christian's language. . . . the Governor spent ten days in traveling from Autiamque to the province called Ayays; and came to a town that stood near the river that

Province located in Northern Louisiana.

passeth by Cayas and Autiamque. There he commanded a barge to be made, wherewith he passed the river. When he had passed the river there fell out such weather that four days he could not travel for snow. As soon as it gave over snowing, he went three days' journey through the wilderness, and a country so low and so full of lakes and evil ways, that he traveled a whole day in water, sometimes knee deep, sometimes to the stirrup, and sometimes they swam. . . .

Marquette and the Arkansas Indians

Nearly 150 years after DeSoto discovered the Mississippi River at the lower end, a French expedition set out from the northern end to explore the reaches of the Great River, as it was called by the indians living near the Great Lakes. In the spring of 1673 the expedition, led by Louis Joliet and Jacques Marquette left St.Ignace, Michigan to explore and claim the river territory for France. They traveled down the river to within 700 miles of the Gulf of Mexico, near the the confluence of the Arkansas River, and turned back. The following extract taken from the journal of that expedition relates their encounter with the Arkansea Indians, who entertained them as honored guests.

I spoke to them in six different languages, but they did not understand any of them. At last they brought to us an old man who spoke the Illinois, whom we told that we wished to go as far as the sea, and then made them some presents. They understood what I meant, but I am not sure they understood what I said to them of God, and things concerning their salvation. It was, however, seed thrown on ground which would in time become fruitful. They told us that at the next great village, called Arkansea, eight or ten leagues farther down the river, we could learn all about the sea. They feasted us with sagamite and fish, and we passed the night with them, not, however, without some uneasiness. We embarked early next morning with our interpreters and ten Indians who went before us in a canoe. Having arrived about half a league from Arkansea, we saw two canoes coming toward us. The captain of one was standing up holding the calumet in his hand, with which he made signs, according to the custom of the country. He afterwards joined us, inviting us to smoke, and singing pleasantly. He then gave us some sagamite and Indian bread to eat and going before made signs for us to follow him, which we did, but at some distance.

Hominy.

They had in the meantime prepared a kind of scaffold to receive us, adorned with fine mats, upon which we sat down with the old men and warriors. We fortunately found among them a young man who spoke the Illinois much better than the interpreter whom we brought with us from the Mitchigamea.

This name is still applied to a lake a little north of the St. Francis River.

We made them some small presents, which they received with great civility, and seemed to admire what I told them about God, the creation of the world, and the mysteries of our holy faith, telling us by the interpreter that they wished us to remain with them for the purpose of instructing them.

We then asked them what they knew of the sea, and they said we were within ten day's journey of it, but we could perform it in five. That they were unacquainted with the nations below because their enemies prevented them from visiting them. That the hatchet, knives and beads had been sold to them by the nations of the East, and were in part brought by the Illinois, who lived four days' journey to the West. That the Indians whom we had met with guns were their enemies, who hindered them from trading with the Europeans, and if we persisted in going any farther, we would expose ourselves to other nations who were their enemies. During this conversation they continued all day to feast us with sagamite, dog meat, and roasted corn out of large wooden dishes.

The Indians were very courteous, and give freely of what they have, but their provisions are but indifferent because they are afraid to go ahunting on account of their enemies. They made three crops of Indian corn a year. They roast and boil it in large earthern pots very curiously made. They also have large baked earthern plates, which they use for different purposes. The men go naked and wear their hair short. They pierce their noses and ears, and wear rings of glass beads in them.

The women cover themselves with skins, and divide their hair into two tresses, which they wear behind their back without any ornament. Their feasts are without ceremony, they serve their meats in large dishes, and every one eats as much as he pleases. Their language is extremely difficult, and although I tried, I could never pronounce a word of it.

Their cabins are made with the bark of trees, and are generally very wide and long. They lay at both ends on mats raised on a platform two feet higher than the floor. They keep their corn in panniers made of rushes. They have no beavers and all their commodities are buffalo hides. It never snows in this country, and they have no other fruit but watermelons, though their soil might produce any other, if they knew how to cultivate it. In the evenings the chiefs held a secret council, wherein some proposed to kill us, but the great chief opposed this base design, and sent for us to dance

A large basket.

the calumet, which he presented us with to seal our common friendship. M. Joliet and I held council, to deliberate upon what we should do—whether to proceed further, or return to Canada, content with the discoveries we had made.

Having satisfied ourselves that the Gulf of Mexico was in latitude 31° 40', and we could reach it in three or four days' journey from the Arkansea (Arkansas River), and that the Mississippi discharged itself into it, and not to the eastward of the cape of Florida, nor into the California Sea, we resolved to return home.

We considered that the advantage of our travels would be altogether lost to our nation if we fell into the hands of the Spaniards, from whom we could expect no other treatment than death or slavery; beside, we saw that we were not prepared to resist the Indians, the allies of the Europeans, who continually infested the lower part of this river; we therefore came to the conclusion to return, and make a report to those who had sent us. So having rested another day, we left the village of the Arkansea, on the seventeenth day of July, 1673, having followed the Mississippi from the latitude of 42° to 34°, and preached the Gospel to the utmost of my power, to the nations we visited. We then ascended the Mississippi with great difficulty against the current, and left it in the latitude of 38° north, to enter another river [Illinois], which took us to the lake of Illinois [Michigan], which is a much shorter way than through the River Mesconsin [Wisconsin], by which we entered the Mississippi.

CHAPTER

2

Explorations of the Louisiana Purchase

William Dunbar Corresponds with President Jefferson

William Dunbar, of "The Forest," Natchez, Mississippi, was a Scotsman who settled in Mississippi in 1773 after coming down the river in a crude flatboat. He was a successful planter, stave maker, experimenter, and scientist. He introduced the square bale for the packing of cotton and was the first to extract the oil from the cotton seed. Under the Spanish government he held the office of surveyor for some few years. Following the formation of the United States of America, he became one of the advisors to Commissioner Ellicott and in 1798 was appointed by Gayoso, governor of Louisiana, to act as astronomer for Spain in running the line of demarcation between the United States and Spain. A correspondence between Dunbar and Jefferson began after Jefferson learned of Dunbar's interest and capability in scientific researches. At the request of Jefferson, Dunbar explored the Ouachita River country and made the first scientific report of the Hot Springs. Later he supervised the Red River Expedition. It is to Jefferson's interest in Louisiana that the following letters are addressed and they undoubtedly influenced to some degree Jefferson's decision to make the Louisiana Purchase. Transcription of the letters is somewhat choppy, due most likely to the difficulty of reading the old papers. In some instances we have supplied words which make the sentences clearer.

Natchez 13th. May 1804
Thos. Jefferson P. U. S.
Washington

Dear Sir

I am honored with your letter of the 13th. March. I am extremely obliged by your condescension in communicating your remarks on some part of my imperfect sketch of the Mississippi: from what you have written I see the necessity of a short appendix which I shall consider as an apology for dissenting from the opinions of so many great mathematicians who have written on the theory of rivers:. . . I found myself obliged to abandon the theories . . . believing them contrary to . . . hydrostatual laws;. . . I have read attentively the examination into the boundaries of Louisiana. The arguments respecting the periods as an Eastern boundary seem unanswerable, and if the french Gov. agree that such was also their understanding of the treaty, they must be conclusive: the general idea by the Gov. & people of Louisiana seems to have been that this portion of W. Florida was not yet actually transferred, but soon must follow as being no longer of any use to the Spaniards, hence those great & extensive sales which have been made by the Spanish Gov. between the Iberville and Perdido: with respect to the Western boundary, it is a subject not so clearly defineable.

The Surveying & exploring expeditions undertaken at public expence must be gratifying to all lovers of Science and natural research; it would have been very desirable that congress had been more liberal with respect to pecuniary provisions for certainly the number and talents of the gentlemen to be employed must be greatly circumscribed thereby: the report of the committee which preceded the Law seem to have contemplated services to be rendered to the public by the patriotism of men of Science & Genius: I hope but it is to be recollected that men of small fortune who engage in such enterprises, however congenial to their feelings, however flattering to the order of their youthful minds, they cannot be accomplished without great sacrifices of precious time and when a great Empire talks of compensation, this ought to be adequate to the importance of the Service and honorable both to Gov. & to the Selected individuals.

It will give me great pleasure to contribute every thing in my power to promote the proposed expedition on the Red & Arcansaw rivers: of the two gentlemen Gelespy & Waller I conceive the first to have been best qualified by education, the last perhaps superior in natural genius etc. but he is not now here. . . . The precipitation with which I was obliged to write by last post prevented my giving you the result of my inquiries which is; that the Marquis de Casa Calva Commis. of limits on the part of Spain conceives that the Western limits of Louisiana are to be designated by a line drawn along the Sabine river from the sea passing by an ancient post called the Adais, thence falling upon a creek called bayu pierre about 5 leagues above Nachitosh & down said creek to the Red river that there it will cross the red River & take a northerly course not yet ascertained; the Comt. of the Spanish post Nacokdosh about 125 miles west of Nackitosh has the most positive orders not to suffer any american or other Stranger to pass beyond what they conceive to be the limits of Louisiana. The Spanish officers are further possessed with a belief that some exchange will take place by giving the floridas for the West side of the Mississippi excepting as they presume that the U. S. may remain possessed of both sides of the Mississippi below the Chafalaya. . . . Such being the present Si . . . people, we cannot Suppose from their habitual jealousy they will with . . . pedition into a country they suppose to be their own. . . . We might go up the Arcansaw river & come down the red river without any great probability of the Spaniards obtaining a knowledge of the expedition, but in the progress of this enquiry we discover other difficulties to be encountered, numerous bodies of warlike Indians inhabit up the Arcansaw river; the Ozages hunt between that & the Missouri, & are not understood to be friendly [with any] white whom they find in their country. M. Shutok [?] of the Illinois has enjoyed an exclusive privilege of trading with those indians, & if time had permitted it might have been very proper to have obtained from him a person of this recommendation possessing the confidence of the Indians to serve as guide & interpreter and hunter There is no doubt that interpreters (old hunters) may be found both upon the red & arcansaw rivers, sufficiently well acquainted with the Natives & their language to a certain extent on both rivers, but it does not appear that advantage can be taken of this circumstance on the river which the party descends, unless, a person from each river be engaged from the commencement of the expedition, which may be very proper, but demands time: on the upper branches of the red river, it is understood that natives reside, always at war with the Spaniards and as they probably know of no other white persons, the approach to those Savages will require precaution.

Nacogdoches, Texas.

Natchitoches, Louisiana.

Major Stephen Minor who tho' yet in the pay of Spain is a Sincere friend to his native country, is of opinion that the Marquis of Casa Calva, who is proud & highspirited but easily flattered might readily be induced by a polite application to consent to the exploring those rivers upon the principle of promoting Science & geographical Knowledge, I however doubt it.

But as we have no authority of this kind, & moreover it might seem as improper condescension to ask the approbation of any man to explore our own rivers I have thought it necessary only to communicate to you these particulars. It appears that the Spanish Comd. & officers are now in waiting for orders to run the line of demarcation, Major Stephen Minor who has long since signified his desire of retiring from the Spanish Service is yet retained.

Natchez 9th. June 1804
Thos. Jefferson P. U. S.
Washington

Since you did me the honor to communicate to me the intentions of Gov. to send an expedition to explore the rivers to the West of the Miss. I have been endeavoring to procure such information as is to be employed, & . . . services & connections with the Spanish Gov. . . . we shall proceed to organize . . . with every precaution . . . circumstances may enable us to adopt an order [assuring] ultimate success; hoping if time permits to receive [instructions] upon those points of difficulty which present themselves.

The Red River being thought to be the most interesting of the two to be explored, ought to be ascended as there by more time will be given to explore than can be obtained in descending provided that no imperious circumstance decides in favor of the arcansaw river. . . .

Dunbar on the Indians of Louisiana

There are at least besides the foregoing at least 4 to 500 families of Chactaws who are dispersed on the west side of the Mississippi, on the Ouachita & Red River as far west as Natchitoches, and the whole nation would have emigrated across the Mississippi had it not been for the opposition of the Spaniards and the Indians on that side who had suffered by their aggression.

Between the Red River & the Arkansas there are but few Indians the remains of tribes almost extinct. On this last River is the nation of the same name consisting of about 260 warriors. They are brave yet peaceable and well disposed and have always been attached to the French & espouse their cause in their wars with the Chicasaws whom they have always resisted with success. They live in 3 villages, the first is at 13 leagues from the Mississippi on the Arkansas River, and the others are at 3 and 6 leagues from the first.

A league, in English speaking countries, is approximately three miles.

On the River St. Francis, New Madrid, Cape Girardeau & Revere a la environs [sic] are settled a number of vagabonds, emigrants from the Delawares, Shawanese, Miamis, Chicasaws, Cherekees, Piorias, and supposed to consist in all of 500 families, they are at times troublesome to the boats descending the river and have even plundered some of them and committed a few murders. They were attracted to this country by the Spaniards some years ago when their views were hostile to our country. . . . Col. Vego of Vincennes states that, in 1771 and 1772, he was engaged in the Indian trade on the Arkansas;—that he ascended that river about 750 miles, and then entered and ascended one of its westerly branches for a considerable distance. One of his hands or engages, at that time an old man, pointed out to him a Bayou, as they passed the mouth of it, and said that at the head of it there was a curiosity, and invited the Colonel to ascend and examine it. He said that, when he was a young man and a soldier, he was one among others who assisted in running the boundary line between Louisiana and North Mexico, that the line crossed the Bayou already mentioned at the head of it; where, on a large tree, the officers and surveyors fixed a large plate of lead or other metal, with inscriptions on it, and also made several marks or figures on the tree itself. Colonel Vego is ready to conduct any person to the Bayou, which, he says, he can easily find, and should know as soon as he could see it.

Texas.

Dunbar's Journal

Thursday 10th

We made this day by the Pilots accot. 14 leagues and encamped at 'Auges d'avelon' [or d'arclon] 3 leagues below the Missouri; slept near this place on the 23d Novr.,—it appears by reference to the Journal that we were 13 days in going up from this place to Ellis Camp, which has required by 3 broken days to come down, having made several stops to examine the rocks &c., and to day we made a considerable one at the Camp of a M. Le Fevre. This was an intelligent man, a native of the Illenois now living at the Arcansas, he is come here with some Delaware & other Indians whom he has furnished with goods & receives the peltry, fur &c in payment as it is brought in by the hunters. This Gentleman informed us that a considerable party of the Osages from the Arcansa River have made an excursion round by the prairie towards the red river, & down the little Missouri as low as the fourche d'Antoine, & there meeting with a small party of Cherokees, are supposed to have killed six and four more are missing; Three Americans and ten

Chicasaws went a hunting into that quarter, who are also supposed to have been in danger and have not yet returned. M. Le Fevre possesses considerable knowledge of the interior of the Country; he confirms the accounts we have already obtained that the hills or mountains which give birth to the various sources of this river, are themselves insulated and entirely enclosed by the immense plains or prairies which extend from the red to the Arkansa river & are supposed to reach to the feet of the great chain of Mountains which separate the water flowing into the Mississippi from those which discharge themselves into the Western pacific. This prodigious plain is supposed to be 200 leagues in breadth due west, & extending probably from the heads of the rivers to the South of the red river, which fall into the bay of Mexico, as far northward as the Missouri & perhaps farther. One branch indeed of the Great Missouri called the Riviere platte [Shallow river] takes its source so far South that it is found in the neighbourhood of the sources of the red and arcansa rivers, both of which last run a very long course thro' immense regions of the richest and most fertile lands, and are likewise both navigable for flat built & well constructed boats to an unknown distance; the great obstacle upon the Red river, has already been mentioned, viz the covering which has been laid over it by drift logs, which is continually increasing from above, and is said to

The Great Raft, an extensive log and debris jam.

A snagboat at work on the Great Raft of Red River

extend it 17 leagues, it exists between the Nakitosh and the Cadaux nation, about 150 leagues above the first: but no obstacle of any kind is found on the arcansa river; the navigation of which is safe and agreeable without shallows or rapids; the lands on either side are of the best quality well watered with springs, rivulets & creeks sufficient for the turning of Mills. About 200 leagues up the Arcansa is an interesting place called the Salt prairie; at that place during the hot dry weather of summer, the salt may be raked up on the ground into heaps as it often forms a crust of a handsbreadth in thickness; it is not often approached on account of the danger from the Ozage Indians; much less do the white hunters venture higher to visit the silver mines, which all agree are to be found upon that river. The plains to the westward are not to be understood as a dead flat, but as a country almost without [sic] wood, with gentle eminences & valleys in which last is found abundance of water, with rich soil; very little rain falls upon those plains, but the dews are extremely abundant, and the rivulets may be led all over the valleys; such also is the situation of the Spanish settlements at Nacodoches & others westerly, & their crops are generally made without the aid of rain; depending on the dews and the industry of the people in conducting the water of their brooks over their rich level lands. . . . Every account demonstrates that immense natural magazines of salt must exist in the great chain of Mountains to the westward; all known rivers flowing from these mountains during the dry season, are more or less charged with salt, until that property becomes imperceptible by the accession of the waters of many other rivers. M. Le Fevre informed us also that some of the Indians of the Osage nation & belonging to the tribe of White hairs visited the Arcansa river about the beginning of December & robbed all the white hunters upon that river, scarsely leaving them a shirt. All the old french hunters best acquainted with the Indian nations agree in accusing the Osages as being the most faithless of all ; they will pretend to make peace and enter into terms of amity, but on the first favorable occasion, they rob, plunder & even kill without any hesitation; the other Indians speak of them also in terms of great abhorrence, & have been already concerting plans for the destruction of that part of the Nation settled on the arcansa river: if the United States should ever find themselves constrained to chastise the insolence of those faithless savages, a handful of men hoisting the Standard of the U. S. would be attended by the warriors of many nations more than sufficient to bring them to reason.

The Arcansa Nation always waging a defensive war with those robbers, propose sending in the spring of the year a deputation of three chiefs to the Government of the U. S. they say that the Country from the Washita river on the South, including the lands of the arcansa river, white river and St. Francis, termination on the north above the last mentioned is wholly their property; that they propose to say to the Gov[t]. of the U. S. "We will relinquish to your people all the lands to the North of the Arkansa river, on the white river & on the river St. Francis; we will also relinquish the country to the South of the arcansa river upon the Mississippi far beyond the settlements which have ever been attempted by white people, the limits of which we will fix; but we request that the powerful arm of the United States will defend us in the possession of the remainder of our hunting ground lying between the arcansa & Washita river."

William and Persis Lovely

William Lewis Lovely served as the first agent for the Cherokee Indians in their new country from 1813 until his death in 1817. Lovely was a native of Dublin, Ireland, who immigrated before the American Revolution to the Colonies. He joined the Continental Army in 1776, rising to the rank of Major. After the war, Lovely secured the position of Assistant Agent to the Cherokees in Tennessee under Col. Return J. Meigs, who recommended that he be named Agent in Arkansas after the number of emigrating Cherokees grew so large that it was deemed necessary to provide them with an agent. He arrived at Arkansas Post in June of 1813 and ascended the Arkansas River, arriving at the Cherokee settlement in late June or July of that year. In 1813, Lovely was only one of three Indian agents west of the Mississippi; another agent was at Fort Osage, near Kansas City, and there was one at Natchitoches, Louisiana. It has been said that Major Lovely "was the sole representative of the United States Government from Arkansas Post to the setting sun." In a letter dated September, 1815, Lovely wrote to then President James Madison, in whose boyhood home he had served as a servant:

> . . . . When I took leave of you in the year 1774 you were sitting on your father's fence; . . . My situation is I can assure you disagreeable living at upwards of three hundred miles from a post office no ways of procuring information but those which are owing to chance and those seldom happen. So I may say with propriety that I am entirely secluded from the land of the living surrounded on all sides by Indians together with the Worst of White Settlers living just

> below me betwixt whom there are daily disturbances arising & against whom there are no possible means in my power of enforcing any laws. . . .

The Major was apparently a man of strong convictions and was prone to act upon what he considered necessary without waiting for orders from Washington. He showed a strong ability to recognize future problems and to attempt to rectify situations of impending danger. He was, it seems, genuinely concerned for the Indians under his supervision, who evidently saw in him a friend and protector in their new home. Lovely was aware of the dangers to the peace from the "lawless" whites who lived below him on the Arkansas River, which must have prompted the Notice of 1813 that appears below.

Major Lovely and his wife settled among the Cherokees on a tract of land purchased from the Osages and called the "Lovely Purchase." Most of the purchase lay in the lands which were ceded to the Cherokees in the Treaty of 1828 that established the present western boundary of Arkansas, so most of the "Lovely Purchase" was lost to Arkansas. However, in the Major's lifetime it was his home and the home of his wife, Persis, until her death in 1842. Mrs. Lovely remained on the land after the death of the Major in 1817 by permission of the Cherokees. The Treaty of 1817, made by the U. S. government, granted a large tract of land north of the Arkansas River to the Cherokees in exclusive ownership and forbid any whites to occupy those lands. However, the Indians requested that Persis Lovely be allowed to remain and she is specifically named in the treaty as the only white person given such permission. Her Memorial to Congress and the letter addressed to President Jackson reveal something of the regard for the Major and the problems encounted by Mrs. Lovely in the Cherokee Nation.

July 20th, 1813

Notice

Is hereby given that a temporary [boundary] is agreed to be drawn between the Cherokees and the White people in order to keep peace and harmony between them and their white brothers—until the Aprobation of the President, their father be known, the line to be drawn as follows first, Beginning on White river where the line intersects the river that was agreed on between General Clarke and the Osage Nation from thence down the middle of said river, to the junction with Little red river to the mouth of Cedar Creek from thence up to the source of sd creek from thence in a direct line to Budwell's Old Place—upon the Arkansas river at the mouth of point remove byo Thence a southwesterly course so as to include the waters of the Pete, John Byo to a point claimed by Other Tribes that is to say the line between the Territory of the Missouri and State of Louisiana, thence a westerly Course till it intercepts the affore said Osage boundary—I do here recommend it to all inhabitants—not to intrude upon the peaceable demeanor of the Cherokees, the Sages, and Other tribes, according to the wish of their father The President.

It will be neccessary that recourse may be had to the treatys subsisting between the United States and the Several Tribes of Indians taken under the protection of General Government, if any such intrusion shall be made.

The Cherokees do pledge themselves that no enemy white or red shall influence them to action inimicable or contrary to the wish of their Great Father the President. The present war existing between America and Britain will Justify their best endeavors, for peace with both white and red.

For WmL Lovely Agent for the Cherokee

Memorial to Congress by Persis Lovely

(NA:HF.,21 Cong., sess.: DS)
(Referred December 16, 1829)

TO THE HONORABLE THE SENATE AND HOUSE OF REPRESENTATIVES OF UNITED STATES OF AMERICA IN CONGRESS ASSEMBLED.

The Memorial of the undersigned Persis Lovely humbly sheweth. That, she was the wife, and is the relict of Maj. William L.S. Lovely who was an officer pending the Revolutionary War for seven years, and afterwards employed in the Agency of the Cherokees East & West of the Mississippi for upwards of nineteen years.—Maj. Lovely was ordered West of the Mississippi as agent to the emigrating Cherokees in the year 1813 as the records of the War Department will attest.—During all the term of his service as agent, Your Memorialist has the proud satisfaction accompanied with sorrowful recollection of saying, that she was his consort.—In leaving his station at Hiawassee in Tennessee, in the year above stated, he abandoned a pleasant residence and improvements, worth from 7. to $800, situated where civilized society was always at hand, for one in the Wilderness wherever the whim or fancy of the Indians might make it neccessarily compulsary on him to locate himself & his family.—After a tedious passage which threatened famine & danger from the many hostile parties of Indians that Surrounded us, Maj Lovely fixed his residence on the Illinois Bayou one mile above its junction with the Arkansas, and about the centre of the Settlements made by the Cherokees:—Where under circumstances the most disadvantageous, he erected buildings and opened a small farm, purchasing flour at the rate of twenty dollars per barrel, and all other description of provision and supplies at a like proportion, half of which your memorialist States with truth, he was compelled from Charitable feeling, to bestow on the suffering and perishing Cherokees; finding that his salary would not support him under such exorbitant though neccessary expenditures and being daily exposed to hostile & beligerent parties of Indians, as well as every other privation of Civilized life; he at one time made a declaration that he would Resign his appointment; this was no sooner known and understood by the Cherokees then on the Arkansas River, than they assembled around him & asserted, if he did so, that they would re-cross the Mississippi and never return. Knowing that it was the policy of the Government to place the Indians West of the Mississippi, his love of Country spoke his imperious duty, and under all the bereavements of Comfort, privations and dangers of life, he remained till 1817 when he paid the debt of nature, and was interred upon the spot where he located himself, and the spot which destiny has since fixed your Memorialist upon, and from which, she now utters her prayer.

Russellville.

Under such circumstances, can it be doubted that your Memorialist was left in a helpless, bereaved, and forlorn situation; without a neighbor but the savages, without a friend or relative closer than Massachusets, and even without the pecuniary means of conveying herself to them.—Thus situated, she formed the resolution of obtaining permission to remain where she was for life, looking upon the tomb that held the remains of her husband, until time and will of Heaven should call her hence, and to have her ashes mingled with that of his.—This Resolution met with the approbation of the Cherokees, and at the Treaty of Hiawassee in 1817 where Gen Andrew Jackson was one of the Commissioners, a life estate was guaranteed to her with the privlege of Cultivating as much soil as she chose.

Thus had your memorialist remained in a situation desolate indeed, but one which a fixed & tried detirmination had reconciled her to, until the late

Treaty at Washington City with the Cherokees; in which Treaty the former Compact is entirely forgotten, her name not even mentioned, and herself disposed of as though she was a Cherokee.—This is not the only hardship accompanying the many misfortunes of the widowed woman; The only reserve of Land made by the last mentioned Treaty was one of about 3000 acres for specified purposes and objects; within this reserve your memorialist residence falls, the reserve has been sold and become private property, and she now finds herself a tenant at will to an individual, instead of being Sheltered under the wing of Government, and secure in the attachment of a whole Nations of Indians who universally looked up to her and called her mother:—It is true that the improvements of your memorialist was appraised (in like manner of those of the Indians) at the inconsiderable sum of five hundred Dollars; Should she ever receive this pittance, which she has not yet; She would ask in the name of justice if it could be considered equivalent to a life estate (however precarious that might be) together with the privilege of cultivating as much soil as she might see proper? She would ask if her landlord should compel her to leave the spot of all others she is most attached to in nature, if five hundred Dollars would compensate her for the losses she would have to sustain for disposing of her Stock and other personal property that she could not take with her, or procure any price for where she is?—She would ask if $500 would purchase her a comfortable home for life with unlimited privilege of soil elsewhere? She would imploringly ask if the Justice and humanity of Congress would not shudder, if the wife & Widow of a faithful officer of Government who pioneered the way to the acquisition of this portion of Country which has just been permanantly secured by Treaty, Should be turned out of doors at her advanced stage of life to wander in search of a home and shelter, without child to comfort or assist her, and without anything to subsist on but the *prospect* of five hundred dollars for life? A life which under such circumstances would almost become a burthen, but which under the dispensations of heaven might be protracted for a number of years.—She feels convinced that the philanthropy and magnaminety of Congress will avert such a catastrophe; and therefore prays that your Honorable bodies will make such other and farther provision for her support and assistance, as in their Justice & Wisdom they may deem meet; and your memorialist as in duty bound will ever pray &c

Persis Lovely

Persis Lovely to the President

Pope County A. T. January 9, 1830—

Sir I intrude to Solicit redress for what I feel as a wrong. You Sir, was comissioner to negotiate a treaty with the Cherokees held at Highwassee 1817 in which treaty the place where I then lived was secured to me for life—Maj Lovely my husband died a few months previous to that treaty: and there I have lived unmolested, until 1828 when another treaty with the Cherokees took place, at Washington in which treaty a reservation of land was given to the Cherokees, that reservation included my home: which reservation has Since been sold intire, and in consequince I am a houseless wanderer at Sixty years of age. As soon as I saw the treaty I adress'd a note to the Secretary of War, and an other to the Agent for the Cherokees, who was then at Washington: it was several months before the Agent returned to this countrey, when he told me he had been instructed to let me know that I might Select a place made vacant by the removal of the Cherokees; or have my place valued; and receive the amount in money: it was too late to select a place as all the places worth any thing were taken up, my place was valued by the Gentlemen appointed to value Indian improvements, it was Valued to five-hundred dollars, which sum I have not received and am led to believe I never shall. I have prepared a petition to Congress which I hope is in the hands of The Honourable Member for Arkansas Territory; in which my claims are set forth: in which Sir I have to Solicit your aid and influence if you consider the low voice of a distressed, & she thinks— injured widow an intrusion Sir for which you must blame your own exalted character for benevolence and Justice; for her attempt to interest you in her favour. I have obtained permission to shelter my Self in a house built by a Missionary: one mile from their former establishment, called Dwight where the reverend A Finney lived with the little mill attached to it, which mill does not run more than four months in the year and receive the valuation of the place I was obliged to relinquish I shall be content: but Sir five hundred dollars is a Small remuneration for a home for life, especially to a woman who is a widow childless and lone in the world I confidently hope my Government will do me Justice: and pray your Excelency will interpose your aid that I may Obtain relief.

I am Sir with Respect & Esteem yours &c
Persis Lovely

Addressed: His Excellency Andrew Jackson President of the United States of America Washinton City.
Postmarked: Tekatoka, A.T. Jan 26, 1830 Free.

From *The Arkansas Gazette*: February 16, 1842

Departed this life, at the residence of Mr. Kirkbride Potts in Pope County, Arkansas, on the 18th of January, after a short illness, Mrs. Persis Lovely, aged 71 years, 6 months, and 17 days. She was born in Middleton Connecticut, and was the daughter of Mr. Thomas Brown, who afterwards removed to New Hampshire. She died regretted by all who know her. Eminent in all the social relations of life, her numerous friends will long deplore their loss, and society will mourn for one of its brightest gems. The New Hampshire papers will please copy.

Recollections of Timothy Flint

Timothy Flint lived, worked and traveled in the Mississippi Valley from 1815 until 1825. An ordained minister from Massachusetts, Flint moved with his family into Ohio and Kentucky from which he later moved to Louisiana. He had been attracted to the West even as a child, so his travels fulfilled a lifelong dream. His Recollections provide for the reader accurate and detailed impressions of the country he travelled. Although he was plagued by ill health most of his life, he never tired of visiting new places and recording what he witnessed. He was a sensitive observer, though not always a tactful one, and his Harvard education provided him with the tools to write in a vivid style.

St. Charles, Missiouri.

A regular customer.

I propse therefore to throw together the result of my observations in the southern parts of this state, though they were made on my return from the Arkansas, and to reserve my remarks on that part of the country, as a portion of my observations of the southern part of the Mississippi valley. I will only remark, that in my trip from St. Charles to Arkansas, we went in a very large keel-boat, with an ignorant *patron*. The whole way was one scene of disasters. We ran aground near Belle-Fontaine, and were extricated by the help of a file of soldiers from the garrison. We were carried among the sawyers at the mouth of the Missouri, and narrowly escaped wreck. We were like to be sunk in the harbour at St. Louis by a leak in the bottom of our boat, which commenced in a dark and stormy night. . . .

We were afterwards driven by wind and by mismanagement into an eddy opposite the middle Chickasaw bluff, in which our boat of an hundred feet in length, was whirled about so rapidly, as to create dizziness in the passengers, and in which the centre sunk like a basin, and of course bent the boat, so as that it would have broken, had we not availed ourselves of a fortunate filling of this basin, to get a cable to the trees on shore, by which, with great difficulty, we extricated ourselves. A barge, but a little while before, had been broken in two, in this same eddy. This closed the series of our unpleasant accidents, before we reached the fort of Arkansas. . . . *Memphis.*

~~~~

Letter XXII—Arkansas

May 5, 1819. We were swept round by the strong current of the Mississippi in our keel-boat between two green islands covered with rushes and cotton-waters of White River. This is all a region of deep and universal inundation. There was from six to ten feet water over all the bottoms; and we had a wide display of that spectacle so common in the spring on the Mississippi,—a dense forest of the largest trees, vocal with the song of birds, matted with every species of tangled vegetation, and harbouring in great numbers the turkey-buzzard, and some species of eagles; and all this vegetation apparently rising from the bosom of dark and discoloured waters. . . . It is late in the season before the floods recede; and fever, musquitoes, alligators, serpents, bears, and now and then parties of hunting Indians, are the only tenants of these woods.

The river received its name from the Indians, on account of its pellucid waters. They are in appearance rather green than white; and we could see the huge cat-fish gamboling in the waters, among multitudes of fishes of all classes. . . . We continued to float on through this deep and inundated forest six or seven miles, when at right angles to our course we discovered another opening. It was the Arkansas moving on with a majestic current of waters of the colour of Arnotto die. *Yellowish-red dye.*

This is, next to the Missouri, the largest and most interesting tributary of the Mississippi, and from its mouth by its meanders to the mountains, is commonly computed about two thousand miles. Its course has been traced in these mountains at least five hundred miles, and it is believed that the sources of the Arkansas have not yet been explored by our people. One
~~~~

singularity distinguishes this river from any other of the United States. Where it winds along among the mountains, all agree that it is a broad and deep river, and carries a great volume of water. But no sooner does it emerge from the shelter of woods and mountains, into a boundless and arid plain,—composed to a great depth of quicksands,—than it begins to disappear; and in a hundred miles from the very elevated mountain, near which it enters upon the plain, it is fordable during the summer. Still lower down it is a stream, according to the well-known phrase of this country, "sunk in the sand"; that is, it trickles amidst the banks of sand and pebbles, so as in many places to exhibit a dry channel of burning sand from bank to bank. here, on these vast sandy plains, which will for ages be the Syrtes of America, the home of elks and buffaloes, are the wide fields of those rich native grapes, that all travellers in these regions have spoken of in terms of such admiration. They are said to be conical in shape, large, of a beautiful blue, and transparent. The driving sands rise round the stem that advances still above the sand. . . .

Muscadine.

Over the whole of these vast plains salt seems to be distributed, even of the surface. In fact, one of the peculiar features of the whole country west of the Mississippi, is these licks,—places where the wild and domestic cattle have beaten firm roads in all directions round them; and by continually licking for the salt, intermixed with the clay, which they swallow with the salt, there are often wide cavities, sometimes to a considerable depth, occasioned by the consumption by this continual licking. . . .

Arkansas River.

At the distance of fifteen miles below the Post of Arkansas, settlements begin to be thinly established along the river; and from this distance to the mouth, about forty miles, the bottoms of the river are too much and too long inundated to be susceptible of cultivation. In fact, up to the first bluffs, by the course of the river, is a hundred miles. This singular river has a very narrow skirt of soil, sometimes but a few rods in width, and then extending half a mile back, which is elevated so as to be above the ordinary inundations. At the distance of a mile or two from the river, there are first thick cane brakes, then a series of lakes, exactly resembling the river in their points and bends, and in the colour of their waters. When the river is high, it pours its redundant waters into these lakes and Bayous, and the water is in motion for a width of twenty miles. These lakes are covered with the large leaves, and in the proper season the flowers of the "nymphea nelumbom," the largest and most splendid flower that I have ever seen. I have seen them of the size of the crown of a hat; the external leaves of the most brilliant white, and the internal of a beautiful yellow. They are the enlarged copy of the new England pond lily, which has always struck me as

Water Lily.

the most beautiful and fragrant flower of that country. These lakes are so entirely covered with these large conical leaves, nearly of the size of a parasol, and a smaller class of aquatic plant, of the same form of leaves, but with a yellow flower, that a bird might walk from shore to shore without dipping its feet in water; and these plants rise from all depths of water up to ten feet. . . .

The Post of Arkansas is situated on a level tract of land, which has a slight elevation above the adjacent bottom. It lies between two *Bayous*, that are *gullied* very deep, on the bend of the river. The soil about the town is poor and heavy, and covered with shrub-oaks and persimon trees. So perfectly level is the country, that there is not a hill or a stone in forty miles distance. The highest point of land in all this extent is scarcely ten feet above the highest inundations of the river. The court-house is situated within three hundred yards of the river in front, and about the same distance in the rear from a swamp, into which, in high water, White River flows, which is distant thirty miles. In all directions the country is a dead level, and there are innumerable communications between the rivers, in high water, by one of which, a little below the Post, a canoe has gone out of the Arkansas into the Washita, and from that again into Red River, and from that into the *Bayou Chaffatio*, and from that into the Gulf of Mexico, a communication eight hundred miles in extent. . . .

[T]hese open plains are more swept by the winds, and are more free from musquitoes, and healthier than the bottoms; all the planters, who prefer raising cattle to cotton, are settled on the edges of the prairies.

When I first arrived at the Post, the population of the territory,—for it had been recently separated from Missouri, as a territory,—amounted, probably to about ten thousand. These were in long and detached lines, the one along the Mississippi, called the St. Francis settlement; the other on the Mississippi below the mouth of the river, called point Ohico settlement, the settlement on the waters of White River, a settlement far up the Arkansas, called Mulberry settlement, and the settlements on the table land between the Arkansas and Red Rivers, called Mount Prairie.

I did not travel as extensively here as in Missouri; but I travelled enough to see an ample specimen of the people and the country. The valley of the Arkansas, with very little exception, is sickly. Remittents and intermittents are so common, that when a person has no more than simple fever and ague, he is hardly allowed to claim the immunities of sickness, and it is remarked that he has only the ague. The autumn that I was there, it appeared to me that more than half the inhabitants, not excepting the Creoles had the ague.

Beards Town appears on early Arkansas maps west of Little Meto Creek and opposite a village no longer on maps, Heckatoo. It was upstream thirty-five miles from Arkansas Post.

South of the thirty-fourth degree the lands are fine for cotton. I have no where remarked finer fields of cotton, than at the settlement of Bairdstown, about forty miles above the Post, on the river. The season cannot be quite so long as it is on Red River, but the cotton seemed not inferior in luxuriance of growth. . . . The uplands of the country are, with few exceptions, miserable; being either flint knobs, bare hills, or shrubby plains. Mount Prairie is a most interesting exception. This is a circular eminence of table land, perhaps sixteen miles in diameter, rising considerabley above the adjacent country. The soil is a texture of marl and clay, as black as ink, rather inclined to bake and upon it fissures, but very rich. Through this extraordinary stratum of earth, apparently the deposit of a lake or swamp, they dig nearly an hundred feet in order to find water in their wells. What is still more extraordinary, on this curious mound, nearly equidistant between Red and Arkansas Rivers, and at five hundred miles distance from the Gulf of Mexico, are found large marine shells, bleached to the purest white, and in the greatest abundance. . . .

The plains far up the Arkansas, and at a sufficient distance from the influence of its waters, are very dry, have an atmosphere of great purity, and must be healthy. They are the resorts of the Osage and Cherokee Indians. Still farther up, the Pawnees of the northern waters of the Arkansas meet those of the southern waters of the Missouri; and they are sometimes joined by the wandering tribes of the interior provinces of Spain. Here their principal object is to hunt the buffaloe, which is here found in greater numbers than in any other region.

I was at Arkansas at the setting up of the territorial government; and it exhibited a scene sufficiently painful and disgusting. Our government cannot be supposed to be omnipresent or omniscient. Yet if all favouritism were avoided in the appointment of officers in these distant regions; if they took pains to learn how these organs of their will performed their functions, things would be different. But as it is, the recommendations are made by members of congress who have cousins perhaps qualified, but who perhaps have been a burden on their hands, and they are happy to get rid of them by sending them to these remote regions to fill the new offices, created by the erection of a territorial government. The persons who procured the appointment have an interest in withholding unfavourable views, and the parties are not disposed to betray themselves; and these men, dressed out in a "little brief authority," perform deeds to make "the high heavens weep."

They were re-enacting in that distant and turbulent region, what they would call "the blue laws" of old Virginia, relating to gambling, breach of the Sabbath, and the like; and having promulgated these laws, on the succeeding Sabbath,—in the face of their recent ordinances, and of a population who needed the enforcement of them,—the legislators and judges would fall to their usual vocation of gambling through the day. . . .

I saw a noble looking Quawpaw chief, rather advanced in age, who was universally reported to have performed a noble action for the last Spanish commandant. It seems that a party of Muskogee Indians,—as the Creeks are called by the tribes, and by themselves,—had penetrated to the Post, found the only child of the commandant,—but just advanced beyound the age of infancy,—so unguarded or so far from the house, that they seized on him and carried him off. The commandant, upon learning the fact, was, as may naturally be supposed, in an agony. The Quawpaw in question proposed, for some trifling compensation, to follow the party down the Arkansas, and recover the child; and he fulfilled his promise in this way:—he descended behind them to the grand "cut-off," the *Bayou* that unites White River and the Arkansas; and at the point of the vast island made by this *Bayou*, the Arkansas, and the Mississippi, he found the savages encamped, holding high jubilee over the roasted carcass of a bear. It is the custom of the savages of these regions to send forward some noted warrior, like the herald of the Romans, who, at the commencement of the first battle, threw a javelin into the enemy's camp, and devoted them to the infernal gods. This warrior, as the "avant courier" of his tribe, rushes upon the enemy, singing the war-song, and shouting defiance. So did this intrepid Indian,—and the Muskogees, supposing the united Spanish and Quawpaws to be behind, sprung to their canoes, leaving their utensils, their unfinished feast, their whiskey, and the child, behind, and the crafty savage immediately seized the child, and began his return up the river. The same savage performed an office, scarcely less dangerous, for me, in recovering a valuable yawl from the ferocious Choctaws, who had stolen it and carried it far up the river. *Saracin.*

The remaining period which I spent in this country was, from a hundred circumstances, a time of gloom and dejection. Every member of my family was visited with fever, except myself. The lives of two were in jeopardy for a number of days. All the neighbours were sick, and many were dying about me. A negro child died in my family. Our only servant was sick and in this season of general distress no other could be procured. The only physician in whom we had confidence, and who had been a member of my family, was sick. The air was excessively sultry, and the musquitoes troublesome to a degree, which I have not experienced before nor since. I was obliged to rise from my bed at least ten times a night, for forty nights, I soon would become oppressed for want of breath under the curtain, and when I drew it up and attempted to inhale a little of the damp and sultry atmosphere, the musquitoes would instantly settle on my face in such numbers that I was soon obliged to retreat behind my curtain again. Thus passed those dreadful nights amidst the groans of my family, calls for medicine and drink, suffocation behind my curtain, or the agony of musquitoe stings, as soon as I was exposed to the air. These were gloomy days indeed; for during the day the ardours of the sun were almost intolerable. My accustomed walk, to change the scene and to diversify the general gloom a little, was down a breach towards the upper *Bayou* under the shade of some lofty cypress trees; and even here, the moment I was out of the full heat of the sun, the musquitoes, which, during the heats of the day, took shelter in the shade, would rise in countless swarms from the grass to attack me.

During all this gloomy summer, we could not take our food until a fire, kindled with the most offensive materials, and under the table, dispersed its suffocating fumes to drive them away. Even when I wrote a letter, it was necessary that some one should be at hand to brush off the musquitoes. In truth, the lower course of the Arkansas is infested with these tormenting insects in a degree in which I have never seen them elsewhere. The inhabitants, while jesting upon the subject, used to urge this incessant torment as a excuse for deep drinking. A sufficient quantity of wine or spirits to produce a happy reverie, of a dozing insensiblility, had a cant, but very significant name,—"a musquitoe dose. . . ."

I had preached regularly every Sabbath, in the court-house, up to the time when my family was taken sick. My congregation was principally French, and although at that time my pronunciation of their language was defective, I attempted in the best manner in my power to address them in their own language. They are always in such circumstances polite, and seem attentive. But in regions like this, where the habits, unchecked by any serious influence, unawed by any example, have been gathering stability for an age, a few sermons, be they impressive or otherwise, cannot be expected to have much effect. One thing has been indelibly impressed in my mind by deep conviction;—that religion nowhere has much influence unless its rites have some degree of uniformity, unless the associations of awe, of tenderness, and of piety, are established by frequent and long repetition. Hence it is, that the transient labours of itinerants, manifested in earnestness and exclamation, seem to operate on a region over which it passes like the flames of a stubble field. There is much appearance of flame and smoke; but the fire passes slightly over the surface, and in a few days the observer sees not a trace of the conflagration left. I did not flatter myself that my services were of much utility.

The French people generally came to the place of worship, arrayed in their ball-dresses, and went directly from worship to the ball. A billiard room was near, and parts of my audience sometimes came in for a moment, and after listening to a few sentences, returned to their billiards. Nor is here the only place, where the preacher has to endure the heart-wearing agony of having an audience interchanging their attention repeatedly between the sermon the billiard-room, in the delivery of one discourse. . . .

Before I left the country, I crossed the river to view the wretched remains of that singular class of enthusiasts, known in this country by the name of the "Pilgrims." This whole region, it is true, wears an aspect of irreligion; but we must not thence infer, that we do not often see the semblance and the counterfeit of religion. There is no country where bigotry and enthusiasm are seen in forms of more glaring absurdity, and, at the same time, of more arrogant assumption. There were, I think, six persons of them left,—the "prophet," so called, and his wife, and another woman and perhaps three children. They were sick and poor; and the rags with which they were originally habited to excite attention, and to be *in keeping* with their name and assumption, were now retained from necessity. The "prophet" was too sick to impart much information, and the others seemed reluctant to do it. But from the wife of the prophet I gleaned the information which follows, of their origin, progress, and end. I have collated her information with the most authentic notices of them, which I obtained at every stage on the Mississippi where they were seen, and where they stopped.

It seems that the fermenting principle of the society began to operate in Lower Canada. A few religious people began to talk about the deadness and the unworthiness of all churches, as bodies, and they were anxious to separate from them, in order to compound a more perfect society. The enthusiasm caught in other minds like a spark fallen in flax. A number immediately sold every thing, and prepared to commence a course towards the southwest. In their progress through Vermont they came in contact with other minds affected with the same longing with themselves. There can be no doubt that most of them were perfectly honest in their purpose. The "prophet," a compound, like the character of Cromwell, of hypocrite and enthusiast, joined himself to them, and from his superior talents or contributions to the common stock of the society, became their leader. They went on accumulating through New York, where their numbers amounted to nearly fifty. Here they encountered the Shakers, and as they had some notions in common, a kind of coalition was attempted with them. But the Shakers are industrious and neat to a proverb, and are more known to the community by these traits, than any other. But industry made little part of the religion of the Pilgrims, and neatness still less; for it was a maxim with them to wear the clothes as long as they would last on the body, without washing or changing; and the more patched and particoloured the better. If they wore one whole shoe, the other one,—like the pretended pilgrims of old time,—was clouted and patched. . . . [E]ach party claimed the victory, and lamented the obduracy, blindness, and certain tendency to everlasting destruction of the other; and they probably parted with these expectations of each other's doom.

I knew nothing of their course from that place to New Madrid below the mouth of the Ohio. They were then organized to a considerable degree, and had probably eight or ten thousand dollars in common stock. The prophet was their ruler, spiritual and temporal. He had visions by night, which were expounded in the morning, and determined whether they should stand still or go on; whether they should advance by land or water; in short every thing was settled by immediate inspiration. . . .

Their food was mush and milk, prepared in a trough, and they sucked it up, standing erect, through a perforated stalk of cane. They enjoined severe penances, according to the state of grace in which the penitent was. For the lower stages the penance was very severe, as to stand for four successive days without reclining or sitting, to fast one or two days. In fact fasting was a primary object of penance, both as severe in itself, and as economical. They affected to be ragged, and to have different stripes in their dresses and caps, like those adopted in penitentiaries as badges of the character of the convicts. So formidable a band of ragged Pilgrims, marching in perfect order, chanting with a peculiar twang the short phrase "Praise God! Praise God!" had in it something imposing to a people, like those of the West, strongly governed by feelings and impressions. Sensible people assured me that the coming of a band of these Pilgrims into their houses affected them with a thrill of alarm which they could hardly express. The untasted food before them lost its savour, while they heard these strange people call upon them, standing themselves in the posture of statues, and uttering only the words, "Praise god, repent, fast, pray." Small children, waggish and profane as most of the children are, were seen to shed tears, and to ask their parents, if it would not be fasting enough, to leave off one meal a day. . . . At Pilgrim Island, thirty miles below, and opposite the Little Prairie, they staid a long time.

Here dissensions began to spring up among them. Emaciated with hunger, and feverish from filth and the climate, many of them left their bones. They were ordered by the prophet, from some direct revelation which he received, to lie unburied; and their bones were bleaching on the island when we were there. Some escaped from them at this place, and the sheriff of the county of New Madrid, indignant at the starvation imposed as a discipline upon the little children, carried to them a pirogue of provisions, keeping off with his sword the leaders, who would fain have prevented these greedy innocents from satiating their appetites.

While on this island, a great number of boatmen are said to have joined, to take them at their profession of having no regard for the world, or the things of it, and robbed them of all their money, differently stated to be between five and ten thousand dollars. From this place, reduced in number by desertion and death, in their descent to the mouth of the Arkansas, there were only the numbers surviving, which I saw. When I asked the wife of the prophet, why, instead of descending in the summer to the sickly country, they had not ascended to the high and healthy regions of Cape Girardeau, in order to acclimate themselves before their descent; their answer was, that such calculations of worldly wisdom were foreign to their object; that they did not study advantage, or calculate to act as the world acts upon such subjects, but that suffering was a part of their plan. . . . this history of the delusion and destruction of between thirty and forty people, most of them honest and sincere, left a deep and melancholy impression of the universal empire of bigotry, and its fatal influences in all ages and countries. . . .

In a cabin at the mouth of the Arkansas, I saw a woman, apparently very sick of fever and ague, lying on the floor of the cabin, on a bear skin, with an infant babe also sick by her side. She had been evidently a beautiful woman, and by her countenance, and her manner, as well as by remnants of tattered lace and finery, I saw that she had not been born and reared in this country. I asked her for her story. With great labour and exhaustion, and with accents often interrupted, she told me the following tale. She was born in London, and had married a sergeant in the British army. He had been ordered on the service against New Orleans. After the defeat of the eighth of January, he was a prisoner, and chose to remain in the country. She had crossed the Atlantic in pursuit of her truant husband, had landed at New York, and made her way to Cincinnati; being here in extreme misery and want, and in despair of ever finding her husband she had, as the horrid but familiar phrase of this country is, "taken up with a man" at Cincinnati, by whom she had this child. After living with her a few months, he had deserted her. She then came down in a boat, until within sixty miles of the Arkansas, had then and there been taken extremely ill of fever and ague, and had been taken in by a family who kept her as long as she had any clothes or trinkets left. The men of the family had then taken her from bed after sunset, put her in a pirogue, and rowed her down during the night to the mouth of the river, and there left her on the sand-bar. The bank which it was necessary to mount, before arriving at a house, was sixty feet high. She made various attempts, as the morning sun began to beat upon her head, to mount this bank, in hope of finding either a house, or shelter. All her exertions failed, and she laid herself down and tried to resign herself to die.

It happened that some men, who cut wood for the steam-boats, boarded at the house above the bank. They were crossing the river a third of a mile above the mouth, to go to their morning task. They heard the wailings of the infant that was lying by its mother. One of the men insisted that the cries were those of a child. The rest ridiculed the idea, and insisted that it was the scream of owls, that in these countries often utter their notes in the morning. He would not be ridiculed out of his persuasion, crossed back to the side of the river from which he started, descended it to the mouth, and there on the bar found the woman and her babe. She was taken in at the house on the bank, and treated as kindly as their circumstances would admit. We gave her counsel, and a small sum of money, collected in common from all who heard her story, and left her. I know nothing of her history beyond that time.

The Thomas Nuttal Journal

Thomas Nuttall provided for the scientific world the first extensive record of the botanical wonders of Arkansas when he published his journal in 1821. A self-taught botanist from Liverpool, Nuttall would earn the respect of botanists in both England and America before his death. He would, for a time, serve as the botanist for Harvard University and become an honorary member of the American Philosophical Society and of the Academy of Natural Sciences. He arrived in Philadelphia on April 23, 1808 and in 1810 joined the John Jacob Astor land brigade in exploring the northern portion of the Louisiana Purchase. It was on this trip that he determined to travel through the southern portion of the Purchase to continue his botanical research of the North American Continent. The War of 1812 forced him to return to England and his plans were not realized until after that war. He returned to America in 1815 and immediately set about implementing his ambitious project to write a volume on American flora. This project, as well as the necessity to acquire some funds, kept him from his desired plan until fall of 1818. He left

Philadelphia on October 2, 1818, with $150 from his patrons, a few personal belongings, his pocket microscope and a firearm which he used to dig plants and roots. He went by stage to Lancaster, Pennsylvania. From that point he chose to travel on foot and alone. For a little over a year, Nuttal walked through the country, inspecting and examining plant life. His acuteness as an observer, his ability to gather information from acquaintances, his interest in Indian antiquities and contemporary life make his journal rich and revealing.

To-day I was detained at Mr. M'Lane's, waiting the drunken whim of the Yankee, whom necessity had obliged me to hire. In the course of a few hours he had shifted from two bargains. At first, I was to give him five dollars for his assistance, and in case that should prove inadequate, I had agreed to hire an additional hand on the Arkansa. Now he wished to have the boat for bringing her completely to the Port, and next he wanted 10 dollars. . . . Today we proceeded up White river with considerable difficulty, and hard labour, the Mississippi not being sufficiently high to produce any eddy. . . . I now found the boatman whom I had hired, one of the most worthless and drunken scoundrels imaginable; he could not be prevailed upon to do any thing but steer, while myself and the other man I had hired, were obliged to keep constantly to the oar, or the cordelle (tow-rope). In the evening we left the boat without any guard, intending to repair to it in the morning from Mr. M'Lane's, where we returned again this evening, being only three miles distant across the forest. Here I discovered that the Yankee intended to proceed to the boat in our absence and rob me, pretending some business to the mouth of the Arkansas, for which he must depart by moon-light. Unknown to him, however, and accompanied by a young man whom I had hired in his place, we repaired to the boat, waiting under arms the approach of the thief, but unable to obtain a boat, he had relinquished the attempt, and saved himself from chastisement . . . .

[15th]We continued with hard labour ascending White river to the bayou, in a direction of west to north-west, the bayou or cut-off continuing to the south-west. In this distance, there are no settlements, the land being overflowed by the back water of the Mississippi. We passed nearly through the bayou, in which there are four points of land and a half; the current carrying us almost three miles an hour towards the Arkansa, which it entered nearly at right angles, with a rapid current, and a channel filled with snags. The length of the bayou appears to be about eight or nine miles.

[16th] Leaving the bayou, we entered the Arkansa, which was very low,

but still red and muddy from the freshets of the Canadian. Most of the larger streams which enter into it from the south, are charged with red and turbid water, while those of the north are clear . . . . The Arkansa had here a very gentle current, and was scarcely more than 200 yards wide, with its meanders on a small scale, similar to those of the Mississippi. In consequence of the unrestrained dominion of the inundation, no settlements yet appeared in this quarter. We proceeded chiefly by means of the cordelle, but at a very tedious and tiresome rate, for, after the utmost exertion, with our unwieldy boat, we were this evening only six and a half miles above the outlet of the bayou.

[17th.] We found the labour of towing our boat exceedingly tiresome, in consequence of the sudden falling of the river . . . With painful exertions, and after wading more than three hours in the river, we passed only two bars in the course of the day.

[18th] To-day we towed along two bars, much more considerable than any preceding bends, but had the disappointment to spend the night only a single mile below Madame Gordon's, the place of our destination with the boat, and only 16 miles above the bayou, by which we entered the Arkansa. This house is the first which is met with in ascending the river . . . .

The land, although neglected, appears in several places, below Madame Gordon's, high enough to be susceptible of cultivation, and secure from inundation, at least for some distance from the immediate bank of the river.

No change, that I can remark, yet exists in the vegetation, and the scenery is almost destitute of every thing which is agreeable to human nature. . . . All is rude nature as it sprang into existence, still preserving it primeval type, its unreclaimed exuberance. . . .

A mile and a half from Madame Gordon's there was a settlement, consisting of four or five French families, situated upon an elevated tract of fertile land, which is occasionally insulated by the overflowings of the White and Arkansa rivers.

Possibly yellow rocket mustard.

[20th.] . . . . [O]n the high and open bank of the river near to Madame Gordon's, I had already the gratification of finding flowers of the same natural family as many of the early plants of Europe; the Cruciferae; but to me they were doubley interesting, as the first fruits of a harvest never before reaped by any botanist.

In the afternoon, I walked about a mile from the river to the house of Monsieur Tenass, and honest and industrious farmer. The crop of cotton, and of corn, here the last summer was, I understand, very indifferent, for want of rain, The first sold here, at five to six dollars per hundred weight, in the seed; and flour at 10 dollars per barrel . . . .

The land on which this gentleman and his neighbours resided, in tolerable independence, is very considerably elevated and open, bearing a resemblance to the lands about the Chicasaw Bluffs, and at first view, I thought I discovered a considerable hill, but it was, in fact, an enormous mound, not less than 40 feet high, situated towards the centre of a circle of other lesser mounds, and elevated platforms of earth. The usual vestiges of earthenware, and weapons of hornstone flint, are here also met with, scattered over the surrounding soil . . . .

Prehistoric temple mound, surrounded by grave mounds, is representative of the Middle Mississippi Culture (A.D. 1300-1700).

Towards evening, two keel boats came in sight, one of which was deeply loaded with whiskey and flour; the other, a small boat fitted out by a general Calamees and his brother, two elderly men out on a land speculation, who intended to ascend the river as far as the Cadron, which is 300 miles from hence by water, or to the Fort, which is 350 miles further. I perceived that they noted down every particular which came to their knowledge, but appeared to be illiterate men, and of course, I found them incapable of appreciating the value of science. On application, they merely condescended to offer me a passage, provided I would find my own provision, and work as a boatman. Such was the encouragement, which I at length wrung from these generous speculators; not, I dare say, exploring the Missouri territory with the philanthropic views as the generous Birkbeck. . . .

[22d] The path, which I this morning pursued to the Post, now town of Arkansas, passed through remarkably contrasted situations and soil. After leaving the small circumscribed and elevated portion of settled lands already noticed, and over which were scattered a number of aboriginal mounds, I entered upon an oak swamp, which, by the marks on the trees, appeared to be usually inundated, in the course of the summer, four to six feet by the back water of the river. . . . After crossing this horrid morass, a delightful tract of high ground again occurs, over which the floods had never yet prevailed; here the fields of the French settlers were already of a vivid green, and the birds were singing from every bush, more particularly the red bird . . . and the blue sparrow. . . . After emerging out of the swamp, in which I found it necessary to wade about ankle deep, a prairie came into view, with scattering houses spreading over a narrow and elevated tract for about three miles parallel to the bend of the river.

On arriving, I waited on Monsieur Bougie, one of the earliest settlers and principal inhabitants of the place, to whom I was introduced by letter. I soon found in him a gentleman, though disguised at this time in the garb of a Canadian boatman. He treated me with great politeness and respect, and, from the first interview, appeared to take a generous and active interest in my favour. Monsieur B. was by birth a Canadian, and, though 70 years of age, possessed almost the vigour and agility of youth. This settlement owes much to his enterprise and industry.

The town, or rather settlement of the Post of Arkansas, was somewhat dispersed over a prairie, nearly as elevated as that of the Chicasaw Bluffs, and containing in all between 30 and 40 houses. The merchants, then transacting nearly all the business of the Arkansa and White river, were Messrs. Braham and Drope, Mr. Lewis, and Monsieur Notrebe, who kept well-assorted stores of merchandize, supplied chiefly from New Orleans, with the exception of some heavy articles of domestic manufacture obtained from Pittsburgh. Mr. Drope, to whom I was also introduced by letter, received me with politeness, and I could not but now for awhile consider myself as once more introduced into the circle of civilization.

The improvement and settlement of this place proceeded slowly, owing, in some measure, as I am informed, to the uncertain titles of the neighbouring lands. Several enormous Spanish grants remained still undecided; that of Messrs. Winters, of Natchez, called for no less than one million acres, but the congress of the United States, inclined to put in force a kind of agrarian law against such monopolizers, had laid them, as I was told, under the stipulation of settling upon this immense tract a certain number of families.

Nuttall's 1821 sketch of Cadron Settlement

The cotton produced in this neighborhood, of a quality no way inferior to that of Red river, obtained this year from six to six and a half dollars per cwt. in the seed, and there are now two gins established for its preparation, though, like everything else, in this infant settlement of the poor and improvident, but little attention beyond that of absolute neccessity, was as yet paid to any branch of agriculture. Nature has here done so much, and man so little, that we are yet totally unable to appreciate the value and resources of the soil. Amongst other kinds of grain, rice has been tried on a small scale and found to answer every expectation. The price of grain brought from New Orleans, was no less than 25 to 37 1/2 cents per pound by retail. Under the influence of a climate as mild as the south of Europe, and a soil equal to Kentucky, wealth will ere long flow, no doubt, to the banks of the Arkansa.

I again made application to the land speculators, trying to prevail upon them on any terms, to take up my baggage, as far as the Cadron, which would have enabled me immediately to proceed on my journey, across the great prairie, but they remained inexorable.

[24th] This morning I again proceeded up the river with my flat boat, by the assistance of two French boatmen, full of talk, and, at first, but indifferently inclined to work. . . . The following day in the evening, after a good deal of hard labour and wading, on my part, and that of the negro in my employ, we arrived at Monsieur Bourgie's, and the next day I parted with a sort of regret from the boat, which, with all its difficulties, had afforded me, through the most inclement season of the year, no inconsiderable degree of comfort and convenience.

On the 26th, I proceeded with my baggage and property to the village in Monsieur Bougie's perogue, accompanied by one boatman. . . .

In the meanest garb of a working boatman, and unattended by a single slave, I was no doubt considered, as I had probably been by the land speculators, one of the canaille, and I neither claimed not expected attention; my thoughts centered upon other objects, and all pride of appearance I willingly sacrificed to promote with frugality and industry the objects of my mission.

Riff-raff.

An insignificant village, containing three stores, destitute even of a hatter, a shoe-maker, and a taylor, and containing about 20 houses, after an existence of near a century, scarcely deserved geographical notice, and will never probably flatter the industry of the French emigrants, whose habits, at least those of the Canadians, are generally opposed to improvement and regular industry. During my stay, I took up my residence with Dr. M'Kay, and found in him an intelligent and agreeable companion. . . . Blanket, capeaus, moccasins, and overalls of the same materials, are here, as in Canada, the prevailing dress, and men and women commonly wear a handkerchief on the head in place of hats and bonnets. . . .

[*February* 3d] This afternoon I walked to Mr. Mosely's, six miles distant by land, and 15 by water. . . .The first attempt at settlement on the banks of the Arkansa, was begun a few miles below the bayou which communicates with White river. An extraordinary inundation occasioned the removal of the garrison to the borders of the lagoons near Madame Gordon's, and, again disturbed by an overflow, they at length chose the present site of Arkansas. The first band of hunters who attempted to reside here, were, it is said, obliged to remove, in consequence of the swarms of rats, with which they found the county infested. These animals, which are native, differ specifically from the European species, are much larger, and commit the most serious depredations . . . .

The love of amusements, here, as in most of the French colonies, is carried to extravagance, particularly gambling, and dancing parties or balls. But the sum of general industry is, as yet, totally insufficient for the support of any thing like a town.

The houses, commonly surrounded with open galleries, destitute of glass windows, and perforated with numerous doors, are well enough suited for a summer shelter, but totally destitute of comfort in the winter. Without mechanics, domestic conveniences and articles of dress were badly supplied at the most expensive rate. Provision produced in the country, such as beef and pork, did not exceed six cents per pound; but potatoes, onions, apples, flour, spirits, wine, and almost every other necessary article of diet, were imported at an enormous price, into a country which ought to possess every article of the kind for exportation to New Orleans. Such is the evil which may always be anticipated by forcing a town, like a garrison, into being, previous to the existence of necessary supplies. With a little industry, surely every person in possession of slaves might have, at least, a kitchen garden! But these Canadian descendants, so long nurtured amidst savages, have become strangers to civilized comforts and regular industry. They must, however, in time give way to the introduction of more enterprising inhabitants.

The enormous claim of Messrs. Winters, containing about a million of acres of this territory, and which will yet probably for some time remain undetermined, proves a considerable bar to the progress of the settlement. Besides a great portion of the neighbouring prairie, it embraces much of the finest land on the northern border of the river, and continues for near one hundred miles along its bank.

The great prairie . . . contains an invaluable body of land, and, where sufficiently drained, which is pretty generally the case, except during the rains of winter, would produce most species of grain in abundance. As a pasture it is truly inexhaustible, though in the hottest months of summer occasionally deprived of water . . . .

For several miles in and round the town, the accumulation of low mounds or Indian graves, scattered with those fragments of pots, which were either interred or left on the graves with offers of food, by the affectionate friends of the deceased, mark the ancient residence of the natives. In one of the tumuli, on the bank towards the bayou, intersected by the falling away of the earth, a pot of this kind, still employed by the Chicasaws and other natives for boiling their victuals, had fallen out of the grave, and did not appear to be of very ancient interment. Whether these monuments had been the slow accumulation of natural and casual mortality, or the sad remains of some overwhelming destruction, was now impossible to determine. From the ashes of fires, and fragments of charcoal, besides the accompaniment of many indestructible weapons, utensils, and pots broken into fragments by force, I suspect that these mounds are merely incidental, arising from the demolition of the circular dwelling in which the deceased had been interred, a custom which was formerly practised by the Natchez, Cherokees, and other of the natives. Indeed, the sacrifices and offerings which the Indians formerly made to the manes of the deceased father, were sometimes almost ruinous to his family, though no manes longer blackened by the immolation of human victims. Father Charleviox relates, that . . . the same with the Quapaws (or, as they call themselves, O-guah-pas), then living near the confluence of White river with the Mississippi, he found them in great distress from the ravages of the small-pox. Their burying-place appeared "like a forest of poles and posts newly set up, and on which there hung all manner of things: there is every thing which the savages use." The men and women both continued lamenting thoughout the night, and repeating without ceasing, "*Mihahani*, as the Illinois do, and in the same tone." A mother weeping over the grave of her son, poured upon it a great quantity of Sagamitty (or hominy). Another kindled a fire near one of the tombs, probably for the purpose of sacrificing food, as I have seen practised by the Pawnee-Rikasrees of the Missouri.

Spirits of ancestors.

The aborigines of this territory, now commonly called Arkansas or Quapaws and Osarks, do not at this time number more than about 200 warriors. They were first discovered about the 1685, by Chevalier de Tonti. From what source Father Charlevoix ascertains that they were very numerous in the time of Ferdinand de Soto, I am unable to learn . . . .

French Explorer, merchant, and colonizer of the Mississippi valley.

In a council held with the Quapaws some years ago, concerning the boundaries of the lands which they claimed, a very old chieftain related to the agent, that at a very remote period his nation had descended the

Mississippi, and after having proceeded in one body to the entrance of a large and muddy river (the Missouri), they had there divided, one party continuing down the Mississippi, and the other up the miry river. The descending band were checked in their progress by the Kaskaskias, whose opposition they at length subdued. In their further descent they were harassed by the Chicasaws and Choctaws, and waged war with them for some considerable time, but, at length, overcoming all opposition, they obtained the banks of the Arkansa, where they have remained ever since. Some of them, reverting apparently to the period of creation, say, that they originally emerged out of the water, but made many long and circuitious journeys upon that element, previous to their arrival on the banks of this river. . . .They bear an unexceptionally mild character, both amongst the French and Americans, having always abstained, as they say, from offering any injury to the whites. Indeed, to do them justice, and to prove this opinion concerning them is no modern prejudice, I cannot do less than quote the testimony of Du Pratz, made about a century ago. Speaking of the Arkansa territory, he adds, "I am so prepossessed in favour of this country, that I persuade myself the beauty of the climate has a great influence on the character of the inhabitants, who are at the same time very gentle, and very brave. They have ever had an inviolable friendship for the French, uninfluenced thereto, either by fear or views of interest; and live with them as brethren, rather than as neighbours ." . . .

The social regulations, as well as the superstitions and ideas of the supernatural entertained by the Quapaws, are no way materially distinct from those which are practised by their eastern and northern neighbours. The most simple testimonies of attachment, without the aid of solemn vows, are thought sufficient to complete a conjugal felicity, which, where all are equal, in wealth and property, can only be instigated throughout the desire of personal gratification or mutual attachment, and can but seldom be attended with that coldness and disgust, which is but too common, where this sacred tie is knit by avarice. Neither is this contract controlled by any unnatural and overruling policy. The obligation to decorum and the essential ties of society are not abandoned by the Indian, in consequence of his being freed from the perpetual restraint, which appears to have been requisite in civilized society. The father can recall his daughter from the habitation of one who has rendered himself odious to his child. The husband can abandon the wife who has made herself obnoxious to his house and family. They are only united by the bonds of mutual esteem and reciprocal friendship; they will, of course, endeavour to deserve it of each other, as affording a gratification to themselves, no less than to their parents and relatives. . . .

That any ceremonies, more than the celebration of a frugal and sober feast, are constantly practised by any of the natives of this country, is much more than can be satisfactorily proved. Among the Quapaws, I have been informed, that the husband, on the consummation of his marriage, presents his wife with the leg of a deer, and she, in return, offers him an ear of maize, both of which are so many symbols of that provision against the calls of necessity, which they are mutually accustomed to provide.

The young and unmarried women of the Quapaws, according to a custom equally prevalent among many other tribes of Indians, wear their hair braided up into two parts, brought round to either ear in a cylindric form, and decorated with beads, wampum, or silver. After marriage these locks are all unfolded, the decorations laid aside for her daughters, and her hair, brought together behind in a single lock, becomes no longer an assiduous object of ornament. . . .

Small cylindrical beads made from polished shells.

The ideas of supernatural agency, entertained by the Arkansas, are very similar to those which prevail among the natives of the Missouri. Every family, for example, chooses its *penates*, or guardian spirit, from among those various objects of creation which are remarkable for their sagacity, their utility, or power. Some will perhaps choose a snake, a buffaloe, an owl, or a raven; and many of them venerate the eagle to that degree, that if one of those birds should happen to be killed during any expedition, the whole party immediately return home. The large feathers of the war-eagle, which they consider talismanic, are sometimes distributed throughout the nation, as sacred presents, which are expected to act as sovereign charms to those who wear them.

The cure of diseases, though sometimes attempted with rational applications, is not unfrequently sought, among the Quapaws, and many other natives of the continent, in charms and jugglery.

As to the future state, in which they are firm believers, their ideas are merely deduced from what they see around them. Their heaven for hunters is at least as rational as that of some of our own fanatics.

For some considerable time after the interment of a warrior and hunter, his grave is frequented with provision, which, if still remaining, after a reasonable lapse of time, is considered as a sure presage that the deceased has arrived at a bountiful hunting ground, and needs no further supply from the earth.

The Quapaws though no greater proficients in music than the rest of the Indians, have, however, songs appropriated to love, to death, and to battle, but which are merely so many simultaneous effusions of the heart, accompanied by rude and characteristic airs and dances . . . .

[T]he dress of the Arkansas . . . are, as usual, moccasins for the feet; leggings which cover the leg and thigh; a breech-cloth; an overall or hunting shirt, seamed up, and slipped over the head; all of which articles are made of leather, softly dressed by means of fat and oily substances, and often rendered more durable by the smoke with which they are purposely imbued. The ears and nose are adorned with pendents and the men, as among many other Indian tribes, and after the manner of the Chinese, carefully cut away the hair of the head, except a lock on the crown, which is plaited and ornamented with rings, wampum, and feathers. Many of them, in imitation of the Canadian French, wear handkerchiefs around their heads, but in the manner of a turban. Some have also acquired the habit of wearing printed calicoe shirts next to the skin.

The younger Indians, as I am informed, notwithstanding the neglect of renewing their dress, are so partial to cleanliness of the skin, that they practice bathing both winter and summer.

From Arkansas to the Cadron, a distance of about 300 miles by water, I now understood there existed a considerable line of settlements along the north border of the river, and that the greatest uninhabited interval did not exceed 30 miles. . . . [T]he want of society and of employment induced me to embrace the earliest opportunity of continuing my journey into the interior of the territory, where I hoped to find additional employment and gratification in my researches connected with natural history. For this purpose I again embarked on the river in a large skiff, which was proceeding to the Baird's-town settlement; but as most of our company were fond of whiskey, the only beverage in the country, except water or milk, it was difficult to get them parted from their companions and conversation; however, after many efforts to make a start, we at last got off, though merely to make one or two miles . . . . Our encampment was a sand-bar or beach, skirted by willows, and though in itself a situation by no means interesting, yet far from disagreeable to him who can enjoy the simple fare of the hunter, and the calm and unsullied pleasures of nature.

On the following day (February the 27th)we proceeded about 21 miles, or seven points up the river, and in some places against a current of considerable velocity, which had been augmented by a southern freshet, communicating a muddiness and chocolate-brown colour to the stream.

. . .

Arkansas Post. On the 28th, after ascending about 13 miles, we arrived at the settlement begun by colonel Mooney, consisting of three of four families. I was here very hospitabley entertained by Mr. Davison. Near this house, and about

200 yards from the river, there was a fine lake of clear water, of considerable extent, communicating with the river by a bayou, which enters a few miles below. Its bed appeared to be firm and sandy. The neighbouring land was of a superior quality, either for corn or cotton, but all conditionally held on the uncertain claim of Messrs. Winters. Notwithstanding the extent of inundated lands, the climate was considered unusually healthy, and the soil, with but little labour, capable of insuring a comfortable independence to the cultivator. . . .

[4th] The middle of the day, and early part of the afternoon, felt warm and sultry as summer. About noon I arrived at the cabin of Mr. Joseph Kirkendale, four miles above the cut-off in the river, where I tasted nearly the first milk and butter which I had seen since my arrival on the banks of the Arkansa. This farm, like those below on Old River, was situated upon a small and insulated prairie or open and elevated meadow, about 15 miles from the Great Prairie. The drought which was experienced last summer throughout this territory, proved, in many places, nearly fatal to the crops of corn and cotton, so that the inhabitants were now under the necessity of importing maize for provision, at the rate of one dollar and a quarter per bushel.

At Mr. Kirkendale's, I had an interview with the principal chief of the Quapaws, who landed here on his way down the river. His name, to me unintelligible, was Ha-kat-ton (or the *dry man*). He was not the hereditary chief, but received his appointment as such, in consequence of the infancy of the children of the Grand Barbe. . . . Being told that I had journeyed a great distance, almost from the borders of the great lake of salt water, to see the country of the Arkansa, and observing the attention paid to me by my hospitable friend, he, in his turn, showed me every possible civility, returned to his canoe, put on his uniform coat, and brought with him a roll of writing, which he unfolded with great care, and gave it me to read. This instrument was a treaty of the late cession and purchase of lands from the Quapaws, made the last autumn, and accompanied by a survey of the specified country. The lines of this claim, now conceded for the trifling sum of 4000 dollars in hand, and an annuity of a thousand dollars worth of goods, pass up White river, until a south line intersects the Canadian river of Arkansa, then continuing along the course of this river to its sources, afterwards down Red river to the great Raft, and thence in a north-east direction to point Chicot, on the Mississippi, and so in a north-west line to the place of commencement, near White river. Their reservation (situated exclusively on the south bank of the Arkansa) commences at the post or town of Arkansas, and continues up that river to the Little Rock, thence in a southern direction to the Washita, which continues to be the boundary, to a line intersecting the place of commencement. To this deed were added the names of no less than 13 chiefs. This tract contains probably more than 60,000 square miles. Such are the negociating conquests of the American republic, made almost without the expense of either blood or treasure. . . .

A form of water lily, water chinquapin.

This morning I observed the wife of the chief, preparing for her family a breakfast from the nuts of the Cyamus (or Nelumbium). They are first steeped in water, and parched in sand, to extricate the kernals, which are afterwards mixed with fat, and made into a palatable soup. The tubers of the root, somewhat resembling batatas of sweet potatoe, and are penetrated internally and longitudinally, with from five to eight cavities or cells. . . .

On the 7th, we proceeded to Mr. Morrison's, a few miles distant, but did not accomplish it until the succeeding morning, in consequences of the prevalence of a violent storm from the southwest.

Yellow buttercup.

On the 8th, I remained at Mr. Morrison's farm, agreeably situated on a small prairie, continuous to the river, surrounded with an extensive body of good land, continuing a considerable distance from the bank. These small prairies often appear to have been the sites of ancient Indian stations . . . . The adjoining forest was already adorned with flowers, like the month of May in the middle states. The woods, which had been overrun by fire in autumn, were strewed in almost exclusive profusion with the *Ranunculusmarilandicus*, in full bloom, affording with other herbage, already an abundant pasture for the cattle. Towards evening, Mr Drope, with his large and commodious trading boat of 25 tons burthen, passed this place on his way to the garrison, with whom I was to embark on the following morning. . . .

[11th] Passed Mr. Embree's, and arrived at Mr. Lewismore's. Six miles above, we also saw two Indian villages, opposite each of those settlements. The land is here generally elevated above the inundation, and of a superior quality; the upper stratum a dark-coloured loam, rich in vegetable matter.

The Indians, unfortunately, are here, as usual, both poor and indolent, and alive to wants which they have not the power of gratifying. The younger ones are extremely foppish in their dress; covered with feathers, blazing calicoes, scarlet blankets, and silver pendents. Their houses, sufficiently convenient with their habits, are oblong square, and without any other furniture than baskets and benches, spread with skins for the purpose of rest and repose. The fire, as usual, is in the middle of the hut, which is constructed of strips of bark and cane, with doors also on the latter split and plaited together. . . .

We spent the evening with major Lewismore Vaugin, the son of a gentleman of noble decent, whose father formerly held a considerable post under the Spanish government. . . .

[12th.] This morning we met captain Prior and Mr. Richards, descending with cargoes of furs and peltries, collected among the Osages.

The former was one of those who had accompanied Lewis and Clarke across the continent. Six miles above Mr. Vaugin's, at Monsieur Michael LeBoun's, commences the first appearance of a hill, in ascending the Arkansa. It is called the Bluff, and appears to be a low ridge covered with pine, similar to the Chicasaw cliffs, and affording in the broken bank of the river the same parti-coloured clays. Mr. Drope remained at the Bluff, trading the remainder of the day with the two or three metif families settled here, who are very little removed in their habits from the savages, with whose language and manners they are quite familiar. In the evening, a ball or dance was struck up betwixt them and the *engages*. The pine land is here, as everywhere else, poor and unfit for cultivation. Over this elevated ground were scattered a considerable number of low mounds. . . .

Of mixed Indian and French-Canadian ancestry.

[14th.] We proceeded to Mons. Bartholome's, where Mr. D. stayed about two hours. Mons. B. and the two or three families who are his neighbours are entirely hunters, or in fact Indians in habits, and pay no attention to the cultivation of the soil. These, with two or three families at the first Pine Bluffs, are the remains of the French hunters, whose stations have found a place in the maps of the Arkansa, and they are in all probability the descendants of those ten Frenchmen whom de Tonti left with the Arkansa, on his way up the Mississippi in the 1685. From this place we meet with no more settlements until our arrival at the Little Rock, 12 miles below which, and about 70 from hence, by the meandering course of the river, we again meet with a house. We proceeded about eight miles from Bartholome's, and about sun-set came in sight of another pine bluff of about 100 feet elevation, and a mile in length. On the right hand bank the land appeared fertile and elevated. Near our encampment there was a small lake communicating with the river by a bayou. The horizontal beds of clay in this cliff or precipice are precisely similar to those of the Chicasaw Bluffs. . . .

[15th.] The territory watered by the Arkansa is scarcely less fertile than Kentucky, and it owes its luxuriance to the same source of alluvial deposition. Many places will admit of a condensed population. The climate is no less healthy, and at the same time favourable to productions more valuable and saleable. The privations of an infant settlement are already beginning to disappear, grist and saw-mills, now commenced, only wait for support; and the want of good roads is scarcely felt in a level country meandered by rivers. Those who have large and growing families can always find lucrative employment in a country which produces cotton. The wages of labourers were from 12 to 15 dollars per month and boarding, which could not then be considered as extravagant, while cotton produced from five to six dollars per hundred weight in the seed, and each acre from 1000 to 1500 pounds. . . .

[18th.] We now passed an island or cut-off two miles long, and forming a point four or five miles round. Near its commencement we were again gratified with the sight of a human habitation . . . . [B]etwixt the lower settlement and Mr. Twiner's, where we now arrived, the surveyor found considerable tracts subject to the overflow, and in one place a whole township so situated. On the opposite side, or Indian reservation, the hills approach within six or eight miles of the river, and, like most of the southern pine lands, promise but little to the agriculturist, but the intermediate alluvion is as fertile as usual. . . .

Towards evening we arrived at Monsieur La Feve's, where two families reside, at the distance of about eight miles above Mr. Twiner's; these are also descendants from the ancient French settlers.

[20th.] Two miles further lived Mr. Daniels. . . . The land in this vicinity appeared to be of a very superior quality, and well suited for cotton. Some of it, obtained by the grant of the Spaniards, and since confirmed by the United States, is held as high as ten dollars the acre. From this place proceeds the road to St. Louis, on the right, and Mount Prairie settlement, and Natchitoches on Red river, on the left. From all I can learn, it appears pretty evident that these extensive and convenient routes have been opened from time immemorial by the Indians; they were their war and hunting-paths, and such as in many instances had been tracked out instinctively by the bison in their periodical migrations. It is in these routes, conducted by the Indians, that we are to trace the adventurers De Soto and La Salle, and by which we may possibly identify the truth of their relations. . . . The distance from Mr. Daniels', on the banks of the Arkansa, to Red river, is believed to be about 250 miles. . . .

In the course of the day we passed the sixth Pine Bluff, behind which appeared the first prominent hill that occurs to view on the banks of the river, is called the Little Rock, as it is the first stone which occurs in place. . . . In the evening we arrived at Mr. Hogan's, or the settlement of the Little Rock opposite to which appear the cliffs, formed of a dark greenish coloured, fine-grained, slaty, sandstone, mixed with minute scales of mica, forming what geologists commonly term the *grauwacke slate*. . . . There are a few families living on both sides, upon high, healthy, and fertile land;

and about 22 miles from Hogan's, there is another settlement of nine or ten families situated towards the sources of Saline creek of the Washita. . . . [21st] In the distance of two miles we arrived at the younger Mr. Curran's, nearly opposite to whose house appeared gentle hills, presenting along the bank of the river beds of slate dipping about 45 [degrees] to the north-west. . . . About eight miles from Mr. Curran's, appeared again, on the left, very considerable round-top The Mamelle, at the mouth of hills, one of them, called the Mamelle, appeared insulated and conic like a like form. volcano. The cliffs bordering the river, broken into shelvings, were decorated with the red cedar (*Juniperus verginiana*), and clusters of ferns.

Nuttall's 1821 sketch of Mamelle

After emerging as it were from so vast a tract of alluvial lands, as that through which I had now been travelling for more than three months, it is almost impossible to describe the pleasure which these romantic prospects again afforded me. Who can be insensible to the beauty of the verdant hill and valley, to the sublimity of the clouded mountain, the fearful precipice, or the torrent of the cataract. Even bald and moss-grown rocks, without the aid of sculpture, forcibly inspire us with that veneration which we justly owe to the high antiquity of nature, and which appears to arise no less from a solemn and intuitive reflection on their vast capacity for duration, contrasted with that transient scene in which we ourselves only appear to act a momentary part. . . .

[22D] From Mr. Blair's, at which place and in the neighbourhood Mr. D. spent the remainder of the day, I proceeded down the river about eight miles, in order to examine the reported silver mine of that place. The pretended silver-mine is situated about one mile below White Oak bayou or rivulet. The search appears to have been induced by the exposure of the rocks in the bank of the river, which present indeed an appearance somewhat remarkable . . . and the whole texture of the rock, is similar to that which we have already noticed. The principal and lowest stratum, is a dark coloured, sandy, but fragile slate-clay; the upper beds are a fine-grained, siliceous sandstone, containing grains of mica, and occasionally traversed with veins of quartz. In one of these veins, about a foot in breadth, were abundance of rock crystals, scattered over with round masses or imperfect crystals of a white and diaphanous talc, collected into radii, each plate forming the segment of a circle.

I was for some time unable to ascertain the character of the pretended ore of silver, as the whole concern lay abandoned. I observed, however, that the slags of their furnace betrayed a considerable proportion of iron in their operations, and at length I discovered a heap of what appeared to have been the ore, containing pyrites, some of the crystals of which were cubic, like those so common around Lancaster (Pennsylvania), in the cholrite slate. Whether these pyrites did indeed contain silver or not, I could not absolutely determine, though nothing extraordinary could reasonably have been expected from their very common appearance and unequivocal character. On showing these specimens to the neighbours, they informed me, the pyrites was the ore in question, while others asserted it to be sulphur, and considered the siliceous matrix as the silver ore. It did not, however, to the microscope betray the smallest metallic vestige which could be taken for silver. Like all the rest of this rock, it indeed contained abundance of magnetic iron-sand, which on the disintegration of the stone, appeared scattered along the strand of the river. Upon the whole, I am inclined to believe that some imposition had been practised upon the ignorance and credulity of those who were enticed into this undertaking. Monsieur Brangiere is the person who first made the experiment, or attempted to bring the project into execution.

Ever since the time of Soto, reports concerning the discovery of precious metals in this territory have been cherished; we see them marked upon the maps, and although the places are easily discoverable, the gold and silver they were said to afford has entirely vanished like a fairy dream. . . .

[23D] Mr. D. remained nearly the whole day at J. Piat's. . . . About a quarter of a mile above Piat's I amused myself in sketching a view of the romantic hills that border the river, and which are not less than 5 to 800 feet high, . . . In the afternoon I crossed the river, and ascended to the summit of these lofty cliffs of slaty and siliceous sandstone, where, from an elevation of about 600 feet, I obtained a panorama view of the surrounding country, checquered with low mountains running in chains from the north of west to the south of east. The meanders of the river appeared partly hid in the pervading forests of its alluvial lands, still fertile and expansive. To the west, the lofty, conic, and broken hill called the mamelle now appeared nearly double the elevation of that on which I stood, probably more than 1000 feet in height. Two miles above, it presented the appearance of a vast pyramid, hiding its summit in the clouds. . . . These mountains appear to be connected with the Mazern chain of Darby, as they continue from hence towards the sources of the Pottoe of Arkansa, and the Little river, and Kiamesha or Red river. . . .

Here and earlier Nuttal had been looking westward at the mountains running in chains from the Ouachita Mountains.

On the 27th we arrived at the Cadron settlement, containing in a contiguous space about five or six families. Mr. M'Ilmery, one of the first, is at present the only resident on the imaginary town plot. . . . No village or town, except Arkansas, has yet been produced on the banks of this river, though I have no doubt, but my remarks may ere long be quoted and contrasted with a rising state or more condensed population. Town-lot speculations have already been tried at the Cadron, which is yet but a proximate chain of farms, and I greatly doubt whether a town of any consequence on the Arkansa will ever be chosen on this site. Some high and rich body of alluvial lands would be better suited for the situation of an inland town, than the hills and the rocks of the Cadron. Modern cities rarely thrive in such romantic situations. . . .

[28th.] It is to be regretted that the widely scattered state of the population in this territory, is but too favourable to the spread of ignorance and barbarism. The means of education are, at present, nearly proscribed, and the rising generation are growing up in mental darkness, like the French hunters who have proceeded them, and who have almost forgot that they appertain to the civilized world. This barrier will, however, be effectually removed by the progressive accession of population, which, like a resistless tide, still continues to set towards the west.

Nuttal left Fort Smith on May 16, crossing into what is now Oklahoma.

Schoolcraft Travels the Ozarks

The journal of Henry R. Schoolcraft was first published in London in 1821 in a series entitled Voyages and Travels *collected by Richard Phillips. The information given here is from the Preface to a later publication in this country thirty-four years after the journey. The journal entries, however, come from the Phillips publication and were reprinted in 1955 by Hugh Parks of Van Buren. Schoolcraft, in his Preface to the later volume, states that his expedition of 1818 followed a six month sojourn in the lead-mine district of Missouri. He also states that his expedition was "the first and only attempt to identify De Soto's march west of the Mississippi." In 1852 that claim was most probably true, but since that time others have attempted the same objective with a more thorough result. For our purposes Schoolcraft is included not as an authority of De Soto's march, but as still another observer of Arkansas in its earliest days. An interesting circumstance to be noted is that while Schoolcraft and his companion were traveling from the north to the south studying rock formations and alluvial conditions, Thomas Nuttal was proceeding from south to north in search of botanical specimens. That both men kept detailed journals and encountered much the same travel conditions confirms the accuracy of their journeys. Schoolcraft traveled with a friend identified only as "Mr. Pettibone, a Connecticut man," and their findings compliment those of Nuttal, who published his journal also in 1821, but in Philadelphia.*

From Chapter I

I begin my tour where other travellers have ended theirs, on the confines of the wilderness, and at the last village of white inhabitants, between the Mississippi river and the Pacific Ocean. I have passed down the valley of the Ohio, and across the state of Illinois, in silence! I am now at the mines of Missouri, at the village of Mine a Barton. . . .

~~~~

From Chapter V

Thursday, Nov. 19th.

The valley we are now in is bounded on each side by bluffs of lime-stone over-laying sand-stone. The mineralogical character of the country has been
~~~~

quite uninteresting since last noticed. From this spot we shall no longer travel by the compass, but pursue the stream, which I shall for the present call Lime-stone River, in all its windings down. . . .

~~~~

Sunday, Nov. 22nd.

The difficulties attending our progress along the banks of the river induced us this morning to take the highlands, where we found the travelling much easier, both to ourselves and our horse. On quitting the valley of the limestone we held a due-west course for about two miles, in order to completely disengage ourselves from the pine-forest, the ravines, and the brush, bordering the right bank of the river, when we found ourselves on an open barren, with very little timber, or under-brush, and generally level. We now altered our course to south-south-west, and travelled in a direct line fourteen miles without meeting anything worthy of remark. . . . For two miles we pursued our way without the prospect of finding a suitable place to encamp. Night was closing fast around us, and as the sky darkened, the wind began to rise, and as it murmured among the pines which crowned the high bluffs by which we were encompassed, seemed to forbode that we were destined to pass a cheerless night. We almost involuntarily stopped to survey the scene around us, and at this moment observed a small spring of water trickling among the stones at our feet; and turning toward its source, a cave in the rock, situated about midway up the bluff, yawned before us.

Elated with this sudden discovery, we immediately scrambled up to explore it; found it habitable, with a spring issuing at its mouth, and encamped. It was a spacious cave, and when we kindled our fires, the reflection of light upon its high and rugged roof, and the different apartments into which it separated, produced an effect of aweful grandeur which it is impossible to describe. The train of reflections in which we are apt to indulge is not always the effect of a previous resolution, nor is it always within the power of control; and while we partook of our frugal meal of dried venison, bread, and water, we were almost imperceptibly drawn into a conversation on the nature and objects of our journey, the hardships of the hunter's life, its advantages and disadvantages, and comparison between savage and civilized society. This carried us to other scenes, the land of our nativity, which seemed dearer in being at a distance; the
~~~~

conversation dropped, and we spread our skins and prepared for sleep. While the light alternately glared or faded upon the terrific walls of the cave, I engraved the date of our visit with a knife upon a smooth calcareous rock, and transcribed from my journal a part of the following inscription, previously penciled for the purpose:

O thou, who, clothed with magic spell,
Delight'st in lonely wilds to dwell,
Resting in rift, or wrapt in air,
remote from mortal ken or care.
Spirits of Caverns, goddess blest!
Hear a suppliant's fond request . . . .

~~~~

From Chapter VI

Thursday, Nov. 26th.

It is necessary here to note, that we have for several days been in the expectation of striking the hunter settlements on White River, having already been in the woods more than double the time contemplated. Our supplies have consequently been failing for several days. Our bread gave out more than a week ago, and we have not Indian meal enough to last more than one day more. Our dried meat and our shot are also nearly expended, so that there appears a certainty of running out of provisions very soon, without the possibility of getting a supply, unless we should be fortunate enough to arrive at some hunter's cabin in the course of one or two days. We have, in fact, already been on short allowance for two days past, and begin to feel the effects of an unsatisfied appetite. . . .

A circumstance has been noticed this evening, which proves that the climate we are in is adapted to the growth of cotton, several stalks of which were found growing spontaneously among the woods encircling our camp. The bowls were handsomely filled with cotton of a fine quality, and we picked some of it, for the purpose of kindling a fire, as we find it preferable to tow, which we have heretofore used. . . .

Cotton bolls.
~~~~

Saturday, Nov. 28th.

We this morning finished the last morsel of our provisions. . . . November in this region may uniformly be characterized by mild, serene, and pleasant weather. Distance fourteen miles. Acorns for supper.

~~~~

Monday, Nov. 30th.

We obtained little sleep last night on account of the cold, and commenced our journey at a very early hour this morning. After travelling two miles we fell into a horse-path with fresh tracks leading both ways, and after some deliberation followed the left-hand end of it, leading to the north-east.

There was no doubt now of our being on a path occasionally travelled between two settlements, but it was impossible to tell to which of them we were nearest. We first concluded to follow to the north-east; but, on going about three miles, altered our minds, and had returned about half a mile on the same path we went, when we met a man on horseback. He was the first human being we had encountered for twenty days, and I do not know that I have ever received a greater pleasure at the sight of a man on horseback. He proved to be a person who had formerly resided as a hunter at a remote settlement on White River, and was now returning from a visit to that region, where he had disposed of a small improvement. From him we learned that the stream we had been following down, was the Great North Fork or White River; that we were then within ten miles of its mouth, and that we were within a few miles of a house either way. Elated with this information, we turned about and followed our informant, who, in travelling about seven miles in a north-west direction, brought us to a hunter's house on Bennet's Bayou, a tributary stream of the North Fork, where we arrived about three o'clock in the afternoon.

The Great North Fork is now Norfolk Lake.

Our approach was announced by the loud and long continued barking of dogs, who required repeated bidding before they could be pacified; and the first object worthy of remark which presented itself on emerging from the forest, was the innumerable quantity of deer, bear, and other skins, which had been from time to time stretched out, and hung up to dry on poles and
~~~~

trees around the house. These trophies of skill and prowess in the chase were regarded with great complacency by our conductor as we passed among them, and he told us, that the house we were about to visit belonged to a person by the name of Wells, who was a forehanded man for these parts, and a great hunter. He had several acres of ground in a state of cultivation, and a substantial new-built log-house, consisting of one room, which had been lately exchanged for one less calculated to accommodate a growing family. Its interior would disappoint any person who had never had an opportunity of witnessing the abode of man beyond the pale of the civilized world. Nothing could be more remote from the ideas we have attached to domestic comfort, neatness, or conveniency, without allusion to cleanliness, order, and the concomitant train of household attributes, which make up the sum of human felicity in refined society.

The dress of the children attracted our attention. The boys were clothed in a particular kind of garment made of deer-skin, which served the double purpose of shirt and jacket. The girls had buck-skin frocks, which it was evident, by the careless manner in which they were clothed, were intended to combine the utility both of linen and calico, and all were abundantly greasy and dirty. Around the walls of the room hung the horns of deer and buffalo, rifles, shotpouches, leather-coats, dried meat, and other articles, composing the ward-robe, smoke-house, and magazine of our host and family, while the floor displayed great evidence of his own skill in the fabrication of household furniture. A dressed deer-skin, sewed up much in the shape the animal originally possessd, and filled with bear's oil, and another filled with wild honey, hanging on opposite sides of the fire-place, were too conspicuous to escape observation. . . .

We now sat down to a meal of smoking-hot corn-bread, butter, honey, and milk, a diet we should at anytime have relished, but in the present instance very judiciously set before us; and after eating as much as we supposed two hearty men ought to, arose unsatisfied, not more from a regard to moral than physical propriety. . . .

In the course of the evening I tried to engage our hostess and her daughters in small-talk, such as passes current in every social corner; but, for the first time, found I should not recommend myself in that way. They could only talk of bears, hunting, and the like. The rude pursuits, and the coarse enjoyments of the hunter state, were all they knew.

The evening was now far spent; we had related the most striking incidents of our tour, and had listened in return to many a hunting exploit, in the course of which, the trophies on the wall were occasionally refered to as proof, when a motion was made for sleep, and we lay down on a skin before the fire, happy in the relection that we had a roof to cover us. . . .

~~~~

Tuesday, Dec. 1st.

We had concluded to spend this day in preparations for recommencing our journey on the next. Our dress now required attention. Our shoes were literally cut to pieces by the stony region we had crossed, and we had purchased a deer-skin for the purpose of making ourselves a pair of mockasons a-piece. We also had purchased some corn for bread, some wild honey, and a little lead. The former required pounding in a mortar, and the latter moulding into bullets, or shot. . . . [W]e began early in the morning to beat our corn into meal, by means of a wooden mortar and pestle he kept in the top of a firm stump, and a large wooden pestle attached to a spring-pole, adapted to play into it. It was an unwieldly apparatus, and worked with a tremendous clattering, attended with incredible fatigue to the operator. . . .

~~~~

From Chapter VII

Thursday, Dec. 3rd.

While Mr. Pettibone completed the preparations necessary for recommencing our journey tomorrow, I sallied into the adjoining woods with my gun, with a determination to kill something. But after spending several hours in endeavoring to elude the sagacity of the birds and beasts of the forest, and making three unsuccessful shots, I returned to camp in a plight infinitely worse than I left it. Mr. P. then took the gun, and also made an unsuccessful shot at a turkey. We had now but one ball left; it was near night, and a flock of turkey betook themselves to roost on a cluster of oaks at no great distance.

As we had been unsuccessful during the day, we resolved to try our fortune at night, and endeavour to accomplish that by strategem which we had been unable to do in any other way. The night was dark, and we presumed this animal would not be frightened from its roost by our approach. To prevent all accidents, I cleaned up my gun thoroughly, put in a new flint, and charged it with great care, with the remaining ball, having first cut in thirty-two parts by way of shot. Then taking a torch, we proceeded into the midst of the flock, and selecting a large one, which sat low, Mr. P. fired, while I held the light above the barrel, and the turkey dropped. With joy we returned to camp, and prepared a sumptuous repast.

Saturday, Dec. 5th.

The weather being clear this morning, we got our horse packed at an early hour, and fording the river, pursued a west course for Sugar-Loaf Prairie, on White River. After travelling two miles across a high ridge, we struck a small river, tributary to the Great North Fork, which we followed up seven or eight miles, and encamped in a cane-brake on a low point of land, formed by the junction of two streams, near its head. Travelling had been excessively bad, owing to the hills, the roughness of the country, and the thickets along the margin of the stream. A proportion of cane-brake and swamp had also been encountered, in crossing which, our horse got mired, an accident which cost us great labour, and threatened one of the most serious calamities which had yet attended our journey. All attempts to rescue him seemed fruitless, our exertions only served to sink him deeper in the mire. We at last succeeded in getting off the pack, piece after piece, but after spending two hours in vain endeavours to extricate the horse, gave up the attempt. We now carried our baggage to a contiguous spot of dry ground, and set down to rest, and to contemplate our own situation, which, deprived of our horse, was truly deplorable. Our skins, our cooking-utensils, axe, some part of our corn, meal, &c. must be abandoned. Without these we could not progress with any degree of comfort, and in resolving to renew with any degree of comfort, and in resolving to renew our attempts, exhibited, perhaps, less of reasonable perseverance than of desperation, for on returning to the horse, he was now sunk in soft black *Quicksand.* mud so deep, that the upper part of his back and head and neck were only visible. Nevertheless we succeeded, with less than a hour's work, in drawing him out, and cleaning the mud from his body, so that we were enabled to re-pack him, and travel on about three miles before encamping. Some tolerably good lands have been observed on the stream we came up. But generally there is want of timber. . . .

Monday, Dec. 7th.

We had been told by the hunter to travel toward sun-set, that is, nearly due-west, and that in going fifteen miles we shoud reach a settlement of hunters on the banks of White River. We had now gone double that distance, and as we could not, from the elevated peak on which we now stood, discover any signs of White River, or of human habitations, had reason to conclude we had received wrong directions, and therefore, resolved to alter our course of travelling. Returning to our horse, we turned directly south, making a right angle with our former course, and had not proceeded more than a mile, when we fell into a faintly-marked horse-path, and in following this three miles, it led into another and a plainer path, which led us on a high bluff of rocks, forming the eastern bank of the White River, which ran a broad and beautiful stream below. Elated with this discovery, made so soon after we were ready to conclude ourselves lost, we followed down the river's bank about a mile, and discovered a house on the opposite bank of the river. We lost no time in fording it at a ripple, where the water was only half-leg deep, and were received with hospitality by the occupant, a white hunter, by the name of M'Gary. He had a field of several acres under cultivation, where he raised corn, with several horses, cows and hogs. The house was built of logs after the manner of the new settlers in the interior of Ohio, Indiana, and Illinois. He was provided with a hand-mill for grinding corn, a smokehouse filled with bear and other meats, and the interior of the house, though very far from being either neat or comfortable, bore some evidence that the occupant had once resided in civilized society. I noticed a couple of odd volumes of books upon a shelf. Some part of the wearing apparel of himself and family was of foreign manufacture. Upon the whole, he appeared to live in great ease and independence, surrounded by a numerous family of sons and daughters, all grown up; received us with cordiality, gave us plenty to eat, and bid us welcome as long as we pleased to stay.

In the evening, conversation turned on the length and object of our journey, the difficulties we had encountered, the game we had seen, &c. he told us we were 800 miles above the juncture of White River with the Mississippi; that the river was navigable with keel-boats all the way; that there were several settlements along its banks, the river bottoms being very rich; and that traders sometimes came up with large canoes to that place, and to the settlements above at the Sugar-Loaf Prairie. . . .

He also informed us, that a deadly and deep-rooted hostility existed between the Cherokees, who had lately exchanged their lands in Tennessee for the country lying between the Arkansas and Red River, and the Osages, and that they were daily committing depredations upon the territories and properties of each other. Having but a short time before witnessed the conclusion of a treaty of peace between these two tribes, made in St. Louis under the auspices of Governor Clark. I was surprised to hear of the continuance of hostilities. To prove what reliance is to be placed on the faith of such treaties, he mentioned, that when the Cherokees returned from the council which included that treaty, they pursued a party of Osages near the banks of White River, and stole, unperceived, twenty horses, and carried them safely off. Before going to sleep we determined to leave our horse, who had fallen away very much, and indeed all our baggage which cannot be put into Knapsacks, with M'Gary, until our return. . . .

~~~~

From Chapter IX

Sunday, Dec. 13th.

We are now at the last hunter-settlement on the river, which is, also, the most remote bound to which the white hunter has penetrated in a south-west direction from the Mississippi river, toward the rocky mountains. It consists of two families, Holt and Fisher by name, who have located themselves here within the last four months. They have not yet cleared any land for corn, nor finished their houses, notwithstanding the advanced season. They have fixed the site of their habitations on the east banks of the river, on the verge of a very large and rich tract of bottom land, occupying a bend in the river. . . .

~~~~

Monday, Dec. 14th.

[We] have just concluded a bargain with Holt. He is to have our horse, and ten dollars, to accompany us as guide and hunter, with the benefit of all skins or furs he may collect on the tour. He is first to go about 100 miles down the river, to purchase corn from some wealthy hunter there, for the use of his family. In the meantime we shall remain, and employ ourselves in making a canoe to descend the river on our return, or in completing the hunters' cabins, so that they may leave their families in a comfortable situation while we are absent. Fisher concludes to accompany us gratuitously, but would not go unless Holt went as guide, from which it is evident they have a perfect understanding of each other's views. . . .

~~~~

Thursday, Dec. 17th.

Employed in chopping wood, clearing land. Our day's work, during the hunters' absence, will be much the same, and made up chiefly of the following particulars: in the morning, rise at, or before day break, and build a large cabin-fire, of logs eight feet long; then pound the corn which is to serve the family during the day. This is done in a wooden mortar, with a pestle attached to a spring pole. The time from this to breakfast is employed in patching mockasons, &c. We then sally out into the forest with our axes, and chop and clear away cane and brush until dinner, which answers also for supper, and happens about five o'clock, so that we never sit down without an appetite. Our bill of fare presents no variety. We have homony, that is, corn boiled until it is soft, and bear's bacon for dinner, without any vegetables. The same for breakfast, with the addition of sassafras-tea. The day's work closes with the building a large night-fire, and packing up, from the adjoining forest, wood enough to replenish it during the night, and succeeding day. We then lie down on a bear-skin before the fire, and enjoy the sweet repose from daily labour. . . .

~~~~

Friday, Dec. 18th.

Employed as yesterday. We are sometimes led to contrast the force of habit on different persons, or different classes of society; but it is only on comparing the manners and customs of people widely separated, and whose modes of life and of thinking are wholly dissimilar from our own, that the power of moral or physical habit is rendered striking, or extraordinary. We have had frequent occasion, while sojourning among the hunters in this region, to draw such comparisons. A few instances may here be mentioned. We had furnished our travelling pack with a quantity of choice young hyson-tea, and this morning made a pot of it, and invited Mrs. Fisher to partake, presuming it would be highly relished, but were surprised to hear her declare it was bitter, and unpalatable stuff. She could not drink it. She preferred dittany, sassafras, and spiced tea, to our hyson. We had not before imagined that there was any part of the white population of the United States strangers to this plant, so universally in use in our country.

Some days ago, a young child of Mrs. H. Being taken violently ill with what I considered a bilious attack, I administered one of "Lee's pills," which gave effectual relief, and the child suddenly recovered. This incident served to give them great confidence in my skill, and led to further applications.

. . .

Justice, which in civilized society is administered through all the formalities of the law is here obtained in a more summary way. Two hunters having a dispute respecting a horse, which one had been instrumental in stealing from the other, the person aggrieved meeting the other, some days afterwards, in the woods, shot him through the body. He immediately fled, keeping in the woods for several weeks, when the neighbouring hunters, aroused by so glaring an outrage, assembled and set out in quest of him. Being an expert woodman, he eluded them for some time, but at last they got a glimpse of him as he passed through a thicket, and one of the party fired upon him. The ball passed through his shoulder, but did not kill him. This event happened a few days before our arrival, but I know not how it has terminated. In all probability several lives will be lost before a pacification takes place, as both parties have their friends, and all are hot for revenge. . . .

~~~~

Wednesday, Dec. 23rd.

About ten o'clock this morning, Holt and Fisher returned, laden with corn. The day has been mild and pleasant, the dense fog having entirely disappeared, giving place to a clear blue sky.
~~~~

Thursday, Dec. 24th.

Employed in hewing out a table daubing and chinking the house, &c. We this day left Fisher's, and removed to Holt's, a distance of half-a-mile, having now got his cabin in a comfortable condition. The hunter, although habitually lazy, and holding in contempt the pursuits of agriculture, so far, at least, as is not necessary to his own subsistence, is nevertheless a slave to his dog, the only object around him to which he appears really devoted. . . .

~~~~

Friday, Dec. 25th.

Christmas-day. Employed in splitting oak-boards, &c. At our suggestion, the hunters went out to kill some turkeys, as we wished for a Christmas-dinner, and after an absence of a couple of hours, returned with fourteen. I prevailed on Mrs. H. to undertake a turkey-pie with Indian meal crust, which we partook of under a shady tree on the banks of the river, the weather being warm and pleasant.

~~~~

Saturday, Dec. 26th.

Employed in beating meal for bread on our tour. We have, at last, obviated every difficulty opposing our progress, and got matters in readiness for continuing our journey, tomorrow being fixed upon for starting, should the weather prove favourable. . . .

~~~~

From Chapter X

Sunday, Dec. 27th.
~~~~

Rain, which began last night, prevented our starting this day, which has been improved in reflection and rest. The sabbath is not known by any cessation of the usual avocations of the hunter in this region. To him all days are equally unhallowed, and the first and the last day of the week find him alike sunk in unconcerned sloth, and stupid ignorance. He neither thinks for himself, nor reads the thoughts of others, and if he ever acknowledges his dependence upon the Supreme Being, it must be in that silent awe produced by the furious tempest, when the earth trembles with concussive thunders, and lightning shatters the oaks around his cottage, that cottage which certainly never echoed the voice of human prayer. In conversation a few days ago, with our host, on the subject of religion, he observed that when living on the banks of the Mississippi, some years ago, he occasionally attended a methodist-meeting and thought it a very good thing, but had found as many rogues there as any where else, and on account of a particular act of dishonesty in one of the members of the church, had determined never to go again, and had since thought there was no great use in religion; that a man might be as good without going to church as with it, and that it seemed to him to be a useless expense to be paying preachers for telling us a string of falsehoods, &c. He said, that itinerant preachers sometimes visited the lower parts of White River, and had penetrated within 300 miles of the place where we then sat, but had not found much encouragement.

Schools are also unknown, and no species of learning cultivated. Children are wholly ignorant of the knowledge of books, and have not learned even the rudiments of their own tongue. Thus situated, without moral restraint, brought up on the uncontrolled indulgence of every passion and without a regard of religion the state of society among the rising generation in this region is truly deplorable. In their childish disputes, boys frequently stab each other with knives, two instances of which have occurred since our residence here. No correction was administered in either case, the act being rather looked upon as a promising trait of character. . . . Among all classes superstition is prevalent. Witchcraft, and a belief in the sovereign virtue of certain metals, so prevalent in those periods of the history of the progress of the human mind, which reflect disgrace upon our species, have still their advocates here. Mr. F. related to us an amusing story of a rifle he had, that was bewitched, so that he could kill nothing with it, and sold it on that account. He had fixed his suspicions upon a neighbor, and was full in the belief that he had, out of malice, laid a spell upon his rifle.

Mrs. H. had a brass ring which she had worn for several years, and declared it to be an infallible remedy for the cramp, which she was much troubled with before putting on the ring, but had not had the slightest return of it since. . . .

~~~~

From Chapter XII

Monday, Jan. 11th.

It rained hard during the night, but ceased a little before day-break, when we embarked in our canoe, and descended the river forty miles. This brought us to M'Gary's, where we first struck White River, on crossing the wilderness from Potosi, and where, on the 8th December, we left our horse, and part of our travelling pack. . . . Immediately after passing Big Creek we met a petty trader coming up stream with a large canoe, in which he had the remains of a barrel of whiskey, and a few other articles intended to be bartered off for skins among the hunters. Of him, anxious to hear how the civilized world was progressing, we inquired the news, but were disappointed to learn that he himself resided at no great distance below, where he had purchased his articles from another trader, and knew nothing of those political occurrences in our own country, about which we felt solicitous to be informed. . . . He knew, forsooth, that he was living under the United States' government, and had some indefinite ideas about St. Louis, New Orleans, and Washington; but who filled the presidential chair, what Congress were deliberating upon, whether the people of Missouri had been admitted to form a state, constitution, and government, and other analogous matters, these were subjects which, to use his own phraseology, "he had never troubled his head about." Such a total ignorance of the affairs of his own country, and indifference to passing events, in one who possessed enterprise enough to become a river pedlar, surprised us, even here, in this benighted corner of the union. . . .

~~~~

Tuesday, Jan. 12th.

We were cordially welcomed at M'Gary's, and congratulated on our perseverance in visiting a region where travelling was, in their estimation, attended with so much hazard from Indian hostility, and our progress to which had been attended with such accumulated difficulties. . . . On learning from us that the Osage Indians had broken up their hunting encampments in the region about James' River, and retired upon the Grand Osage some weeks previous to our arrival, one of the sons of M'Garys manifested a strong inclination to go out upon a hunting excursion into that quarter, which on further learning that we had found game abundant, he immediately determined upon, and was ready to set out toward that country at the same time we embarked in our canoe this morning. . . .

Having spent some time in our passage over the rapids and got thoroughly wetted, so that we felt chilly and uncomfortable, we determined to stop at the next cabin which presented itself on the banks of the river. This happened to be the house of Augustine Friend, situated five miles below the shoals, a man of some intelligence, and who has the honor of giving name to a settlement which is forming around him. . . . Mr. Friend has lately been detained a prisoner by the Osages; but although they stole his beaver traps, and some other articles, he was treated humanely in other respects, and suffered, after a confinement of several weeks, to depart. In relating the particulars of his captivity, and in repeating several anecdotes illustrative of savage life and manners, the time passed imperceptibly away, so that although wet and fatigued on our arrival, it was after ten before we betook, ourselves to rest.

~~~~

from Chapter XIII

Monday, Jan. 18th.

Much had been said along the river, respecting a tin mine reported to exist on the north bank of the river in this vicinity, and although not prepared to find this metal among secondary rocks, I had determined to make a point of particular inquiry, and after descending the river five miles this morning, stopped about the hour of breakfast, at the house of the person (Mr. Jones) on whose lands the discovery was reported to have been made. He confimed all we had heard on the subject; and said that a very large body of singular ore, supposed to be tin, had been found some eight or ten miles north of his house, on the high-lands; that it lay in a valley upon the surface of the earth, upon a kind of rotten lime-stone rock, with a small
~~~~

stream running by, &c. He now produced some lumps of the ore. It was a species of the mountain iron-ore (iron glance) of a bluish grey colour, great weight, and possessed considerable metallic lustre; destitute, however, of those tarnished colours which serve to beautify the surface of certain varieties of specular iron glance. This incident seems to show how readily persons who have devoted little attention to the subject, are deceived in the appearance of a mineral, and how prone they are to ascribe to it a value which it does not possess.

At the distance of fifteen miles below Jones's, we passed Hardin's Ferry; dwelling-house on the south bank. Here the main road from Missouri to Arkansaw crosses the river, and a mail is carried from St. Louis to the post of Arkansaw, (now the seat of Territorial Government, March 1820) once a month. Two miles below is Morrison's Ferry, a branch of the same road crossing there, and eight miles farther Poke Bayou, a village of a dozen houses, situated on the north bank of the river, where we arrived at about four o'clock in the afternoon, and were entertained with hospitality by Mr. Robert Bean, merchant of that place. . . .

~~~~

Tuesday, Jan. 19th.

Before leaving the banks of White River, it is due to the hardy, frank, and independent hunters, through whose territories we have travelled, and with whom we have from time to time sojourned, to say, that we have been uniformly received at the cabins with a blunt welcome, and experienced the most hospitable and generous treatment. This conduct, which we were not prepared to expect, is the more remarkable, in being wholly disinterested, for no remuneration in money for such entertainment, (with a very few exceptions,) was ever demanded; but, when presented, uniformly refused, on the principle of its not being customary to accept pay of the traveller, for any thing necessary to his sustenance. Nor can we quit the house at which we have here been made to feel our return to the land of civilization, after an absence of several months, without a grateful expression of our sense of the kind civilities and generous attention with which we have been treated. . . . I had wrenched my ankle in such a way as to render it extremely painful in walking, and we stopped early in the afternoon, at a small plantation fortunately at hand.
~~~~

Wednesday, Jan. 20th.

An application of dissolved muriate of soda and flannels, surcharged with microcosmic salts in natural solution, did little to mitigate the swelling of my foot; and, after a night passed in sleepless anxiety, I arose without feeling any sensible diminution of pain, and without the ability to continue the journey on foot. This accident could not have happened at a spot where medical aid, or the conveniency of transportation, was in all probability more completely out of reach, and one of the most unpleasant delays threatened to ensue. Here chance supplied, as it frequently happens, what could not have been procured in any other way. A traveller passing on horse-back agreed, for a trifling compensation, to let me ride his horse to the banks of the south fork of Strawberry River, while he himself performed the journey on foot. This helped me twelve miles, and we arrived about noon. The road lay across an uninhabited tract, much cut up by little valleys, worn out of shelly limestone, and covered with a stratum of gravelly clay, bearing post oaks and black oaks. A mile before reaching the river we entered upon an alluvial plain, which continued to the village seated upon its margin. Here were fifteen buildings, scattered along the banks of the stream, including a small grist-mill turned by water, a whiskey-distillery, a blacksmith's-shop, and a tavern. Feeling somewhat relieved, I concluded to hobble on four miles farther to the main stream of the river, where we arrived before night, and stopped at a farmer's house, my foot having in the meantime become exceedingly painful.

~~~~

Thursday, Jan. 21st.

It was in vain to attempt travelling under such circumstances. I determined to halt, and await the recovery of my foot, while Mr. Pettibone, anxious to terminate a journey which had already been protracted to an unexpected length, concluded to proceed alone toward St. Louis. . . .
~~~~

Friday, Jan. 22nd.

Left alone, my impatience of delay increased, and I lost the benefit of no application which circumstances, diligence, or the united skill of my hostess and myself could supply. Forty-one hours thus devoted, superadded to the advantages of rest, abated the swelling of my ankle, and enabled me without great inconvenience to walk. I determined, therefore, to proceed by easy stages for several days until it became sufficiently invigorated to permit a bolder step, and crossed the Strawberry River this morning at nine. Proceeding with an easy pace, and by frequent resting, I gained ten miles by night, and stopped at the Dogwood Spring, a noted resting-place on the dividing ridge between Strawberry and Spring Rivers. . . .

~~~~

Saturday, Jan. 23rd.

Ten miles beyond this brought me to the banks of Spring River, a large and beautiful stream, which originates in one large spring forty miles above, and, after receiving the river Elevenpoints, unites with Black River ten miles below. It is a clear stream, and affords considerable bodies of choice intervale. A mile before reaching it the alluvial soil commences. Here Indian corn, wheat, rye, oats, cotton, and tobacco, all flourish in the same field.

~~~~

Sunday, Jan. 24th.

I was carried across the river in a canoe. A mile beyond, the river bottom terminates, and I ascended the calcereous ridge of secondary rock which separate its waters from those of Elevenpoints. Neither the soil, the vegetation, nor geological character of the country, present any variations entitled to notice. At twelve o'clock I reached the banks of Elevenpoints, and was ferried over in a canoe. This stream is nearly as large as Spring River, with which it unites three miles above its junction with Big Black River. Its waters are beautifully clear, and it affords a strip of alluvion a mile across from hill to hill.

Davidsonville, the seat of justice of Lawrence county, is situated seven miles eastwardly, on the point of land formed by the junction of Spring with Black River. It unites the advantages of an uninterrupted water-communication through White with the Mississippi, and through that with the ocean, but is a place of little note or importance at present. Half a mile beyond the north bank of the Elevenpoints, the ridge of secondary calcerous rock, separating its valley from that of Fourche a Thomas, is struck, and the road winds along through a sterile and uninhabited country for nine miles. On one of the highest elevations of this intervening ridge, and equidistant from both streams, I passed a bed of black oxide of manganese. It possesses little weight, is earthy, and soils the finger like soot. Some red oxide is in combination. The quantity is immense. As daylight withdrew, I entered the valley of Fourche a Thomas, having travelled nineteen miles.

PART TWO
Arkansas Territory
1819—1836

In 1803 President Thomas Jefferson purchased from Napoleon Bonaparte of France extensive land holdings on the North American continent. The Louisiana Purchase, in fact, consisted of virtually all the land from the Mississippi River to the Rocky Mountains from the Gulf of Mexico to Canada. It therefore incorporated the entire part of America which we call the Great Midwest. Within this purchase, then, were the lands which we know as "home": Arkansas. Until 1812 all of the Purchase was known as Louisiana Territory, or the District of Louisiana. When Louisiana was admitted to the Union in 1812, the remainder of the lands were designated as the Missouri Territory. In 1813, the Missouri Legislature changed the District of Arkansas into Arkansas County. Six years later, in 1819, Arkansas became a separate territory, with its own legislature and its own governor.

An act of Congress creating the Arkansaw Territory was approved by President James Monroe on March 2, 1819. The spelling is attributed to the petition, drawn up at Arkansas Post in 1818, seeking territorial status for Arkansaw County of the Missouri Territory. "Arkansaw" appears 10 times in the act creating the territory. The modern spelling, which derives from the Arkansa Indians, was not established for several years. The boundaries of the Territory were almost the same as the state's boundaries are today, with the exception of what was called the "western boundaries," constituting the western boundary of the Louisiana Purchase. Those western boundaries extended, in 1819, into what is now Oklahoma and part of Colorado. Subsequent treaties with various Indian tribes continued to erode the western part of the Arkansas Territory until the final Cherokee treaty in 1828 fixed the western boundary of the Territory to what is now the western boundary of the State of Arkansas.

President Monroe appointed as the first Territorial Governor, General James Miller, a hero of the War of 1812. The first Arkansas legislature convened at Arkansas Post on Wednesday, July 28, 1819, to enact laws for the new territory. The first legislature was unlike any other in the history of the territory: it was composed of the governor and three judges of the Superior Court–at that time the highest court of the territory. Because the governor had not yet arrived in the territory, he was represented by the territorial secretary acting as governor. The members of this first legislature were Robert Crittenden, acting governor, and judges Charles Jouett, Andrew Scott, and Robert P. Letcher. All of these positions were appointed by President Monroe.

The first General Election in Arkansas was held on Saturday, November 20, 1819. The voters on that day elected a delegate to Congress, James Woodson Bates, five members of a legislative council, and nine members of a house of representatives. Stephen F. Austin was one of the six candidates for the delegate's position to Congress. The holding of its first general election also produced another first for the territory: the first issue of the *Arkansas Gazette* was released that day from Arkansas Post.

Unfortunately, too much from these early proceedings has not been preserved, so the earliest formation of government has been lost to posterity. Enough material has been collected, however, to determine the most pressing issues of the territorial period of Arkansas' history. Travel conditions were of general concern. Acquisition of land was another topic of broad interest; the materials found on this topic, and there were many, consisted of business transactions which would not be of interest to a general reading public and have been eliminated. One of the most vital concerns of the territory was the Indians and the disposition of their grievances, which can be read in the first hand accounts reprinted herein. Toward the end of the territorial period, politics became the burning issue as application for statehood approached. Much of the material centering on politics deals with this issue as it proved to be the most interesting to the editors.

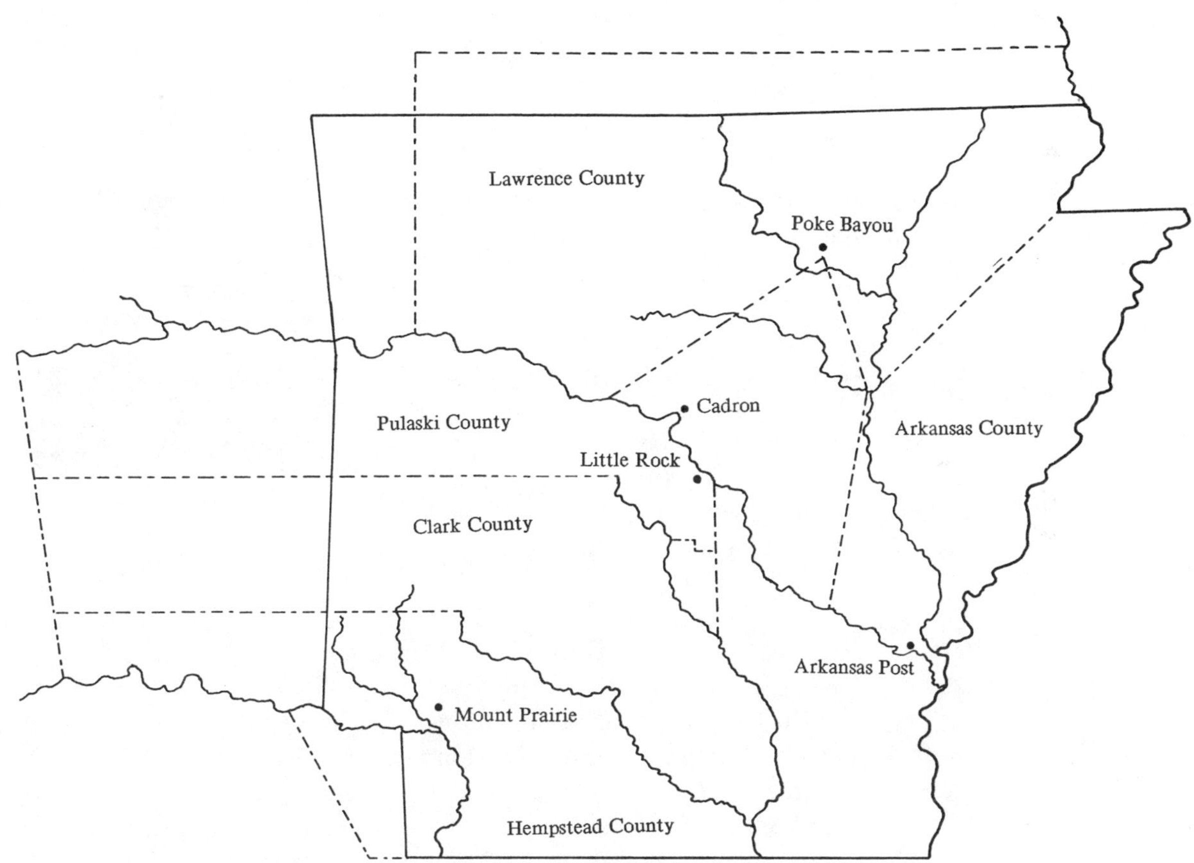

Five Counties of The Arkansas Territory, 1819

CHAPTER

3

The Indians

Cephas Washburn

The Reverend Cephas Washburn journeyed into the wilds of the Arkansas Territory in 1820 under the auspices of the "American Board of Commissioners for Foreign Missions." His task was to establish the first American Mission for the Cherokee Indians west of the Mississippi River. The story of the establishing of Dwight Mission is told in a series of letters written by Washburn years afterward at the request of a friend, a Reverend Moore, Presbyterian minister of Little Rock. The following excerpts are portions of those letters, first published in 1869, and later edited by Hugh Parks.

Perilous Journey—Organization of the Mission

Very Dear Brother: Among the misteries . . . in our American Zion, is the fact that she remained asleep so long in reference to the Saviour's ascending command,"Go ye into all the world and preach the Gospel to every creature." I was nineteen years old when the first foreign missionaries sailed from our shores. And when the Churches were imbued with the spirit of Missions. . . . [T]he whole field of vision seemed filled with the idol worshippers on foreign shores. When brother Kingsbury started on his mission to the Indians, he was regarded by a majority in the Church as little better than a second Don Quixote. The Indians were regarded as outcasts in

Divine Providence, who had been forgotten in the exuberance of Divine love, and overlooked in the provisions of redeeming mercy. . . .

Brother Kingsbury had a faith which brought these poor outcasts within the pale of Christ's power to save, and annimated by that faith he took his lonely way to the Cherokee Nation. He commenced a mission there in the autumn of 1816. . . . God was with him and blessed his labours. Souls were converted to God among the Cherokees before any of our other missions had been blessed by the converting power of the Holy Spirit. . . . That Mission among the Cherokees was visited in the spring of 1818, by Jeremiah Evarts, Esq., at that time Treasurer of the American Board. During that visit he had an interview with Tol-on-tus-ky, the principal chief of the Arkansas Cherokees. That chief expressed a wish to have a mission sent to his people, and Mr. Evarts promised to comply with his request as soon as it could be done. In the autumn of that same year I was accepted as a missionary of that Board, and sent out to the State of Georgia as an agent.

. . .

In the autumn of 1819 I was instructed to commence my journey to Arkansas to commence a mission among the Arkansas Cherokees. . . . I was joined by my brother-in-law, Rev. Alfred Finney, who was associated with me in the establishment of the Arkansas Cherokee Mission. On the 19th of November, 1819, we took up our line of travel from Brainerd for the wilderness of Arkansas.

Brainerd was the mission in Georgia.

Our whole company consisted of Rev. Mr. Finney, wife and one child, myself, wife and one child, and Miss Minerva Washburn, afterwards Mrs. Orr. We had a two-horse wagon and a one-horse wagon. We were instructed to go through the Chickasaw and Choctaw Nations, and to leave our wives and children and Miss Washburn at Elliott, a mission station among the Choctaws, and to proceed, ourselves, to Arkansas, and make some preparations for our families, and then to return for them. Had we been a month earlier in the year, we might have made the journey to Elliott without difficulty; as it was we had a most labourious, tedious, and trying journey. We reached the Chickasaw Nation on the "Old Natchez Trail," amid the rains of the winter solstice. . . . Our first day's travel in the Chickasaw Nation was over a high pine country and was comparatively pleasant. Hitherto, we had found a house at which to stay every night but one, and then were where we could easily get fire, but now we were in the midst of the forest and must lie out. Our fireworks proved to be defective, and we utterly failed to make fire. . . . From the experience of the night, we learned some lessons about "camping out," which have been of use to us ever since. The next day we took the swamps. These we shall never forget.

Elliot was located in Mississippi, near the River.

The whole country for miles was almost a dead level, and at that time covered with water from the great rains of the season.

Before reaching Elliott, an axletree of one of our wagons was broken. This could not be repaired there. Mr. Finney remained with the wagons, and I obtained Indian ponies, and started with the ladies and babes and a missionary brother, sent to us from Elliott. Thus, toil-worn and weary, we reached the station a little after midnight on the 2nd, or rather very early in the morning of the 3rd of January 1820. The next day Mr. Finney arrived with the wagons in safety. . . .

At that time Arkansas was a perfect *terra incognita*. The way to get there was unknown; and what it was, or was like, if you did get there was still more an unrevealed mystery. We traveled in company with an Indian trader who was taking peltries to market on pack horse. Our progress was slow, but after a journey of fourteen days, during which we had camped out every night but one, we reached the Mississippi river at a place then known as the "Walnut Hills," the site of the present city of Vicksburg. Here we learned that twelve miles down the river there was a man who had been to Arkansas. We went to visit him and sure enough we saw a "live man," who had seen Arkansas. He had ascended the Arkansas river to very near the Cherokee country. All he could tell us of the country was very little indeed. He, however, perfectly satisfied our minds that it was utterly impracticable to make the journey by land at that season of the year. We therefore retraced our steps to Elliott, making the journey pleasantly in five days. At this station, labouring with the devoted band for the improvement and salvation of the Choctaws, we remained till the 16th of May following, when again, leaving our ladies and babes, we started a second time for Arkansas.

We went to Walnut Hill as before on horseback, and sent back our horses, to be taken by two men we had hired to the Post of Arkansas, a settlement on the Arkansas river forty miles from its mouth, where we were to remain until the men with our horses should arrive. After a detention of some days at Walnut Hills, we got aboard a steamer, and landed in Arkansas at the mouth of White River, on the 2nd of June, 1820.

Here we purchased a skiff, and, for the first time, tried our skill as watermen. We ascended White river a few miles and then, through the "Cut Off," entered the Arkansas river. To us, unpracticed as we were, it was very laborious to row the skiff up stream; and at night our rest was prevented by myriads of mosquitoes, against whose torturing bites and hateful buzz we had absolutely no protection. Sleep under such circumstances, was utterly out of the question. Notwithstanding, we made the trip in safety in two days and a half. At the Post we found hospitable friends, and a quiet and comfortable boarding place, in the family of a Methodist local preacher. . . .

We waited at the Post for our hired man and horses till we began to fear that the swamps of the Mississippi or the alligators had swallowed them up; or that they had perished with hunger. At last, after we had been at the Post several days, they arrived. They had encountered the most incredible hardships in the swamps. We now fixed upon the day to start up the river to the Cherokee country. It was to be on Monday, but on Sabbath evening two men assigned by the Board as our helpers, Messrs. Orr and Hitchcock, arrived at the Post. They had heard of us at the mouth of White river, and fearing lest we should leave the Post before they could overtake us, they had traveled in in a skiff as we did, on the Sabbath. This, though totally unexpected (for we had heard nothing of their appointment,) was a most joyful meeting.

After another day's detention to purchase another pack horse, on Tuesday morning we started. Our caravan consisted of three pack-horses loaded with our clothing, a few necessary tools and cooking utensils and provisions, and six men of us on foot. Our nearest route lay through the "Grand Prairie," and on this route we commenced our pedestrian journey. The weather was very hot, and the meridian sun beat with such tremendous power upon us that we were compelled to seek the shelter of the timber. We turned into what was then called the "River Trail." This would increase the distance we would have to travel some thirty miles but we would all the way except here and there a clearing, have shelter of the dense foliage of the trees on the river margin.

Before night the first day we had all blistered feet, and legs more weary than I had ever felt before. Our day's march amounted to no more than twenty-five miles. We found a comfortable habitation and very hospitable entertainment. The next day we pursued our journey as diligently as we were able, and camped in the midst of an extensive swamp, on the margin of what was called a lake, but was in reality only water, which had collected in a vast hollow during the spring overflow of the river and was not yet evaporated by the sun. The whole surface was covered with a thick green scum. Our thirst compelled us to drink it, as charged as it was with malaria. Of it also we made our coffee.

Here we had the pleasure of the company of innumerable swarms of mosquitoes, but we were so fatigued with the day's travel that we were neither disposed or able to show much attention to our buzzing visitants. We slept till near day, when some of our company began to show some symptoms of disease. We resumed our toilsome journey in the morning, and continued for a day and a half longer when we were compelled to stop on account of the serious sickness of Messrs. Finney and Orr. We found shelter and the most kind and hospitable entertainment at the house of a Mr. Embree. Mrs. Embree will never be forgotten to us. She "took us in," and treated us with all the kindness of a mother. She was also of very great benefit to us as a doctress and a nurse. She will not lose her reward.

The second day after our arrival at Mr. Embree's, both our hired men were taken down, leaving only Mr. Hitchcock and myself well. We now heard of the high lands and good water at Little Rock, and were assured that if we could get there we might hope to recover the health of all the party. But how were we to get there? It was manifest we could not proceed in the way we had hitherto travelled. Messrs. Finney and Orr were utterly prostrate with bilious remitting fever. The two hired men had the ague and fever, or as the people in the country called it, they had "regular shakes." At last it was concluded that one of the hired men could ride on horseback, and that the other could steer a canoe. So it was arranged that Mr. Hitchcock and one of the hired men should take the horse through by land to Little Rock. I procured a canoe and hired a waterman to assist me. In the back part of the canoe we fixed up an awning of blankets to protect the two sick brethren from the scorching sun, quite in the stern the hired man was placed to steer, and in the forward part, with poles and paddles, was the waterman and myself to work the craft up the river. In this way, with much toil, we accomplished this part of our journey. Our sick brethren suffered much, but were no worse on our arrival at the Rock than when we left Embree's. Little Rock, at that time, did not look much like the capital of a sovereign state.

"Bold-face" is a term for whiskey.

Just by the Rock, and near the spring, was a little framed shanty, containing at that time a very scanty supply of "drugs and medicines," and a more liberal supply of "bold-face." Back considerable distance from the river, near, as I should think, the present site of the Campellite Church, was a small cabin made of round logs, with the bark on. These were all the buildings at that time at Little Rock.

We had stopped on the other side of the river, at the house of Mr. Martin, opposite the Rock. I immediately crossed over to the drug-store and procured some medicine for the sick, which abated the violence of their symptoms in all cases, and broke the paroxysms of the ague on the hired man. It was the 3rd of July when we arrived opposite to Little Rock. On the next morning, the glorious fourth, I was waited on by a committee of gentlemen, among whom were Dr. Cunningham and Colonel Austin, requesting me to preach a Fourth of July sermon at Little Rock. I accepted the invitation and preached in the aforesaid log cabin to an audience of fourteen men and no women.

This was the first sermon ever preached at Little Rock. From the Rock to Cadron, we travelled in a variety of ways. For the sick, horses were provided; the rest went part of the way by water in a canoe, and the rest of the way on foot. Cadron at the time was the county seat of Pulaski county, and loudly talked of, at least by its own-citizens and holders of property, as permanent capital of the Territory. There we found comparatively comfortable quarters for our sick, a supply of needed medicines, and the attentions of a young man who was preparing for the practice of medicine. Here Mr. Hitchcock was taken down with the bilious fever, leaving me as the only healthy one of our company. It was now decided that the sick should remain here till their fever was broken, and that I should proceed to the Cherokee Nation, and make arrangements for a council of the Nation, before which we might present ourselves and our object.

One of the hired men, whose fevers were broken up, accompanied me. I had thus far enjoyed good health, but by reason of hard toil, watching, and anxiety for the sick, etc. I was very much fatigued. Hitherto in all the journey, I had either walked or laboured as a waterman. Now to be permitted to mount a horse and ride, seemed to me like "Taking my pleasure." With these feelings, in good health and spirits, I left the brethren, and started for the Cherokee Nation. . . .

My pleasure trip soon became one of great pain. I had not been more than an hour on my way before I was attacked with the most violent pains in the head and back and all my bones, accompanied by severe rigours. . . . At night we reached a house on Point Remove creek, within the limits of the Nation. The family were very kind, and urged me to stay until I could recover from my fever; but I was very anxious to reach the residence of Mrs. L, for whom I had letters from the United States Agent in the old Nation, and where I intended taking medicine to remove my fever.

Mrs. L. is most probably Persis Lovely.

After a sleepless night . . . I hired a guide to conduct us to Mrs. L's. He accompanied us about eight miles, and then paused. He said he could go no further, but pointed to a mountain some six or eight miles in advance, where he told us we would find a trail which would lead us to our place of destination. When we reached the mountain, we found a trail, but it led us off our course. We followed this trail for many weary miles. At last we came to an Indian cabin. The man could speak a little broken English. From him we learned that we were now further from Mrs. L's than when we started in the morning. . . .

The hospitable Indian put us into a path or trail, which he said would lead us to a village only four miles from Mrs. L's. On this trail we started, but had traveled but few miles, when night overtook us. We lay down on the ground to wait the return of day. My thirst was extreme, but no water could be found. In the morning early we resumed our weary way . . . and a few miles brought us to the village. Here we enquired for Mrs. L. The chief furnished us a guide to show us the way. This chief had a strong dislike of the Governor of Arkansas, and supposing me to be an agent of the Governor's, he determined to lead me astray.

Gov. James Miller.

The guide conducted us to a little blind path, which he said would lead us to our destination. Not suspecting any treachery, we followed the path. It soon led us into the mountains and there gave out. We tried to retrace our steps but were soon bewildered in the mazes of the mountain wilderness, and thus we wandered, utterly lost, without refreshment for ourselves or horses and without so much as the sight of water for two days and nights. All this time my fever raged with increasing violence. . . .

About noon the third day after leaving the village as good Providence would have it, we heard human voices. We descended the mountain in the direction of the voices. Soon we came upon a company of Cherokees collected at a spring for the purpose of making arrangements for a ball play. They manifested a deep interest for us in our suffering state. . . . After taking us to a house where our horses were fed and food given to my companion a guide conducted us to Mrs. L's, where we arrived about nine o'clock in the evening. I introduced myself to Mrs. L. and presented her letters of introduction. Though commiserating my condition, and disposed to afford me all the aid in her power, she manifested great terror. My appearance was such as to fix the belief in her mind that I had the yellow fever, and she was apprehensive that the contagion might be communicated to herself and servants. I was immediately conducted to a separate apartment, and I saw her no more for two weeks. . . .

The next morning my hired man left me, as he said, to find some one to give me medicine, and aid in taking care of me. I saw him no more till the brethren came up. He sent me word that he was sick, but I afterwards learned that he found whiskey and friends to drink with him, and so he forsook me. Mrs. L. was afraid to see me. Morning and night she would send her servant, her mouth filled with linsey, lest she should catch the fever, to ask if I wanted anything. I had to be my own physician and nurse. Cook I need not. I passed a week in this way. Then a half-breed Cherokee, who afterwards became a most dearly beloved Christian brother, came to see me. . . . He staid with me day and night till the brethren came. . . . [M]y disease had taken the form of a daily ague and fever. I

Linsey is probably cotton or linen cloth.

had been at Mrs. L's two weeks. . . .

Our whole company were now together again, and we all had the ague and fever. We were, however, able to help each other to some extent, and could hold fraternal intercourse and pray together. At that time the specific remedy for ague and fever was Peruvian bark; but there was none of this article nearer than the Post of Arkansas, a distance of more than two hundred miles. We had an opportunity to send for this indispensible remedy. One pound of it cost us thirty-six dollars, sixteen dollars for the bark and twenty dollars we had to pay the bearer.

Soon after the reception of this tonic febrifuge, we were all restored temporarily to health. We made the best use we could of our time. A council was convened, at which all the chiefs but one were present. The absent chief was Ta-kah-to-kuh. This was the same chief who had mistaken me for an agent of the Governor. . . .

Any substance for reducing or removing fever.

On the day of the council, Mr. Finney and myself repaired to the ground, and were soon and very formally introduced by the public crier into the presence of the chiefs and warriors. At first, they gave us but a cold welcome; but when we told them that we came from the same good people who had established a mission among their brethren in the old Nation, and that we came in fulfilment of a promise made to their late beloved, but lamented chief, Tolontuskee, the whole aspect of things was changed. . . . [W]e were allowed to visit any part of their country, and to select any site we might choose for our first and principal mission; to erect such buildings, improve and cultivate such lands, introduce such stock and other property, as the wants of the Mission might make necessary; and whenever, in our judgment, the advancement of the Cherokees might require it, we might establish other schools and mission stations.

When all these preliminaries were agreed upon, and committed to writing, we were about to retire. We were then requested to wait, that all the chiefs and warriors might give us their hands in token of the ratification of all the matters agreed to, and as a token of fraternal regard, and our adoption as Cherokees. This was quite an imposing ceremony. Each of the chiefs made a speech, on giving us their hands, and a cordial shake came from all. . . . When all was completed, we parted with the council, greatly interested and encouraged; and fervently praying that the God of missions would bless our undertaking and greatly bless the Cherokee people.

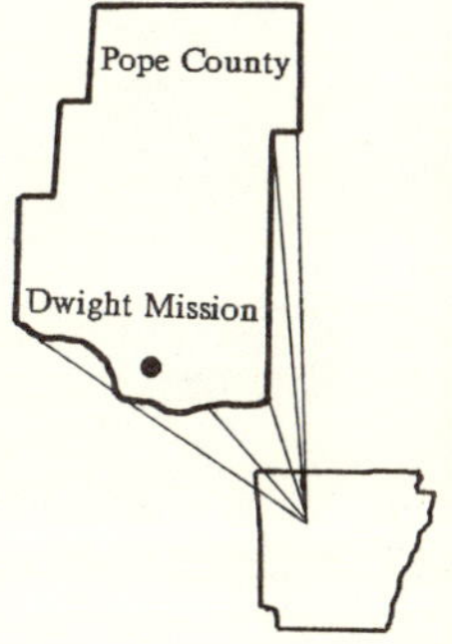

This prayer has been abundantly answered. Soon after this, we selected as the site of the Mission, the place now known as Dwight, in Pope County. . . . The name was given in honour of the Rev. Timothy Dwight, President of Yale College, who was the first corporate member of the

American Board, now deceased. . . . By the first of October we had erected two comfortable cabins, and made other preparations for the reception of our families. Early in October, Mr. Finney and myself left the station to return to the Choctaw Nation for our ladies and children; and we did not get back to the station till the 10 of May following. . . .

When the last removal of the Cherokee Nation was made to the Indian territory in 1828, the mission was moved also.

Dwight Mission, from a drawing made in 1824

Asa Hitchcock traveled with Misses Stetson and Brown. Jacob Hitchcock joined Washburn at Arkansas Post.

During the ensuing summer, much was done in the way of putting up buildings, and making arrangements for the commencement of a boarding school. We all suffered again from sickness, especially our ladies. In December of this year, our Mission was reinforced by the arrival of Miss Ellen Stetson, and Miss Nancy Brown, and Mr. Asa Hitchcock. A few days after their arrival, we had two weddings. Mr. Orr and Miss Minerva Washburn had, by and with the advice of their fellow-labourers, concluded that their happiness and usefulness would be promoted by continuing no longer twain, but by becoming one flesh; and Mr. Jacob Hitchcock and Miss Brown had been affianced previously to his leaving New England. . . .

On the lst of January, 1822, the school was opened with fifteen scholars; and such was the earnest entreaty of the people, that this number was soon increased to fifty.

In the early part of the following spring–in March, I think–the Dwight Mission Church was organized. Its membership embraced only the missionaries. From the arrival of our families at the station, the preceding May, stated public worship was established every Sabbath, and preaching in different parts of the Nation, both on Sabbath, and on other days, was ever continued. Thus the Arkansas Cherokee Mission was established; and those influences set in operation which so greatly changed the aspect of the Nation, and which have resulted in the salvation of precious souls. Here, then I close this long and dry detail.

Reminiscences of Individuals—Ta-kah-to-kuh.

My Dear Brother: I shall now occupy several letters with reminiscences of individuals. . . . The subject of this letter is Ta-kah-to-kuh, a chief already frequently referred to.

When I first saw this chief he was, I should judge, sixty-five years old. . . . I never saw a finer face. It was of the Grecian model, with a little stronger marked features. His forehead was high and very well developed. . . . His mouth and lip expressed great determination and force of character. But his eye was the most striking and awe-inspiring feature in his very fine and interesting countenance. . . . When any subject of profound importance occupied his mind, his eye would send forth scentillations of most magnificent powers of thought. . . . Ta-kah-to-kuh was lineally descended from their ancient priesthood; and before his immigration to Arkansas, often conducted the religious ceremonies of his people, and several times, after his removal, he officiated in that capacity; hence he was usually designated as "The beloved man."

. . . A few weeks before the commencement of our school, I met him at the house of Colonel Webber; there was but one door of ingress and egress, and he could not avoid me, and I determined he should speak to me, or refuse to do so. I approached and extended my hand, addressing to him the customary salutation. He gave me his hand and returned the salutation, but with an averted face, showing that there was no cordiality in it. By this act the ice was broken, and the way opened for farther intercourse; and shortly after, when passing his residence with an interpreter, I called to visit him. He gave me a polite, hospitable, but at first, rather cold reception.

He set me a stool, and desired me to be seated; next he handed me a gourd of pure cool water, and then said, "go and eat." On the form which served in the place of a table, was an ample supply of wholesome food, cooked after the Indian custom, but palatable. I partook of it freely and with good relish, which seemed to afford the old chief great gratification, as he regarded it as an act of friendly communion, a kind of seal to cordiality afterwards. There was no plate on the quasi table, nor fork; a single knife, such as is usually carried by the Indians in their belts; and a spoon, manufactured by himself from a buffalo horn, with which to help myself to hominy, or con-noh-ha-neh, in Cherokee, were all the eating implements used. When my interpreter and myself had done sufficient justice to the viands before us, Ta-kah-to-kuh filled his long pipe with ta-lo-neh, (a mixture of the dried leaves of the sumack and tobacco,) and lighting it, he first took two or three whiffs, and then passed it to me. I did the same, and passed it to the interpreter. After this, the chief took me again most cordially by the hand, and said, "Now, we are friends forever." The utmost frankness and freedom of conversation followed, and our intercourse ever after was of the most unreserved and friendly character.

I embraced this opportunity to state to him minutely our object in coming to reside and labour among his people, and to speak of the advantages of civilization and education, and especially of the advantages of Christianity, both in respect to the present and future world. He gave me a respectful and dignified hearing; and when I ended, he said,"We are evermore friends, personally; but I differ with you and with the other chiefs on these subjects. Nor," said he,"do I believe that our great father, the President of the United States, wishes us to be civilized and educated. If he so wished, why, when we emigrated from our old homes, did he not give us a hoe and spelling-book, instead of a blanket and rifle? No; as missionaries, (his word for this, Tin-tah-ous-keh, comprehended our whole character of preachers and teachers.) you belong to the other party. . . ." He designated them as the breeches, or pantaloons party. . . .

From this time the old chief was a frequent visitor at the Mission, and often ate at our common table. On one occasion, he had come to get some work done at our smithery, and was in the shop when the bell rung for dinner. I stepped out and invited him to dine with us. "Yes," said he; "but I do not like your way. When you come to my cabin I always say to you, 'go and eat,' and there is always food for you close at hand, and you may eat whenever you choose. But when I come to see you, I never see any food in any of your dwellings; and it is only at certain definite hours that I can find any food; then that bell rattles, ding, ding, ding,! and all must go then and eat, or all will be soon out of sight. I don't like it, but I suppose it is your way; and all the breeches party among my own people are following your fashion. I say I don't like it."

George Guess, whose Indian name was Sequoyah, was a leader among the Cherokee. His Cherokee alphabet made it possible to write in the Cherokee language.

For a long time Ta-kah-to-kuh maintained his hostility to the arts of civilization, as well as to schools. When George Guess, the Cherokee Cadmus, first visited Arkansas, he was at once patronized by Ta-kah-to-kuh; and the first class taught to read by Guess, were men of his village. He afterwards learned to read and write himself. His views soon underwent a change. . . .

About this time the Mission was in receipt of supplies from Boston. Ta-kah-to-kuh was present when these supplies were opened. Among them was a pair of globes. . . . I observed that they attracted the old man's attention; but true to the characteristics of his race, he manifested no curiosity. . . . He then carelessly inquired what kind of birds laid those eggs? I answered they were not eggs, and told him of what and how they were made; and placed the terrestrial globe in its frame, and showed him how it represented the earth and its motions. "Ha!" he replied, "what is that you say; that the earth moves?"

I told him; and illustrated it on the globe that the earth turns on its axis every twenty-four hours. "That's a lie," says he; "for if the earth should turn over, all the water would spill out, and all the rocks would fall off." This I also endeavoured to explain. After a few minutes of deep thought, he sent a young man, who was with him, to the spring for a bucket of water. This he took by the bail and swung it rapidly around. The water did not spill out.

"Oo-kuh-squah-tuh (my own name in Cherokee) is right," said he. "The earth turns over every day; and it is this which causes the rising and setting sun. This subject has always troubled me. When I was a child, I was told that the sun went back to the east in the night when we could not see it, and was ready to rise in the morning. This I knew could not be true; because the sun afforded us light, and was the cause of day. When my people have inquired of me, I have told them that there must be a hole in the foundation of the earth through which the sun passed, and so got back to the east. But this never satisfied my own mind; for I knew the sun must be immensely large, and a hole of such magnitude must weaken the foundation of the earth so much, that it could not support the earth. But now I am satisfied."

From this time he frequently visited me to study astronomy by the aid of the globes, until he perfectly understood the motions of the earth and other planets of our system, and the causes of the season, etc. . . .

For a long time Ta-kah-to-kuh stood aloof from religious instructions, and at first seemed disposed to treat it with contempt and ridicule. He was often present at our domestic worship in the common family, but would never take the posture of prayer. . . . He never attended any of our appointments for preaching. . . . Whenever any of the more intelligent of the village population attended, he would be very inquisitive as to what they heard. It was this way that he obtained some outline of Christian doctrine and morals. . . . But when he had opportunity to witness the reforming and elevating influence of Christianity, as illustrated by the spirit and life of those who professed it among his own people, he was constrained to acknowledge that this influence was good, and that our religion was from God. He no longer ridiculed, but ever spoke in favour of the word of God.

He now commenced attending upon the preaching of the gospel. He was first present at an appointment in his own village. The subject was, "God's love to the world, as manifested in the gift of His only Son." The next Sabbath he was present at Dwight; and from this time he was a very frequent attendant upon public worship; and became an interested inquirer upon the subject of Christian doctrine. At one time, when I had preached at a house, a short distance from his village, he requested me to go home with him, saying that he had many questions which he wished me to answer. I had another appointment to attend the same day, so that I could not comply with his request; but I promised to visit him the next day, and spend as long a time in conversation as he might desire. Accordingly, I was at his house the next day at an early hour.

He seemed glad to see me, and at once entered into conversation . . . . He then desired me to tell him the very way by which he himself might become a Christian. This was the very question, above all others, which I desired to hear him ask. His manner was dignified and serious; yet I was not fully satisfied with the mental state indicated by the question, and by his previous interrogatories and remarks. He seemed more like a philosopher asking after the *rationale* of Christianity, than a burdened sinner asking for relief. Still I addressed myself to the answer of his question. . . . I think he comprehended the Christian scheme of salvation, and that his judgment approved; but he gave me no evidence that his heart embraced it.

At the conclusion of my answer, with a very serious aspect and tone of voice, he remarked, "It is a great and wonderful way; and I believe it is the right way. Our young people will learn it, and will walk in it and be saved." And with a most desponding air he added, "I am like the sun away down there (pointing a very little above the horizon.) I shall go down to the night of death. It is too late for me."

I laboured earnestly and affectionately to dispel this desponding conclusion, but apparently without effect. This was but a few months before the old man's death; and I do not know that anything more hopeful was ever indicated as to his moral state and future prospects. . . .

As ever, yours,
C. Washburn

Reminiscences of the Indians. Cephas Washburn. Ed. Hugh Park. Press-Argus, Van Buren.

Washburn's Eulogy

The Arkansas Gazette *published a lengthy and florid obituary upon the death of Rev. Washburn. The following is an excerpt taken from the* Arkansas Valley Historical Papers *of June, 1955, No 8.*

DIED–In this city [Little Rock], at the residence of Dr. R. L. Dodge, on the 17th inst., Rev. Cephas Washbourne, of Pneumonia, in the 68th year of his age.

Truly a good man has passed away. This melancholy intelligence will fill the hearts of thousands with sadness. The deceased was born in Vermont, and received his education in the university of his native state. He studied theology in Andover Theological Seminary. Having dedicated himself to the service of God for the work of the ministry, he was ordained as a missionary for the Cherokee Indians. . . .

For nearly twenty years he labored as a faithful and devoted missionary of the Cross among the red men of the forest; and doubtless many of them will rise up in the judgment to call him blessed. When Christ shall come to make up his jewels, how many will be found as the fruits of his labors among the poor Cherokees.

When Mr. Washbourne left the mission work among the Indians, he came to labor as a missionary in our state. His first settlement was in Benton County. Here he taught school and preached the blessed gospel of the Son of God, for about 10 years. His next settlement was at Fort Smith. And, about this time, he joined the presbytery of Arkansas–his ecclesiastical relations having been hitherto with a Congregational Association. In 1855 he removed to Norristown, where he continued to reside until his death. . . . It is not possible for us to describe the many blessed consequencies, direct and indirect, resulting from his abundant labors, for so many years, among so many people. Eternity alone will reveal the good he has done. . . .

Letter from H. R. Wilson

Rev. J. W. Moore undertook to compile memoirs of Rev. Washburn after his death. What follows is a letter to Rev. Moore from Rev. Henry R. Wilson, who was at one time Washburn's assistant at Dwight Mission. The letter provides us with some insight into Washburn's devotion to his mission and to the Cherokees whom he loved.

Springfield, Ohio, Feb. 2, 1861.

Rev. J. W. Moore:

Dear Brother: It affords me sincere pleasure to learn that, at the request of your Presbytery, you have undertaken to prepare a memoir of our beloved brother Washburn so long and faithfully a member of the Cherokee mission. As it was my privilege to be associated with brother Washburn in missionary labour, you have asked me to furnish you with some reminiscences of that good man, and the mission with which he was connected, and, indeed, of which he may be justly deemed the founder. In complying with your wish, I have only to regret that the infirm state of my health, and the multiplied cares which press upon me, wholly unfit me for doing so as I could desire.

It was near the close of the year 1832 that I joined the Cherokee Mission at Dwight. After a long journey I landed at Fort Smith (consisting then of some five or six log cabins) on a Friday evening. Here I found brother Hitchcock, of the Mission, awaiting Miss Smith and myself with horses. On Saturday morning we set off on horseback for Dwight, carrying what baggage we could, and leaving the rest of our things behind us. After a tedious ride of some thirty miles through an almost trackless forest, we reached the mission in the twilight. Just as we emerged from the dense forest, our ears were saluted by the delightful sound of the church-bell—the church-bell in the midst of a heathen land! It thrilled me to my inmost soul, and stirred up feelings there which I shall never forget. It was their communion season. On the next day, the last Sabbath but one of the year, the sacrament of the Lord's Supper was to be administered. The converted Indians, and the missionaries from the neighboring stations, were assembled for the purpose, and had been engaged in worship during the day. After taking a little refreshment, I hastened to the church, or rather the school-house, where they were assembled. There I had my first interview with brother Washburn and the dear Cherokees who had been redeemed by the blood of Jesus.

When I entered, they were singing a hymn in the Cherokee language. Never before did music appear half so sweet to me. The language is music itself. The air is a sweet one, and the deep feeling of devotion with which it was sung rendered it truly refreshing. When the hymn was ended brother Washburn announced to the congregation that the new missionaries, for whom they had been praying that day, had arrived. God had sent them; and then called upon one of the Indians to give thanks for our safe arrival. An old gray-headed warrior arose, with love and gratitude beaming in his face, and poured forth his feelings in such a manner and with such fervor as I had never witnessed before. I could not understand a word that he spoke, but I felt deeply moved to see one who had often led his benighted countrymen to war and deeds of cruelty and blood, now leading them to the throne of grace through the atoning blood of Jesus Christ. I was next called upon to address the congregation through an interpreter, which I did from a full and overflowing heart. When the religious exercises were closed, the Indians pressed around me to shake hands and give me their cordial welcome; and never did I receive a more cordial greeting.

The next Sabbath was a day long to be remembered. We had prayer-meeting, conference-meeting, preaching, and the Lord's Supper. I was permitted not only to break the bread of life to a large number of converted Indians, but to put into their hands the emblems of the Savior's body and blood, as they renewed their covenant engagements with God. In this one day's enjoyments, I felt amply repaid for all the toil and trial of my journey.

Such was my introduction to missionary life among the red men of the forest. How different from the experience of my dear brother Washburn, into whose labours I was entering, and who had been the honoured instrument in the hands of God in effecting this delightful opening. But my auspicious introduction to the Cherokees was not yet completed. On Monday morning, after a season of prayer, we all set out on horseback, in number about twenty-five or thirty, to the residence of Colonel Webber, one of the chiefs of the nation, who, although not yet a Christian, had invited the missionaries and his Christianized Indians to spend Christmas at his house, in preaching and hearing the gospel, instead of drinking whiskey and dancing, as had been their custom for many years. The distance was some fifty-odd miles through forests and swamps. Unable to make the journey in one day, we were obliged to camp out. This was the first time I had ever been obliged to sleep on the ground and under the broad canopy of Heaven. As it was winter and cold, we built fires, around which we gathered in groups and talked of the love of Jesus. After our frugal meal, for which our day's ride had given us a good appetite, we enjoyed a delightful prayer-meeting, and then laid ourselves down and slept as best we could. In the morning after breakfast and worship, we resumed our journey, and in the afternoon reached the house, or rather cabin, of our kind, warm-hearted host. Here we found probably two hundred or three hundred Indians all assembled, like those in the house of Cornelius, "To hear all things that were commanded of God." As there was no building large enough to hold us all, we had to meet out of doors during the day, and in different cabins in the evening, when it was too cold to be out.

On our homeward way, many were the delightful communions we enjoyed, and like the two disciples of old, our hearts burned within us as we talked by the way, and Jesus graciously manifested himself unto us. By this time I felt so well acquainted with brother Washburn as if I had known him for years; and indeed to know him was to love him, for he was no ordinary man. He possessed a mind far above the ordinary standard and that mind had been admirably trained and cultivated. My first impressions in my ignorance were, that it was a pity such talents and scholarship had not been employed in some city pulpit, or theological chair, instead of being unappreciated and unprofitably employed among the untutored and ignorant savages. But it was not long before I learned through my own deficiences my mistake; for a clear and well-disciplined mind is necessary to a clear and simple exhibition of truth to the minds of the uneducated and uncultivated. Just such men as brother Washburn are, of all others, the men needed to tear away the rubbish of heathenism, and lay broad and deep the foundations of truth upon which the Church of God must stand, and against the gates shall not prevail.

But brother Washburn was not only a man of talent and scholarship, he was also a man of great modesty and unaffected humility. With talents which might have raised him to eminence and distinction he was as humble and unaspiring as John the Baptist. Instead of endeavoring to attract the admiration of his fellow men to himself, he sought only to direct their admiring gaze to the lamb of God that taketh away the sin of the world. But it was his consistent, ardent and unwavering piety which distinguished him above every thing else. He never seemed to be in ecstacy, nor much depressed in spirit, but enjoyed a degree of equanimity to which few attain. I have seen him under almost every variety of circumstances—in trials, afflictions, disappointments, and vexations, but never have I seen him ruffled or out of temper. His was uniformly a happy, cheerful, hopeful disposition. Many a wearisome mile have we traveled together in our missionary tours, but his cheerful instructive, and edifying conversation beguiled the time and refreshed my spirits, when my body was sorely jaded, and never that I can now remember the slightest disagreement or disputation, not withstanding the disparity in our years, my youth and inexperience making me liable to many blunders. . . .

But he was not merely a scholar, a theologian, and a preacher; he was also a man of sound practical wisdom and judgment, which was of vast importance to the Mission in those times of trial and perplexity. The Mission, as you know, had been established some fifty or sixty miles farther down the river, and when the territorial line of Arkansas was run, the Indians were driven farther west. The Mission had to be abandoned, and another location selected still farther west. In the selection of this site, the erection of the buildings, the settlement of business with the Government officers, and, above all, in maintaining the confidence and friendship of the Indians themselves, wisdom and prudence of brother Washburn was of incalculable service. He was the man for the times, and God had raised him up for this important work. The Mission, situated on the Salaiseau, a beautiful tributary of the Arkansas river, was well located and most economically conducted. It embraced five families, four unmarried members, with two boarding-schools, one for males and one for females, numbering in all not less than seventy-five persons; and yet I suppose the annual expense for all did not exceed one thousand dollars. A few boxes of clothing, sent out by the board, furnished our wardrobe. Our bread and meat we raised on a farm connected with the Mission, and these, with a very few groceries sent out by the board, constituted our whole supply. We had no luxuries, but few comforts, and yet we were happy; happy in our work, happy in the confidence of each other, and above all, happy in the favour of Him who had called and commissioned us to labour in that dreary wilderness. We had our trials, and they were neither few nor small. . . . Sickness and death visited our family again and again, and in these sore bereavements none so calm, so tranquil and submissive as brother Washburn. . . . He was a man of patience and untiring perserverance. . .

Salaiseau is probably the Salisaw River in Oklahoma.

May God abundantly bless you and this work in which you are engaged.

Sincerely and truly, yours,
Henry R. Wilson

Biography of the Rev. Cephas Washburn

The Cherokee Petition

The following petition to Governor James Miller, first Territorial Governor of Arkansas, was discovered in the Small Manuscripts Collections of the Arkansas History Commission. The Cherokee had confidence in Governor Miller's ability to settle their differences with the Osage indians so that they could reside peaceably within the Territory.

Cherokee Nation, in Arkansas
April 22nd, 1820

To Gov. Miller

My father,

We have seen you in our council house and have heard you talk, We thought more than well of your address and advice to us. We do not wish to do anything contrary to your inclinations. If your desire in relation to a settlement between us and the Osages can be accomplished we shall be glad, and at all events we shall be grateful for your friendly disposition and thankful for your endeavors to bring about a reconciliation between us and our neighbors the Osages. We wish to have our differences with that nation settled as soon as possible.

We had made up our opinion and determination upon this subject under the influence of passion, which is not extraordinary for men laboring under a sense of unprovoked injury from those with whom they are willing to be at peace, but since we have seen you we feel relieved; and are willing to wait the result of your endeavors to make peace between us and our neighbors the Osages. We shall bear you in mind every moment until your return to us. We wish you to think of us, and hasten a settlement of this business as much as possible consistent with your (undecipherable word). You may rest that we will wait your motions before we take any step to redress ourselves for the wrongs which we have suffered from the Osages. We are about(?) selecting some of our men to accompany you in your visit to the Osages and they can witness, if that nation refuse to surrender to us the murderers of our people, These men whom we send with you are fully impowered to investigate our difficulties and to receive restitution for any depredation which we have suffered from the Osages.

Te-keh-to-ka	his mark X
John Jolly	his mark X
The Fox	his mark X
John Maclemore	his mark X
Watermina	his mark X
Thomas Maw	his mark X
Walter Webber	his mark X
John Rogers	his mark X
Big Canoe	his mark X

Attest:

James Rogers, Interpreter

Small Manuscripts Collection: Arkansas History Commission

The Letters of George Izard

General George Izard, Arkansas' second territorial governor, was a well educated man from Philadelphia. When he accepted President James Monroe's appointment to the territory in 1825, the most pressing issues with which he had to deal were establishing boundaries of Indian lands and organizing the government of the territory. The following letters concerning the Indian movements were found in a letter book by the Secretary of State in the basement of the Old State House in July, 1905. The original letters were never found.

To the Secy at War

Little Rock,

June 18, 1825

Sir,

Major E. W. Duval, the Cherokee Agent, passed through this place a week ago, and delivered to me your letter of the 16th April. Conformably with your instructions, I will open negotiation with the Cherokees residing within this Territory. From what I can learn however, it seems improbable, that these Indians will accept the first proposal mentioned by you, of removing entirely beyond the limits of Arkansas. Their object is to exchange the lands they now occupy for those lying south and west of them and immediately adjoining the former. Even this will be very advantageous to the Inhabitants of Arkansas & Missouri, as it will open a direct communication between the settlements on White River & those on the Arkansas & Red Rivers. From the part of the country to be ceded to the Choctaws I have not heard since my last of the 6th inst–In a few days I expect precise information from that quarter. . . .

Towson was a military facility near the border of what is now Oklahoma and Texas.

I am at present engaged in organizing the Militia of this Territory. Nothing has been done on this important subject, except commissioning a number of officers. The Brig. Gen'l. resides at Cantonment Towson, where he holds the office of Sutler to the Garrison. The Adj't. Gen'l is sheriff for the county of Arkansas and lives about 100 miles from this place. . . . It is very desirable that Arms and ammunition should be transmitted to the Territory before winter. . . .

Sutler is a storekeeper.

The arrival of the Choctaw, the removal of the Quapaws and the excitement among the Citizens who are ordered away from their settlements west of the new Choctaw line, render preparation for defence or coercion indispensible. In my opinion the establishment of an Arsenal with a competent detachment of Ordnance officers at or near this town, would be highly advantageous to the public interests.

I am & C.

~~~~
~~~~

To the Secy. at War.

Little Rock, July 2nd, 1825.

Sir: –

On the 20th of last month, the Principal Chief of the Quapaw Tribe, attended by a small suite, visited me at this place, and in a formal conference requested that I would communicate the wish of his people to their great Father, that they may remain a few years longer on the land ceded to the United States, by the Treaty of November, 1824. I expressed to Heckaton (the hereditary Chief) my conviction that such permission would not be granted, but that I would nevertheless comply with his request, and would inform him of the President's decision. The Deputies were satisfied with their reception, and I have no doubt that the removal of the tribe to the Cadean Country will be effected without difficulty, even before the time stipulated. They asked permission to send a few of their Chiefs to investigate the lands which they are to settle on, previously to the migration of the whole nation. To this I consented.

Cadean Country is lands belonging to the Caddo Indians south of the Arkansas River.

They will be attended by an acting Sub-Agent M. Barraque, an intelligent Frenchman, who has lived much among them, and who was particularly designated as the person they wished to accompany them.

The arrival of Mr. Crittendon, Secretary of the Territory, has relieved me from some uneasiness respecting the pecuniary supplies required for this Superintendency. The specie which I mentioned as being in deposit at the mouth of White River (Three Thousand Dollars), has arrived at this place, and is stored in a private warehouse. For the security of the public funds here it is indispensible that an Iron Chest be provided, and some plan adopted for their safe keeping. The few commercial houses in Little Rock are rarely able to cash the bills sent by the Treasurer of the United States.

Safe.

I shall probably be under the necessity of employing a confidential messenger to proceed to New Orleans for the amount of those now in Mr. Crittendon's hands and payable to his order. The sum is $10,500. . . .

I am & C.

~~~~
~~~~

To the Secretary at War,

Little, Sept. 3rd, 1825.

Sir –

I have been honored in the course of the last month with several letters from the Department of War. . . .

I informed you on the 2nd of July that a small party of Quapaw (more properly Gappa) Chiefs were to visit the country of the Cadeans to examine the lands on which they are [to] settle themselves next winter. They returned 10 days ago and I was gratified to hear from themselves that they were pleased with their destined residence and with their reception by the Cadean Tribe. In this transaction the characteristic independence of the Indians is strongly exhibited. . . .

The Cadean and Gappas have a tradition of having been allied in some wars many years ago, but they have had no intercourse with each other for a long time and their languages are totally different. The accidental circumstances of a Gappa Hunter's having resided some months with the former tribe, furnished them with an Interpreter. . . . From a humane regard for the weak and infirm part of their population the Emigrants are desirous of commencing their removal early in the Autumn. I am in daily expectation of learning the time of their departure, which was to be fixed upon at one of their Councils. . . .

Military posts west of the territory in what is now Oklahoma. Fort Gibson was opposite Fort Smith.

Of the Choctaws I have heard nothing. Major McClellen, whose appointment as Agent to the Tribe you gave me notice of under date of 1st July, has not yet made his appearance here. So soon as I have conferred with him the orders of the Department on that subject shall be executed. I trust that before the arrival of those Indians steps will have been taken to remove from the Frontier Posts at Cantonments Towson & Gibson, the whole of the present garrisons, officers and men. Further outrageous scenes have taken place at the former of those stations: the animosity between the Citizens and Soldiers is carried to excess, and the *Esprit de Corps* has rendered the troops at Post Gibson as violent on the subject as if they were immediately concerned in it. In my opinion the whole of the two detachments should be replaced by others; and if possible the relief should be effected without permitting the new-comers to have any intercourse with the others, lest they should imbibe the same feeling of irritation. . . . The sanguine expectation which I entertained of effecting an exchange of the Country occupied by the Cherokees for lands west of our territorial boundary has been entirely defeated by the caprice of that people. Your letter on the subject transmitted by Major E. W. Duval, the Indian Agent, and the conversation I had with that gentleman on this passage up the country, led me to believe such a negotiation was desired by themselves. In consequence I instructed him to invite the Chiefs of the Cherokee Nation to a Conference at this place at some convenient time.

In the few weeks after Mr. Duvall's arrival at his agency he wrote me the note No. 1, of which forwarded you the original. Nothing more was said by me on the subject. I availed myself, however, of occasional visits made to the Indian settlements by citizens of my acquaintance to inquire into the sentiments of those people, and from their reports I inferred that the greater number were disposed to seek better hunting grounds in the Western Country, but that the measure was vehemently opposed by the half-breeds and whites established among them. This description of persons form no inconsiderable part of the Cherokee population, with some property, more intelligence than the pure Aborigines, monopolizing the trade and advantages resulting from the periodical disbursement of Annuities and entirely free of the numerous burdens inseparabale from a civilized State, as well as all check upon the indulgence of the passions in their domestic relations, it is not surprising that this class of inhabitants should be strongly opposed to any arrangement which would disturb their present situation.

. . .

I should regret the course which the intended negotiation with the Cherokees has taken had I not become better acquainted with the country which it was intended to offer in exchange for their present possessions, in the contingency of their declining to migrate to the westward. The portion of the Arkansas Territory which is interposed between the Indian Settlements and its western boundary is invaluable from its mineral treasures. Salt springs abound in that district. . . .

In a few days, I shall have the Honor, Sir, of laying before you some of the views for the improvement of this promising Country, which have presented themselves to my mind during my residence in it. Entirely unaided in any of the official situation, the multiplied correspondence which I am obliged to keep up with every part of the territory, especially on the subject of the Militia, engages much of my time. . . .

I am & C.

~~~~
~~~~

Little Rock,
Jany. 28, 1826

The Secy. at War,

Sir: –

A letter from Mr. McKinney covering a report from him to you relative to the memorial of the legislature of this territory to the President soliciting permission of the citizens to settle the tract known by the name of Lovely's purchase, came to hand by the last mail. I have the honor to address you in answer to the reference made to me by your direction on this subject.

By the Treaty of Sept. 25th, 1818, with the Great and Little Osages, they ceded to the United States the tract of Country within the following bounds, viz:–Vide Laws U.S. Vol. 6, page 743. The original negotiations were entered into, as I am informed, by one Lovely, then an agent or Factor in the Osage Country, and from him the tract has taken its appellation, though his name nowhere appears in that Treaty.

When the Cherokees established themselves on the Arkansas River conformably to the treaty of July 8th, 1817, the lines which were run under the directions of Govr. Miller, my predecessor, did not satisfy the Indians and on their representations, the boundaries were re-surveyed. The course of their line Eastward of their present location is from Point Demon Remove on the Arkansas River to the Cathoochee Mountain on the White River above Batesville, a distance of 71 miles. On the Western side a line parallel to the last was drawn from the mouth of a bayou about 20 miles from Fort Smith on the Arkansas, which strikes the White River not far from the junction of the Little North and South forks of that stream. This cutting off of a triangular tract of land from what is called Lovely's Purchase of about 200 square miles. What remains of the purchase in question is the country which our citizens are desirous of settling. It contains numerous and valuable salt springs, and there are strong reasons for believing that it abounds with metallic substances. The whole tract between the falls of the Verdigres River (at the point where our Territorial Boundary on the west crosses that stream) and the East and West line which bounds us on the North as far east as the headwaters of White River, is unappropriated by the Government of the United States and offers a commodious outlet to the Cherokees for their hunting parties to the Westward. The probable consequence of settling the above designated Country, which is the subject of the memorial, will be a disposition on the part of the Cherokees to negotiate for their final removal from our limits. This measure will be warmly opposed by the Whites and half casts of the tribe, from motives widely differing from the views of the United States, for the improvement and civilization of the Indians. The Indigenes themselves are fast migrating to the upper waters of the Arkansas and Red Rivers, many have already removed to the neighbouring Mexican Province of Texas.

I am etc.,

~~~~

Little Rock,
June 6th, 1827

Honoble Secy at War.

Sir: –

On my arrival here ten days ago I had the honor of receiving several letters from the War Department. That of the 26th March relative to the treatment of the Quapaws by the Cadean Tribe and agent was particularly gratifying, as I have stong reasons for believing that gross mis-conduct has been exercised in that quarter towards these unfortunate people. I was informed last summer that many of these Indians had re-crossed Red River and were in a state of starvation. Several of them had died of hunger before it was possible to relieve them. The citizens of Hempstead County conducted themselves with humanity and even liberality towards them and communicated to me by express the circumstances of their distress. I lost no time in taking measures to provide them with a supply of corn, which was delivered to them in parcels, in order to avoid the consequences of their improvidence and habits of waste. . . . A small party of the Quapaws, with their war chief, Sarrazin, returned to their ancient habitation on the Arkansas River in the course of last winter. I am in hourly expectation of a visit from them, when I will communicate to them your letter of the 26th March. . . .

I am, etc.,
~~~~

Little Rock,
29th June, 1827.

The Secretary War,
Sir: –

It was not until the 27th inst. that I had an opportunity of seeing Sarrasin, the Quapaw Chief, to whom I delivered your letter of the 26th March last. I had two conferences with him, the result of which was that he declined for himself and his band consisting of 120 men, women, and children, the proposal of joining the Cherokees on the Arkansas. Having learnt that the Osage were desirous of receiving them into their nation on the ground that they were a kindred tribe I sounded Sarrasin on that head. He assured me that although a few words of their respective languages had the same meaning, yet this did not extend to such similarity as to render them intelligible to each other. That their Fathers (and he who is an aged man himself, had conversed with many of them in the course of his life) disavowed any such connection and on the contrary had always regarded the Osage as enemies. He said that he and his followers were desirous of assimilating themselves to the whites, that several of their children now went to a white school near their village; that they wished their women to be taught spinning and weaving and their young men to learn husbandry and forsake their wild habits. They wanted to buy some small tracts of land for cultivation, they were indeed very poor but they were able to provide for their wants on the spot where they were now located. That he himself was half a white man by birth and entirely white in affection and inclination. It is certain that the presence of these people on the Arkansas is not disagreeable to the white settlers in their neighborhood, many of whom are of French descent and are of a mixed breed themselves. I am not aware of any law by which after relinquishing their Indian title to the soil they can be prevented from establishing themselves on it as American Citizens. They have planted crops of corn which will be sufficient for their subsistence this year, and probably they will require little or no aid from Government for the future. I informed Sarrasin that I would communicate what he had said to their great father, whose decision should be made known to them, as soon as I should be made acquainted with it, and in the meantime they might remain on the present habitations. The poor creatures suffered greatly in the Cadean country. Many died of actual starvation. Of these several were of Sarrasin's own family.

I am, etc.,

Long Prairie, 17th Apl. 1826

To his excellency, the Govr. of the Territory of Arkansas:

My object in now writing is to inform you that I am not at all satisfied in my present situation, that the man who I am informed is our agent does not please or suit the Quapaws.

My Father, I have always been obedient to your Government, as a proof of which I have moved from the Arkansas to the Red River agreeable to their request which was agreeable to my promise, and it is my wish and hope that your Government will comply with all their promises. In our present situation we are surrounded by Red Skins of the tribe of several nations, besides the Cadeans, who threaten to steal or take from us not only our beef, and other provisions but also our land, and we have reason to believe that the Agent (Mr. Gray) has and will encourage them to do so. We want to have nothing to do with any other Red Skins than the Cadean nor do we want any other about us. Your Government promised to give us an agent and an Interpreter, which promise I want them to comply with. The Interpreter appointed by Mr. Gray is one that we can not understand and in consequence thereof we are unable to do business with our brothers (the Cadean). We want such a one as we can understand, to enable us to do business easy and right. We also want a good man for our agent. Mr. Gray does not suit us. When we sold you our land and started for the Country we are settled on, it was our wish and hope that the Agent and Interpreter who accompanied us would continue with us. . . . Those now appointed are to us and we to them, like men without ears. We can not understand one another at all, and are unable to do any business. Mr. Gray has insulted me and all of my children. He told me that I was not Chief and that My red brother at the head of the Cadean nation was not chief. That he, Gray, was the only chief. That he was the only big man in all this part of the country. That there was only one man any where in all this Country that was above him and that he was very little, and said he lived at Nachatosh or somewhere in that country, that all the rest both white and red were below him, they were no more than so many dogs.

I now think that I will very soon have to come and see you and think it probable that I will go on with Bernard Bonne.

I am,
(Signed) Hekatton,
his mark.

Arkansas Terry, Hempstead County.
17th April, 1826

I do hereby certify that I was present at the meeting between Capt. George Gray and Antoine Baraque, about fifteen days since at the Quapaw village in Trease prairie at which time and place Mr. Gray was very insulting to Mr. Baraque. Told him his agency and power was from that time at an end. Sd. Baraque told him that he had settlement to make with the Indians and money to pay over to them. Gray told him that he had no power in that agency. Sd. Baraque told him that he was sent there by the Government and that he knew his duty. Sd. Gray observed that the Governor had nothing to do there and that he cared not for him.

Given under my hand in Long Prairie the day and date above.

(Signed) Morris May.

Evidence #1
Caddo Prairie, Red River
Ind. Agency, March 1826.

The Big Chickasaw has my permission to pack three kegs of whiskey through the Caddo nation to the Saline River.

(Signed) G. Gray,
Indian Agent

Evidence #2

I certify that I saw an instrument of writing in the hands of the Big Chickasaw of which the above is a true copy, and that it was the handwriting of Geo. Gray.

April 17th, 1826.
(Signed) I. Poston.

Evidence #3

I certify that I saw the above mentioned passport in the hands of the Big Chickasaw the day it was given and that I saw a part of the whiskey sold to the Caddo Indians, by the Big Chickasaw in the Caddo Nation April 17th, 1826.

(Signed) John Wynne.

Publications of the Arkansas Historical Association: Vol. I, 1906.

Before General Izard left his home in Philadelphia to assume his duties as Governor of the Arkansas Territory, he approached the American Philosophical Society about gathering information on the Quapaw Indian tribes who were living in the territory. The Society indicated some interest in such a study and provided Izard with guidelines to follow. In January of 1827 Izard presented the following report when he returned to Philadelphia because of the death of his wife. The report was never completed because Izard himself died ten months later in Arkansas.

"A Report on the Quapaw: The Letters of Governor George Izard to the American Philosophical Society, 1825-1827."

Philadelphia
January 10, 1827

Sir,

I beg leave through you to lay before the American Philosophical Society some brief notes respecting the Territory of Arkansa and the late possessors and occupants of the greater part of that country. You will also receive a specimen of their language which entirely differs from that of any of the Indians in their neighborhood, the Cherokees, Choctaws, Chickassaws, Shawnees, Osages, etc.

The Quapaw interpreters are exclusively French Creoles or Half-breeds. I was therefore under the necessity of using the French language in the first instance to explain the Indian words.

In order to fix the pronunciation, I originally wrote the Indian words as they were uttered successively by two individuals, one the interpeter, the other an Indian Chief, in the German alphabet, giving to the vowels and consonants their value in the latter language; and where the words were long and the quantity of the syllables difficult, I used the usual prosodical signs to distinguish them. Thus:

Baÿou	Creek	Uàhtīschkā
Dix	Ten	Gĕdēh-bŏnāh

Official occupations and want of health prevented me from making a larger collection for the information of the Society. I have however, in several parts of Arkansa taken measures to obtain such objects as may be interesting, and which will be transmitted as opportunities shall occur. I have for the present only to solicit the indulgence of the Society, and to express my regret at the scantiness of the tribute which I offer them.

I am respectfully,
Sir,
Your most obed. serv.
Geo. Izard

Notes respecting the Arkansa Territory, January 1827.

The only tribe of Indians which had inhabited the country, now designated as the Territory of Arkansa, before its cession to the U. States, remaining on the banks of the River Arkansa in 1825, was that called by themselves Gappa and by the Americans Quapaws. A treaty was made with them in 1824 by which they yielded their lands to our Government for certain considerations; and in February, 1826, the whole tribe consisting of 158 men, 123 women and 174 children emigrated under the conduct of an Indian agent, specially appointed for that purpose and selected by the Chiefs, to the country of the Cadeaux (improperly called in our public documents Caddoes), lying south of Red River within the limits of the state of Louisiana and adjoining the Mexican state of Texas.

The following account of the Gappa nation was received from Paheka (dry-head), grandfather of Heckaton, the present principal chief.

When we abandoned our former lands we set out without knowing whither we were going. Our motive for leaving the country we occupied was the scarcity of game. We were too numerous at the time; we had as many as 1600 warriors. On arriving at the mouth of the Ohio River (Ny-Tonka), our chiefs determined on separating the nation, in order to procure the means of subsistance with greater facility. Our former name was Mahas. Those who followed the chief *Wajin-ka-sa* (Blackbird) retained that appellation and now inhabit the country on the upper water of the Missouri. Our chief whose name was Paheka, chose to alter our name, and called us Gappa.

After our separation, our party followed the course of the *Ny-Tonka* (Mississippi). The first red skins whom we met with were settled some way below the *Ny-Whoutteh-junka* (the little Muddy River, now the St. Francis); they were called *Tonnika*. We attacked and put them to flight. Some time afterwards we entered this river, which we called *Ny-jitteh* (Red River, now the Arkansa). We soon discovered that there were other red skins (Indians) in the country. Parties were sent out to look for them. They were found encamped in the Great Prairie (between the Post of Arkansa and the town of Little Rock). We attacked them; they made a valiant resistance, but we beat them and drove them away. This nation called itself *Intouka*; the whites at that period gave them the name of Illinois. Then we were left entire masters of this country. The Osages alone have made war on us; but we have always beaten and driven them beyond the Canadian River.

The river Ohio is called by the Gappas *Ny-Tonka* (great river) which is also their name for the Mississippi.

To the foregoing summary of the history of the tribe little is to be added. They appear to have been always on friendly terms with the whites, whether French, Spanish or American. Not withstanding their constant intercourse for nearly a century with the colonists, there is not among them the slightest approximation to a civilized state. They are said to have been noted among the Indian Nations for courage and valor. Their religion is an unintelligible farrago of superstition and barbarous rites. They have several idols, the sight of some of which is prohibited even among themselves. . . . Human sacrifices were, till a few years ago, frequent among them. On their departure from the Cadeaux country, they burnt to death an orphan child belonging to the tribe in order to propitiate their deities. Aware however that the performance of this horrid act would be prevented if the whites had notice of it, they carefully concealed their purpose.

Some of their ceremonies are too disgusting for recital. Indeed they are in their habits and persons among the filthiest of their degraded race.

On the other hand, they are remarkable for strict honesty. Subject in consequence of their idleness and want of foresight, to suffer frequently from the scarcity of provisions, they have never been known to plunder the grain of the farmers, around whose open barns they remain sometimes for weeks, content with the scanty pittance which charity doles out to them.

The Small Pox committed great ravages among them a few years ago, and the prevalence of the use of poison, to revenge injuries and affronts among themselves, has hastened the decline of their population. Like almost all the other savages on our continent, they are immoderately fond of spiritous liquors and neglect no opportunity of drinking to excess.

Subjoined are two of what they call songs, the accompaniment to which, like all their music, is as monotonous and fatiguing to the ear as sounds can possibly be. They were selected from among his numerous productions by a half-breed, named Sarrasin, who is the most distinguished of their warriors. This hero, poet and musician ranks as a chief in some respects; he is permitted to wear medals and assist at their councils, but his honors are altogether personal and will not descend to his eldest son, as in the case with the other chiefs whose blood is purely Indian.

~~~~

The following account of an early exploit of Sarrasin was given by himself in The presence of the assembled chiefs. When he was a youth (correct dates are out of the question with these people) the Post of Arkansa was surprised by the Chickassaws. The Spanish commandant, Villar or Villers, and his two infant daughters were carried off by the assailants. Sarrasin casually visited the Post a few hours after this event; he found Madam Villar in the deepest distress at the loss of her husband and children. Moved by her tears, he determined to attempt the rescue of the prisoners and immediately followed the trace of the Chickassaws. After a pursuit of several miles he overtook two of the latter, who were reposing under a tree, and to his joy and surprise beheld the two babes lying on the ground near them. He sprang forward without uttering a word, seized and threw the two latter over his shoulders and retraced his steps to the Post, unmolested by the Chickassaws
~~~~

who were either too much fatigued or astonished to interrupt him. As he approached the little Spanish Fort the mother flew to meet him; but when within a few steps shrieked with agony at seeing one of her infants, as she thought, dead on its preserver's shoulder. The child had fallen asleep and its little head nodded with every step of the warrior. She was soon relieved from her fears, and poured out thanks to her benefactor.

Villar, the father, was yet to be restored to the family. Sarrasin undertook to bring him back or perish. "If I am killed," said he, "There will be but one dog less on the earth; but if I succeed, a whole family will be made happy." A brother of the commandant gave him a sack of dollars as ransom for his relation; with this he set out, and on his way towards the Chickassaws, who were encamped at some distance above the mouth of the White River on the Mississippi, he called on an uncle of his. The latter, when he had learned his destination, declared that the project was impracticable unless the demand for the captive were supported by a force from their tribe. All of the latter who were in the neighborhood were immediately assembled; they approached the Chickassaw camp and after some negotiation, Villar was returned to liberty and his family.

Song #1

	English translation:
Vikudah uschkonn kuttabih Uattechheh uattintah	I will strike my foe, If I find him, I will not spare him.

Song #2

	English translation:
Schentawah shosheh Kommadeh nikeh	I intend to do mischief today, I will attack my enemy.

A vocabulary (French and Indian) of the Gappa or Quapaw Indians, otherwise called the Arkansas, or Arkansa, German pronunciation.

By General George Izard.

(The English translation of the French in the middle column has been added by the editor of the PCHR and verified by Rosalie M. Cheatham, Foreign Language Dept., UALR)

FRENCH	ENGLISH	QUAPAW
Américain	American	Ŭatschinni
argent	silver, money	moseska
arbre	tree	yon (french sound of on)
arc	bow	mōktēh
bon	good	huckton
buffle	buffalo	teh
boeuf sauvage	wild cattle	teh-hukah

Submitted by David W. Bizzell. Pulaski County Historical Review *Winter, 1981. Vol. 29.*

The Cherokee Phoenix

The Cherokee nation east of the Mississippi was a highly civilized nation. They held large tracts of land and enjoyed much success as farmers. They had a distinct form of government which gave to their nation a means of ruling with justice. They also had an official newspaper which was published weekly. The following are excerpts from that newspaper, written by members of the nation who had emigrated to Arkansas before the entire nation was removed in 1838. Copies of the Cherokee Phoenix *are on file in the Library of Congress, which provided these excerpts.*

New Echota: Georgia
Wednesday, Sept. 17, 1828

The following extract of a letter from an intelligent Gentleman residing among the Cherokees of the Arkansas, addressed to a friend of this place, will be read with interest.

Ere this I presume you have seen the new compact entered into by the Cherokee Delegation from this nation. From the documents we have received it appears that the Delegation labored faithfully to accomplish the business for which they were sent to Washington, and when they found that was impracticable, they were pursuaded to accede to the proposals made by the Sec. of War to enter into a new compact. Very general dissatisfaction prevails among the people. At first their feelings were excited to a very high degree against the Delegation, who were threatened with the full weight of the nation's indignation. By many, their lives were threatened as soon as they should return. At this time, the excitement has nearly subsided, and I think that no other punishment will be inflicted upon the Delegation than depriving them of their offices and influence. Nearly all the people are still dissatisfied with the treaty, and think the delegation exercises a most unwarranted stretch of power in making it. What will be the ultimate effect of the new treaty upon the general interests of the Nation it is impossible to foresee. When, however, the disastrous influence and confusion arising from breaking up from their homes and moving shall have subsided, and they shall be settled in their new homes, I do hope the provisions of the new compact will be favorable. This will certainly be the case, if the Nation exercise prudence and wisdom in the regulation of their internal affairs, and in regulating their intercourse with whites. By the new compact, whites can approach them only on one side and all the navigable waters will lie in an Indian country. These circumstances, I do hope, will greatly restrain, if not entirely prevent the introduction of ardent spirits into the country, as well as put a stop to many unpleasant collissions with whites. I hope, however, that no other Indians will be induced to try the same experiment.

On May 16, 1828, the Cherokee representatives negotiated a treaty in Washington which resulted in their giving up their lands in Arkansas and removing to the Indian Territory.

~~~~

Wednesday, October 29, 1828

Letter from Arkansas

The following is a translation of a letter from one of our brethren in Arkansas, the original of which we also publish. We suppose that such translations may be of some interest to our English readers, not simply for the information which they contain, but as affording occasional specimens
~~~~

of the manner of communication between those who are only beginning to be versed in this new species of literature, and ignorant of all other.

In August and the beginning of September I write.

I will relate to you what is done here on the Arkansas river.

Last fall certain Chiefs were appointed to visit the city of Washington. Three days after Christmas they set out. They were sent for the purpose of settling a claim for land due to the nation—This object was not accomplished.—They exchanged away the country which we already possessed. Consequently there is great disturbance—The people were exceedingly exasperated. When the delegation returned they came very scattering. Then a council was held. Two did not attend—John Rogers and Geo. Morris. Two only were present—Thos. Graves and Geo. Guess. I did not however see any difficulty arise in the council. Several tribes of us were present—Shawnees, Mohawks, Delawares, Creeks—so many different tribes met with us. It was all very peaceful. We are soon to have another council, at which I understand they [the delegation] are to be tried for not following their instructions—for what they have done in regard to the land, whereas they were directed to go and see respecting a debt. They were instructed, if any other proposal should be made, not to accede to it. On this account their conduct gave offence. It has been very near creating mischief. But what is not to be will not be. At present the people are beginning to look out for themselves building spots.

Now I have done giving you an account of this one subject.

Now I will relate to you what things have taken place at the West. Last Fall a party of men, thirty five in number, set out on a hunting expedition. When they had gone far, three of their number returned. On their way they were taken prisoners, and detained five days. They were, however, set at liberty, and returned. The company who went farther had proceded some distance, when they saw Pawnees. The Pawnees were many. Now they rushed upon them, and surrounded them. Then a battle commenced. Three were lost—Tee-le-tah-ta-gee of the A-nee-sah-haw-nee Clan, another called the Squirrel, the other the Horse. This is a true account. Many of the other party were lost, for they had no guns, but only bows and arrows.

Secondly, Another company of seven persons set out for the Pawnee towns. There they arrived at a populous village. They were discovered, there they were attacked, and three of their number were lost. Four only returned, belonging to one town, called Piney-town. Of those that were lost, one was of the Long Savannah Clan, viz. Oo-lah-stoo-hah, another of the Deaf Clan, Tung-ne-no-lee, of the family of Wau hatch-ee, the other of the Wolf Clan, James, a half Creek. This happened in the month of June.

Thirdly, The Council has now just adjourned. Many were together–There was a great variety of people and a great variety of business. It was with difficulty that affairs were settled. Now they have completed their business. The land which has become ours is not far off, and is good land.

Fourthly, we hear that there will be war. I believe it will prove true; for we have suffered much injury during the past winter.

At the West there is much war. –There is no prospect of peace. What you hear of bloodshed is true. . . .

My friends I relate to you something of importance. We learn here that there is likely to be disturbance in the Spanish territory. . . . People from the United States are much engaged in forming settlements within the Spanish dominions. We understand also that they cross over to the North side of our line. A great variety of people of different nations are now crossing over.

Here in our country the Cherokees have disposed of their lands. But the land is good. There is no fault to be found with it. . . . Exert yourselves, members of Council. I wish it might again belong to us Cherokees on the Arkansas River. I hear that such a thing is possible. My friends, I relate this to you.

The Creeks are about crossing into the Choctaw country to settle. The river is the boundary between us. –They do not like the Fork, they say. When they have settled, then they will go to Washington to tell that they like their land.

This is addressed to you all;–John Miller, John Watts, John McIntosh, Cul-sa-tee-he, Hair Conrad, Bushy-head Thos. Field.

Now, my friends, Farewell. Be thankful that all is well here in Arkansas. This is all. Send me in turn some information, that I may hear what is done among you.

I The Glass write this. I am well.

~~~~

Fort Smith, Sept. 13th 1829.

Dear Brother,–I embrace this opportunity to inform you that I and my family are all well, hoping these times may find you and family enjoying the
~~~~

same. I can inform you that I had a tiresome journey. I was a long time on the way, and now I got here I am very much dissatisfied. I find no good land, bad water, very little good timber, and my advice is to you, stay where you are. I find the country sickly and a number of the people are dead that came with me and a number more sick, and I do not know where I shall settle.—I dont think I shall live on Arkansaw.

I am dear brother, yours with more than common respect.

John Wilson.

The above simple statement of facts is corroborated by hundreds of other testimonies. Major Long the authorized agent of the General Government to ascertain the nature of the country must also have entertained "the most unnatural and improbable fancies" in regard to it, for he considers it "uninhabitable," and styles it an "American desert." The Cherokees and Creeks are not the only ones of the southern tribes who entertain such fancies. . . .

John Ross
a Cherokee Chief

CHAPTER

4

Travel & Life Styles

Daniel Witter Reminiscences

The following letter was written by Daniel Witter, and published in the Arkansas Gazette *on October 26, 1873.*

Editors Gazette: In November, 1819, your humble servant, then residing in St. Louis, Mo., left that city on his way to a point on the Arkansas River, then known as "The Little Rock."

Meeting with a series of delays and misfortunes that clouded and changed the whole course and pursuits of his subsequent life, he finally reached the incipient city and anticipated state capital in May of the following year. He found on his arrival the following named gentlemen who comprised, at that time, the entire population of the future city, viz: Capt. Amos Wheeler, of St. Louis, one of the proprietors and sole monarch of the survey, Dr. Matthew Cunningham, Chester Ashley, Stephen F. Austin, James Bryan, E. Austin Elliott, Charles H. Pelham, Henry Sanford, and some three or four laborers and employees. Upon the arrival of your correspondent, the name of Daniel T. Witter was added to the human muster-roll, and who is now the sole survivor of those early pioneer citizens. He scarcely then dreamed that he would live to see those lofty pines and impenetrable jungles give place to refinement and roses, with all their hallowing and purifying influences. . . . The only buildings then erected were a small one-story frame, some thirty by eighteen feet square, divided into two rooms, one of which was used as a store, with a small remnant of dry goods, etc., and the other was used as a sort of general headquarters. . . .

In addition to this building, there were three or four huts built of round pine logs, one of which was used as a cooking room and dining saloon, and the others as sleeping apartments. No lots had then been sold, and the ground was in the possession of the proprietors of the New Madrid claim that had been located thereon. About the lst of June, Major Noah Lester, then late of the United States army, and who had come to the country with Gov. Miller, reached here from the Post, and within a few days thereafter was taken sick, and in a few days died. His was the first death and the first burial at Little Rock.

A few days later, two keel boats, each containing a company of Missourians bound for the Indian country west, under direction of Rev. Messrs. Vail and Chapman, and numbering some thirty or forty persons in all, reached here. They were suffering greatly from sickness contracted on the river, and I think one or more of their number had died before they reached here, and probably one or more shortly after their arrival.

Our little forlorn community suffered a good deal with ague and fever during the summer. Indeed no one escaped. Your correspondent, never having witnessed that form of disease before, could hardly understand how any one could shake with cold in such excessively hot weather, and was rather disposed to think it a sort of mental delusion. But he soon had his skepticism shook out of him. We had the services of our good Dr. Matthew Cunningham, but he soon ran short of the usual curative remedies, and as quinine was then unknown, our only reliance was Boneset tea, and we were drenched with that to our heart's content.

Another small building, with two or three rooms, was put up by the proprietor during the summer . . . which was temporarily used as a public house, and was kept by Sam Collins. Standing near the line of the land, the title of which was then in litigation, between the proprietors then in possession, and William Russell, claiming that possession. This building was moved across the line previous to William Russell getting possession of the land on which it was erected. Being at the residence of Gov. Fulton at Little Rock, some ten or twelve years later, the governor told me that this building formed a portion of his then residence. This, with the buildings named in a former paper, constituted the entire buildings of the city at the time your narrator left there in the fall of 1820, after which date he was there no more until October, 1825. During this interval, the seat of government, with all its offices and officers, had been removed there, great changes had taken place, many worthy and enterprising gentlemen, with their families, had become permanently settled there, and both place and people were putting on quite city-like appearances. . . .

Dr. M. Cunningham was at that time the only married man of our company. He came to Little Rock in February, 1820, leaving his family at Herculaneum, Missouri, until he could make suitable arrangements for their removal; and having made such arrangements, Mrs. Cunningham and family joined him there in September following. This was the first family, and Mrs. C. the first lady that had a permanent residence in Little Rock.

I remain, your obedient servant,
OLD SETTLER

Washington, October 22, 1873.

"Early Times: Reminiscences of Little Rock in 1820," Pulaski County Historical Review *Vol. 1, June, 1953.*

Blissville, Little Rock, Arkansas

The Stephen H. Long Expedition: Captain John R. Bell Journal

The following excerpts are taken from the journal of Captain John R. Bell, journalist for the Stephen H. Long Expedition to the Rocky Mountains, 1820. The expedition was approaching the Arkansas Territory from the west, which accounts for their reaching Belle Point, known today as Fort Smith, before other points in the territory.

Friday, Septr. 8th. We were annoyed and suffered more from the misquetoes and ticks last night, than we have been any night on our tour. It was impossible to sleep, from the great number of ticks crawling over the skin in gangs of hundreds. At 6 oclock a.m. we marched, glad to leave a place where there was no rest–not until we had stripped off our clothes & picked off the ticks from our bodies and clothes before we had any comfort.

. . .

The country abounds in ticks, it is diverting to see each of our party endeavoring by a variety of means to avoid or keep them off. The Corpl. killed a turkey and brought to camp. In the afternoon crossed two small creeks branches of the skin Bayou, at about 6 miles, the trace forks one leading to plantations cultivated near the mouth of the Skin Bayou, the other to Belle Point, two or three saplings are blazed at the forks of the trace. The country in that distance is hilly & rocky unfit for cultivation–after passing the forks of the trace, descending from the high lands, we came into a handsome undulating prairie & timbered land of fine soil and well adapted for cultivation after crossing a Bayou we halted for the night.

Saturday, Septr. 9th. Marched at 6 oclock a.m. The country similar to that passed yesterday afternoon–cross two small streams, was hailed by an Indian, who came up and spoke to us, he was a Cherokee & belonged to a small hunting party encamped on the Skin Bayou. Travelled 5 miles and arrived at where the trace forked again, one to the right leading through a heavy timbered and thick cane brake bottom of the Arkansas about 3 miles to Belle Point situated on the opposite side of the river–the other trace continued down the north side of the Arkansas to settlements of the Cherokees & some white families–after travelling over the bottom we arrived at a plantation opposite Fort Smith, thence on the margin of the river, hailed the guard of the Fort, a scow was sent over ourselves & horses was soon transported across to the long look for Belle Point where we were very politely & hospitably received by Captain Ballard of the Rifle Regiment, the only Officer at the Post. . . .

Friday, Sept. 15th. Major Long complains of being unwell, Lieut. Swift, continuing his astronomical observations and copying a map for Major Bradford–with much difficulty, shod my Indian horse, by throwing him and keeping him down 3 hours.

Saturday, Septr. 16th. Received pay & subsistence from Captain Kernay for the month of April 1820. Accompanied Major Long to examine our horses, found the Indian horse lame from the exertions and struggles he made yesterday while shoeing him. . . .

Sunday, Septr. 17th. Belle Point is situated below the confluence of the Porteau river with the Arkansas, about 130 miles from the Osage Village on the Verdegris and 100 above the Cherokee settlements on the Arkansas and 75 miles below the Trading house at the mouth of the Grand river. It was selected as a site for a military Post, by Major Long in 1817. . . . After selecting it, Major Long furnished a plan of a work to be constructed of timber, on a square whose sides were to be 132 feet, and two block houses in two opposite angles of the work, the whole to be surrounded by a ditch. The two block houses and two sides of the square next the land are completed– and timber collected for erecting the other two sides next the water. No settlers are permitted to establish themselves above the Porteau, of the Arkansas & Cayamecha of the Red river. I understand a negociation has been on foot with the Osage Indians for the sextion of country above the Cherokee boundary & below the rapids or falls of the Verdegris river; it is said this section embraces some of the finest lands in the Arkansas country, well watered by a number of streams, on which are mill seats, salt springs and Iron oar.

Monday, Septr. 18th. This place is remarkably healthy, and . . . the country generally for 100 miles about Belle Point, will prove so to settlers. Its surface is hilly & in many places broken, lime stone is to be found, I am told, and where that is their(sic) is pure water and a healthy country. The diseases of the country are ague & fevers & bellious complaints, which seldom prove fatal, I have not heard of any physician in this part of the country, there is none belonging to the garrison, the Soldiers are all in fine health. Last night a Soldier's wife of the garrison, was delivered of a fine boy weighing 12 pounds & this morning she is about her usual avocations.

Fruit & vegetables of every description grow here with cultivation, in the greatest abundance and of the finest flavor, and perfection.

Tuesday, Septr. 19th. By permission of the Commanding officer of the expedition, I started in advance of the party, at 9 oclock this morning, for Cape Geradeau on the Mississippi, accompanied by Oakly & Daugherty, discharged from the expedition. We followed the trace on the South side of the Arkansas river, and at the distance of 12 miles crossed the Vashgrass a considerable bayou which discharges into the Arkansas. Six miles from the Bayou we arrived at the house of a Mr. Billingsly where we halted for the night. . . . Mr. Billingsly who is from Kentucky, has resided 10 years on the Arkansas river, the last 2 years at his present plantation–his corn raised on the bottom land of the Arkansas will produce 70 bushels the acre, on the upland will produce 60 bushels. Cotton will produce at the rate of 800 lb the acre. He also stated to me that after he was married he resided 16 years in Kentucky, and every year his family was more or less sick–that since in this country he had raised a family of eleven without sickness, that he had not paid four pence half penny for medical aid in the time. . . .

Wednesday, Septr. 27. My horse travelling with more speed than any other of the party, I started before 6 oclock a.m. in advance, following the trace, the country is hilly and broken, thin soil, producing scrub oaks which appear to have had a fire through them this spring, 12 miles, crossed the 2nd fork of the Cadron, water a light blue colour, good place to encamp. . . . In the afternoon, crossed a hill, after which descending, until I struck the Cadron road on which a wagon may pass–continued over a fine tract of country to Little Red river, where I stopped at the house of Mr. Gills, family just recovering from attacks of ague and fever and billious fever. . . .

Friday, Sept. 29th. Marched about 6 oclock a.m. over a very hilly and rocky part of the country. . . . Arrived at Mr. Adams plantation two miles from Hardins ferry on White river, where we halted to refresh ourselves and to feed our horses with corn. The Major exchanged horses with Mr. Adams. In the afternoon we proceeded taking the road leading to Morris ford 5 miles from Adams'–begin to see plantations under cultivation and in good order–but the inhabitants all appear sickly with the prevailing complaint of ague & fever. It is said to [be] an unusual sickly season. Arrived at Morris on the bank of White river and put up for the night–he has a beautiful plantation of bottom land, the buildings are temporary & in bad order–he is an exception to sickly faces–the blossoms on his nose bid defiance to agues.

Sunday, October lst. . . . Proceeded early in the morning, taking what is called the upper road across Strawberry river–leaving the flourishing town of Davidsonville to our right. Crossed William's Creek a fine stream, on it is a mill, the first we have seen, the house is constructed of logs–crossed Strawberry river 50 yards wide, bottoms subject to inundation–breakfasted at Mr McKnights, the first family we have seen since we left the Arkansas river, whose members were enjoying good health.

The Journal of Captain John R. Bell: Official Journalist for the Stephen H. Long Expedition to the Rocky Mountains, 1820. The Arthur H. Clark Company, Glendale, California, U.S.A.: 1973.

The Ellen Stetson Journal: Sept. 3 - Oct. 22, 1821

Ellen Stetson left Brimfield, Massachusetts on Sept 3, 1821, enroute to Dwight Mission in the Arkansas Territory to serve as missionary with Rev. Washburn. All we know of her is the journal which she kept while traveling and that she left the Mission in 1841. We pick her up at Cape Girardeau,

Mo. on the 29th of September.

29. Left Cape Girardeau and passed through Jackson, a considerable village, 12 miles from Cape Gir. having heard of a Mr. Hunt, a Presbyterian minister who had recently left the place, called on Mrs. Ginnell, formerly of Boston, to make some inquiries in relation to him, and found there Mr. Hunt, formerly of Leavenburd Mass. We learned he had not been placed in a situation congenial to his feelings. He has a numerous family and has suffered much he has lately removed from this place to St. Charles on the Missouri. After we left Jackson we rode on expecting to reach a house 13 miles distant and should have succeeded, but we mistook the road. It was a rainy afternoon, and darkness overtook us in the midst of the forest in a path so obscure that we could keep it with difficulty by daylight. After a time the rain fell in showers and the moon tho' small, gave at intervals some light. We were afraid to ride as the path was newly cut and thickly set with stumps of trees; and now the rain fell without intermission.

We came to the bed of a creek and in the steep pitch I went forward and thought I saw the road before me, and I had the pleasure of seeing a light glimmering thru the trees at a distance. Before I was aware I was seperated from my company. I went back to the place I had left but could hear no sound excepting a distant hallo, this I imagined proceeded from some hunter, and returned to the path I had left with silence almost breathless. I thought I would go to the light and as I could find no other opening I kept the bed of the brook. Owing to the rough, rocky bottom I had repeated falls, nothing was now visible but the gravelly way a few yards forward, for the light had disappeared. I heard at a distance the barking of dogs, and Indians, and wolves, and panthers and the more savage hunters into my mind. The hallowing still continued and I thought possibly it might be Brother Asa looking for me and I ventured to answer, but I was so much exhausted that my answer was merely an indistinct murmur.

I went on tho torn with briars and wet to the skin. I soon again perceived the light still distant, but as the country was full of creeks and fallen trees, I felt uncertain whether I should reach it. As I approached the light I thought I would go cautiously on and obtain a view of the habitation and if possible of the inhabitants before I ventured to make myself one among them, but when within 20 yards of the cabin my intention was frustrated by my falling down a steep bank. I struck the back of my head which stunned me for a moment and when I recovered my recollection I thought myself unable to rise. I forgot all my prudent resolutions and cried for help, but I cried in vain for the dogs set up a full chorus and ran in every direction. After a little reflection I arose and groping about to collect my garments which had been scattered by my fall, proceeded toward the hut calling Asa at every step. I met him near the dwelling, but instead of finding him with the carriage and Sister Nancy, I found he had left them half a mile back. He went in to find if we have lodging for the night but found no kindness or hospitality. The man whose cabin we entered merely inform'd him where he might find entertainment and went in shutting the door behind him. We made the utmost haste toward the waggon, thro' a wood filled with underbrush. On reaching the spot we "held a talk" on the best course to be pursued, and as we had entirely lost our path we came to the conclusion, that Br. Asa should go and endeavor to find the house of Capt. Young, to which we had been directed, and there if possible obtain assistance and a light. As we were destitute of food for the horses we could not think of stopping for the night without further effort. Brother Asa commenced his walk and we seated ourselves in the waggon to wait the result. Many gloomy apprehensions were before us, the rain fell in torrents and the darkness was intense. How then could Asa find or keep the path? but we kept these fears within our own bosoms, and waited quietly for his return, not without many dismal forebodings on his account. At length we heard his voice and saw the welcome light of a lantern. He was accompanied by Capt. Young who led the way and we proceeded toward his house, which we reached about midnight. These kind people had provided us an excellent supper and fire and lodging and waited on us with the utmost cheerfulness, dried our soaked garments, and we had a sweet night's rest after our fatiguing evening.

30 Arose this morning refreshed and after breakfast recommenced our journey. We were informed there was a stage twenty miles from this place we left and we hoped to reach it easily. Bro. Asa had the precaution however to take feed for the horses. We did not reach the place till after dark, we walked about five miles after it became evening. We passed several Indian encampments and deliberated whether we had best go on or stay for the night. At length we concluded on the former and reached the place safely. . . .

Oct. 5. We have crossed the little black river and gone on about twenty miles today. I have walked about half the day. I find that, tho' much fatigued I do not feel that lassitude and depression that I do when I ride.

Commend me to the simple Moravian. Could I find others like minded, I would dismiss the horses "minding myself to go afoot." It is wonderful to see the indolence of this people. We tarried last night at a house which had neither doors nor windows, the night was winter in her shortest mood. We had nothing but a feather bed without a sheet, and coverlid, laid just between two open door ways. We have staid in several houses that had neither windows nor doors. We have ridden 25 miles today besides crossing Current's river in a ferry boat.

Oct. 7 Made to Davidsonville, the seat of justice for Lawrence Co. Ark. Crossed Hadlock's ferry at the junction of Spring river and Eleven points and rode eight miles further to the house of Col. Stewart and concluded to tarry tho it was not night, as we could not reach the next house, which was ten miles on, and a broad river to cross. We had a cold snow storm today, and we would favor the horses as much as possible.

Oct. 8 Cross'd the Strawberry river ten miles from Col. Stewart's, and took breakfast on the other side, proceeded by a rough road 16 miles farther to the house of an Irish emigrant by the name of St. Clair, they inform'd us that two of the missionaries, from Arkansaw were here last week and went as far as Davidsonville in hope of meeting us, but hearing no tidings they returned. It seems the letters which we sent from Lexington were not received, as one of them mentioned his expectation of meeting a brother whom he suppos'd to be on his way to the Cherokee nation. They confirm'd the report respecting the war between the Cherokees and Osages, and the slaughter made among the women and children of the Osages. The Cherokees rush'd upon them while their warriors were absent and destroy'd and made captive near one hundred. It would have been great joy to us, if we could have met the brethren, but it seems the design of Providence that we should explore the desert alone, and why should we refuse, He who has preserved us in six, yea in seven troubles is still near us and we shall not sink, supported by an almighty arm. . . .

10 We have cross'd White River at the mouth of Poke Bayou. This is a very large and beautiful river, the waters are as transparent and bright as those of Connecticut. We were repeatedly told that the fording it was safe and we ventur'd without much fear, but Br. Asa, from not understanding the manner of crossing large streams, made his curve the wrong way and before we were aware of the danger, the dearborn was nearly filled. We were wet and frightened and we thought that was all, as we got out safely.

A form of wagon or buggy.

After we had ridden a mile we stop'd for the night (it has been a rainy day and we have to prepare something for our journey. 2 miles carry us out of the settlements, and we have near 50 miles without so much as an indian hut) On examination we find that the wetting and fright were not all the injury we sustained. The water had found its way into our trunks so as to wet nearly every thing they contain and we have the labor of unpacking and drying to employ us this evening. Brother Asa & Miss B. had books in their trunks which are very much injured.

11 After we had ridden a mile a gentleman spoke to us, and on learning who we were gave us a letter which was left by our Missionary friends, Hitchcock & Orr. The letter contained particular directions respecting our course, and they engaged Col. Johnson with whom the letter was left, to render us all needful assistance, but he was now confin'd to his bed by a rheumatic fever and in most excruciating distress, so that he could render us no assistance on the way. His son was necessary to him every moment, so that we seem destin'd to pursue our path alone, contrary to the advice of Brother H. in his letter, and he little knew how much alone we are. Col. Johnson's family treated us with greatest kindness and urged our stay so earnestly that we could not doubt but they desired it. The horses were to be shod and we concluded to stay untill this was done and then the day was so far spent that we concluded to accept their invitation and not stay needlessly one night in the forest. We think we never knew December colder in New England than this has been so far. We shiver with the cold even while sitting by a good fire, but there are no warm houses.

12 In the wilderness a day's journey from any human habitation. We left the settlement on White river early and have proceeded by mark'd trees as far as we are able towards Little Red River where is another settlement.

We have stop'd for the night near a creek which contains good water. Our first object was fire, as the weather was severe and there was no little in our commencing housekeeping. The horses were brought into the same assortment and fed and watered, and wood was to be collected for the night. We made tea under a spreading mulberry tree, boil'd potatoes and toasted our cornbread. We had an excellent supper and have sat down cheerfully by a good fire with no shelter beneath the azure canopy of Heaven. If wolves and panthers do not give us a serenading, we shall be quite comfortable—far more so than in many houses where we have lately been receiv'd and why should we fear?. . . Unless God had preserv'd us we should long ere this have been destroyed by man. . . . We have had more freedom for social conversation and devotion this evening than we have enjoyed for a long time.

13 We had a comfortable night tho' the snow fell to a considerable depth. We made our beds in the waggon which was drawn near the fire, and a chest with a buffaloe robe and some blankets. This Brother Asa took. We rose early and after breakfast prepar'd to depart but soon found an unexpected trial. The horses, unaccustom'd to standing out all night without shelter were rather unruly and in attempting to go up a rough hill, near which we had encamp'd, they ran back and broke the waggon. As it was impossible to go on we thought no time was to be lost, and Asa took one of the horses and set out to ride to Little red river; and there to endeavour to procure some assistance. We two were left alone in the wilderness. The waggon was left part way up the hill in a place where we could not make a fire. The snow was falling fast and we had no shelter. We had the horse to take care of and wood to obtain. There was no fallen wood and we could obtain none without crossing a considerable creek and at almost every step the water would run over the tops of our shoes. Our clothes were heavy with snow and ice. We had consum'd all our cooked provisions, and had nothing left but fat pork and potatoes, no meal or bread. Our situation seem'd comfortless and forlorn. As Asa rode a tired horse without a saddle we had no expectation of his return till morning and perhaps not till midday. We labor'd hard to collect a scanty portion of fuel during the day, and went every step our shoes in snow, and brought the wood which we collected through the creek which was now considerably deep and rapid, being swell'd by the storm. We found up the hill a thicket of pines and went to work with only a little hatchett, and dug up enough of the nots[?] around the decay'd roots to give us a light during the night. We clim'd the steep, rocky and snowclad hill and brought down with great fatigue a heavy waggon seat and chest for our seats, and then, as the ground was wet and cold, so that we could not possibly dry or warm our ice-covered feet we collected some flat stones to make a kind of hearth. All that we had to do must be done before dark as we were sensible that neither fear nor cold would permit us to leave the fire afterwards. Our minds were tolerably tranquil yet we had many gloomy and some dismal feelings which we labor'd to suppress. This was the place of encampment for all the travellers of every description, white, red, and black. Between White and Red rivers every one knew of Salador Creek, and we were a feeble company, and it has often been observed "it was well known missionaries must have money." We both felt that "there was but a step between us and death."

We were unable to drive poles of sufficient length to sit upright under our blankets which we fastened to them, but we did the best we might and at the close of the day prepar'd our solitary supper and sat down under the blanket which was a partial shelter, and now seated by the fire we have time to feel our fatigue. The storm has clear'd and is succeeded by a cold, northwest wind which almost blinds us by driving the smoke into our eyes, and with all our efforts we cannot be warm, tho we have put on dry warm garments. The horse, us'd so long to standing by his fellow keeps an incessant noise and seems every moment ready to break away. We fear his loud neighing will attract some of the tenants of the forest.

There follows a rather long unfinished poem which Miss Stetson was writing in her journal.

14 About midnight as were sitting cheerless and cold, trying in vain to sleep, we heard voices, and soon found that Br. Asa had return'd with a man he had hired to assist him, and some provisions. The man was one who had been employ'd by the missionaries at Dwight and had prepar'd to return there. He would have commenced his journey the same morning on which Asa began his to go in quest of a guide, but was prevented by the storm. He will assist the remainder of our journey with a fresh horse. This is peculairly favorable as we shall have no marked trees, and nothing but an indian trace or footpath the remainder of the way. We are now about 85 miles from our future home. We think we have felt something what it is to be pilgrim, the last day and evening. After the waggon was repaired and loaded, and breakfast over, we prepar'd to go forward, but the rough hill was still before us and it was long before we could ascend it. The men carried up all the baggage on their shoulders and after reloading, at one o'clock we took our farewell look of Salador creek. Would that some of those people who say that "Missionairies go for the sake of maintenance in case" were here a day and night. We have this evening been saved from the trouble of cooking as there is no water to be had. We are now five or six miles from Giles ferry. We do not find our path improved by this constant recurrence to "Hog and Hominy," that with the hardship of yesterday has render'd us somewhat unwell.

15 We have this day cross'd little Red River and have put up at the house of Mr. Giles to stay over the Sabbath, we feel ourselves much worn out, the way is full of peril, but we do not yet fear. Yet we have not either a gun or dog with us.

Mr. Giles observes that they felt much solicitus on our account while Brother Asa was absent from us. He mention'd a circumstance which had recently occurred, of a man who had left the Garrison to go eastward with four little children. A few days after their bodies were found in the Arkansaw, barbarously mangled, but the Lord is our keeper, therefore will not we fear.

17 We have this morning commenced our journey across the wilderness in a severe and cold storm of rain. The addition of provisions for ourselves and cattle enlarges the load more than the additional horse can draw. We had a very difficult mountain to ascend and felt some fears, but our kind hearted landlord without mentioning his design to us rode after and overtook us before we reached the elevation, and by unloading and carrying up part of the baggage they were enabled to ascend, this was ten miles from Mr. Giles' house. We proceeded slowly along, cold, spiritless and drench'd to the skin. At evening we were so benum'd that we found it difficult to kindle a fire. The screech owl, and the raven gave us their music but we were no otherwise annoyed. The rain clear'd about midnight and was succeeded by violent west wind. We suffer'd [?] considerably with cold this and the following day and night.

19 At dark a storm commence'd, but we were seated round a good fire, tho' somewhat smoky, and tho' we were in the very spot where a short time ago, a young man was terribly mangled by a catamount and we heard the panther screaming near us, yet we slept soundly.

20 Our waggon top was this morning completely broken down by a tree in which it was caught. We have walked the principal part of the day in a heavy rain. We often have a water course to cross twenty times, in riding two or three miles. One of the men constantly drives while the other goes forward to explore the path. The banks of the creeks are steep and rugged, and the way rocky and mountainous. We have reached the house of one Glass a Cherokee and think to tarry thro' the night. It is better than most of the cabins in this country, tho' there is no cleanliness except on the dressing[?] which make quite a display of blue and white. There are enamel'd dishes and little [containers?] curiously striped white and red and fill'd with milk. The room is adorn'd with the spoils of the savage inhabitants of the forest, and "weapons form'd for savage fray." Under the beds they threw their game as they came in from hunting. We have on the whole a wretched night. The dogs and hogs keep up a continual din, enough to turn stronger

heads than ours. We are now 25 miles from Dwight and 60 from Giles' ferry. We have seen no human being since we left that place except that we had a distant view of some Chickasaw Indians in their encampment. Their discordant noises made the forest ring.

21st We have not been able to reach home, and must pass another night in the open waggon. We have just quitted a large Prairie and have no shelter from the keen biting wind.

22nd We rose early and commenced what we hoped to be the last day of our journeying. As we walked slowly along the [?] road, we recollected the day of which this is the anniversary, the birthday of dear New England. In imagination we saw the little company of Pilgrims who landed on the long remembered *Plymouth Rock*, and compared our state with theirs, and saw, we hope with gratitude, how much the balance was in our favor. Oh! may the spirit of the Puritans hover over the Missionaries of Arkansaw. Two hundred years ago, how large a part of this land was only the abode of wild beasts, and savage men. Now Jesus reigns over thousands of hearts and is still increasing his kingdoms in this land, while thousands who have had their garments washed, and made white in the blood of the Lamb are already gone to their rest, and join the chorus of all the redeemed in Heaven and on earth.

. . . We walked along several miles of the Illinois creek, and about eleven o'clock came in view of the little missionary establishment and after crossing the creek in a canoe, we closed our journeying and found ourselves at home. . . .

William Pope's Impressions

Judge William F. Pope came to Arkansas from Virginia as the private secretary to Governor John Pope, Third Territorial Governor of Arkansas from 1829 to 1835. His book Early Days in Arkansas *(Little Rock: Frederich W. Allsopp, Publisher, 1895.) relates his experiences and impressions from the time of his arrival in the territory until 1861. Judge Pope finished the book on the eightieth birthday, long after he had lost his eyesight.*

Early River Navigation

The first craft of any description navigated by civilized man to ply the waters of the Arkansas, of which we have any accurate information, was the fleet of keelboats and barges used by the adventurers from New Orleans in their search for gold in 1809. . . . This fleet of boats was commanded by one Captain Hillare, a Frenchman.

In the latter part of 1815, a fleet of keelboats and barges, under command of Major Gibson, United States Army, bearing troops, supplies and material for establishing forts or military posts along the upper Arkansas in the Indian country, passed up the river. These boats were *cordeled* up stream. This method of ascending a river was slow and laborious. A strong rope was attached to the boat, amidship, and one end of the rope carried ashore, where men walked along the bank and towed the boat. A man stood at the prow of the boat and with a long pole kept it out from the shore and parallel to it. . . .

The next craft of any importance to ascend the Arkansas river was a finely fitted up keelboat from St. Louis, enroute for Fort Gibson, with military supplies for the garrisons there and at Arbuckle, Towson and other places. This boat was called the "Arkansas," and had as passengers Gov. James Miller, first Governor of Arkansas Territory, and suite. The Governor and party disembarked at the Post of Arkansas, the seat of government, and the boat proceeded on her trip up the river.

The first boat propelled by steam to ascend the Arkansas was the "Comet," commanded by Capt. Byrne. She arrived at the Post of Arkansas on April 1, 1820, eight days out from New Orleans. . . .

The *Gazette* of March 22, 1822, announces the arrival at Little Rock of the steamer "Eagle," Capt. Morris in command, seventeen days from New Orleans. She was bound for Dwight Mission. Says the *Gazette* of the above date: "This is the first steamboat that ever ascended to this place. . . ." She returned on the 19th, having ascended to within twelve miles of her destination–low water prevented her from reaching it.

A Unique Ferry Boat

The ferry boat in use at this early date (1832) deserves more than passing notice. In construction it . . . [consisted] of a long flat bottomed hull, with two bows. It was the method of propulsion that made it unique. This was accomplished by means of buoys or buoy boats, as they were called. These buoy boats were about twelve feet long and some four or five feet wide amidship, the two ends coming to a sharp point. These buoy boats were some fifteen or twenty in number and were staunchly built, and entirely floored over. In the center of each of them was a post, varying in height from three to ten feet, according to the location of the buoys. At the top of each of these posts was a large pulley, through which a large rope, one and one-half in diameter, ran. This rope was attached to a huge cottonwood tree on the north side of the river, opposite the foot of Main street and about fifty feet above the ground. The other end of the rope was passed through the pulleys on the buoy boats. These boats were distributed along at regular intervals, the last one being located about one hundred and fifty feet above the ferry landing on the Little Rock side. The rope passing through the pulley on the last buoy boat had a slack of about fifty feet. To this part of the large rope a pulley was attached, through which a smaller rope ran and was fastened to each of the upper corners of the ferry boat. At each end of the boat was what was called a lee board, some fifteen inches wide, and which was raised or depressed by a lever. On starting from either shore this lee board was so depressed as to swing the end of the boat quartering up stream, the buoy boats assuming the same position. The action of the water against the lee board gave the necessary impetus to the ferry boat to carry her across the river. On coming to within forty or fifty feet of the shore a vigorous pull upon the rope would straighten the course of the boat directly across the river and bring it to the landing. To prevent the buoy boats from drifting together, a smaller rope was tied to the same cottonwood tree lower down, and attached to the bottom of the posts on the buoy boats. The speed of a ferry boat propelled in the manner I have attempted to describe was very rapid, indeed, almost equal to that of steam. This unique ferry boat, with her attendant buoy boats, was destroyed by the heavy drifts in the river during the tremendous overflow of 1833.

The Bowie-Knife

In the minds of some . . . the words "Arkansas" and "Bowie-knife" are synonymous terms, and that weapon has been classed as an important part of every Arkansan's personal outfit.

In 1827, or 1828, there came to Washington, Hempstead county, Arkansas, from where, I do not know, a man named Black, who was an expert workman in all kinds of metals, being also a gunsmith, and who possessed the secret of tempering steel to a hardness that has never been equalled since.

There was then living at Walnut Hills, Lafayette county, a wealthy planter named Reason Bowie, a brother of the celebrated James Bowie, who afterwards fell at the storming of the "Alamo."

Reason Bowie was a keen lover of the chase and spent most of his time in hunting the bear and deer, in which the country then abounded. On one of his visits to Washington, Bowie called on Black, the artificer, and engaged him to make a hunting-knife after a certain pattern of his own designing. Bowie whittled out of the top of a cigar box the exact shape of the knife he desired made. He told the smith that he wanted a knife that would disjoint the bones of a bear or deer without gaping or turning the edge of the blade. Black undertook the job and turned out the implement of the hunt which was afterwards known as the Bowie-knife. The hilt was elaborately ornamented with silver designs. Black's charge for the work was $10, but Bowie was so pleased with the excellence of the knife that he gave the maker thereof $50.

I have seen hand-made needles of the smallest size produced by this man Black. I do not hesitate to make the statement that no "genuine" Bowie-knives have ever been made outside of the State of Arkansas, for when Black died, sometime after the late war, his secret of tempering the steel . . . died with him. Many imitations have been attempted, but they are not "Bowie-knives."

A memorable event

A memorable event in the history of Little Rock was the stopping there, for a few hours only, of the noted author, Washington Irving, and the celebrated ornithologist, John James Audubon. These gentlemen were returning east after having been with the expedition sent out by the Government, under command of Capt. B. L. E. Bonneville, United States Army, to make a reconnoissance of the plains. . . .

It was during this expedition that Washington Irving obtained material for his highly interesting book, entitled, "Adventures of Captain

Bonneville." Audubon also secured on this trip many sketches and descriptions of the native birds of the far west, to be used in the preparation of his world famous work, "Birds of America."

The citizens of the town tendered these distinguished authors a complimentary banquet, which they were obliged to decline on account of the inability of the boat, the steamer "Little Rock,"on which they were passengers, to lay over for the necessary length of time.

The Duel

One of the most unique affairs of honor, so called, in the annals of duelling, occurred at Little Rock in the month of October, 1833, and took place at the corner of Main and Markham streets, then the heart of the town. . . . The parties to this strange duel were Robertson Childers, a man of some prominence as a lawyer, and one Stewart, a professional gambler. The quarrel grew out of a dispute at cards.

Childers and Stewart agreed to meet on a certain day and hour at the corner of Main and Markham streets, the one to take position on the southeast corner . . . and the other on the northeast corner. . . . It was further agreed that double-barrelled shotguns, loaded with buckshot, were to be used first, and, if neither was injured, then pistols were to take the place of the shotguns; if they still remained unhurt, dirk knives were to be drawn and they both to advance to the middle of the street and proceed to carve each other after the most approved fashion.

On the day and hour fixed these two men met as per agreement, and proceeded to carry out their bloody programme. At the first fire, Mr. Childers received a slight flesh wound in the leg. The remaining barrels were discharged, without effect, when the shotguns were thrown aside and pistols resorted to, with bloodless result. The pistols were then discarded and the murderous dirk knives drawn, but just as the now infuriated combatants were advancing for the final encounter, Judge Benjamin Johnson, Judge of the Superior Court, appeared upon the scene. He commanded the peace and summoned the bystanders—a large crowd had gathered by this time—to assist him in arresting the parties.

Thus ended, without serious injury to either party, what promised at the outset to be a fight to the death of one or both of the participants. Childers and Stewart were heavily fined and put under large bonds to keep the peace.

An Amusing Scene

The Legislature of 1833 met in a one-story frame house near the northwest corner of Main and Mulberry (Third) streets. . . .

An exciting and at the same time an amusing scene occurred during this session of the Legislature, between Dr. Matthew Cunningham, an early settler of the town and a prominent physician, and J. Alexander, a representative from Washington County. Dr. Cunningham had written and had published in the *Advocate* an article severely criticizinng Mr. Alexander's career as a legislator, charging him, among other things, with stupidity and ignorance; and also taking the people of Washington county to task for sending such a man to the Legislature.

Eliza Cunningham

Alexander demanded of the editor of the paper the name of the writer of the article, and was informed that Dr. Cunningham was its author. That afternoon, upon the adjournment of the Legislature for the day, Alexander discovered Dr. Cunningham crossing the street in the direction of the Legislative building. He advanced to meet the Doctor, and as he came within striking distance dealt him a blow with a stick which felled him to the ground, and stood over his prostrate enemy raining blow after blow upon him. The Doctor's wife, who was standing in the doorway of their family residence, just across the street, observing the state of affairs, seized a large stick and went to her husband's rescue. Before Alexander could realize what was about to happen, he received a furious blow over the head and another in the face which brought him to the ground and put a stop to the fight. The old Doctor was considerably bruised but had no bones broken. Alexander, however, was prevented from attending to his Legislative duties for several days.

Early Days in Arkansas. *William F. Pope. Little Rock: Frederich W. Allsopp, Publisher, 1895.*

Early Batesville

The two letters below come from the Arkansas Gazette *of November 26, 1857 and provide a glimpse of Batesville and the White River in 1826. "N" is probably C. F. M. Noland, who figured quite heavily in the politics of the Territory. Noland published a newspaper in Batesville for several years and provided humorous sketches of life in Arkansas for* The Spirit of the Times, *a paper in St. Louis. These sketches were collected in 1957 by Ted R. Worley and Eugene A. Nolte into a volume entitled* Pete Whetstone of Devil's Fork. *The tone and style of these letters is so similar to the sketches that the assumption that Noland wrote them is fairly reliable.*

Fairway, Nov. 26, 1857

Dear Captain–Herewith you will receive the beginning of an early history of Arkansas. I write for neither profit nor pay–nor do I intend to make any efforts at display. I shall write when inclination prompts me, and leave off from the same cause. I shall try, nothing to extenuate, nor aught set down in malice, yet, I am not free from prejudice, and to err is human.

Truly yours, N.

Early Times in Arkansas by N.–It was in the Fall of 1826, that I reached the Town of Batesville, in the county of Independence. It was just after the great September freshet of that year, which had been so destructive to the settlers on White river. At that period, Batesville was the second town in importance in the then Territory of Arkansas. It was the county seat of Independence, and one of the two Land offices to which the Territory was entitled, was located there. The Batesville Land District was very extensive–even Little Rock, at which point the office of the other District was located, belonged to it. The whole of Town, one North, Range Twelve West, being in the Batesville district. . . . At that time there were no towns or villages on White River, from Batesville to its mouth. The points of any note, were mouth of Black River, Chickasaw Crossings, Nigger Hill, and Mouth of Cache.

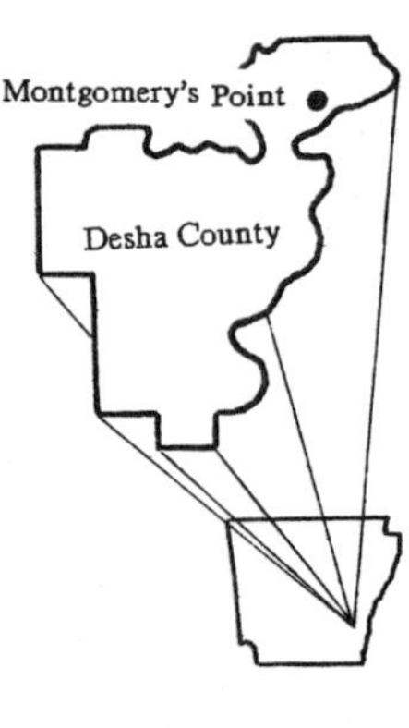

Montgomery's Point on the Mississippi river was the great trading point for all Arkansas, North, and for a great portion South, of the Arkansas river. For many years, all boats passing out of either the Arkansas or White rivers, touched at Montgomery's Point, and what was remarkable, persons passed down those rivers into the broad Mississippi, and yet never passed through the mouth of either. Arkansas boats invariably came into White river through the cut off, while a chute of the Mississippi, just below Montgomery's Point, enabled them to reach the father of waters, without passing out at the mouth of White river.

At that early day, there were shipped from Batesville one hundred bales of cotton and upwards. Hartwell Boswell was the great merchant of that region, and people came hundreds of miles to trade with him—two pounds of coffee for a dollar. I remember when a new comer arrived with a keel boat of goods, and sold it at 3 pounds for a silver dollar. There was great rejoicing among the old women.

The first Territorial election took place in the month of November, 1819. James Woodson Bates, A. S. Walker, Henry Casseday, Perly Wallis, and Robert T. Slaughter, were candidates for Delegate. The first named was elected. The members of the first General Assembly of the Territory, were as follows, viz:

Members of the Legislative Council—

Sylvanus Phillips, Arkansas county.
Edward McDonald, Lawrence county.
David Clark, Hempstead county.
John McElmurry, Pulaski county.
Jacob Barkman, Clark county.

House of Representatives—

Wm. O. Allen, and Wm. B. R. Horner, Arkansas county
Jo. Hardin and Joab Hardin, Lawrence co'y.
Wm. Stephenson and John English, Hempstead county
Radford Ellis and Thos. H. Tindell, Pulaski co.
Thos. Fish, Clark county.

The first Legislature met at the Post of Arkansas on the 20th of Feb. 1820, and organized by electing Stephenson, speaker, and Sam C. Roane, clerk of the house. McDonald, President of the Senate, and Richard Searcy, clerk.

Gen Wm. O. Allen, who had been elected to the Legislature, had once belonged to the army. He was appointed Brig. Gen. of the Arkansas militia.

A misunderstanding between him and Col. Robt. C. Oden, resulted in a duel, which was fought on the 10th of March, 1820. Elijah Morton was the second of Oden, Geo. W. Scott, of Allen. At the first fire Oden received a severe wound in the hip, which at first it was supposed would prove mortal. In falling, his pistol went off, and the ball from it struck Allen on the head. The wound was not deemed dangerous, and Allen was careless about it–fever ensued, however, and Allen died eleven days from the day on which they fought. Oden recovered, but suffered a great deal. He was under the impression that Geo. Scott purposely failed to neck the bullet with which he was shot. . . .

Dueling pistols have a barrel extension called a forcing or necking cone to properly seat the bullet to assure the accuracy of the weapon. Improperly "necked," Allen's pistol was believed to be erratic.

And now of mail facilities at Batesville. In 1826, and for some thereafter, we had a weekly mail north, and one south. Jim Russell and Booker Bennett were the mail riders on the northern route, at different times. They left Batesville in the morning of one day, and in three and a half days, reached Greenville, Mo., a distance of some 140 miles, and in 3 1/2 days more returned to Batesville. They were as faithful as men could be, and the mail rarely ever failed. . . . There was a little cross-mail occasionally, once, I believe, in two weeks, to Liberty, the county Seat of Izard county. A great change in mail facilities since then, but there was less complaint then than now. In a file of the "Gazette" I noticed that the President's message was published in it, on the 22d day of February, 1820, though delivered to Congress on the 7th day of Dec., 1819.

[No. 2]

Early Times in Arkansas by N. . . . The first and only newspaper up to the year 1830, was the "Arkansas Gazette," published and edited by Wm. E. Woodruff. The first No. was issued Nov. 25th, 1819. Gen. James Miller, a distinguished soldier, and a native of New Hampshire was the first Governor. He returned to his native State on a visit and for his health, in the year 1824, and while there was elected to Congress. He resigned the Governorship and was succeeded by another gallant soldier, and most accomplished gentleman, Gen. Geo. Izard.

In 1829 . . . there was a considerable business done in peltries. The Delawares and Shawnees, some of whom lived on Crooked Creek, now in Marion county, came annually to Batesville with their peltries, and white hunters were quite numerous. There were but two practicing lawyers. . . . There were two physicians, Dr. Jonathan Isom, a good honest man, with but little education, and Dr. Caleb S. Manley, one of the–and it requires a great effort not to finish the sentence.

Such was Batesville in 1826. How changed in 1857, when I last visited it.

From the state Gazette and Democrat

Hiram Whittington's Letters

Hiram Abiff Whittington was a young printer from Boston who arrived in Little Rock on Christmas Eve, 1826. He worked for William E. Woodruff, publisher of the Arkansas Gazette *until 1832, when poor health forced him to move to Hot Springs. In 1836 he brought his bride, Mary Burnham of Boston, to make their home. Whittington became active in the business community and in the politics of the Territory. In the following letters, written to his brother Granville, we find amusing anecdotes on social customs, politics, the life and people of the early times in Arkansas. Hiram died at Hot Springs in 1890. His brother joined him in the Territory in 1837. The letters were found in Granville's home in Mount Ida when it was being dismantled and have been preserved by his descendants. Dallas T. Herndon copied the letters from the originals.*

Little Rock, A.T., April 21,1827

Dear Brother (Sunday morning):

This morning as I was shaving your letter was laid under my nose, postmarked Boston, which surprised more agreeably than anything which has taken place in this wide world in the last six thousand years, and came within an ace of sending me to the Indian Valley. Just as I was drawing the razor down under my chin I caught sight of the postmark, and the sudden jerk I gave it at that moment raised the skin from my throat at a great rate; however, I do not think it will prove fatal, and you may think yourself a lucky fellow in not cutting my head entirely off.

I had a rascally time in getting here from New Orleans, or rather from the mouth of the Arkansas. The first seven hundred miles after leaving New

Orleans was very fine, being on one of the best steamboats on the Mississippi. We stopped at Natchez and about 20 other places before we arrived at the mouth of White river, where we left the boat, two others besides myself. From that time on we had to get along the best way we could, sometimes in a dugout and then afoot. We were 5 days from the mouth of the Arkansas to Little Rock, about 150 miles; at night we slept in log cabins, except one night when we slept on the ground in the woods. By making a big fire and wrapping our cloaks around us, we slept very comfortably. At the log cabins we were obliged to sleep in the same room with the man and his wife. The first time I slept in the room with the women, I felt foolish enough, you may be sure. The women would not leave the room to give me a chance to get into bed, and I finally had to go to bed before them. I did not take my pantaloons off, however, until I had got between the sheets.

In the afternoon of Sunday, the – day of December, we arrived at Little Rock. It is situated on the south bank of the Arkansas, contains about 60 buildings, 6 brick, 8 frame, the balance log cabins. The best building in the place is the printer's; it is built of brick and is as good an office as any in Boston. Little Rock Academy is a log hut and the State House is a little low wooden building about 10 feet by sixteen. The town has been settled about eight years, and has improved very slow. The trees are not cut down in the town yet; instead of streets we walk in cow trails from one house to another. The town, and I believe the whole Territory, is inhabited by the dregs of Kentucky, Georgia and Louisiana, but principally from the former, and a more drunken, good for nothing set of fellows never got together. The Secretary of the Territory and the Judges of the Supreme Court drink whiskey out of the same cup with the lowest born, and roll together in the same gutter. There have been more than a dozen murders committed here, but the murderer was always acquitted. The greatest drunkards fill the most responsible offices. In August, the election of a member for Congress and the members of the General Assembly takes place. The opposing candidates never meet in the street without stopping to blackguard each other, and very often fight. Most of the inhabitants carry dirks or pistols in their pockets, but the greater part of them are too cowardly to use them. Mr. Woodruff, my employer, being an honest and sober man, the majority of the people are his bitter enemies, and he has frequently been threatened. About a month ago, three worthies got into such a fury, owing to a piece published in the Gazette criticizinng the conduct of the Secretary, that they threatened to annihilate all the printers; and one of the judges of the Supreme Court swore that he would pulverize every printer in the Territory in less than a month.

Of the female part of the community, I have not much to say, as there are five grown girls in the township and they are as ugly as sin and as mean as the devil. It is a famous place for parties. I have been to three since I have been here, where they have a violin and dance all night, and as there are not girls to form a set, all the old women dance, and lie in bed the next day. The men get drunk and generally have a fight before they get home. Last Sunday I saw two French ladies walking out, each with a young coon in her arms; they are used instead of lap dogs.

The bushes in the woods, likewise in the town, are covered with ticks, which are the greatest curse I have yet discovered. . . . They are worse than bed bugs, and in a very short time get under the skin and make a very bad sore. If the girls feel a tick biting them at a party, and even if they are on the floor dancing, they immediately stop and unpin and scratch themselves until they find it; it would do your heart good to see how expert the dear little good-for-nothing creatures are at catching ticks. This is a good country for peaches, melons, sweet potatoes, etc. . . .

The steam boats arrived here last week, which never happened before. One of them returned to New Orleans yesterday, and the other proceeded up the river with provisions for the garrison. It is altogether uncertain when I will leave this Territory; probably in the course of a year. It is fashionable to be sick in the summer in this town, and most of the people engage a physician by the year. I expect to have the fever, if nothing worse. We live entirely on corn bread and salt pork, which are the staples of the country. The Indians sometimes bring deer and buffalo meat to town and try to sell it, but the folks are such intolerants that they seldom purchase any. They think there is nothing like a dead hog.

When you write, which I shall expect you to do as soon as you get this, you must fill your sheet; the last I got from you was not more than one quarter filled up.

Your affectionate brother,
H. A. Whittington.

~~~~~

Dwight Mission, Indian Nation,
A.T. August 15, 1828
~~~~~

Dear Brother:

You will be surprised to find by the caption of this letter that I have left Little Rock, but so it is. I am now in the heart of the Cherokee Nation of Indians, about 100 miles from Little Rock.

Mr. Brown, the Principal of the Little Rock Academy, has a sister attached to this Mission, and being about to visit her during his vacation, invited me to accompany him, which I immediately agreed to do. We left Little Rock on the 4th inst. and arrived here on the 7th. This Mission was established by the Presbyterian Board about 8 years ago for the purpose of civilizing the Cherokees. There are eight families attached to the Mission, all from New England, All Yankees. There is one old lady from Boston, Miss Stutson, who has charge of the female scholars. She appeared to be very glad to see me, merely because I was Boston born. She is very severe with her scholars, many of whom are women grown and as handsome as any women I ever saw, notwithstanding they are squaws.

Possibly Ellen Stetson.

There are about 30 or 40 girls that belong to this school, from 5 to 20 years of age. Some can talk as good English as I can, and some of them a good deal better; all that have been in the school one year can talk some English. Some of them have light hair and as white skins an any white girls in Cohassett. There are a great many white men married to Cherokee girls, and settled in the Nation. Most of the girls who receive their education here marry white men, and generally make the most affectionate and industrious kind of wives. There are about as many boys as girls who go to school here. The Missionaries chose a very good place to locate themselves; it is on the Illinois creek, about the center of the Nation. They have about 30 buildings of one kind and another; a dining room about 100 feet in length where all the scholars, amounting to from 60 to 70, and everyone attached to the Mission, as well as those who visit them, sit down together.

There is a young man here by the name of Thornton, a Cherokee who is studying medicine, and he has been very attentive to me since I have been here. We ride out every day or two and visit his friends and relatives, where we generally see some pretty little girls and get as many melons and peaches as we can eat. Day before yesterday, we rode about 7 miles to a friend of his where we stayed all day. The man is French and his wife Cherokee. They have one very pretty daughter, about 14 years old, who speaks and understands three languages, French, Cherokee and American. She is as white as anybody and is the most interesting little thing I ever saw.

Next Thursday there is to be a Grand Council, about 40 miles from here, at a place called the "Horse Head," at which I shall attend with Mr.

Washburn, the Superintendent of this Mission. You will recollect that the Treaty which was made with the United States by the Cherokees last winter in Washington, one thousand dollars was appropriated for the purchase of a printing press and types for the use of the Cherokees, which will probably go into operation as soon as the Cherokees get moved to their new land, which is about 200 miles farther up the Arkansas. My object in attending the Council is to get the appointment of printer to their paper when it is put into operation. Should I succeed, it will not interfere with my intended visit to "Sandy Cove" next summer, as the press will not go into operation before a year or 18 months from this date. As soon as the Council adjourns I shall return to Little Rock.

The paper will be similar to the one printed in the old Nation, part in English and part in Cherokee language, and in Cherokee characters as invented by George Guess, one of the chiefs. When I return to the Rock I will send you one of the Cherokee papers printed in the old Nation. I hope I may succeed, as I like the Indians better than any people I have seen for the past three years. My health has improved since I left the Rock, which I believe is owing to good company more than anything else.

"Old Nation" refers to the Cherokee nation located east of the Mississippi River in Alabama and Georgia before the removal.

I will write you as soon as I get to the Rock and tell you something about the Council. I anticipate a great deal of sport there with the Indians, as there will be a great many present. I hope you are all well at home. Give my best respects to Father, Mother, and all the family.

Yours, etc.
H. A. Whittington.

Little Rock, Aug. 30, 1828

Dear Brother:

I returned last Friday from my trip to the Indians, in good health and spirits. I believe I mentioned in my last letter that my object was to get the appointment of Printer to the Cherokee Nation. I now have to state that I succeeded. I left the Missionaries in a few days after I wrote to you, and proceeded up the country about 40 miles to a place called the Horsehead, where a Grand Council of the chiefs and head men were convened. I waited three days before the Council met and three days after it had met before I could transact my business. I stayed part of the time at the home of Mr. Jolly. He is the principal chief of the Nation; some of the natives call him king and some call him president. He is a real fine old fellow, and has a large double house surrounded by china trees; about 50 acres in corn and a large peach orchard, etc. I likewise stopped 2 days at Mr. John Drew's. He is a half-breed and talks as good English as you or I do. He is also a first-rate fellow, and took me one night about 3 miles to see what is called an "Eagle Tail" dance, which I will tell you about when I get home. . . .

The business is all done in council. The Nation is divided into four districts, and each district chooses annually two committee-men, who prepare all the business before the people at large. They have a log house in which they meet to do their business, which is called the council house. Outside of the house is a large smooth space, where the Indians, men, women and children, amuse themselves by dancing while their chiefs are transacting the business of the Nation. I went before the committee and stat[ed] to them, through an interpreter, that I wished to be employed to superintend their printing office. They smoked and consulted their chiefs a few hours, and agreed that I should have the appointment. It will probably be a year before they get ready for their office. I expect to be authorized to purchase the office [for] them when I return in the spring. . . . My salary is to be decided on when I commence my services. I am principally indebted to Mr. Woodruff and Mr. Washburn, the superintendent of the Dwight Mission, for the appointment. . . .

Whittington's appointment as printer for the Cherokee paper was never finalized because plans for the paper were delayed until 1844 after the Nation's removal into Indian territory.

There were about five hundred Indians present at the Council, who appeared to enjoy themselves very well, and during the three days the Council was in session I did not see one who was not in a good humor. There was not a fight nor any angry words passed between any of them the whole time. Never in my life before have I seen a hundredth part as large a concourse of people assembled together without witnessing more or less broken heads and bloody noses. I felt ashamed for my own color, and thought of the angry passions I had seen excited among them on election day and the 4th of July in different parts of the Union. The difference between the Cherokee Indians and the Nantucket oil boys is not so very great, but there is no comparison between the Cherokees and the people of Little Rock, this sink of iniquity. There all was harmony, all was peace.

I was so well pleased with them that I was sorry when I was obliged to return to this town, and almost wished I was an Indian. The first thing the Indians ask us when we stop at a house is to eat, and whether we stay one day or two weeks, they will take no pay; which I believe is not the custom among white people. . . .

I forgot to mention that the Missionaries at Dwight are all Yankees; we lived in the usual Yankee style. They fed us upon suckertash, baked beans, salt fish, etc. Give my best regards to Father, Mother, and all the family, and accept, yourself, my best wishes.

H. A. Whittington.

~~~~

Gazette Office, Little Rock,
Dec. 1, 1828

Dear Father:

. . . I am now waiting for Major Duvall, the Cherokee Agent, who is in Washington City, and is expected here some time during the winter. As soon as he arrives, I expect to set off for Boston for the purpose of procuring the materials for the printing office, and shall probably be home all summer.

There has been a great change in this place within a few weeks. We have had a minister of the Gospel preaching here for some time past, and his labors are likely to be crowned with success. The female part of the community were the first to interest themselves about religion, and several joined the Presbyterian and Baptist churches. Later the young men have been affected, and several that a few weeks since were a pest to society, are now an ornament to it. Instead of drinking and gambling at the taverns, they are reading the Bible and conversing with the preacher. Among the young men is Col. Oden, a lawyer who was a candidate for Congress a year ago, and is probably a man of better talents than anyone in the Territory; but he has heretofore been one of the most haughty, proud, self conceited, good for nothing fellows I ever knew, continually in some drunken frolic, quarreling with every person he met. He is now changed, and such a change as is seldom seen; his former enemies are now his best friends, and I should not be surprised if ere long he should become the pride and boast of Arkansas. Should the present excitement continue to increase, this place will be as famed for morality and piety as it has heretofore been for wickedness and vice. . . .

And be so good as to remember me kindly to Mother and all the family, and accept yourself my best and fervent wishes for the speedy recovery of your health, and believe me ever to be
~~~~

Your affectionate son,

Hiram A. Whittington.

Gazette Office, Little Rock.
May 8, 1832 (1831?)

Dear Brother:

Agreeably to promise, I sit down to write you the news, Arkansas news. I have forgotten what it was you wished me to communicate, but I recollect something about a bet. If you have more money than you know what to do with, you can bet that I will marry, but unless you have, don't bet. What has put such an idea into your head I am at a loss to divine. I expect you are in a hurry to commit matrimony yourself, and don't like the notion of waiting for me any longer; if so, go ahead and prosper. There are two things, however, I would suggest for your consideration, i.e. never marry unless you love, and never love where there is no money unless you are in a situation to support a family yourself.

I recollect of spending a part of a day last summer with the young ladies, and after leaving them came home, and as it was very warm and sultry, I took a little nap and dreamed I was married; but to who I knew not. . . . If I had been awake and just been sentenced to the gallows, my feelings would not have been more acute than they were in this, as you would call it, pleasant dream. . . . I awoke, and the pleasantest moment I ever experienced in my life was then. If by any accident you should chance to be left on Barrel Rock in a thick foggy day, the tide rising, the night approaching, the wind increasing, the waves running high and apparently opening their hungry jaws to suck you in, exalting in anticipation of their intended victim, until they become so high that your feet could but just hold on; if at this moment a boat should shoot out from the mist and take you off, you will then know how I felt when I awoke. Oh! the luxury of that moment; I shall never forget it. I then came to the determination never to marry, and I have no idea of departing from that resolve. . . .

We have had one arrival since I last wrote you. Miss Binum from Mississippi, worth, they say, about $25,000, amiable, accomplished, etc.

I see the New Yorkers have been giving our countryman Webster a dinner. The Jackson press talks of a coalition between Webster, Clay and Calhoun, and one of the Boston papers thinks there would be no harm in a league with the devil himself to put down Jackson. He is half right. By the way, this rupture in the Jackson ranks between Jackson and Calhoun must tickle you Yankees at a great rate. Whether it will affect Jackson's re-election or not is hard to tell, but at all events it is likely to have one good effect, and that is to break down Duff Green.

We have had the smallpox in this place for six months past, but to no considerable extent. I feel in no dread of it, having been vaccinated before I left home (thanks to a provident mother). There has been but one murder since I last wrote; a boy about 18, by a man of 50, in the woods about 10 miles from town. Both families were respectable.

Our election for Delegate to Congress and members of the Legislature comes on in August, and the candidates are out lectioneering, making stump speeches, etc. We have an entirely different manner of managing our elections from what you have. You do it all by caucus. Here the candidate comes out on his own bottom, tells the people he is a candidate for such an office, and then goes on to tell them how he will serve them with fidelity, energy, etc.; not forgetting to set forth his claims to their support in the most dazzling light, and if he knows of any little sins of his opponent he will not be apt to let them pass unnoticed. They attend all public gatherings, and mount a stump and make speeches two or three hours long. It commonly costs them about twice as much to get an office as the office is worth after they get it. It is expected of a candidate that they are to treat all their friends as often as they see them from now until election, find them in segars, tobacco, etc. . . .

One thing I like to have forgotten to mention, i.e. that I joined a temperance society about a month ago; not because I was in a habit of drinking, but merely to please the ladies, who said they wanted the temperate men to join for the sake of their example. About twenty men, all the ladies in the place, old and young, have joined; and I have no doubt Little Rock will soon experience its good effects. I hope you will go and do likewise. . . .

Your affectionate brother,
Hiram

Little Rock, A.T., June 25, 1831

Dear Brother:

You are the most perverse, obstinate and unbelieving brother man was ever pestered with. You will neglect writing to me for some six or eight months, whilst I am constantly writing and wondering that you do not answer some of my letters –until at last after I have given up all hope of ever hearing from you again, here comes a letter, when the first thing I see on opening it is a page of complaints and invectives against me for not writing to you oftener. . . . O, imprudence, what a wonderful convenient thing thou art!

You wish to know what chances there would be for a book-binder and book-seller in Arkansas. In reply, I will say that as there are no books printed here, of course there could be nothing for a binder to do. There are some books sold here, such as school books, law books, etc., but not enough to justify a book store unless a man could do something else. Most any other kind of a mechanic would do better here than a book binder; still he could get some little work, such as binding up files of newspapers, old law books, novels, etc. If you know of any carpenters, brick masons or saddlers, you may inform them that they could do a good business here, and a silver smith and a tinner are very much wanted at present. A silver smith came here about three years ago and remained about a year and cleared upwards of a thousand dollars, but he had a wife in New York and must fain go to her.

It is the best place in the world for farmers. If the Yankees only knew this country; that they can purchase the best of land for a dollar and a quarter an acre; that corn grows without hoeing; all you have to do is to plant it and plow it a little; you can build a good log cabin for 10 dollars; fire wood you never have to buy; and besides getting a good price for everything you raise, corn has always since I have been here brought from 50 cents to one dollar per bushel. We have a most miserable lazy set of farmers. A farmer to come here and be as industrious as they are in New England, they could not help getting rich. If you are anything of a philanthropist, you will advise all persons who wish to turn their attention to farming to come to Arkansas, where they can be independent, no matter how poor they are if they are not too lazy. I believe if John J. Lathrop were to migrate to this country, he would be worth more in five years than he would in Cohassett in a thousand; tell him so.

If you should think seriously of coming to Arkansas, and will let me know what your prospects are, I will cheerfully give you all the information in my power, not only as regards your trade, but anything else you may wish to know. However much I might wish to have you settled along with me, I cannot advise, for if you should come and anything should happen to you whilst here, I should never forgive myself for being instrumental in your coming. I will, however, pledge myself that so long as you behave yourself, you shall neither be shot, dirked or gouged; the only danger, then, you would incur will be from the climate, and as regards that, I can only say I have enjoyed as good, and perhaps better, health here than I did in Nantucket or N. York. Be so good as to write me further on this subject.

H. A. Whittington.

~~~~

Hot Springs, June 28, 1833

Dear Brother:

I recd. yours of May as I was on my way to Little Rock a few days ago. I spoke to my friends at the Rock in relation to your proposition to send out some blank books, but Woodruff is the only man there who sells any of account, and he has made arrangements to be supplied for a long time, and cannot take any. In this country books of any description are a curiosity. Two thirds of the people here can neither read nor write.

Of course, I could sell no books here, but I should like to get a tolerable library for my own use. . . . I would be glad to get Scott's works, Cooper's, Byron's, Bulwer's, etc, and in fact any novels that are interesting and of the modern school, all the American novels that are of any account, history, biography, etc. . . .

We have got cholera in its most aggravated type in this country. Every boat that comes up the Arkansas is full of it. I got to the Rock on Saturday last, and on Sunday eve, a steamer came up in great distress. She had lost four of her crew and two passengers in 4 days. She only had six passengers on board. The balance of the crew and passengers were sick. . . .

The cholera is five times as bad as it was last season. . . . The whole Mississippi Valley is full of it, and the poor slaves die like rotten sheep. Some of the planters have turned their negroes out into the woods to take
~~~~

care of themselves the best way they can. It spares neither age, sex, nor condition, but like a deluge, sweeps everything in its course. Where and when is this mighty scourge to be arrested in its deadly march? I hope and pray it may not visit you this season; and I believe it will not, as it appears to hover about the low, sickly parts of the country, and to leave the more healthy regions free.

Great parts of our country have been inundated. All the large rivers have been from five to 20 feet above high water mark. All the farmers on the rivers are injured, and some completely ruined. But this you can see in the papers, and I refer you to the Gazette. This overflow will be another great source of sickness for those on the rivers.

Whittington sought and won the position of clerk of Hot Springs County.

Our election is approaching rapidly. In one little month the tale will be told. I am very easy as to the result, notwithstanding the formidable opposition I have had to contend with. I have not lived in Arkansas all this time without knowing something of the dispositions of the people, and how to manage them. I go the whole hog for Sevier and, notwithstanding this county has always been opposed to him, and my opponent is opposed to him, still I shall beat him. This county will vote about 120 votes. As often as I can get an extra paper, I shall send it to you. Farewell.

H. A. Whittington

Letters of Hiram Abiff Whittington. PCHS. Number 3: December, 1956. edited by Margaret Smith Ross.

Featherstonhaugh in the Territory

G. W. Featherstonhaugh, an Englishman, made a 3000 mile geological tour of the southern states, the slave states, in 1834 and 1835. What follows is a portion of his report on his travels through the Arkansas Territory.

Featherstonhaugh traveled with his son and interspersed among his geological findings their reactions to the people and conditions encountered along the way. His comments throughout are critical, even caustic, but provide a bit of humor as well. In his introduction, Featherstonhaugh explains that friends advised him not to publish his report in this country because of the criticism. The final chapter of the report is a defense of that criticism which he states is honest and accurate. He states that people in the United States are oversensitive to any criticism of "the country they love," and are unwilling to recognize the primitive and "uncivilized" life styles of the country he traversed. His report Excursion Through the Slave States *was published in England in 1844.*

Military Road . . . was distinguished by blazes cut into some of the trees standing on the road-side, so that it could not be mistaken; a great comfort to travelers in such a wilderness. For a few miles we pursued it through a fine bottom, then got upon the horizontal limestone we had seen at the Currant . . . and at length rose to the level of our old friend the calcarco-siliceous rock. . . . Fourteen miles from the Currant we crossed "Fourche Thomas." . . . We passed it by an excellent wooden bridge constructed in the best style, and had a good view of the ledges of horizontal limestone cropping out on the bank . . . One or more settlers here having quarrelled about the direction of the Military Road, have taken liberty to cut roads resembling it, and blaze the trees to their own cabins; in consequence of this we got out of our way, and after driving sixteen miles, reached at a late hour a Mr. Russel's, who moved his family in here about twenty-four years ago, among the earliest Americans who came to the territory of Arkansas. As we were approaching the place, we saw two wild-looking urchins of boys trailing a beeve's head through the woods to bait a wolf's trap; that animal abounding here, and frequently being caught in that way.

Last night we had the pleasure of Mrs. Harris's company in our bed-room, and this night after we had retired, old Mrs. Russel, a discreet matron of at least seventy, accompanied by a sickly, unhappy looking girl, of, perhaps eighteen, came into our room, where there were three beds, upon one of which I was laid down, and my son upon the other. Without uttering a word, these amiable ladies very deliberately went through the ceremony of unrobing and getting into the other bed. This to be sure was an unexpected treat; I thought my son would never have done with laughing, and certainly I never saw anything done with more nonchalance. . . .

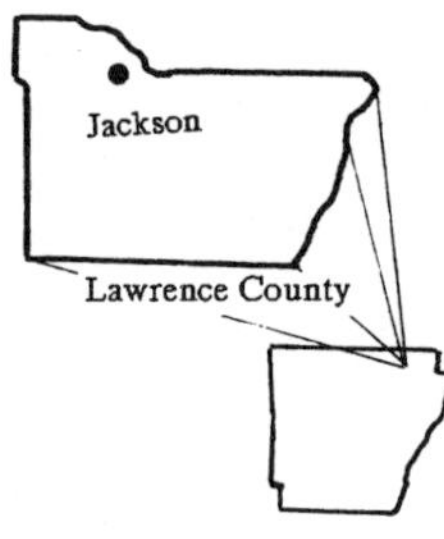

Pursuing our journey the next morning . . . at Eleven-mile Point River, another beautifully pellucid stream about 130 yards broad, running through a fertile bottom, we stopped to breakfast upon our own provender, in a sorry hovel. There was no man to attend the ferry, and we were obliged to cross the stream in an awkward flat boat conducted by a girl about 16: the landing was an an exceedingly bad one, and in making it we barely escaped ruining both horse and carriage. The country from hence was rough and hilly for six miles to Jackson, a wretched place which passes for the county town, and which is situated–why I know not–at the inconvenient distance of a mile from a beautiful transparent stream called Spring River. From hence we drove fourteen miles over a country somewhat less hilly, and part of it in open woods, to a widow Newland's, where we were most miserably provided for, and shown to a wretched flock-bed, neither long enough nor wide enough for two to lie down upon; which, perhaps, was the reason why the good, considerate old lady did not favor us with her company. . . .

Early in the morning we gladly started again; we had passed a bad night and got nothing to eat, and it was clear we should have fared much better if from the first we had relied entirely upon ourselves, and had "camped out" at nights. We could have purchased meal and chickens' at some of the farm houses, and could have made a hearty repast of them at the end of the day.

. . .

We are now on rather a flattish country with open woods, and flocks of parroqueets screaming around us. Being in advance about a mile, and very near the bank of *Strawberry River*, I heard the cry of a wild goose . . . I took for granted he was calling us to breakfast, and firing at him put a ball into his neck close to his head, a lucky shot I could not have made perhaps once in twenty times. I immediately rushed through a ripple of the river to secure my prize, and seeing a cabin not far off went there to wait for my son and inquire if they had any meal, but the people were steeped in poverty and broken down by fever and ague. We however made a breakfast of what we had, and were too glad to procure a feed of corn for our horse. . . . After breakfast I drove the horse, my son preferring to walk, and proceeding through a fertile flat country, a very heavy rain set in; the old saying, that it never rains difficulties but it pours, was now verified, for in ascending a hill the coupling pin of the fore part of the carriage came out, and the front and hinder wheels again separated, and brought us to a stand. This was a day of great trouble: we contrived, however, soaked through as we were, to drag our waggon on with various luck, and in the evening took shelter at a settler's called Meriwether, ten miles from the Strawberry.

Mr. Meriwether's cabin was at the top of a hill a short distance from the main road; he seemed to be a hearty good-fellow, for he assisted us us with great alacrity to get our things out of the rain, and to take care of our poor horse, who was very much jaded. On going into the house we were made acquainted with a person he called Mrs. Meriwether, but who from her great height, which was six feet two inches, an extraordinary dark, bony, hairy face, and trimmings to match, I should've taken for some South American grenadier in women's clothes. Here, seated before a rousing fire, we contrived to dry ourselves, and with the aid of some of their milk, cornmeal, and fried pork, and our tea and sugar, managed to make a hearty supper. Our appearance was the greatest godsend imaginable to these worthy people; they were two of the greatest talkers I ever heard, had not seen any travellers for a long time, and now a fine opportunity occurred of delivering everything they had to say. The only great difficulty they labored under was, that both wanted to talk at the same time. When Mr. Meriwether had fairly entered upon one of his yarns, she would cut in upon him with "Well, but John, I've heer'n that so often now;" upon which he would say, "Just give me a chance to git through, and I swar you shall have a chance too; ride and tie, you know, that's fair."

Our host said he had been once a soldier, and that he was a relative of Captain Meriwether Lewis, the associate of the venerable Captain Clarke of St. Louis, in the exploration of the country west of the Rocky Mountains, and that he was with Captain Lewis when he destroyed himself in Tennessee. He told me he had led an adventurous and merry life, had not laid up a dollar, and was one of the earliest settlers in Arkansas, where he got along as well he could by hunting, and trading, and raising a patch of corn. He said the track by which we had come to his cabin from the main-road, was part of the ancient Indian path or trail from Vincennes on the Wabash to Nachitoches in Mexico. . . .

He said that although there were a great many respectable settlers in the country now, yet there was a "heap of villans" in it; and mentioned a place on the Mississippi, called Helena, which was the territory of Arkansas, where all sorts of "negur runners," counterfeiters, "horse stealers," "murderers, and sich like," took shelter "agin the law" . . . . He followed with a relation of the story of Mr. Childers, which was harrowing enough.

The person, it appears, was an old bachelor, and a man of some property;

a few years ago, being on a journey, he slept at a man's on the southside of White River, whose name was Couch, and pursuing his journey the next morning, was dogged to within two miles of Meriwether's cabin, and murdered when he was asleep at his bivouac; "and there the old man's bones are to this day," said Meriwether. I expressed here in strong terms my surprise to him, that knowing these things he had not given the remains a decent burial. He replied that he had often thought of it, but had never done it.

The hour of rest being come, we were shown to a part of the cabin which was quite out of repair, and where the weather came in freely enough, for it rained torrents the whole night. We were, however, alone, and did not neglect our host's advice to be vigilant. Placing, therefore, our trunks against the door, we prepared ourselves as well as we could for any emergency before we laid down to sleep; but daylight broke with a clear sky, and on going into the kitchen we found our two hosts just as talkative and obliging as ever. I therefore soon got over my suspicions; and finding that Meriwether was not only able but willing to mend our waggon I restored him entirely to my good opinion. . . .

Whilst Meriwether was assisting my son to repair our waggon, I went under the guidance of a little boy, the only one of their who had survived the effects of malaria, and who was recovering from a broken arm badly set, to look for the remains of Mr. Childers We found the place where he had been murdered, and after a very long search admidst the leaves and rubbish, which a little stream called the Curie had carried there. . . . [W]e at length found a sort of heap of what appeared to be soil, and taking some of the earthy matter in my hands, I perceived a rank smell of putrefaction Removing the heap with a spade I had brought, I found the remains of a skeleton. . . . Having collected all the remains I could find, I dug a grave on the spot where he had been sleeping when he was slain, and there deposited them in their proper order, thus rescuing them, as far as I could from further dishonour. . . .

In the morning of November 12th, we started very early . . . [and] we reached a settler's of the name of Morton, who had things rather more inviting around him than we had seen for some time; so finding that we could get good bread and milk, and fried venison—which is tolerably fat at this season—we stopped to feed our horse and boil our kettle again. When we came to pay our bill the charge was a *bit*, or the eighth of a dollar, a little more than sixpence for both of us; but we found a difficulty in paying this, for the smallest coin we had was half a dollar, and Mr. Morton had no coin whatever in the house. He was very fair, however, and said he didn't mind, but that he was out of lead, and if my son had a mind to give him a small bar of lead he had taken out of his pocket and placed on the table, he would be glad to have it, as he thought it was worth a bit. . . .

[Before] we went away we generously made him a present of another bar on the part of Missouri [their horse], and thus became entitled to the respectable apellation of *traders*, which had been deemed to belong to us in various occasions; for the rear part of our vehicle being occupied by a large basket containing our cooking utensils and *munitions de bouche*, attracted general attention when we passed the cabins, which were all accustomed to be supplied by traveling "marchants." . . .

These worthy people think, if you are not looking for land to settle, that you must be pedlars: there are no markets or shopkeepers in the country for them to go to, and therefore the markets go to them—pedlars to sell goods, and tailors to cut out and make their new clothes. As to the Yankee clock pedlars, they are everywhere, and have contrived by an assurance and perserverance that have been unrivaled from the Maccabees down to stick up a clock in every cabin in the western country. Wherever we have been, in Kentucky, in Indiana, in Missouri, and here in every dell of Arkansas, and in cabins where there was not a chair to sit on, there was sure to be a Connecticut clock. The clock pedlar is an irresistible person; he enters a log cabin, gets familiarly acquainted with inmates in the shortest imaginable time, and then comes to business.

"I *guess* I shall have to sell you a clock before I go."

"I *expect* a clock's of no use here; besides, I ha'n't got the money to pay for one."

"Oh, a clock's fine company here in the woods; why you couldn't live without one after you'd had one awhile, and you can pay for it some other time."

"I *calculate* you'll find I ain't going to take one."

The wife must now be acted upon.

"Well, mistress, your husband won't take a clock; it is most a surprising: he hadn't ought to let *you* go without one. Why, every one of your neighbors is going to git one. I suppose, however, you've no objection to my nailing one up here, till I come back in a month or so. I'm sure you'll take care of it, and I shall charge you nothing for the use of it at any rate."

No reasonable objection, of course, can be made to this. It is nailed up; he instructs her how to keep it in order, and takes leave. But what can equal their delight, when with a bright, clear sound it strikes the hours! "Well," they exclaim, "if that don't beat all! Sartin, it is the most delightful company!" The wife now teaches her husband to wind up the clock, and great care is taken of it, as it is a deposit, and must be restored in as good condition as when it was received. Too soon, Jonathan, the wiley tempter, returns, talks of taking the clock down: "It was the best clock he ever had, they were such nice people he almost wishes it was theirs." Such a friendly and disinterested proceeding throws down all the icy barriers that prudence had raised between them and the shrewd Yankee. Before morning the wife gets the husband's consent, and the clock becomes theirs for the mere formality of his giving a note, payable in six months, for some eighteen or twenty dollars. . . .

I was so fortunate to obtain my letters from the post-office before breakfast, and as they all contained agreeable information my satisfaction was complete, and I went to the breakfast-table in high spirits. The territory of Arkansas was on the confines of the United States and Mexico, and as I had long known, was the occasional residence of many timid and nervous persons, against whom the law of these respective countries had a grudge. *Gentlemen*, who had taken the liberty to make the signatures of other persons; *bankrupts*, who were not disposed to be plundered by their creditors; *homicides*, *horse-stealers*, and *gamblers*, all admired Arkansas on account of the very gentle and tolerant state of public opinion which prevailed there in regard to such fundamental points as religion, morals, and property. . . . Such a community I was anxious to see, as well to observe the form society had taken in it. . . .

On entering the breakfast room I found a very motley set at table, and took my seat opposite to a dignified looking person with a well-grown set of mustachios, a round-about jacket, with other vestments made in Spanish fashion, and a profusion of showy rings on his fingers. The gravity of his deportment was quite Spanish, and being informed he was from New Spain, I promised myself a good deal of pleasure of conversing with him in his native tongue about his own country: but after bolting what was before him with an enviable rapidity—a talent I never before had seen in a Spainard— he left the room ere I had an opportunity of speaking to him. . . .

The town of Little Rock receives its name from being built upon the first rock,—a slate which underlies the sand stone and dips S.E. at a great inclination—which juts out into the Arkansa, in coming up the river from its mouth in the Mississippi; it is tolerably well laid out, has a few brick houses, and a greater number of indifferently built wooden ones, generally in staggering situations, which admit of their having a piece of ground attached to them. The population at this time betwixt 500 and 600 inhabitants, a great proportion of them mechanics; lawyers and doctors without number, and abundance of tradesmen going by the name of merchants, Americans of a certain class, to whatever distant point they go, carry the passion for newspaper reading with them, as if it were the greatest end of education. A town in England with a population of 8000 souls will have a few of the lower classes who do not know how to read at all, but those who are not of the educated classes, and who do read, generally apply that noble art, when proper occasions present themselves, to reading the Bible and moral books.

. . .

Newspapers are too expensive for the poorer classes in England . . . [but] in Little Rock with a population of 600 people, there are no less than three *cheap* newspapers, which are not read but devoured by everybody: for for what pleasure can be equal to that which,–through the blessing of universal sufferage,–those free and enlightened citizens called the "sovereign people" are made partakers once a day, or at least three times a week, on finding that the political party which has omitted to purchase their support is composed of scoundrels and liars, and men who want to get into power for no other purpose but ruin their country? It seems impossible that there should be any time or inclination for Bible reading where this kind of cheap poison gets into the minds of human beings; you might as well expect a confirmed Chinese opium smoker engaged in the solution of the problems of Euclid. In this part of the country it has struck me as the worst of all signs, that I have never seen a Bible in the hands of any individual, even on a Sunday. . . .

It was my good fortune to become acquainted with a few respectable and agreeable individuals here. Governor Pope, the governor of the territory, is an unaffected, worthy person: he was once a conspicuous politician in Kentucky, and by some accident has lost one of his arms. . . .

He lives amongst the inhabitants in an unpretending and plain-manner, encouraging them to use no ceremony in talking to him, and appearing to me to carry his affability and familiarity quite as far as it was expedient to do. . . . Soon after my arrival I went to call upon his Excellency the Governor, and being told he lived in a small house in a particular quarter of the town, I went in that direction. . . . [At] last I found it, and knocking with my knuckles against the door, a dame came, who, I found afterwards was the Governor's lady. . . . With the most winning politeness, therefore I inquired, "If his Excellency the Governor was at home?" Upon which, without mincing the matter, she very frankly told me that "he was gone to the woods to hunt for a sow and pigs belonging to her that were missing." Now this might very reasonably happen to a territorial governor in such a practical way of life as he was, and still be, as it really was, creditable to him. . . .

Besides the Governor there were other agreeable persons with whom I became acquainted; Colonel A ——, a clever good-tempered lawyer. Mr. Woodruff, the editor of the principal Gazette of the place, and postmaster was always obliging, and of the most indefatigably industrious men of the territory. At his store we used to call to hear the news of the day, which were various and exciting enough; for, with some honourable exceptions, perhaps there never such a population assembled–broken tradesmen, refugees from justice, travelling gamblers, and some young bucks and bloods, who, never having the advantage of good examples for imitation, had set up a standard of manners, consisting of everything that was extravagantly and outrageously bad. Quarrelling seemed to be their principal occupation,and these puppies, without family, education, or refinement of any kind, were continually resorting to what they called "Laws of Honour," a part of the code of which Little Rock, is said to administer justice with your own hand the first convenient opportunity. A common practice with these fellows was to fire at each other with a rifle across the street then dodge behind a door: every day groups were to be seen gathered round these wordy bullies, who were holding knives in their hands, and daring each other to strike, but cherishing the secret hope that the spectators would interfere. . . .

Mr. Woodruff, like most of the postmasters, kept a store, and thither these desperadoes used to resort; but it became so great a nuisance at last as to be intolerable, and being a firm man he determined to put a stop to it. The young fellow in question dared him to interfere, threatened him more than once, and coming to the store one evening provoked the postmaster so much by his insolent violence, that a scuffle ensued in which the bully got a mortal wound. Mr. Woodruff described the scene to me, and showed me the place where he fell, but said that he got his death by the awkward use of his own weapon. The public opinion sided with the postmaster, who was very popular at the period of our visit.

One of the most respectable inhabitants told me, that he did not suppose there were *twelve* inhabitants of the place who ever went into the streets without–from some motive or other–being armed with pistals or large hunting-knives about a foot long and an inch and a half broad, originally intended to skin and cut up an animal, but which are now made and ornamented with great care, and kept exceedingly sharp for the purpose of slashing and sticking human beings. These formidable instruments, with their sheaths mounted in silver, are the pride of an Arkansas blood, and got their name of *Bowie* knives from a conspicuous person of this fiery climate.

A large building was pointed out to me that had been erected for stores and warehouses, but the owner thinking he could do better by applying it to the uses of a more steady line of business, rented the large store on the ground floor as a drinking shop, commonly called here a "groggery;" here it was the custom of the bloods to convene and discuss the last quarrel, and tell how such a one "drew his pistal," and then how such a one "whipped out his knife;" adjourning when they had drunk to the warehouse up stairs, which they called the "college," and which was converted into a gambling room for faro and rouge et noir. . . . To this place it was the practice to inveigle all the young men they could, who had any property or any credit, make them mad with drink (the youth of these climes become frantic, not stupid, with the fiery potations they use), and then ruin them with the most atrocious foul play. Out of this class they recruit their infamous gang, and teach them how to decoy and ruin others. When they have no one to fleece, they play amongst themselves–having no idea of any other mode of occupying time. Many stories were related to me of a trader at the mouth of *White River*, named Montgomery, a finished *sportsman* in every sense, passionately fond of gambling, excessively addicted to whiskey, and who always used to sit down at the faro table with his Bowie knife unsheathed by his side, to insure fair play. This man, with some others, succeeded in effecting the ruin of a promising young officer in the United States service, a Lieutenant-, who was an acting quarter master . . . a married man, and had his wife with him, became at length their familiar companion. Having government drafts in his possession, they contrived to defraud him, when drunk, of them, to the amount of ten thousand dollars. Such was the infatuation of this man, that finding he was ruined for ever in his profession, he went off with Montgomery and a party of sharpers to New Orleans, to get the drafts cashed that he had parted with, together with others he still had left. But it so happened that an active officer, who was acting in the commissariat service, heard of this movement, and pushing across the country, reached the banks of the Mississippi, far to the south of the Arkansa and White River, where the gamblers were to embark. He had scarce been there an hour when a steamer heaving in sight, he went on board, and to his great surprise found his brother officer and the whole gang of villains on the deck. They were thus frustrated in their nefarious plans, for on their arrival at New Orleans, he immediately stopped payment of the drafts, and the party returned to White River, where the unhappy victim of these scoundrels afterwards died of delirium tremens.

So general is this propensity to gambling in the territory, that a respectable person assured me that he had seen the judges of their highest courts playing publicly at faro, at some races. The senators and members of the territorial legislature do the same thing; in fact, the greater part of these men get elected to the legislature, not to assist in transacting public business, but to get the wages they are entitled to per diem, and to gratify their passion for gambling. A traveller, whom I met with at Little Rock, told me had been lodging in an indifferent tavern there, and had been put in a room with four beds in it. There he had slept quietly alone two nights, when on the third, the day before the legislature convened, the house became suddenly filled with senators and members, several of whom, having come up into his room with their saddlebags, got out a table, ordered some whiskey, and produced cards they had brought with them. The most amusing part of the incident was that they asked him to lend them five dollars until they could get some of their legislative "wages." Not liking this proposition very much, he told them that he was as hard up as themselves. They therefore proceeded to play on tick, sat up almost the whole night smoking, spittting, drinking, swearing and gambling; and at about five in the morning two of them threw off their clothes and came to bed to him.

. . .

What must forcibly strike a stranger here, is the apparent total indifference of everybody to what we call personal comforts. No one seems to think there is any thing better in the world than little square bits of pork fried in lard, bad coffee, and indifferent bread. . . . Venison, it is true, is abundant, but it is no better than any thing else. A man goes into the woods, kills a deer twenty miles off, skins it, cuts the haunches, or "*hams*," as they are called, off, hangs one on each side of his saddle, leaves the rest behind him for the turkey-buzzard . . . or wolf and rides into town. . . . My hostess took it very ill in me that I would not eat of it. She had "telled the man to bring the saddle in for me, and he had chopped that part of it off with an axe, and had left the thin part behind: she had put it in the oven instead of frying it, and I would not eat it so not no more than I would when it was fried–if I didn't beat all!" . . . Those at the table with me seemed, however, to enjoy their repast as much as if it had been prepared by an artist of the first talent. They ate heartily, and appeared to be cheerful and contented; so true is it that we are the creatures of education and habit, and that the slovenliness and dirt, which are so revolting to those who are not accustomed to them, are not even seen by others. . . .

The town of Little Rock is surrounded by extremely poor land, and from the variety of oncurring causes can never be very populous. The river on which it is situated is hardly navigable four months in the year, and the sandbars upon it are annually becoming more obstructive. As a place of deposit for the immediate neighborhood, and in virtue of its being the seat of government, it may in time become a respectable small town, have good seminaries of education for the youth of the territory, and afford agreeable society; but in a commercial point of view it can only have a limited share of trade. White River will hereafter be made navigable for steamers 200 miles above Big Black River, and will be the avenue of trade to the northern districts, whilst Red River will be the same for the southern. . . . Mountains and soils of inferior quality form two thirds of the whole area, and the rich bottoms which communicate with the Arkansas and the Mississippi, Big Black, White River, and other streams, will in most places require a great capital to be laid out in embankments, or levees, as they are called, to secure the cotton crops from innudation. Cotton will always be the staple production of Arkansas, which is therefore destined to the curse of being a slave-holding state. . . .

During our stay here we made various excursions into the neighborhood. I had heard of the Mammelles, and was desirous of seeing them and the adjacent country, as they were only about twenty miles off up the Arkansas River; accordingly, on the 22nd of November, having procured an additional horse, we took to the woods again. . . . We saw numerous deer on the way, bounding and skipping about with great agility, and then showing us their snow-white tails and haunches. . . . The ridges here run nearly east and west for about twelve miles from Little Rock, when the country becomes more level, with small bottoms of land and narrow streams running through them. . . .

We now entered upon an extensive bottom with numerous streams running through it, one of which, about fifteen miles from Little Rock, is called the Petite Mammelle; and here, in the immediate vicinity of this stream is the magnificent rocky cone called the *Mammelle Mountain*. . . . Its south-west aspect is extremely fine, and resembles a pyramid, the height of which is about 700 feet from its base. . . .

Having ridden our horses through the pinetrees which extend two-thirds of the way up mountain, we dismounted and secured them in order to accomplish the rest of the ascent, which is naked, steep, and rugged, on foot. . . . After a fatiguing ascent we gained the top. . . . The view from this mountain is extremely characteristic of the wilds of America, and would make a fine panorama. . . .

Having scraped our nags a little, we re-saddled and proceeded on admist those never-ending painted trees, that were continually reminding us of the Arkansas, to which, as when men are walking upon the crater of an abated volcano, we felt as if we were too near. . . . On we went, losing and finding where the ground was more beaten, and several other paths appeared. A little embarressed at this, we, in the end, preferred the most beaten of them, and put our willing horses—who seemed as much comforted as ourselves by these signs—upon it.

Night had fallen, when suddenly we heard the comforting sounds of the lowing of cattle . . . [and] guided by them we came to a small house on the river, and were directed to proceed half a mile to a settlement where the mill was, and the proprietor of which we had an introduction.

The owner of the mill, Mr. Starbuck, was from home with his wife, but his father-in-law, a Mr. Elliot from Virginia, and his lady, were there and received us in a very friendly manner. Here we supped and slept, if being awake almost the whole night can be called sleeping, for which there were various causes; Fahrenheit's thermometer fell before midnight to 24 [degrees], a point which is sensibly felt in this latitude, and our room, although not out of doors, felt very much like it. Then came the yelling and howling of wolves, who made incredible noise, especially towards morning, some barking in one tone, some screaming and howling in another, as if each had his tail in a pair of pincers; for stragglers come into the swamp, where they crouch during the day. . . .

In the morning I was glad to get out of doors at the break of day, in order to gratify myself looking around, and to restore circulation by a good long walk before breakfast. . . .

We also visited a place we heard a good deal of wondrous matter about, called *Crystal Hill*. It is distant from Little Rock about 14 miles, and abuts upon the river. . . . At the water's edge the shale contains bands and nodules of ironstone and occasionally pyrites . . . which many persons, ignorant of minerals, who have landed here, have supposedly connected with precious metals, and so have caused the locality to be talked about. Indeed there is another place a few miles lower down, called *Mine Hill*, where some individuals, upon the strength of similar appearances, have actually dug for silver.

Night coming on, we engaged two men to row us back up in a skiff to a Mr. Henderson's, where we had sent our horses in the morning, and here we were very hospitably entertained. Our host, had formerly been a trader with the Indians, and knew this part of America well. On the chimney-piece of the room where we slept, I saw a singular ornament, a compound mirror, composed of near a hundred small ones, all with separate lackered frames, and fancifully arranged into one general frame. He said it was the only remnant of his old stock in trade, and that he used to exchange these trifles with the Indians for their peltry. After breakfast he was kind enough to accompany us for a few miles from his house, in order to see us safe across the Grand Mammelle by another ford, where there was less mud. On reaching the ford, I was amused with the nonchalance with which he commenced upon his operations; merely crossing his own stirrups over the saddle, he led his horse to the stream, and drove him in with a few strokes of the whip, when the animal, partly swimming, and partly walking, soon got over. Then taking the saddles from our horses, and tying the bridles round their necks, he drove our horses across in the same manner, which immediately joined his nag that was cropping leaves of a cane-brake on the opposite side. With our saddles on our shoulders, we now crossed the bayou, over a tree which had been felled for that purpose, and remounting, soon came on the eastern and south fronts of the Mammelle Mountain. . . . Having taken a friendly leave of our guide, and received his directions for our course, we without difficulty got into the old road and reached Little Rock again in the afternoon.

On the 27th of November we again put our little waggon in motion, and directed our course towards the hot springs of Washita (pronounced Washitaw). For the first eight miles the road was very bad, full of rocks, stumps, and deep mud holes, and wound up one of those sandstone ridges that are so common in this country. We frequently came across trees that had fallen across the road, and had lain there many years, exhibiting the indifference on the part of the settlers unknown in the more industrious northern states. When a tree falls on the narrow forest road, the first traveler is obliged to make a circutous path around it, and the rest follow him for the same reason. I have observed this peculiarity both in Missouri and Arkansas. . . .

In the evening we came to a sort of tavern, 27 miles from Little Rock, built on a rich bottom of land, at the north fork of the Saline, a violent stream in the season of *freshets*, or floods which then overflows its banks 20, feet. The place was kept by a sort of she–Caliban, and the tenement consisted of one room with a mud floor, in the various corners of which were four cranky bedsteads, upon which were huddled what she chose to call bed clothes! Then there was a door that would not shut, a window frame with every pane broken, and some benches to sit on before a broken table, to form the sum total of the furniture and appliances of this hotel. She told us we might choose our own bed, and after we had put our horse up, she would give us some supper. As it had already begun to rain, we were glad to be housed for the night, and having put Missouri into a hovel, consisting of open logs, with some boards to cover him, and left him with plenty of Indian corn leaves and some grain, we adjourned to the fireside. The rain now began to pour down in torrents, and before our supper was ready four more travellers joined us, ostensibly on their way to a government sale of land or a distant county. I was glad of this, because one of them was Colonel—— of Little Rock, a very intelligent and agreeable person, with whom I was acquainted.

This accession to her company put our hostess into a great bustle; she had to prepare supper for six persons, several of whom were lawyers, and of course the great men of Little Rock, and she set about it accordingly. We now discovered she possessed resources we had not suspected the existence of; a kitchen–that corresponded to every thing else–was attached to the hotel, and communicated with it by a small door, and that kitchen was her aide de cuisine and factotum, a stunted, big-headed negro girl, that from her size did not appear to be more than twelve, yet was not destined to see her twentieth year again. The grotesque rags this creature was dressed in, and the broken-brimmed man's hat that was cocked on one side of her head, gave such an effect to the general attractions of *Nisby*–for that was her name –that she put us all in the very best possible humour, and we could not but break out into a chuckle of delight whenever she came into a room. Whenever we became better acquainted, we found Nisby was an abbreviation of Sophynisby, as our hostess pronounced it. . . . The appearance of the girl indicated extreme stolidity, yet she did not want for spirit and activity. . . . By and by in came Missus to take a survey before the first entree came in, and affecting a most distressing surprise, commenced the following dialogue with her aide de cuisine at the top of their voices:

"Why, how's this gal laid the table! Nisby?"
"What's awanting, Missus?"
"You ain't laid the table no hayw, you kreeter, you!"
"I reckon I couldn't do it no better."
"Why, whar on arth is all the forks?"
"Why, the forks is on the table thar."
"If you don't beat all–I mean the new forks."
"I niver seen no new forks, you know that, Missus."
"Whar ahs the kreeter put the forks, I say?"

No answer.

"Whahl! if you don't find the forks, I allow I'll give it to you!"

Enter Nisby, agitcia

"I ha-ant put no forks nowhar. I niver seen no forks but them or what's on the table; thar's five on 'em, and thar's not no more; thar's *Stump Handle*, *Crooky Prongs*, *Horny*, *Big Pewter*, and *Little Pickey*, and that's jist what thar is, and I expect they are all that to speak for themselves."

And Nisby was right. . . .

As my son and myself had our own knives and forks, we did not dispute the choice of the remarkable ones on the table; and the guests, excessively diverted with this dialogue, good naturedly adapted themselves to the necessity of the case. We contrived to swallow some of the wretched coffee, by putting a great deal of sugar in it; and we tasted the heavy cakes, one-third of which seemed to be mere dirt. Indeed everything was so dirty that my stomach revolted at what was before us. . . .

[We] returned to Mr. Whittington's to make the very important inquiry of how and where we were to get something to eat, and here we learnt that a Mr. Percival, who lived in another of the log cabins, was the general entertainer of all visitors to this place. He had been a hunter, and having seen the place as early as 1807, had in some year subsequent to that built a cabin in the vale: this fact, as he conceived, gave him a pre-emption claim of right as proprietor of the waters, and finding some advantage in supplying the invalids who had now for some years resorted to them, he had set up a monopoly as general provider to all strangers who had any money in their pockets. To Mr. Percival's cabin therefore we hied, and presenting ourselves at his supper-table. found a quantity of little pieces of pork swimming in hog's grease, some very badly made bread, and much worse coffee, waiting for us. They knew very well that we had no other place to go to, and had prepared accordingly

Nothing could be less tempting and more rude than the fare we got; and if it had not been for the supply of tea and sugar we had laid in at Little Rock our stomachs would have gone to bed very discontentedly. Percival, however, was a good-natured man, could talk about things that interested us, and promise to look up some venison for another time, so we adjourned to our cabin, got up a good fire, and laid down. In the night we were awoke by the weather, which had set in excessively stormy, and we found that our portice, whatever its use might be in the summer, was not upon duty at this season of the year, for the wind came in with such force that we could scarce keep any of the covering upon us, and I discovered that the rain had been pouring upon me for some time before I awoke, We were also mistaken in our calculation of being alone, for it seems our cabin being placed upon a loose wall raised about a foot and a half from the ground, offered a good shelter to the various hogs belonging to the place, all of which had congregated immediately beneath us, and there they were to be sure, grunting, and appearing excessively distressed, as hogs always are in stormy weather, and having every opportunity—if they were so disposed—of seeing what we were doing through the *kiatus valde deflendus*, which separated every plank upon which we trod. This was our first night at the Hot Springs of the Washita, but happily we were not invalids. . . .

One of the inhabitants told me that towards the northern end of the travertine, where there was a considerable pool, he had often seen the fish gliding below, and that upon such occasions when he would throw a few crumbs of bread in, they would dart upwards, and getting their noses into the stratum of hot water at the top, would instantly wheel about and disappear. Frogs and snakes, too, when they fall into it inadvertently, stretch themselves out and die.

We were so charmed with the novelty of every thing around us, that we got some corn bread and a little milk from Mrs. Percival, and sitting down by one of the springs–the temperature of which was 148 [degrees] Fahr.–we made our breakfast there, the water being sufficiently hot for the purpose, and enjoyed ourselves very much. In fact this day, December 30th, 1834, was a memorable one in our journey, for attractive as were the terrestrial rarities we were surrounded with, they were literally eclipsed by a celestial phenomenon of the highest degree of grandeur, an almost total solar eclipse diverting for a while our attention from every thing else. . . .

As soon as this had passed away, we continued our observations upon every thing around us, and were not a little amused with the uses the settlers made of these waters: the facility of obtaining hot water was fully appreciated by them, for they never seemed to boil any water for any purpose, nor to drink any cold water: a tree, smoothed off on the upper side, was laid across the stream at a narrow part, so that they could easily cross and supply themselves for the purpose of washing their clothes, and on a shelf, near the door of each cabin, was always a pail of mineral water with a gourd to drink it from. Some of the springs are quite tasteless, others have a slight chalybeate flavour, but certainly the first neither communicated a foreign taste to tea or coffee. The highest temperature of these springs at the time I was there, did not exceed 148 [degrees]. . . . a particular spring was noted at 156 [degrees] Fahr.

Around the sources of these hot waters the confervae flourish remarkably, but now my attention was particularly drawn to an enamelled lichen-looking substance of a brilliant green colour which was exceedingly mucilaginous; it was not, however, a lichen, for I observed that it began at first by a filament, and that it went on spreading and thickening until it became half an inch thick. In some places it was six inches broad. The settlers finding that this substance keeps warm a long time, and that it feels soft and comfortable like a new poultice, apply it successfully to suppurate wounds. . . .

CHAPTER

5

Politics

The Second Grade Government

Although the exact date of the following petition is not given, we know that it was executed sometime during the governorship of James Miller (1819-1825). Several similar petitions were discovered in the Small Manuscripts Collection of the Arkansas History Commission, indicating that a considerable number of Territorial residents were eager for self-government almost immediately upon becoming a territory. Initially, a territory had no elected officials: all positions coming from Washington in the form of political appointments. The second grade government requested in the petition granted to the populace of the territory the right to elect a Legislative Council to represent them in formulating laws of the territory. The second grade government also provided for a representative of the territory to sit with the national House of Representatives in Washington.

These particular petitions were addressed to the governor "or in the case of his absence" to Robert F. Crittendon because Miller was most frequently absent from the Territory. Crittendon finally called for the election as Acting Governor, an action which created some doubt as to the legality of the election. Such doubt, however, could not deter Arkansans and their petitions were granted as will be noted in the next item.

To his Excellency James Miller, Governor of the Territory of Arkansas (or in case of his absence) Robert F. Crittendon, Secretary, acting as Governor thereof.

Freeholders and preemptioners were classifications given to land holders.

The "second grade government" established a general assembly of the Territory with representation by public election.

The petition of the undersigned inhabitants, Freeholders, Preemptioners, respectfully sheweth that whereas the Government of the United States, have extended unto your Excellency the Power of admitting us to a second grade of Government by the organic Law under certain condition, therein named and taking into consideration the vast extent of our boundaries. The thin population spread election over almost its whole surface. The unsettled and uncertain Tenour by which a great number of our fellow citizens hold their possessions. The many artifices which intriguing, jealous, and interested politicians, and companies of speculators have devised to nulify and destroy our bona fide and legal claim to land and to do away or draw a shade over our preemption claims and thereby mislead the general Government. For these causes as well as for concentrating more prompt, correct, and necessary information, we have thought proper to make known unto your Excellency that it is our wish to be admitted unto a second grade of government, which, if it should be consistent and meet with your approbation, and such a measure be adopted, We pray your Excellency that you will cause an election to take place throughout the Territory as far as may be for a Delegate to represent us in Congress and that your Excellency will cause all such other and necessary measures to be adopted and things done as may be necessary for carrying the prayer of this petition into effect, with full assurance that your Excellency will extend unto us every benefit in your power with propriety to grant as pertinent for us to ask. We here unto subscribe our names.

Auzel Brown
Wm. Stuart
James M. Kuykendall
William Cox
Nevil Wayland
Andrew Cox
Amos Roark
John Antoine Easq.

John Cox
Mishel Johnease
Gilbert G. Stuart
Jas. C. Whitehead
James Robinson
C. H. Pelham
Reuben Richardson
Samuel Brickers
John Brickey
John Charlonne
John de Cass
Reding Stoks
George Ditterein
Reece Price
Francis Lefeve
Geo. Turner
George Turner Jr.
Paul Lefevre

The following document was found in the Small Manuscripts Collection of the Arkansas History Commission.

IN SENATE OF THE UNITED STATES
April 11, 1820

Agreeably to notice given, Mr. Johnson, of Kentucky, asked and obtained leave to bring in the following bill, which was read and passed to the second reading.

A BILL
Relative to the Arkansas Territory.

Be it enacted by the Senate and House of Representatives of the United States of America, in Congress assembled, That the act of Congress passed on the fourth day of June, one thousand eight hundred and twelve, providing for the government of the territory of Missouri, as modified by the act of Congress passed on the twenty-ninth day of April, one thousand eight hundred and sixteen, entitled an act to alter certain parts of the act aforesaid, shall be considered as applicable to the government of the territory of Arkansas, and shall have reference to the proceedings of the said territory, in the organization of the second grade of the territorial government assumed by said territory, under an act of Congress of the second of March, one thousand eight hundred and nineteen, establishing the territory of Arkansas; and all and every step taken under the last mentioned act shall be considered valid, if not inconsistent with the three before recited acts taken together.

From Small Manuscripts Collection: Arkansas History Commission. ("Arkansas Letters to President Polk", Flashback *Vol. 25, May 1975.)*

Governor Izard Speaks to the Council

In what was most likely his first speech to the Legislative Council after assuming his post, Governor Izard presents his achievements since arriving in the Territory. His appointment as the Second Territorial Governor became effective March 4, 1825 and the following speech was delivered on October 4 of the same year. His use of the language is testimony to his education and the tone testifies to his acumen as a politician. The second paragraph sounds quite modern.

~~~~

Fellow-citizens of the legislat: Council of the H. of Repr.

To see you here, assembled for one the most important purposes which can bring Freemen together, is peculiarly gratifying,—as besides the public advantage to be expected from your deliberations, the occasion is afforded me of forming a personal acquaintance with so many of the respectable inhabitants of this Territory. Your united wisdom and experiences will enable you to legislate successfully for the interests of your constituents,—and you may depend on the full exertion of my faculties, feeble as they may be, in cooperating with your attainment of this desirable object.—

We inhabit, fellow-citizens, a portion of the American Empire eminently provided with natural advantages. The fertility of the soil,—a climate favorable to the culture of many valuable productions—the extent of our rivers, which afford a ready communication with the great Emporium of the west,—the mineral treasures with which the Interior of our Territory abounds,—all these insure ample rewards for the exertions of industry, and present attractions which cannot fail in a few years of adding abundantly to
~~~~

our population. To secure for ourselves and our descendants the enjoyment of their blessings, it behoves us to enact and *enforce* such laws as will tend to the improvement of our social state. On the discretion & integrity with which this duty is performed, will depend the safety & happiness of thousands of human beings, now living, and countless numbers yet unborn.—

I am happy to inform you that the last treaty entered into with the Quapaw Indians is about to be carried into effect. In a few weeks the migrations of that tribe to the country south of Red River will commence and a very large body of excellent land, vacated by them will be offered to the enterprize of civilized occupants. It is probable that the possession of this fine tract of country will open new and more convenient communications with the lower settlements on the rivers Arkansa & Mississippi.

Of the expected removal of the Choctaw Nation from the states of Mississippi and Alabama to the western part of our Territory, I have heard nothing very lately. It would be fortunate if an arrangement could be made to establish them beyond our limits,—as the location at present fixed upon for them will produce serious inconvenience to a numerous and valuable portion of our countrymen.

In anticipation of these various movements of the Indian Tribes, I have endeavored to place the militia in a condition to afford immediate protection to our settlements, should any disorder attend the passage of these peoples. In several counties I have met with prompt assistance from the officers;—in others, owing to circumstances probably inseparable from the disorganized state of the regiments and the dispersion of the inhabitants, I have not been equally successful. In the course of a few weeks, however, I hope to have completed such arrangements as will enable us, in case of emergency to call out, for the general defense, bands of our hardy citizen-soldiers, quite competent to repel and punish any insult which might be offered to the Territory.—

The road from our infant capital to Memphis, for opening which Congress made an appropriation, was surveyed several months ago. The documents, necessary for acting on the survey, had not reached the Department of War at Washington in the early part of July. As soon as they should be received, I have been assured that immediate steps would be taken for the accomplishment of this object, which may be considered as one of the most useful to this community and to the neighbouring states beyond the Mississippi that can at present be effected.—

I conclude, Fellow - Citizens, with repeating my confident hope that your council will be successfully directed to the rapid improvement of this interesting portion of our common country,—endowed as it already is by that Being, to whom we must all look in humble adoration and thanksgiving, with many of the choicest gifts bestowed on the works of his creation.—

Geo. Izard
October 4, 1825.

~~~~

As early as 1827, land was being allocated for schools to be established in the Territory. Called "Seminaries of Learning," they were energetically encouraged by the administration of Governor Izard, to whom the following letter was addressed. A public school system was not established until much later, although the groundwork for them had been laid with this letter.

Treasury Department,
August 21, 1827

Sir:

On the second of March last, an act passed Congress providing for the location of the townships of land granted to the territory of Arkansas for the use of a Seminary of Learning therein; and it is understood to be of importance to the value of the grant that the land should be located without unnecessary delay. A copy of the act is enclosed, and I beg leave to request, if it shall comport with the convenience of your Excellency, that you will be pleased to make the necessary selections and transmit them to this Department for confirmation, accompanied by a description of the tracts and their numbers.

Although permission is given in the act to locate tracts of not less than a section, it is not expected that you will find it necessary to make many locations of this kind. You will be pleased to select good lands, fit for tillage, in whatever tracts they may be found, not less than a section, until the whole quantity called for shall be obtained.

I have the honor to be,
With great respect,
Your [?] servant
~~~~

Richard Ruth

His Excellency
Geo Izard,
Little Rock,
Arkansas Territory

Pope's Address to the Territory

Governor John Pope made his last "State of the Territory" address to the Territorial Legislature on October 8, 1833. In this address Pope makes mention of the losses due to late flooding on the Arkansas River; he congratulates the assembly on the territorial improvements they have inaugurated and most interestingly, he defends his opposition to the application for statehood at that particular time. The reasons he cites, perhaps for the first time, verbalize the concerns cited three years later by those who opposed statehood in 1836. Pope in this address also sets forth the steps he had taken to acquire public lands for the erection of a building to house the Legislature and the Territorial Government. This building was to become what we know as "The Old Statehouse." Another interesting point in Pope's address deals with the interpretation of the "Ten section Act" which allocated lands for the use of Seminaries of Learning. There was some difference of opinion between Governor Pope and President Andrew Jackson as to how the sections could be divided. Pope's statements imply some difficulties with partisan politics. Finally, in this address, measures for selling some public lands are stated.

Gentlemen of the Council and gentlemen of the house of Representatives

While we must deeply deplore the losses and suffering of a large portion of our fellow citizens from the late uncommon freshet in the Arkansas river we have reason to be thankful to him who controls and regulates all things for our almost entire exemption from that awful scourge of nations (the spasmodic cholera) which has afflicted many other portions of our common country.

I congratulate you and your Constituents on the rapid march of this Territory in improvement, population and wealth, and on the kind and generous liberality of the National government manifested from year to year toward this infant people. Unlike the oppressed and plundered provinces of ancient Empires, the loving kindness and tender care of the parent government seems to be proportioned to the weakness and necessity of its offspring. In a few years the number and wealth of this Territory will authorize an application to Congress for admission into the Union as a member of the Confederation, but before this step is taken, it would be wise to urge in the consideration of that body, the justice and policy of making ample appropriations for roads from the interior of this Territory to its borders in various directions. All must be aware of the Constitutional doubts and objections, which are constantly interposed to internal improvements in the states which do not apply to a Territory and of the inability of the people for a long period to come if erected into a state government to make those expensive highways which may be justly deemed indispensible inlets to this country. While the people remain in their Territorial condition and the public lands continue under the exclusive jurisdiction of Congress both sound policy and the interest of the nation will prompt those necessary and useful expenditures here which must cease to a great extent upon a change of your political condition. In making these suggestions I beg you to be assured that I am influenced by a sincere and disinterested solicitude for the happiness and prosperity of this people. My present term of official service will expire before the next regular session of this general assembly, and I have no expectation of continuing beyond that period in office.

Pursuant to the authority vested in the Governor of this Territory by act of Congress passed on the 4th day of July, 1832 respecting the ten sections of land granted for a legislative house at Little Rock I have located and sold about eight sections of the land at the rate of $5 per acre subject to a deduction of six percent for prompt payments and one section and a half of the residue has been applied for and will probably be sold in a few days on the same terms leaving only a half of a section to be disposed of. A part of the price has been paid and bonds taken for the residue. A portion of the land has been selected where the surveys have not been completed and the business cannot be closed until the surveys are made and approved. One of my locations must be changed or amended to conform to the views of the president if his objection is adhered to. I indulge a hope that it will be abandoned on the ground of precedent and usage in analogous cases; And if not, the value of the donation will not be materially impaired. . . .

I purchased an eligible site for the State House and am progressing with the building with all practicable dispatch. I deemed it expedient with a view to public convenience and [economy] to place the courthouse and public offices on the same ground. The foundation of the Courthouse has been laid and I shall proceed with the building so soon as funds can be realized from the sales of the public property. I regret that it is not in my power to lay before you at this time a full statement of all the facts, locations, funds and expenditures connected with the public buildings and property. I expect to receive from the Treasury department some additional communication in relation to the lands I have selected and I will as soon as practicable exhibit to this general assembly a view of my brave actions[?] in relation to the matters referred to, for whether particularly accountable to you or not for the exercise of powers delegated to me by Congress it is due to the people and their representatives to give them satisfactory information on subjects which so intimately concern them. As I may not have the honour of addressing the general assembly as Governor of Arkansas after the close of this present session I owe it to my public character as well as to the people to make a full expose of my official conduct during the present session. By an act of Congress passed at their last session the Governor of this Territory was authorized to select 20 sections of the lands reserved for a Seminary of Learning, under the authority of that act I have made the selections and advertised them for sale on the 1st Monday in November next. Most if not all the sections offered for sale lie on or near the Arkansas river, and I fear some of the land has been injured by the late rise in the river and what is more to be apprehended the impression made on the public mind is unfavourable to the value of land on the Arkansas river. Under these circumstances, I incline to believe that it would be expedient to postpone the sale of a considerable part of the land until there shall be a better prospect for selling for a good price and will take that course if your views accord with mine. . . .

I transmit to the Genl. Assembly copies of sundry resolutions of the State of Connecticut, received from the executive of that state, concerning the constitutionality of the laws of the United States imposing protecting duties and other questions growing out of those acts. I transmit also copies of the resolutions of the state of Mississippi on the same subjects, to which you will give that consideration and attention which in your better judgment they merit.

Coming from the several counties of the Territory, clothed with the confidence of your constituents, you must be more intimately acquainted with their grievances than I can possibly be and with the practical operation of the laws upon the various parts, and interest, of the community. I must therefore leave those matters and others of a local nature, to your care and management.

Many subjects of public concern demanding your attention have no doubt been omitted in this communication, but I trust to your more correct knowledge of facts and circumstances to supply the defects[?]. The superior knowledge, constant observation and experience of the judges will afford you much aid in providing appropriate remedies.

For the privileges derived to this people from the genius of our free constitution, for the numerous blessings and felicitations enjoyed in this new country and for the flattering prospects before you, I invite you to join me in returning thanks to the Great Ruler of the Universe.

Assured of your attention to your legislative duties, and ardently hoping for cessation or abatement of that bitter party strife which has for a time to some extent disturbed our social harmony I will conclude by promising you my prompt concurrence in any and every measure lending to promote the interests and happiness of your constituents and the wellfare of the Territory.

Little Rock, Oct. 8th 1833 John Pope

Arkansas History Commission: L. C. Gulley Collection

An Appeal from Archibald Yell

Archibald Yell, in the following letter, is appealing to his friend James Polk for his assistance in securing a Federal Judgeship in the Arkansas Territory. Polk was at that time a Congressman in the U.S. House of Representatives. Because he, like Yell, was a Tennessean, it is apparent from Yell's letter that the two men were close friends and both were strong supporters of President Andrew Jackson. Polk would later become the 11th president of the United States and Yell would serve two terms as Congressman from the new state of Arkansas: from 1836 to 1839 and again from 1845 to 1847. Yell's terms in Congress were interrupted by two terms as Governor of Arkansas from 1840 to 1844. His letter to Polk is reprinted exactly as it was written without alterations in spelling.

My Dear Sir Fayetteville A. T. Nov 10th 1834

I wrote you a few lines by Col Sevier and now write you for fear he may not reach Washington before you may want by posibility some information in relation to my office as late Receiver of Public Moneys &c.

When I left the Territory 2 years since I appointed a Deputy who paid ovr of Pub. Money to my successor Col Chambers the sum of $350. which it seams Chambers nevr deposited to my Cridit & my deputy used $125 so that I am due the Govmt the sum of $475. I fortunately met Capt Bradford of Lexington Ky the Brother of Mrs Chambers & the Executor of the estate who promptely adjusted the account & I paid him the balence $125 cash, all of which he is to deposite at Louisville to my Cridit & has given me a Recept for that amount which will more than square me with the Govmt. From his Character I have no fear of his doing so if no accident befall him on the way. He was also apprised of the impotence to me of the Deposite, and is my frind & will no doubt attend to it promptly. But my Dear Sir if that matter eithr though nigligence or misfortune should not be adjusted do not let that be an obstacle. Advance the mony & you shall be repaid on Notice. Col Sever can inform you all about it. Please give this information to Mers. Grundy & White so that the matter may be adjusted before the senaters makes a first blow. I give you this information for fear of some mishap. Attend to it for me thoughout this matter; you are constituted my true and lawful attorney to do all things according to your own judgmt as if I was personally present, requesting a friendly confidence & cooperation with my frind Col Sevier. You will see from the recommendation forwarded to you or the Presidnt by my frind Judge Fulton, that all things here are easy & to my astonishment found Col Sevier one of my warm friend & signed the recommendations.

William S. Fulton.

Judge Eskridge I fear will not apprise the Presidnt that he will remove this winter, in time to let me hear the result & go to Tennessee & return before the courts commence the (1th Monday in April). Its now said he will not resign as was expected but will hold on until the end of his Term the 4th of March I believe, but without any wish or expectation of a reappointent. Indeed being He could not get 5 members of the Bar in the Territy & perhaps not one in His Circuit to recommend Him for a reappointent; this He knows and will not apply. Col Sever tells me there will be no applicant from the Territory. I did expect Roan would have been thro Col Sever, but he is now otherwise enguaged & Roan can not get a Nomination so that all things here are as safe & easy as I wish them; you & the President & the Senater for the balence.

Yell was petitioning for an appointment as Federal District Judge. He was appointed.

I found hear on my arrival grately to my astonishment all partis willing to receive me; even Governor (John) Pope seamed disposed to be friendly. I did not ask the Governor to interest himself for me because I believe his name would have but little influence at this time with the President, and as I thought it quite likly He would find difficulty enough withe His own case this Winter as it is generally believed Here as well as desired that He should

Andrew Jackson.
Robert Crittenden.

not be Reappointed, the reasons varies according to the Local Parties here—the Sever or Jackson men because he is a whole Hogg Bank man in every shape & no very grate Jackson man, according to my standard. The Crittenden Party because they hate him personally & he has heretofore made war on them. There is a 3d Party here if it ought to be dignified with the name of Party, headed by Govenr Pope in person. Around Him he has a few relations & a few of the disapponted of both the other partis. He is too weak & unpopular to form a strong party but he may pull down & weaken the Jackson party. That He may do to a grater extent than I now imagine, as he has a Press at Command and is himself a man of Talents & will put his shoulder to the wheel. He has now nothing to make by looking back. He will not be received in the ranks of his formr frinds.

If we go into a state govert this Winter, it would be a matter of some doubt whether he ought to be discontinued but if we do not form a state govrmt for a few years to come then I should have no hesitation in determining what would be the policy for the Party.

If Fulton could succeed HIM the people would be sattisfyed. He has been long in the Territory & is popular, but if some Man was sent Here from abroad who would not go into politicks with a view to a state Govemt & to support the anti Bank Measures of the Administration he would do us but little good & might weaken our party. Under present existing circumstances Govr Pope might be less dangerous, as there are many of the Bank Crittenden men who will never recognize Pope as their Head. A Modest Stranger they might, to effect their designs. I am giving you a long letter about things that do not interest you. How do you and Bell get along? Write me often. . . .

A. Yell

Arkansas Becomes a State

The most comprehensive and revealing account of the Territorial bid for statehood comes from Jesse Turner. The following excerpts, interpolated occasionally for clarity, are taken from his extensive article.

Turner came to Arkansas from his native North Carolina in 1831 and made his home in Van Buren. He was a practicing attorney and active in the politics of his day. He served in both houses of the Arkansas Legislature and was elected Associate Justice of the Arkansas Supreme Court.

Ambrose H. Sevier, who was serving as the Territorial member to the House of Representatives, took a rather bold step in January of 1834 by introducing into the House a resolution seeking statehood for the Arkansas Territory. He had in the previous session in 1833 succeeded in gaining a bill whereby the Territory could conduct a census preparatory to admission. The question of slavery was still a burning issue in the Nation and Arkansas would necessarily have to seek admission as a slave state to accompany Michigan into the Union. Now in 1834, he was seeking Congressional approval for a Constitutional Convention and ultimately for Statehood. His concerns and his boldness are made clear in the following letter.

Letter from Sevier to the *Gazette* January 21, 1834.

You will perceive that, on yesterday, I introduced a resolution inquiring into the expediency of permitting the people of Arkansas to form a constitution and come into the Union upon an equal footing with the original states. I have done this for a variety of reasons. Michigan is now applying for admission, and I have every reason to believe that her application will be granted. Michigan, of course, will be a *free* state, and should she go into the Union as such, the happy balance of political power now existing in the senate will be destroyed, unless a slave state should go in with her. The delegate from Florida is not now in his place, but were he here, and were he to press Florida, it would probably exclude us, and, in that event, our admission, in all probability, would be deferred until Wisconsin should apply. When would this application be made? Not for a quarter of a century. Such a procrastination would not be willingly subscribed to by any of our fellow-citizens. Upon the whole, I think this not an unfavorable opportunity for our admission. At this time, also, we should be able to come in without trammels upon the subject of slavery. It may be said, however, that, in the admission of Missouri, the subject was finally

Sevier refers to the Missouri Compromise of 1820. Arkansas was the first state to apply for admission as a slave state.

settled by compromise. It is true that a compromise was made, but I beg leave to reply that no congress has a right to bind a succeeding congress upon the subject of slavery, or on any other subject, and the same body who made the compromise might rescind or disregard it.

It is by no means impossible for political bodies to disregard compacts of compromise, if they have the power, however explicitly they may have been made. It should be observed that any bill upon this subject which congress may pass will not be binding upon us. . . .

Having no memorial from our legislature upon the subject, and no petition from the great body of the people, I have taken upon myself this responsibility. The people cannot be injured by my application, inasmuch as their acceptance or refusal of a state government will depend entirely upon themselves.

Immediately after Sevier made his bid for statehood, delegates from Michigan proposed a like resolution. This action brought into question for the first time the terms of the Missouri Compromise. The Whigs in Congress found the situation quite troublesome. A few days after Sevier's introduction, John Tipton, senator from Indiana and a native of Tennessee, introduced an enabling bill, which would allow the Arkansas Territory to call a constitutional convention. This move created considerable furor in the Senate and Daniel Webster moved that the bill be laid on the table. Webster's motion was accepted by a vote of 17 to 14, and the session adjourned with the Tipton bill remaining tabled. The Advocate *explained the tabling in its July 25, 1834 issue:*

Sevier's bill of 1833 was, at the fag end of the session, laid on the table. Only about thirty senators were present, and the close vote on the question shows that, at the next session, the bill will pass. Webster, Clay and Calhoun voted to lay the bill on the table.

In the second session of the twenty-third congress Sevier called up the house bill and gave notice that he would move to amend it. He succeeded in having it made a special order for December 18, 1834. In a letter to the Gazette *he wrote that there were only three bills ahead of it and seemed confident that it would pass during that session. Sevier, however, was to be disappointed once again, for the bills for both Michigan and Arkansas were defeated. In a letter to Woodruff, Sevier outlined once again his feelings of urgency that Arkansas enter the Union with Michigan.*

Let Michigan get into the Union without us, and we are then completely at the mercy of both houses of congress. Michigan with whose fortunes circumstances have recently connected us, has taken a decisive stand. And, at the next session of congress, her delegate in the house of representatives, with the constitution of his State in one hand and the ordinance of 1787 in the other, will demand, as a matter of right, her admission into the confederacy upon an equal footing with the original states.

Knowing the difficulties she has to encounter, she is imploring us to take a similar step and stand by her in her hour of trial. There is a degree of boldness and spirit in her position well calculated to inspire the admiration of all who take pleasure in seeing a magnanimous people striking for liberty and a free constitution. There is something magical in a name, something enobling in the reflection of feeling, as we walk, that we are citizens of a free and independent state. We have a greater population than had either of four states when admitted to the Union. Our rights are secured to us by the third article of the treaty of April 30, 1803. They are secured to us by the constitution itself. Our ancestors tired of colonial vassalage, and so have we.

The treaty of April 30, 1803 was the treaty whereby Jefferson finalized the Louisiana Purchase with Bonaparte.

(Sevier to Woodruff: June 9, 1835)

Arkansas' quest for statehood became the singular focus for most of the Territory's citizens, and public meetings were called throughout the Territory. On June 13, 1835 one such meeting was held at Little Rock which endorsed statehood and which issued a call for a constitutional convention. The principle figures of this meeting drafted a spirited and highly persuasive statement.

The causes which produced the struggle for American liberty and induced the patriots of '76 to throw off the British oppression can be distinguished by name only from those which should induce their citizens, the free and independent people of Arkansas, to claim the right of emerging from territorial darkness into the light of civil liberty and national independence * * * Has the word liberty, which urged your ancestors to deeds of noble daring, lost its charm for you? Has it ceased to be the spell for the patriot to conjure with? Would it be nothing for you to be represented in the halls of congress? Have you no desire or ambition to have a voice in choosing the president and vice president of the United States? Would it be a small privilege that you should elect your rulers and your judges, instead of having appointed over you such overseers and task-masters as a distant master may see fit? Would it be worth nothing to form a consistent and just code of law and to regulate and purify the system of your courts? If men have fought to the death for less things than these, will we make no effort to gain and possess them. . . .

We possess a rich country, but while we remain a territory we are looked upon with a distrustful eye. When we become a state, emigration will increase and for the first time since the discovery of America a boundary has been fixed beyond which the tide of emigration may not flow: for the Indian country west erects a barrier. Thus, no other asylum for the emigrant will be left except Arkansas. . . .

But we are told that, if we become a state, we must bid farewell to the liberal expenditures of the general government for the improvement of our rivers and roads. This is like telling a young man of twenty-one that he had better stay with his father a while longer for the food and clothes he will give him. But this is not true. . . .

Poor, indeed, is the plea of poverty, when liberty and man's dearest rights are at stake. Craven-hearted and unworthy American must he be who could be contented to remain a bondman and a hewer of wood to escape paying the paltry pittance of twice his present tax.

While public sentiment was largely disposed toward statehood, there were those who were strongly opposed to the move for a variety of reasons. The Territory's third newspaper The Times *appears to have led the opposition. The following excerpts from three letters to the editor of the* Times *and all signed with pseudonyms address three different opposing views.*

"Peregrinus" was concerned with the question of timing:

Must the State of Arkansas be like a sickly plant forced into unnatural growth by a kind of hothouse cultivation? Rather, let her take her stand among her sister states with the mature powers of an adult, not being at too tender an age weaned from the parent nurse.

"Jefferson" took issue with Sevier's term "colonial vassalage":

The good people who form the great mass of the community, and who are quietly pursuing the different occupations common to a new and thriving country, must be struck with astonishment at the picture presented of their abject and intolerable condition, which they never before could have dreamed of. The ridiculous outcry about colonial bondage, love of freedom, and the chivalrous call, at all hazards, to strike for independence is well understood to be only a gull for the ignorant.

"Arkansas" touched on the major cause for dissension: the question of admission as a slave state:

True; but who will stigmatize the enlightened and liberal delegations of the north as fanatics? A few religious fanatics in the heat of misguided zeal made a recent effort to urge our northern brethren on to the commission of acts of injustice and injury against us. But, did they succeed? The democracy of the north stood up as one man and cried: "Down with the traitors to their country" and down they went. . . . The "Missouri question" can never be revived. . . . Of the whole white population, for one who has twenty slaves, we will find you twenty who have no slaves. The one, then, will be the sufferer by the abolition of slavery in the Territory, and to enable him to loll in ease and affluence and to save his own delicate hands from the rude contact of the vulgar plow, the twenty who earn their honest living by the sweat of the brow are called upon with the voice of authority assumed by wealth to receive the yoke. They must consent to a tenfold increase of tax for the support of a state government, because my lord is threatened with danger of desertion from his cotton field if we remain as we are.

To this the nonslaveholders who compose, as will appear by the new census, an overwhelming majority of the population of the territory, cannot submit. They are willing to forego the advantage to themselves of the abolition of slavery, and to smother their dissent from the principle, as a matter of right, religion and ethics, but a greater sacrifice cannot, in justice, be expected. Our slave population is to the white as one to five, and we are in a cold sweat at the idle fear of losing the little we have.

The normal procedure for calling a constitutional convention consisted first of Congressional approval, then a call from the territorial governor, and finally a legislative resolution setting up the constitutional committee. Arkansas had already lost her chance for Congressional approval in the second session of the twenty-third Congress. The Territorial Governor, William Fulton, had doubts as to the legality of calling a convention, and there was political differences with the leaders of the statehood movement, so he refused to issue the call. Finally, the legislature took the initiative and introduced a resolution in what was to be the last session of the Territorial Legislature. On October 7, 1835 a resolution was adopted, appointing a joint committee of fourteen members from the Council and the House to draft a statement in reply to Governor William Fulton's opposition to calling a convention.

On October 14 the committee submitted its report, which Turner called an "exceptionally lucid, comprehensive and well-sustained argument, rising, on the whole, to the dignity of a weighty state paper." Like Turner we hesitate to "emasculate it with an epitomizing lancet."

In the investigation of the subject, two prominent points presented themselves to your committee–the right and the expediency of immediate admission into the Union as a sovereign, free and independent state.

As to the latter, although a branch of the subject upon which many of our most intelligent citizens differ, as motives of interest or patriotism, whether misguided or properly directed, prompt, your committee are of the opinion that, whether viewed as a matter of pecuniary loss or gain, or as one in which the natural feelings of self-respect and capability of self-government are more intimately blended, the case is not materially varied. The great and continuous influx of wealth and population, the recent unparalleled increase of the sales of public lands, as well as the accumulation and concentration within our borders of other fit and permanent subjects of taxation, the better prospect of establishing under a state government, a permanent system of revenue laws and other institutions calculated to advance the prosperity of the country, free from the influence, direct or indirect, of those higher powers, who now frequently have no immediate interest in the welfare of the people, and are, in no case, directly responsible to them–the legitimate source of all power–connected with other important subjects, are entitled to great weight and high consideration. In opposition to them, it might be urged that appropriations by the general government for the convenience and improvement of our country after we throw off the chrysalis and assume the character and powers of a state will cease to be made.

But in the opinion of your committee, those bountiful donations and expenditures will not be materially affected by the change. Nearly all the subjects of expenditure from the United States treasury in Arkansas, upon examination, are found to be, in a military point of view and otherwise, such as the constituted authorities of the Union, by the settled rule of construction, would pronounce national highways and navigable streams, connecting points of defense important to the republic; and, under a state government, with a representation in congress, would be more likely increased than diminished.

Further, the pacification and quiet of a people is one of the indispensable bases to the prosperity and happiness of their country. The restless spirit of men born free, who for a time, in order to carry into effect, in a becoming manner, the constitutional stipulations of their common country, have submitted to the curtailment of a portion of their inherent privileges, when awakened to a sense of their rights by their condition and number, and resolved to claim the stand to which they believe themselves entitled, according to the evidence of every age and country, will continue to agitate a question so vitally important to them until it meets with a final and satisfactory adjustment.

In relation to the right of Arkansas with her present population to admission into the Union, upon an equal footing with the original states, your committee, after a deliberate and calm investigation of the subject, are equally clear and satisfied with the propriety of their conclusion. Without resorting to the abstract and unchangeable principle, founded in nature, and indelibly incorporated in the American code, by our fathers in the war of Independence, that all men are born free and equal, and are, by nature, sovereign and entitled to self-government, they find ample guarantee in written stipulations for the right which the people of this Territory now claim.

Then, without relinquishing the former, they are, for the present, willing to rely upon the latter, as furnishing a sufficient safeguard to the liberties of their constituents, while the congress of the United States retains its high character for justice and uniform respect for the rights of man.

That it was the intention of the people of the original states, who created the federal constitution, to permit an increase in the number of states, is evident from a clause in the constitution itself, declaring that "new states may be admitted by the congress of this Union," and conclusively established by the admission of many "new states" under that constitution.

In addition to this general provision in the constitution, there is a special guarantee to this Territory, as constituting at that time a part of ancient Louisiana, found in the treaty (and treaties by the constitution are declared to be "the supreme law of the land"), ceding that province of France to the United States, under the auspices of Mr. Jefferson, then president of the United States, and Napoleon Bonaparte, then first consul of the French republic.

Territorial governments, as connected with that of the United States, are necessarily in their nature, as also declared by the acts of congress organizing them, "temporary," and only designed to protect the liberty, property and lives of infant communities until they acquire sufficient confidence and numbers properly to avail themselves of their right to admission into the Union as states. This right, your committee believe, may be exercised by a territory situated as Arkansas is, and under the same stipulation on the part of the United States, whenever its population is equal to the ratio of representation in the congress of the Union. With that number of citizens–and Arkansas has more–she, in the opinion of your committee, has a clearly defined right to demand admission into the Union; and congress, as the agent of the people of the several states, is under a concurrent obligation to fulfill their constitutional and treaty stipulations, and in justice bound to grant admission whenever it is thus demanded. It is also true that, should the United States be unjust, they have the power to exclude us from the benefits of the federal constitution; but the exercise of arbitrary power, uncoupled with right, by a mighty people to crush the native and absolute rights, insisted on in a respectful and legitimate manner, of a younger and kindred community "not yet attained to the bone and gristle of manhood," would present a spectacle of injustice not to be apprehended from a government whose faith has never been violated or pledged in vain. Your committee, after viewing every prominent aspect which the subject of admission seems to present, cannot but look upon the main point as clear; and disrobed of the involving mists which sophistry, at the first glance, seems to have thrown around it, as a matter of right, under the constitution and laws, on the part of the Territory; and as one of concurrent obligation, under the same, on the part of the United States; and as a matter of interest, according to the fundamental principles of American liberty, equally desirable and important to both.

If the builders of the constitution had seen the necessity of nurturing the "new state" by a colonial code of laws, they would, in that instrument, most certainly have prescribed the basis or fundamental principles for such a system; but those sages well knew that colonial government, at best, was but ameliorated slavery, and, in respect to the rights of the citizens, refrained from prescribing any rule of action to the new community, leaving them wholly untrammeled to select their own time and manner of admission. To admit the principle, that a territory could not make the first proposition in the matter, even were the right to sovereignty in her people, and her right to admission doubted, would be an extension of the inability in communities to make contracts and stipulations for their security and for the improvement of their political condition, not heretofore known to exist.

Even a slave has the right to stipulate with his master for his freedom, and to propose the terms upon which he wishes it granted. A community, then possessing many acknowledged political rights and powers, would surely have the power and right to treat for more, without first imploring the higher power for an endowment of sovereignty to enable her to make a valid contract.

The true construction of the entire subject is resolved into this, that the first proposition for admission into the Union may be properly made either by Arkansas or the United States; that congress may pass a law declaring her willingness that Arkansas may form a constitution and become a state, which, when Arkansas assents to, the matter is complete; or, that Arkansas may, of her own free will, form a constitution and apply for admission, which, when approved by congress, becomes of equal validity; and, that in either case, Arkansas becomes legally and constitutionally one of the United States of America.

~~~~

This report passed the house with a vote of Yeas 29, Nays 2, and a bill for the calling of the convention was drawn up. When the bill was brought before the house, angry debate ensued over apportionment of delegates to the convention. Of major concern was the counting of the male slave population in the southern and eastern counties, the cotton counties. Sectional division revealed itself vividly, for the northern and western counties would be outnumbered if the slave population was used to ascertain apportionment. David Walker of Washington County attempted to amend the bill, calling for apportionment on the basis of one delegate for each five hundred white adult males in the county. When this amendment failed, Walker moved that the membership require at least one member from each county. With this concession, both factions reached a compromise which allotted twenty-six delegates to the northwest half of the territory and twenty-six to the
~~~~

southeast. With the passing of the bill on October 19, the machinery for a constitutional convention was in place.

Though the convention bill passed, the controversy continued in the Times. *On November 2 an editorial warned the citizens to consider well before casting their ballots for convention delegates:*

Is there not something ominous in the fact that those who espouse the doctrines of the south dare not discuss the question? At least one of the papers of this city is known to be in favor of this doctrine, yet it is as silent as death. * * * Let them (the *Gazette* and *Advocate*) come out and take sides either for or against free, white, male representation—the only true republican representation * * * Let the people * * * ask their candidates * * * are you in favor of a republican constitution and a representation upon the basis of freemen? * * * Pause and reflect before the yoke of slave, or district, representation is fastened upon your necks.
(*Times* November 2, 1835)

Archibald Yell wrote that he was gratified to learn that the Times *would advocate "the republican principle as contended for by the north upon the basis of representation." Yell wrote, almost prophetically it seems now:*

That will be the all-absorbing question in the convention, the decision of which, should it be in favor of slave representation, will create a split incurable between the two great divisions of the country; and discord and sectional feelings will continue for years to come. The freemen of Arkansas will not tamely submit to such a doctrine. * * * We had better remain under a territorial vassalage than be sold to the south and be controlled by our brethren who were instrumental in placing the yokes on our necks. All we ask in the north and west is a republican constitution and a representation upon the basis of freemen.

David Walker, in a circular to his constituents, attempted to explain his actions in the legislative session, which were construed by some to have been a turning away from his principles. He explained that compromise was necessary if the convention were to be called. His explanations apparently angered one "Senex," who assailed Walker in an anonymous letter to the Times. *Walker penned the following brilliant reply:*

The style and language of Senex's publication, not less than its slanderous falsehoods, point so obviously to the obscure and contemptible source from whence it sprung, that I could not be induced to notice it, but from the evident intent of the writer under the pretext of answering what I had said, to whitewash doctrines which he is unwilling should be presented to the public in their naked deformity. . . .

Who this officious scribbler is may be matter of speculation. * * * Perhaps he is one of those from the north or west who abandoned the interests of their constituents.

I repeat fearlessly, that slave representation was contended for in the legislature; that it was contended that districts of country should have representation independent of their population; that two of the northern or western members, by voting with the south, did give to them a majority; that the northern or western members, with scarcely an exception, did determine to vote against the whole measure rather than sanction such principles; and that there are, to this day, 2,200 white males of the north and west unrepresented in the apportionment. * * *

The people would, in one common assembly, have had the right to have appeared in their own proper persons as well as by representatives, and have formed that convention. Suppose it had been the case. * * * Would slaves, or districts, or dollars have voted there, or entitled their owners to vote? * * * If, then, the people send their representatives to do this for them, will slaves, or districts, or dollars have voice to give to country; or the holders of slaves, or money, an additional voice in electing these representatives? Assuredly not. Then, how can such a doctrine be sustained? * * *

Suppose a line to be drawn from northeast to southwest across the Territory. There are, on the northwest side of that line, 2,200 more white male inhabitants than on the southeast side. What is it that gentlemen would count against these freemen to entitle the southeast to as strong a representation as the northwest would have? Is it slaves, country laid off into districts, or property, or what is it? I deny that anything can. Upon principle, all the slaves in America cannot weigh against one freeman's vote, nor can all the districts or wealth of the world.

Is it forgotten that, in a government like ours, the poorest man in society raises as strong an arm in defense of the liberty of his country as the wealthiest nabob in the land, and is entitled to as much weight in making the constitution and laws that govern him and pass upon the life and liberty of himself and family as he who is a lord of wealth? Are the principles of liberty which cost our fathers their blood and treasure so easily forgotten? Is their example, is the example of our mother states, worthy of consideration? If they are, if we respect their wisdom and experience, look to the constitutions of the several states. I challenge an example in all America, except the State of Georgia (and her constitution was formed at a time when the State was ruled by an aristocracy) where such a course has been sanctioned.

I am charged with having said on the floor of the house of representatives that the slave property, or district representation, was anti-republican. I did say so, and I repeat it. It is anti-republican, and strikes at the liberties of the people. I knew at the time that it would bring upon me the displeasure of some. I care not. Anonymous scribblers may endeavor to defeat my election by slander and misrepresentations, but they can never change my course. * * * . . .

That he (Senex) is small game, no one doubts who has seen the track he makes. I shall, therefore, not trouble myself in future by noticing him. Perhaps, he may, if let alone, write himself a name. He certainly needs one.

Elections of delegates to the convention were held in December and on Monday, January 4, 1836, the convention assembled at the Baptist Meeting House in Little Rock. Subsequent meetings were held at the Presbyterian Church where the delegates worked continuously until January 30 when their mission was completed. C. F. M. Noland was appointed special messenger to carry the constitution to Washington for presentation to Congress. Sevier wrote from Washington that the constitution should be in his hands by mid-February, so Noland and the document were immediately dispatched.

The slavery issue and the weather were to plague Sevier and the constitution in Washington. In the following letter to Woodruff, dated March 1, Sevier acknowledges the receipt of the constitution as it appeared in the Gazette *Extra Edition of February 4 and expresses concern for the whereabouts of Noland and the official document. Noland, it seems, was detained in Virginia by a record snowfall that made travel impossible. After waiting six days, he started for Washington against the advice of the officials.*

I received on yesterday your extra *Gazette* containing the constitution, and on today I presented your extra to congress. I have no doubt but your paper contains an exact copy of the constitution, and I thought it better to have it before the committee without delay. Mr. Noland has not yet arrived, nor am I able to account for his delay.

I think the constitution an excellent one. There are but few things in it, and they are of minor importance, that I would alter. But what has become of the ordinance? If there should be any difficulty now, it will be on account of no provision being inserted upon the subject of taxing the public lands within our limits. I hope that such an important arrangement has not been omitted, but will be brought on by our messenger. (*Sevier to Woodruff: March 1, 1836*)

Woodruff obtained a copy of the missing ordinance and mailed it to Sevier forthwith. Sevier, through a series of letters to Woodruff, provides us with a running commentary on the progress through the mills of Congress.

The committee this morning reported a bill to admit Michigan upon condition of her modifying her boundary line. Mr. Noland has not yet arrived, and, in our case, no report can be made until the official copy of our constitution shall arrive. To save time I submitted your extra *Gazette* containing the constitution, but not the ordinance, nor the signatures of the members of the convention. This will answer for an investigation of the subject, but will not do for the final action of the congress. It is to be regretted that an official duplicate of the constitution and ordinance, if an ordinance was adopted, had not been sent me by mail. If any accident should have befallen the messenger, and the constitution be lost, we shall be in an unpleasant condition. To guard against every accident, please procure and send me by mail forthwith a certified copy of the constitution and ordinance. (*Sevier to Woodruff March 2, 1836*)

Fent Noland arrived in this city a few minutes ago with the constitution. He brought but a single copy of that instrument, and that addressed to the secretary of state. It is likely the secretary will lay it before the president without delay, and I think it probable the president may conceive it his duty to lay it before congress. The convention probably designed that I should have nothing to do with the constitution, and therefore sent me no copy.

Before his arrival we had had the constitution under consideration. A bill for our admission was assented to by a majority of the committee and will be reported on the day after tomorrow. I shall draw it up tonight for the committee. There was no objection as to the mode of our application for admission, but there will be an effort, I fear, on the part of some to revive the slave question. But it will be unavailing. We shall come in with our constitution; but in regard to the ordinance I can assure you thus far in advance that upon that the pruning knife, with a heavy hand, will have to be used, or it will not go through. (*Sevier to Woodruff: March 8 [appeared in* Gazette *March 29, 1836]*)

For several days the bill has been in the hands of Mr. Patton of Virginia, and thus far special orders, having precedence, have precluded him from presenting it to the house. This morning I attended the sitting of the select committee of the senate, and I have the happiness to inform you that the committee were unanimous in instructing Mr. Buchanan, the chairman, to report a bill for our admission into the Union forthwith. He will make his report on Monday next.

In regard to the ordinance, which will be a separate matter, I shall have some trouble. I have no fears of being able to obtain of congress as much as any other state has received. I shall certainly get all I can; and, if I obtain as much as other states have received, I hope my acts as a treaty maker will receive the affirmation and ratification of our legislature. This I shall have a right to expect; and, expecting it, I hope I shall not be disappointed, as the heavy responsibility of adjusting these important interests has been committed to my management without my solicitation or knowledge. (*Sevier to Woodruff: March 17.*)

The bill was referred to a select committee with Andrew Buchanan of Pennsylvania chairman. Having received affirmative votes in the committee, Buchanan sent the bill for statehood to the Senate on March 22, where it was read twice. The senate debated a full day (March 29) on the Michigan bill and finally passed it on April 2, after which they took up the Arkansas bill. The Arkansas bill passed the senate on April 4 with a vote of 31 to 6, 3 members being absent and 8 refusing to vote.

The battle in the senate today upon the admission of Michigan was renewed, and about sunset the bill was passed.

After that the Arkansas bill was taken up, considered in committee, and engrossed for a third reading and final passage in that body on Monday next. (*Sevier to* Gazette*: April 2, 1836*)

The senate have this morning given the final vote upon the admission of Arkansas into the Union. Yeas 31, nays 6, of whom Clay of Kentucky and Porter of Louisiana are two. (*Sevier to* Gazette *April 4:*)

The smallness of the final vote in the senate requires explanation. The senate consists of 48 senators; of this number Webster, Goldsborough and Wall were absent from the city. All the residue were in their places, and when the yeas and nays were called, refused to vote.

Of this number of dumb senators were Leigh of Virginia and Crittenden of Kentucky. Comment is unnecessary. (*Sevier to* Gazette *April 5:*)

Both bills–Michigan and Arkansas–were sent to the house and referred to committee. On June 9 the house, sitting as Committee of the Whole, began a heated debate on the two bills. After a 25 hour session the bills were sent to the house in general session and both were passed on June 15.

This day the president signed the bill for the admission of the States of Arkansas and Michigan into the Union; and today the supplemental bills respecting the grants to the two new States also passed. They will be approved today or tomorrow. (*Sevier to Woodruff: June 15*)

The Gazette *informed an anxious public of the news on Tuesday, June 28, 1836, in this manner:*

POSTSCRIPT
ARKANSAS ADMITTED!!!

After our paper of this day had gone to press, we received, by express from Helena, the gratifying intelligence that Arkansas is now a SOVEREIGN STATE OF THE AMERICAN UNION! The bill passed its third reading in the House on the evening of the 13th June, as will be seen from the following extract from the *National Intelligencer*, of the 14th inst.:

Yesterday, the bills which have passed the Senate, for the admission of the States of Michigan and Arkansas into the Union, being again the special order of the day in the House of Representatives, occupied the whole day. The former of these bills was ordered to a third reading about four o'clock; and the latter about six o'clock. After which the bills were read a third time and passed. Both bills having passed without amendment, have no need of being returned to the Senate, and, being known to be acceptable to the President, they may be already considered as laws of the land. (*Gazette* story : Tuesday, June 28, 1836)

The next issue of the Gazette *on July 5 carried the following editorial:*

ADMISSION OF ARKANSAS. In about half the edition of last week's Gazette, and by an extra, despatched on Tuesday evening and Wednesday morning to the different parts of the State, our most distant fellow-citizens are now apprized of the gratifying intelligence, that Arkansas and Michigan are members of the American confederacy of States–twin–sisters, born at one and the same moment, to add two brilliant stars to the spangled and striped banner. We have now contracted with our sister States, the solemn and high obligation of observing the Constitution of the United States, and of sustaining and defending this great fabric, reared for the Liberty and Independence of man! While incurring these deep and great moral responsibilities, we are also called to share the benefit of this inheritance, in its protection and in its honor.

In proclaiming an event so auspicious to the prosperity of Arkansas, we ought not to be sparing or miserly with just praises to those agents, whose untiring exertions and unremitting industry, have brought about a result so desirable to the citizens of this State–and we do not doubt, that the great body of the people will unite with us in naming the individual, who ought to come in first, for the gratifying acknowledgements of the community – and that man is Ambrose H. Sevier. Nor ought we to forget Gen. Jackson and Mr. Van Buren, both of whom gave their active and powerful aid to all the efforts of our Delegate, to succeed in our admission.

Had the plans of the opposition prevailed in Congress, our admission would have been defeated for the present year, which would have rendered our Constitution a nullity, and imposed on the people of this State the task and expense of forming another. Wise, Slade, J. Q. Adams, Granger, Whittlesey, Waddy Thompson, and the ring-leaders of the opposition to Mr. Van Buren, fought it out against us to the last. After the sitting of the House commenced, June 9th, on the subject of our admission, the session began at 10 o'clock on that day, and continued all night, until 11 o'clock next day!–Wise became so furious at length, that he declared the House to be "tired, sleepy, and drunk." (*Arkansas Gazette*, Tuesday, July 5, 1836)

(*Jesse Turner "The Constitution of 1836."* Publication of the Arkansas Historical Association. *Vol. 3: 1911. pp.78 - 99.)*

The brief and subdued tone of Sevier's letter of June 15 seems most out of character when we turn to the Alexandria Gazette *which thoroughly covers the story of the 25 hour session and the* National Intelligencer *which devoted a short editorial to the session. Both of these accounts were discovered in the Library of Congress.*

Alexandria Gazette: June 13, 1836

MICHIGAN AND ARKANSAS–MISSOURI QUESTION REVIVED–ANOTHER MIDNIGHT OR ALL-NIGHT SESSION.

In the House of Representatives on Thursday the Bill for the admission of Michigan into the Union, was taken up in Committee of the Whole.

After considerable debate and several amendments offered and rejected.

. . .

Mr. Adams said . . . He believed the people of Michigan had a right to admission, but he wanted the question of disputed boundary to be left for future adjustment.

Mr. Thomas suggested that it would be better to let the bill be reported, and offer it in the House.

Mr. Adams said he would if the screws would not be applied. . . .

The bill was then laid aside, and the bill for the admission of Arkansas was taken up.

Mr. Phillips said it was now past midnight.—Exhausted in body and mind, he could not feel that it was his duty to remain and consent to the precipitate action, by which it was evidently intended to force through the committee two bills of the importance of those under consideration. He therefore moved that the committee rise.

The motion having been put, there were ayes 17, noes 92—not a quorum.

Mr. Sevier requested Mr. Phillips to withdraw his motion.

Mr. Phillips said that if, with a knowledge of the fact that a quorum was not present, he could be persuaded to withdraw his motion, or to refrain from insisting that the chairman rise and report the fact to the House, according to its rules, for the purpose of acting upon a bill to admit a State in the Union, he should feel himself unworthy of the place he held.

The committee then rose, and reported the fact, that they were without a quorum.

Mr. Reed moved an adjournment; on which question, on motion of Mr. Sevier, the yeas and nays were ordered.

Mr. Adams requested that the hour (near 1 o'clock) might be noted on the Journal.

The Speaker said it was not in order.

The question on the adjournment being taken, the vote was—ayes 24, noes 98.

There being a quorum, the House again went into committee upon the bill for the admission of Arkansas. . . .

A motion was again made that the committee rise, and the vote was, ayes 15, noes 95—not a quorum; and the members having been counted, 112 were reported present.

Mr. Sevier said he did not wish to press the bill at the late hour of the night. When the committee had risen, he said, he should be satisfied if the House would make the bill the special order for tomorrow (Friday) at 10 o'clock.—Loud cries of no, no.

The committee rose, and reported that they were without a quorum.

The motion was made to adjourn, which was lost.

A call of the house was ordered at half past one o'clock, and was proceeded in, till, at about half past four, 112 members having answered, and several absentees having been sent for, and brought up in custody of the Sergeant-at-arms, a motion to excuse all the absentees prevailed, and the doors were opened.

Many amusing, but unimportant incidents occurred, for which there is no room in this day's paper.

The House again went into Committee of the Whole, and resumed the consideration of the Arkansas bill.

Mr. Adams moved to insert a similar provision in the bill, to that included in the acts of several of the new States respecting the emancipation of slaves.

Mr. Adams moved to amend the bill by introducing a clause "that nothing in this act shall be construed as an assent by Congress to the article in the Constitution of the said State in relation to slavery and the emancipation of slaves."

This motion was debated at some extent by Mr. Adams, Mr. Cushing, Mr. Herd, and Mr. Briggs in favor of it, and Mr. Wise, and was negatived, at about four o'clock in the morning by a vote of 98 to 32.

Mr. Adams moved that the committee rise–Lost–44 to 93. . . .

The Arkansas bill was then laid aside, and the committee took up the bill supplementary to the bill for the admission of Arkansas into the Union, and for other purposes.

Mr. Mason of Virginia, moved that the committee rise, and report the two Michigan and Arkansas bills to the House.

After some confusion which arose from a question whether the Michigan bill was still open to amendment

Mr. Mason withdrew his motion, and

Mr. Underwood moved an amendment prescribing certain other conditions on which Michigan should be admitted. Lost.

Mr. Mason, of Virginia, renewed the motion that the committee rise, and report the bills to the House. (This was about 7 o'clock.)

Mr. Slade moved to amend the bill by inserting therein the following:

After the words in the first section, "that the State of Arkansas shall be one, and is hereby declared to be one, of the United States of America . . ." add, "whenever the People of said State shall by a convention, duly elected, expunge from its present Constitution so much thereof as prohibits the General Assembly from passing laws for the emancipation of slaves. . . and shall also provide in and by said Constitution that no negro or mulatto, born in, or brought into said State after its admission into the Union, shall be held or transferred as property. . . ."

Mr. Cave Johnson made a question of order. The Arkansas bill having been laid aside, was not open to amendment.

After some conversation and considerable confusion,

Mr. E. Whittlesey appealed to the gentleman from Vermont to withdraw the amendment, one of the same tenor having been drawn by the gentleman from Massachusetts, (Mr. Adams,) and rejected.

Mr. Slade declined, and addressed the House in support of the motion.

Mr. Jenifer rose to reply, and proceeded to make some general remarks on the subject of the abolition movement, when he was called to order by

Mr. Bynum and others, on the ground that his remarks were irrelevant.

After some words between Messrs. Jenifer and Bynum,

The motion of Mr. Slade was rejected.

Mr. Wise then rose, and addressed the House, at length, in opposition to the course of the majority, in pressing this question upon a House, sleepy, timid, and drunk. He was opposed to the motion that the committee report the bills, and said he would speak till ten o'clock, when the House would be under the necessity of dropping the subject, as it was not a special order for Friday. . . .

At half past nine, Mr. Wise having yielded the floor, Mr. McKennan suggested that, as the members were much exhausted, the committee should rise with the understanding that the House should then adjourn till tomorrow, when the gentleman from Virginia would resume his remarks.

Mr. Wise said it was true that he was in an unfit condition to continue his remarks; but it was near ten o'clock, and he had it in his power to have his will over this subject, and, so help him God, he would persevere if he died by it.

Mr. Wise proceeded in his remarks till ten o'clock.

Mr. Chambers, of Kentucky, then rose, Mr. Wise having temporarily yielded the floor, and called upon the chair to decide whether the committee could continue to sit, it now being ten o'clock, the hour assigned by the Rules for the House to meet, and the Speaker to take the Chair.

Mr. Wise said he would ask of the Sergeant-at-arms, where now is the Speaker of the House.

"In his room," was answered by some one. . . .

[There followed a lengthy discussion of the Parliamentary procedure in such a situation. One of the questions raised was whether the members would be paid for one day or two days for this session.]

Mr. Mason, of Virginia, suggested, as a mode of freeing the House from its present embarrasment, that the committee should now rise, and let these bills be made the special order for today; so that they would come up again as a matter of course, on the House resuming its sitting after an adjournment.

The question was taken on the motion which had been made for the committee to rise, and determined in the negative.

Mr. Wise then resumed the thread of his remarks upon the bill, and concluded at a little after eleven o'clock. When

Mr. McKennan obtained the floor. The Members of the House were, he said, evidently all worn out by this protracted sitting; many had not slept, and others had not broken their fast. All had need of repose. "We have, (said he) fought the bill manfully, and done our best to stave off the decision upon it. . . . I hope, sir, the committee will rise, and report the bills, and we shall adjourn over till tomorrow.

Mr. McK. made a motion to this effect.

The motion was carried. The committee rose and reported the two bills, and the House then adjourned over to meet on Saturday, at the usual hour (10 o'clock).

~~~~

National Intelligencer
Washington
Saturday, June 11, 1836

The sitting of the House . . . which began at 10 o'clock A.M. on Thursday, and ended at 11 o'clock yesterday, is absolutely without a precedent in our history, if not in all the history of legislation. It was a Herculean task for those members who persevered to the end, and a vexatious and painful trial to the constitutions of those who were at last obliged to seek repose, many of whom were brought out of their beds in the dead of the night, by the officers of the House, to replenish the House, and enable it to keep a quorum.

The purpose of this great effort on the part of the Majority may, we suppose, be stated plainly here, without offence to any one, because it is a purpose which no individual in that majority would desire to conceal. The bills which have passed the Senate, for the admission of Arkansas and Michigan as States into the Union, were before the House as in committee of the whole: that is, the Speaker's Chair is filled, in such case, by another Member, who becomes a Chairman of the House, which, by a legal fiction, is then called a committee. Whilst in committee, the Previous Question is silent, nor can the Yeas and Nays be taken. There is no way, therefore, of ending any debate in committee of the whole, if the minority persist in it, whatever may be the will of the majority, but by sitting it out. The
~~~~

majority in the case before us were determined to get these bills out of committee of the whole, that, being reported to the House (as they have been), they might be subject to the operation of the Previous Question. The majority of the House is anxious, of all things, that these bills should pass, and that they should pass without amendment, apprehending that their final passage would be endangered by having to go back to the Senate with amendments. By resorting to the Previous Question, the majority, having succeeded in forcing the committee of the whole to report the bills to the House, will have it in their power, if they chuse, when the bills again come up, to preclude both debate and amendment, and bring the House at once to a direct question on the passage of the bills.

The territorial wilderness of 1819 had at last in 1836 become a bona fide state of the United States of America. The maturing of the territory was slow and often painful. The "birthing" of the state was difficult and was perhaps a forecast of the pain which was to follow in 1860.

Arsenal Grounds at Little Rock

PART THREE
Arkansas Statehood
1836—1860

The Seal of Arkansas, 1836

Statehood spawned jubilant celebrations, and everyone looked to the future with optimism and excitement. Becoming a state was accomplished by an Act of Congress; making a state would be accomplished by vigorous work and careful planning. After the tumult created by admission to the Union came the sobering realization that no longer could Arkansans look to the

Federal Government for its needs. As citizens of a Sovereign State, the people were responsible for the growth and development which would turn their newborn state into a mature, contributing member of the United States of America. The process would take time, but the people turned to the task with fervor.

The existing 34 counties immediately set election dates and the formation of a state government was begun. The first state elections were held on August 1, 1836, and the first Arkansas General Assembly convened in Little Rock on Monday, September 12, 1836. The work of that first General Assembly consisted primarily of business matters which today are simply taken for granted. Legislation for county government was acted upon; land surveys were instigated; a State Bank was established to handle state monies, and taxes were levied for running the government and beginning state development.

For many Arkansans life went on as usual: crops were planted and harvested, travel was still an uncertain quantity, bartering was a major means of acquiring goods, and the ague still plagued families. There appears to have been a change in spirit and attitude, however. Letters were sent to families and friends living east of the Mississippi River urging them to come West to the new state of Arkansas. And many of them came.

There was a steady stream of emigrants crossing the river and becoming citizens of Arkansas. Family groups began to come where there had been only single men before. Businesses sprang up in even the remote areas and private schools, or Seminaries, were established to educate the children.

While national politics stirred a great deal of interest in Presidential Election years, the more crucial and more frequent interests were on the local and state level. Nearly every letter contained something about a political race or the promise of one.

Social events became newsworthy and the ladies vied with each other for the honor of holding soirees, teas, and balls. Civilization had come to Arkansas. Life was hard, but the family spirit was undaunted as communities worked to bring stability and pleasantries to the Territorial wilderness.

Much of Arkansas was still frontier in 1836. Indians presented problems as they continually strayed back across the western border to their former hunting grounds. The new Republic of Texas was encroaching upon Arkansas land. Health was still a major concern.

But as the Nation moved closer and closer to the rupture of 1860, the State of Arkansas was moving farther and farther away from the frontier. She would be pulled into the War Between the States with reluctance and the general growth would be virtually halted for four years. She would suffer through Reconstruction as did her sister states of the South, but she would not falter. The groundwork laid by the first Arkansans would hold firm.

All of these things are evident in the materials found in this section of *Authentic Voices*. None are stated explicitly in the materials, but the implications and emotions are there. There are many voices omitted here, but we earnestly hope that what is presented will provide a deeper understanding of and pride in the Arkansas heritage.

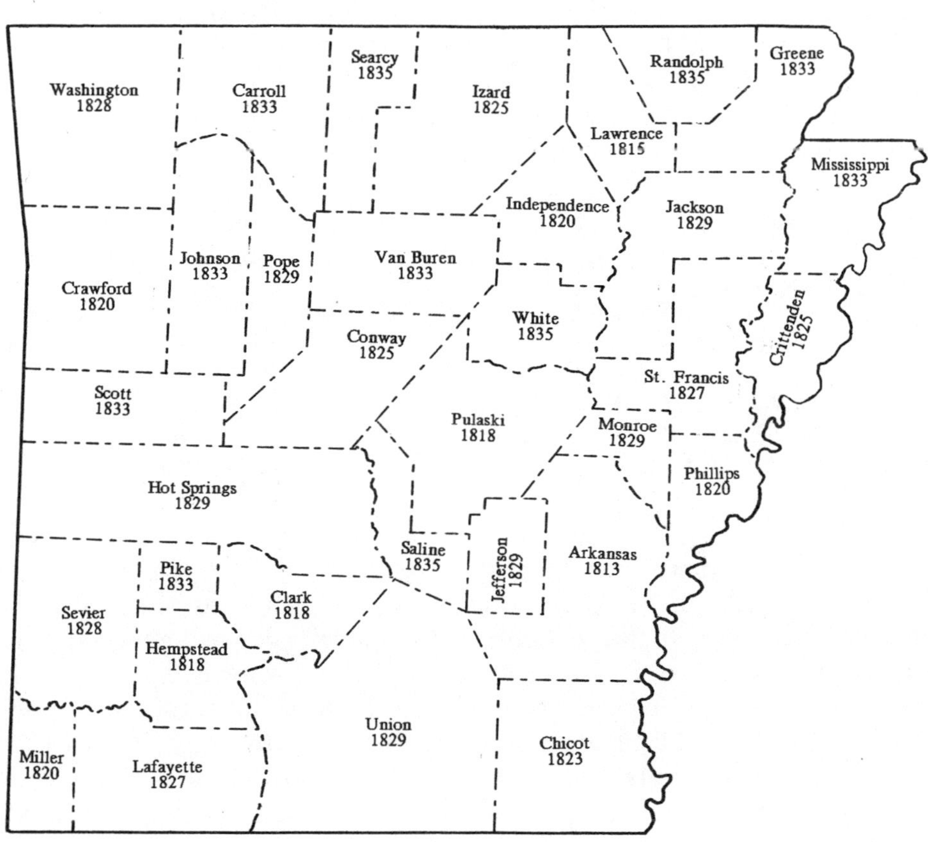

Counties of Arkansas, 1836

CHAPTER

6

Travel and Lifestyles

Incidents of Travel

The Reverend C. A. Morris, one of the bishops of the Methodist Episcopal Church, made his first tour of "the Big Circuit," the Tennessee, Arkansas, Mississippi, and Alabama Circuit which had just been assigned to him, in the fall of 1836, only a few months after Arkansas was made a state. His description of that first trip into the new state is graphic and amusing. In 1841 he made another tour enroute from St. Louis to Texas, and in a series of letters to Brother Elliott, he discusses not only the condition of the church but also what he perceived of the state itself. Both narratives provide interesting reading.

~~~~

I should like to introduce the reader to the Black River Swamp, in the state of Arkansas, but not till I get to it, nor yet exactly as I was introduced to it myself.

St. Louis. In September, 1836, I left the Queen City, to attend the Tennessee, Arkansas, Mississippi, and Alabama conferences. . . . there might be disease and danger in the course; but I was on lawful business, intimately connected with the welfare of redeemed sinners; and why should any man ever fear to go where duty calls, or remain till his work is done. . . ? Far removed, not only from wife, children, and friends, but from the crowds of strangers which usually throng the public lines of conveyance, it was a time for reflection on the responsibilities and difficulties of my new relation, and not wholly unimproved. Lonely reflection, however, was soon superseded by practical duties. While in council with the brethren of Tennessee conference, at Columbia, a call made for volunteers to supply the wants of the new conference just set off in the state of Arkansas, was promptly responded to by some noble-hearted, self-sacrificing young ministers. Three of them were ready to bear me company thither, immediately after the final adjournment. Their names were Randle, Duncan, and Simmons. Passing
~~~~

down through the western district of Tennessee, we came on the fresh trail of fourteen thousand Creek Indians, just then removing from Alabama to their new home in the far-off west. At one of their camping places, then vacated, was seen a standing hollow tree, out of the side of which had been taken a slab, by cutting above and below, and splitting it off, and which had been carefully replaced. A citizen, whose neighbors had made examination, informed us, that in the hollow of that tree was a deceased Indian, standing erect, with his gun, blanket, and hunting costume, as he appeared when living. We subsequently saw several of these depositories of their dead. . . .

After crossing the "Father of waters," at Memphis, we immediately entered the Mississippi Swamp, which, at that point, was forty-two miles across. . . . On the evening of the second day, we emerged from the swamp, and crossed the St. Francis river. At a small, green bottom, two miles beyond the river, two companies of Creeks, numbering some three thousand in all, were camped for the night. We took lodging at a country tavern on the hill, about thirty rods from them. They had nearly as many ponies as people, and almost every pony wore a bell. The camp axes were roaring; dogs and children appeared to be alike abundant and alike noisy. The whole, taken together, produced a singular confusion of sounds, and presented quite a novel spectacle.

Next morning, about daybreak, we rode out through the encampment, in a north-east direction, on the Batesville road. Having cleared the great swamp, and reached an undulating surface, we congratulated ourselves that the worst of the journey was behind. . . . In the afternoon we came by a small company of men engaged in raising a corn-crib near to a cabin, which seemed to be full, and presented no appearance of comfort, when the following conversation ensued:

"How far is it to the next house?"

"Twenty-one miles; and three more to the tavern."

"What sort of road is it?"

"Not very good, nor bad; just middling."

"Is there any deep water to cross?"

"None that will swim, except Bayou de View, sixteen miles from here; and I don't reckon that will swim quite."

Then among ourselves we held a conference, on horseback, the rain still coming down. "It is two o'clock; say four hours till daylight will be entirely gone. Can we reach the point of difficulty before dark?" "Yes, I think we can." "If we fail to get through, we shall need our dinner by to-morrow." "Well, I have a little piece of corn bread," said one. "And I have part of a sweet potato," said another. "That is as good fare as we can get here," responded a third. It was suggested, if we had to camp out, there was no means of striking fire; but perhaps other campers might have left fire on the way. The case was finally summed up thus: our time in which to reach conference is short; there is no use staying here in the rain: come on. And onward we went, ignorant of what was before us. In a few minutes our road disappeared under water. What does this mean? Why, the Black River swamp. "They said, last night, we should cross it, but it looks worse than we expected." The sludge increased, and the horses sank more and more. Presently, while passing a bad place, Nick, better acquainted with M'Adamized turnpikes than swamps, went down till he was nearly buried alive in quicksand and water. After a long and hard struggle, he came out and brought me with him, but my heavy saddle-bags were left behind in the mud. Having recovered them, we resumed the journey, but soon reached another slough, where, to prevent a greater evil, I dismounted, drove the horse, and followed on foot, through mud and water to the knees, by which we made a safe crossing. But the thought of its being twenty miles to the next house, wet and cold, my boots full of water, and the night approaching, was not very cheering. It was about the last of October. The climate was supposed to be unhealthy. We had fairly entered a dismal swamp, thirty-two miles wide, and, in consequence of heavy rains, unusually full of water. Instead of traveling four miles an hour, as we had expected, our horses were unable to make three. The beaten track was the least dangerous, as it always is over quicksand; but for miles together it was wholly under water, varying in depth from six inches to three feet, and the bottom little more than a continuous quagmire, the horses could follow the trace by the old blazes on the sides of the trees; but night closed in upon us long before we reached the main point of difficulty, and the rain still increasing. We lost the track, our feet dragged through brushwood, and the morass shook beneath us; but giving the affrighted horses loose rein, they returned to it. Again we took the wrong direction, and went plunging through water and alder-bushes, in danger, every moment, of being ingulfed in quicksand. . . . A conference was then called to discuss the question, "Shall we give it up, or try to proceed?" It was a solemn conference; and though darkness and storm prevailed without, order and peace were maintained within. The sum of our conversation was briefly this: to stay here all night, wet, cold, and hungry, without shelter, without fire, or a foot of dry ground on which to stand, is perilous: to proceed was only perilous; and the conclusion was, to try it again. . . . But, alas! under the lofty trees and lowering clouds, the darkness was such that we could not see the animals on which we rode. What was to be done? To encounter the turbid stream at random, was bordering on presumption; to wait for daylight, when the stream was rising, was discouraging, and might defeat our whole enterprise. As it was a case in which life might be involved, a regular vote was taken, by calling the roll, and it was unanimous in favor of going ahead. It was also agreed that I should be commander. The line was promptly formed, as follows: brother Randle, having a steady horse, and being a light rider, was to lead off; brother Simmons, second; the writer third; and brother Duncan was to bring up the rear. It was further ordered, to keep two rods apart, so that if we struck a swim, every man might have sea-room, and a chance for life. "All ready?" "Yes." "Proceed. Cry soundings." "Knee-deep; up to the girth; midsides; steady: over the withers, but still feel bottom; more shallow now. Here is the point of the island." "Very well. Now form and angle to the left; down stream is easy." The latter channel was no deeper than the former, and all made safe landing. Thanks to kind Providence. . . !

It was, to our great mortification, soon ascertained that the new way was more miry than the old. As we could see nothing, our quadrupeds had all the credit for keeping the road. Presently brother Randle's horse was heard plunging, at a fearful rate, for some time, when he announced a very dangerous place; "water up to midsides, and the bottom very boggy." Brother Simmons next put in, and was glad when he got out. He advised me to veer to the left; it might be better, and, he thought, could be not worse. It proved to be unfortunate advice, as it threw me on to a heap of logs, that had been rolled in to fill up a deep and dangerous bog, but which were then all afloat. Nick had a terrible scuffle over them. Once his foot hung fast; twice the water rolled over him, and rider was will-nigh unhorsed; but, finally, he righted, and brought me out unhurt. Taking a position, as nearly as I could guess, opposite to where the others crossed, I called to brother Duncan to steer by my voice, and put in. He came near sticking fast, but received no damage. At a late period of the night, while groping amid darkness that could be felt, mingled with incessant showers, we were suddenly aroused by the joyful note, "A light! a light!" Approaching as near as some unseen obstruction allowed, we hailed. An old lady came to the door and demanded,

"Who is there?"

"Travelers."

"Ah! I thought my sons had got back from bear-hunting."

"No, madam, we are strangers; have been belated in the swamp, and wish to know if you will shelter us the balance of the night."

"Why, la, me! I wouldn't turn off a dog such a night as this."

Securing the horses to the trees, we joyfully entered the cabin of poles, about sixteen feet long, and fourteen wide. . . . Four of us, with our wet baggage, added to the family, and two other strangers that were there before us, scarcely left us room to turn round. At midnight we made a comfortable dinner on pork and corn-dodger; and having dried off a little, we held our evening prayers at two o'clock in the morning, and quietly laid us down to sleep, grateful for our kind reception. About daylight we asked the old lady for our bill, which was two dollars. When we inquired if she meant two dollars each, she said,

"La, me! I should be rich if I had that much. I mean two dollars for all four."

Having completed our preparation, we resumed the swamp; but the limbs of our animals were so lacerated by maple-roots and cypress-knees, that they took it very reluctantly. We reached the Cash river tavern, with hard toiling, in an hour and a half, the distance being three miles, where the landlady, in the absence of her husband, first served us with breakfast, and then ferried us over the river. . . .

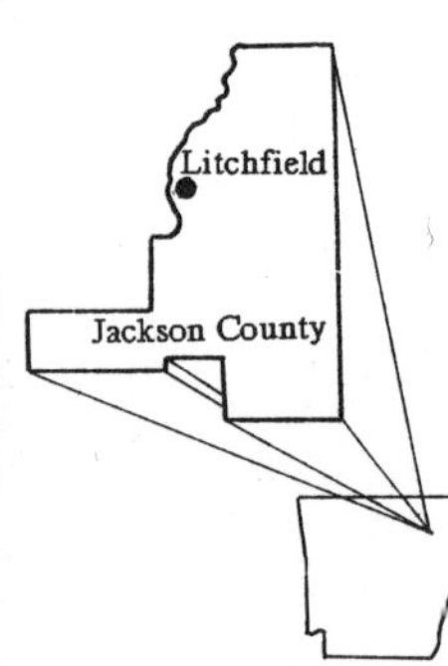

After reaching solid ground, and obtaining lodgings, our first concern was to unpack our clothes, books, and papers, and dry them. This done, we preached, exhorted, and held prayer meeting in the village of Litchfield, where the inhabitants received us kindly, and requested regular preaching, which was of course provided for them. Our little party felt toward each other like a band of patriot soldiers, who had endured a hard and hazardous campaign together, and we distributed among ourselves small presents, as mementos of our mutual regard and providential deliverance. . . .

In this narrative there is not a particle of fiction, nothing thrown in to fill up a chasm, but much omitted to shorten the article. Every man who adventured himself into that swamp in the condition it was then in, did it at his peril. Had I been offered one thousand dollars to retrace my steps, it would have been no temptation. Only for reliance on the providence of God, I should have despaired of getting safely out. . . . How we were to be delivered I did not know, nor feel concerned to know, but felt the most unshaken confidence that God, in his own way, would bring us safely through. And after obtaining that confidence, I felt more of the spirit of rejoicing than is usual for me, even under more favorable circumstances. Such was the beginning of my first regular tour on what is sometimes called "the big circuit;" but I am happy to add, it was not a fair specimen of my journeyings, even in the new country.

The Rev. Morris returned to Arkansas in 1841, enroute to Texas. The letters which follow recount some of his experiences on this trip.

Letter III

Brother Elliott,–

As we are not land-jobbers, nor going on a tour of observation, it will not be expected of me to say much of the country; yet I would like to afford some information for the benefit of our missionaries who may hereafter remove to Arkansas, or Texas, by this route. . . . What I saw, in 1839, of the land north of Missouri river, is generally preferable to what we have seen south of it. The road is often narrow, sideling, rocky, stumpy, and hilly, but free from swamp, and therefore passable. On the morning of Friday, 29th, about fifty miles from Greenville, we crossed the Missouri line, entered the state of Arkansas, and immediately after took the ferry-boat over Current river, at Mr. Pitman's, the place formerly known by the name of Hix's ferry; and in the evening camped some thirteen miles beyond the river, a short distance from the road, back of a field, on the bank of a large creek called Fourche de Mass–pronounced Foosh de Maugh. Mr. Johnson, who occupied the premises, not only gave us leave to camp and gather sticks for our fire, but kindly went and aided us in selecting a pleasant place on which to pitch our tent. We chose rather a romantic site on the point of a sloping ridge, just in the rear of projecting rocks, the strata of which so receded one over another as to afford natural steps to and from the water's edge. The evening was mild and calm; the full moon shone brightly, our log fire looked cheerful, and all the company were in fine glee, except brother Whipple, who was suffering under a severe attack of sick headache, of which, however, he was relieved by a comfortable night's sleep. It is true, our wheat loaf was exhausted, and all efforts to obtain flour had failed, but we had warm corn hoe-cake, fried ham, butter, eggs, sweet potatoes, coffee, and Boston crackers; and considered ourselves among the best livers in the country. We did not, however, pretend to keep fashionable hours, and as soon as we could say prayers and make ready, laid us down and rested to purpose.

Our design was to reach Jackson the next day, and preach there on Sabbath; but a wise Providence ordered otherwise. About midnight the weather changed; a gale sprang up and brought clouds and rain, which pelted our thin habitation the balance of the night, and nearly all next day, so that we could scarcely leave our tent at all without getting wet. Much relief was experienced by putting up a Russia duck awning between the tent and fire, that afforded a shelter under which to sit and eat. Our chief difficulty was from smoke, which occasionally drove in with such violence as to affect our eyes severely, and sometimes force us out into the rain to get a good breath. Here, and in this condition, we expected to remain till Monday; and in view of that conclusion brother Whipple rode some miles in the afternoon, without a saddle, to ascertain whether we could obtain a congregation any where in that region to hear us preach on Sabbath. While he was gone, brother Clark chopped wood to avoid the sin of gathering sticks on the Lord's day. About this time, our camp was visited by a youth, nearly a man in years and size, on the singular errand, as he said, of buying sugar. We did not keep the article on sale, and could not accommodate him; but soon found him better employment. Some of the logs chopped off were very heavy; brother Clark placed a lever under the forepart, put the sturdy youth at one end of the lever, and myself at the other, and taking the tail-end of the log himself, we put forth our strength, straightened, and marched into camp. This operation was repeated till we had collected an ample store of fuel for the Sabbath. . . . Brother Whipple returned, and brought with him old brother Spikes, a native of North Carolina, and for some ten years past a citizen of Arkansas, who insisted on our decamping and going home with him so kindly and earnestly, we had to yield to his entreaty. It was after four o'clock, P. M., when we changed our plan for the night: all possible haste was made in packing up and striking tent; the rain still coming down upon us with increased force. About a quarter past, we bowed out from Camp Fourche de Mass, and reached our new quarters, three miles off, with some difficulty, after dark. The incessant showers of rain on the Sabbath rendered it impracticable to collect any congregation. We sang and prayed at the interment of a neighbor's child on brother Spikes's premises, but had no preaching. Monday we judged it prudent to lay by, in order to dry our tent, and replenish our store of provisions. Brother Whipple went to mill and bought flour, and while sister Clark kneaded and baked, brother Clark made us a portable table out of four new clapboards, shaved and jointed, which we carry on the baggage-rack without any trouble; the legs and frame, consisting of four small forks and two poles laid across, we can procure at any camping-place in five minutes, and the table is complete. . . . Brother Whipple's friends, before he left home, presented him with a rifle and shot-gun, which he accepted for the sake of the small game in this new country. He is what the hunters call "a sure shot" with the rifle, and among hands a fine lot of squirrels and a fat rabbit were here added to our supplies. . . .

Tuesday, November 2nd, we crossed a small, rapid river, called Eleven Pines, because that number of pine-trees grow around the head spring of it, as we were informed. In the afternoon, we passed through Jackson, a small town, and formerly the seat of justice for Lawrence county. . . . while brother Whipple went with the buggy across the river in search of horse provender, we raised a great brush-fire against the fallen trunk of a large sycamore, and when rearing our tent before it, the owner of the land, Mr. S—, rode by, called at the camp, and remarked we had a fine fire. We asked if he had any objection to its being on his land, or kindled with his wood? He replied, "Not any;" and he would be glad if all the timber on his bottom land was removed; as well he might, for it was heavy clearing. On learning that we were preachers going to Texas, he invited us to his house; but not feeling inclined to repack and turn back, we declined accepting the invitation. Here we found our small fry, and other fresh provisions, excellent fare, spent the night pleasantly, and called the place *Camp Sycamore*. . . .

Elevenpoints?

Friday, 5th, we reached Batesville, the seat of the Arkansas conference, where we met a welcome reception, and found excellent accommodation among our Christian friends. I am quartered at Colonel Pelham's, one of the oldest settlers of the place, clerk of Independence county, and a member of our church, and has a pious, pleasant family. Batesville is a considerable town for this new country, and has improved greatly since I was here in 1836. It is situated on the north side of White river, which is navigable for small steamboats a part of the year to this place.

What we have seen of north Arkansas, on this tour, is one of the best watered countries in the United States, and has every appearance of being generally healthy. The upland is mostly poor oak barrens, and the hills quite stony; but the creek and river lands are rich, and covered with lofty forest trees. The climate is mild, and very pleasant. Batesville is situated between thirty-six degrees of north latitude. As to the people, they are quite as intelligent in Arkansas as in other new countries, and generally as well disposed. That there are some desperadoes in Arkansas, as there are in all the states, whose fame has gone abroad, must be admitted; but they are not true specimens of the general state of society. . . . And though a large proportion of them are not professedly religious, many are so professedly and in fact; and the others are generally willing to hear the Gospel preached. Methodism is evidently making some progress among them. Our society have erected quite a handsome brick chapel in this place. But of the general state of the work I may be able to speak more definitely after I shall have heard, in conference, the reports from every part. So far we have had much cause of gratitude on this journey. Providence has favored us in reference to good weather generally. No calamity has befallen us. The Lord has given us some favor in the eyes of the people, and our health has been wonderfully preserved. Sister Clark has been for many years in delicate health; but, by riding moderately each day in the carriage, and the morning and evening exercise of tent-keeping, she is evidently gaining health and strength. Brother Whipple, whose health was very poor before he started, is mending rapidly. Little John, who had long been subject to chills, is becoming strong and hearty. Brother Clark is growing fleshy; and as for myself, though I have no occasion to be any fatter, am nevertheless gaining. . . .

In most of our older conferences we have some good brethren in delicate health, who seem to think themselves unable to endure the toils and exposures of an itinerant life, and under the influence of mistaken notions of self-preservation, incline to linger about those places where roast beef, plum-pudding, and preserves abound in the greatest luxuriance. . . . Now, for the benefit of all such young preachers, though not a professor of the healing art, I venture to make this prescription: Let them form themselves into companies of two, three, or four, and volunteer for the work in Arkansas or Texas conference, not to float down the river pent in the cabin of a steamboat, but to travel in light wagons, such as will carry themselves, tents, and baggage: let them camp out; kill, roast, and eat wild meat; study their Bibles; pray; and sleep with their feet to the fire. A few blankets are easily carried; and as for feathers, every oak and elm produces abundance of such as would be most healthy for them, and which they can have for the trouble of gathering. One such campaign, with the blessing of Providence, would make them sound men, buoyant in spirit, and ready for a frontier circuit, or mission, where they might have the honor of preaching the Gospel to the poor, and of aiding a noble band of brethren in their efforts to save souls. Who will get ready and make the experiment next fall? Healthy brethren are not excluded from the privilege of coming.

By "feathers" Morris is possibly referring to leaves for pillow stuffing.

Yours, sincerely,

T. A. Morris.
Batesville, Arkansas, Nov. 9, 1841

LETTER V

Brother Elliott,–

When taking leave of Batesville in my last, I should have remembered the Male and Female Academy of that place, under the superintendence of Rev. Henry Hunt and his lady. Brother Hunt was formerly a member of the Kentucky conference, but is now in a local relation. His school is situated at the north end of town, in a high and healthy position; the rear ground extends into the edge of a very handsome grove of young cedars, which throws around the place an air of beauty and cheerfulness; the buildings are of respectable appearance, and the institution is favorably spoken of, and pretty well sustained. A committee was appointed by the conference to attend the examination.

On Tuesday, 16th, at a late hour in the morning, we left Batesville in a cold rain, not because we loved it, but for the reason that our engagements ahead required us to be diligent. When we arrived at the ferry, it was difficult crossing, on account of the freshet in White river: however, after being detained two hours, we were safely landed on the opposite side. . . . After we resumed the road, the brethren on horseback passed us, and we were left with our usual company. The afternoon was pleasant; and in the evening we sought and found a retired spot off the road for our camp, with a view to dodge the pigs, as they had been very troublesome on previous occasions; and the experiment was successful–they did not find us till next morning. Our camp was on the north bank of Sally Doe, a name suggested by a singular occurrence. Among the pioneers of the country was a heroine named Sally, who observing a female deer in the water, stood on the bank, and with a gun killed it, from which achievement the settlers agreed to name the creek Sally Doe. . . .

Wednesday afternoon we crossed Little Red river at Crolman's ferry, thirty-two miles from Batesville. It is a deep, rapid stream, about ten or twelve rods over: the boat is worked across by a hand rope, extending from shore to shore, in a very short time; and appears to be profitable to the owner, as I paid for one horse and buggy sixty-two and a half cents in silver. . . . After we left the river, we inquired at each house we passed that evening for corn, but they had none for sale; nor did we blame them, for they appeared to have very little for themselves; till we reached Indian creek, about dark, where Mr. Magness, one of the first settlers, accommodated us with three half-bushels of ears, or about three pecks of corn, for a dollar, which we find to be the usual price of late. This, however, is more than the ordinary price of the country, and is occasioned by the summer drought this year. . . .

A rod is 16.5 feet.

Thursday we lunched at Bayou Dezark, and camped in the evening near Mr. Walker's, where we had nothing to annoy us whatever, except our swine visitors. These ravenous animals appear to be well versed in the art of filching from movers' camps, and have no doubt been practicing their feats of roguery from the time they were weaned. One of the ringleaders of the gang came that night while we were asleep, and dragged our bag of corn from the mouth of our tent, and getting a little the start of us before we awoke, gave us quite a chase to recover it. Friday evening we were kindly received and well treated at Mr. Covvey's. Saturday we crossed Arkansas river in a steam ferry-boat, and arrived at the capital of the state, where the brethren received us with true Christian courtesy. The river here is some six hundred yards wide, and is at present in fine condition for navigation by steamboats. The distance from Batesville to Little Rock by the old military road which we came, is one hundred miles. . . . The inhabitants are few and far between, which, together with the want of time, may account for our having no appointments on the way for preaching. We are here in the midst of Indian summer. The weather last week was frequently too warm to be comfortable. On Friday the temperature was nearly up to summer heat. . . . Such a state of weather the latter part of November is rather remarkable even in Arkansas. Still I have no doubt but this is one of the finest climates in the United States, forming a medium between the extremes north and south, so as to secure its inhabitants generally against the winter fever of the former, and the yellow fever of the latter. . . . but why should people be so difficult to suit in countries? When in the north I am delighted; when in the south, if I had my family with me, I should almost be willing to remain; and when I return to my native west, it still appears to be the best of all. As traveling preachers, the world is our parish, and wherever duty calls, we should be willing to go. On the Sabbath, according to previous appointment, we met the congregation in this city. . . . After sermon the sacrament was administered. All the brethren filled the table around the altar only twice. . . . Little Rock has improved considerable, since I saw it five years ago, in appearance; but our society has not increased in proportion. Still they have peace among themselves, exhibit some fruits of true piety, and there is ground to hope they may so increase in numbers and grace as to become a strong people. To-day we expect to resume our journey, having a series of appointments in advance. At some convenient time you may hear again from

Yours, respectfully,

T. A. Morris.
Little Rock, Arkansas, Nov. 22, 1841.

LETTER VI.

Brother Elliott,—

We left Little Rock Monday, November 22d, and took the military road leading off in a south-west direction. . . . Six miles from the city we passed the cabin in which I slept in 1836, the night before I entered the forty mile wilderness on way to Mississippi conference, which was then occupied by an excellent Methodist family, named Hoover; but on inquiry I learned that the master of the family was dead, and his widow and orphans had removed to a distant part of the country, and the place was in possession of strangers. In one corner of the little field adjoining the cabin, was a neat white paling, which inclosed the remains of brother Wells, who, some years since, came as an itinerant from Tennessee to labor in Arkansas, and died in the work. He was the same brother Wells whose name is identified with the history of the arrest of the missionaries in the Cherokee nation in 1831. While his fellow-laborer was driven on foot before the mounted guards, brother Wells followed on, leading his horse for him to ride back, in case he should be discharged on examination; and for this act of kindness to the prisoner, the heroic Colonel of the guards struck him over the head with a club. He is now where the wicked cease to trouble, where the weary are at rest. These brief but solemn items of the past, afforded for some time a profitable theme of meditation. We spent that evening pleasantly at the house of Mr. T. Rolands, who, some four years since, emigrated from Alabama. He and his family are members of our Church.

Next morning several of his family accompanied us to Benton, the seat of justice for Saline county, where we preached to a small congregation in the court-house. Benton is a small village, twenty-five miles form Little Rock. After dining with Mr. Hockersmith, we proceeded on to the house of brother H. Cornelius. . . . On our way to his house, and near Benton, we forded a heavy stream of water, called Saline river.

Wednesday we ferried the Washita river, where it is, perhaps, one hundred and fifty yards wide, but not navigable for steamboats, though an excellent river for steamers from Ecorefabre down, and ate our luncheon on the south bank. This ferry is twenty-one miles from Benton. In the afternoon we bought provender of Mr. Stubling, entered the Twelve Mile Stretch, so called, because for that distance the road passes over pine hills so poor that no one lives near it. . . . At the south end of this stretch, we came down, on Thursday morning, to Bayou de Roche, which, as its name is intended to express, is remarkably stony in the channel and on either

Escorefabre was the name first given to Camden.

shore, and only a few miles further on, found it sufficiently deep fording a very rapid little river, called Fourche Caddo; and as it was turning cold, we raised a fire, by which to warm and eat, on the other side, in what had been a cane-break. . . .

Saturday morning we resumed our journey. . . . In the evening we forded a large creek called Antoine, and soon after reached Wolf creek, where we had appointed to preach on the Sabbath. We called, as previously advised, on Colonel John Wilson, who keeps a public house, but had the kindness to entertain us gratuitously. His wife, children, and servants, are members of our Church. This was in the corner of Pike county. The Colonel has on his place two valuable springs, one chalybeate and the other weak sulphur, and pleasant to the taste.

Water impregnated with iron.

On Sabbath, at eleven o'clock, we commenced public service in Wolf creek meeting-house with eighteen persons; others came during sermon, some after sermon, while brother Clark was exhorting; and after the congregation dispersed we met others going. . . . It is a free house, where some appoint to commence at noon, and then delay as much longer as suits their convenience. As this is said to be the best chapel in the south part of the state, it may be of some interest to read a brief description of it. The walls are made of hewed logs, about twenty by twenty-four feet in extent, with a wooden chimney in one end, and a place cut out for a chimney at the other end, which is partly closed up with slabs. In the front is a large door, with a center post, and double shutters, on the principle of a barn door. Immediately opposite, on the other side, is a pulpit, which is so high that when the preacher kneels to pray he is nearly concealed from the view of the people. Behind this pulpit is a window without glass, the shutter of which is neither long nor wide enough to close it, and, consequently, lets a double stream of air upon him. The roof is made of clapboards, between which and the floor there is no ceiling, though there are some naked poles laid across on the plates; and the cracks between the logs are partially closed by nailing on thin boards, these have been mostly torn off, to afford light and a free circulation of air. The day was cold, and the people appeared to suffer. In the evening we found a large fire kindled in the front yard near the door, to which the people could retreat when too cold to hear the preaching; when one class were warmed they would return into the house, and another cold set would give place to them. No blame was attached to them for this procedure; for, judging of the feelings of others by my own, it was an indispensable arrangement. We had truly a chilly time that day throughout, temporally and spiritually. Next morning we concluded to measure the temperature of the atmosphere, hung out the thermometer, and the

mercury stood only eleven degrees above zero, which was certainly extraordinary weather for this country the last week in November.

Monday morning we crossed Little Missouri river, about five rods wide, for which we paid $2. . . . That night we staid at Mr. Pates's, and the next morning came into Washington, Hempstead county, where our Christian friends received us cheerfully and treated us kindly. Washington is situated on a high sandy plain, which was, from appearance, originally a pine forest; the town is compact and of respectable appearance, and, except the capital, is one of the largest in the state. There is here a respectable male and female academy, under the superintendence, I learn, of the Rev. Mr. Hodge, of the Presbyterian Church, and a convenient, substantial court-house, in which we preached several times to a congregation respectable in size, appearance, and orderly attention. There is no chapel in the place, nor is there any regularly-organized Methodist society, though we have a few members in the town and its vicinity.

Wednesday evening brother Clark and I, accompanied by brother Gregory . . . went to Columbus, eight or ten miles distant, and preached evening and morning to a small congregation. Columbus is a small village of some taste, and has a male and female academy, both white frames of neat appearance, under the tuition of Rev. Mr. Meloy and his lady, of the Cumberland Presbyterian Church. In this village there is no chapel; and though we have some Methodists there, they are not organized, and have no class meetings. . . .

On our way to Columbus we passed the far-famed Mount prairie, which gives name to this circuit. It is a small prairie, the only one we have seen this side of Illinois, is chiefly under cultivation, and has a notable mound, which is the building-site of the farm. . . . The most remarkable circumstance about it is, the surface abounds with sea-shells–clams, oysters, etc.–so thick, we were told, in places, that a plow can scarcely be forced through. These shells, in many instances, are in a perfect state of preservation, while, in others, they are in a process of decomposition. How they came on a high, dry prairie, more than three hundred miles from the Gulf of Mexico, is a question which I leave for the learned to answer. [footnote–This is the best neighborhood of land we have seen in Arkansas.]

Thursday evening we returned to Washington, where brother Clark preached again to an increased congregation, notwithstanding the evening was rainy.

Yours, truly,

T. A. Morris.
Washington, Ark., Dec. 2, 1841.

LETTER VII.

Brother Elliott,–

We left Washington Friday, December 3rd, and came to Spring Hill, a village on an elevation among the pines in Hempstead county, so called from the fact that numerous springs of excellent water break out of the hill, in various directions, around the village. Many of the citizens of this place are planters, whose cotton farms are on the low lands of Red river, a few miles distant, and afford excellent society for each other. This site, being high and well watered, is healthy and pleasant for family residences; and their children have the benefits of male and female academies, under the superintendence of Rev. Mr. Banks and lady, of the Presbyterian Church. While in Spring Hill we enjoyed a fair specimen of old Virginia hospitality, which of course was very grateful to us weary travelers, and in turn we exerted ourselves to be useful among them. There is no Methodist society organized there, and very few persons who were members of our Church, nor have they any chapel of any sort; but we had the pleasure of preaching two days in the female academy, which accommodated quite a respectable congregation; and from the number present, the attention given, and the interest apparently taken in the preaching, we can but hope that some beneficial effects may follow. Monday, 6th, we left our kind friends of Spring Hill, and took the Minden road, which leads through a country forming a striking contrast with Hempstead county, in some particulars. . . . In the evening we passed Lewisville, the seat of a new county named Fayette. This is a new establishment in the woods, consisting of a log court-house, with a brush arbor in front, and indifferent log school-house, and the commencement of a wooden jail, the walls of which were partly raised. One mile beyond Lewisville, between Dr. Wilson's and Mr. Lemay's, we lodged by a small ravine, where the light-wood was abundant, and called the place Pinot Camp. Here we ate breakfast by candle-light, and at an early hour on Tuesday entered a wilderness of about thirty miles, without a house. Soon after we heard the keen crack of a rifle, and presently saw a buck fleeing as if wounded, and immediately afterward met a young Indian with his hunting costume, attended by a well-trained dog on his track, who, without manifesting any surprise at our appearance, went on in pursuit of his game. While observing him, his father and mother, as we supposed, and some younger children, came up with a train of small ponies packed with skins and meat, in real hunter's style. This was a family of Choctaws returning from their fall hunt, made in the wild regions of the Bodcaw, which is still the abode of wild beasts. . . . Only a few miles on our day's journey, we met a wagon drawn by two mewly oxen, attended with hunters, who informed us they were going after a wild bull, which they had just killed near that place, to bring him into their camp, which we would presently pass; that he was very fat, and they judged would weigh about seven or eight hundred pounds. It is presumed that these cattle originally strayed from the French and Spaniards, and have been increasing in their wild state for ages past. Soon after passing them, we came to the Bodcaw, a large bayou, full of cypress, and difficult to pass. At our crossing, it parted so as to form an island, on which we saw the hunters' camp among the cane, which, in the absence of its owners, was occupied by ravcns and buzzards, fccding on thc offal. Thc banks of thc Badcaw arc nearly perpendicular, and the water so deep that to secure our baggage we had to prop it up on blocks, and then lash it on with ropes to keep it dry. . . . Had we been men of leisure and sport, the temptation to stop here and exhaust our little store of ammunition would have been strong; but we had another and more important object in view than hunting deer, bear, and wild cattle. . . . Why nobody settles along on this road it is difficult to account for, only on the supposition that the land is owned by non-resident speculators. . . . Many flocks of deer scampered before us during this day's journey, but we paid little attention to them. After pushing on all day, we reached Dorcheat at dark, a bayou some forty yards wide, and too difficult crossing to pass in the night, and we were content to stop in rather an inconvenient place on the north side, about two rods from a deserted Indian camp, made of cypress bark; but we preferred our own tent on fresh ground. Our camp was in sight of the house of old Mr. Moss, perhaps the first settler of the neighborhood; but he was buying corn at one dollar a bushel, and hauling it forty miles. However, with some persuasion, he let us have one bushel for two dollars in par funds, but would spare no fodder at any price. . . . While at Camp Dorcheat, the hooting of owls and howling of wolves made us music enough for one night.

Next morning, by blocking up our baggage as before, we forded safely, and, within one mile beyond it, passed two smaller bayous with some difficulty; the ford of one being so blocked up with drift, that we had to seek a new crossing, and cut a road to and from it. The first mile of our road from Dorcheat presented a novel appearance to a northern man: the undergrowth was cane and bay-shrub, shaded by a dense forest of holly, with an occasional pine from three to four feet in diameter. . . . Leaving this flat, we came over poor pine knobs to Mr. Rice's, seven miles, where we bought a nice piece of a fat cub, killed the day before; and half a mile beyond saw a large sweet-gum marked "A. and L.," which we recognized as a line-tree between the states of Arkansas and Louisiana, where we let our horses feed on the cane, while we took our luncheon. This was in latitude thirty-three degrees north.

Yours, respectfully,

T. A. Morris.
State Line, Dec. 8, 1841.

LETTER VIII.

Brother Elliott,—

While taking leave of Arkansas, it may be proper for me to add one or two general remarks to those already made. The south part of the state is a more interesting country, on some accounts, than the north part. The land is rather better, and the climate milder, of course; insomuch that the stock is generally wintered on the wild range, without the expense or trouble of feeding, especially where the cane has not yet been destroyed. This circumstance, together with its China-trees and numerous evergreens, gives it the characteristics of a southern country. It is also a planting region, and produces cotton in abundance, and exhibits more appearance of wealth and intelligence. All that I have said of the civility and hospitality of the inhabitants heretofore, has only been confirmed in my mind by passing through the south-west part of the state. Methodism, I am sorry to say, appears to be less efficient in its operations, and therefore less influential, in Arkansas generally, than it should be, but there is no necessity for this state of things being perpetuated. The people are generally well disposed to receive our views of Christianity, and the teachers of it whom we send to labor among them; and even in the towns, where we have accomplished but little, with few exceptions, much might be done if proper attention was paid to them. I do not know of a better opening for usefulness, by an enterprising Methodist preacher, than in the villages of Hempstead county.

Miscellany: consisting of Essays, Biographical Sketches, and Notes of Travel, *by Rev. C. A. Morris, D. D. L. Swormstedt & A. Poe: Cincinnati, 1854. Discovered at the Arkansas History Commission.*

Gerstoecker Visits Little Rock

Frederick Gerstoecker, a young German of 21 from Hamburg, sailed to America in the spring of 1837 in search of adventure and game. In January of 1838 he arrived in Arkansas where he found game and adventure enough to detain him for four years. He departed Arkansas in September of 1842 and shortly thereafter returned to Germany. His partially fictionalized journal was written in German solely for the pleasures of his family and was later translated for the English reader. Gerstoecker was to later become a widely travelled and world famous author. The following excerpt taken from his first book describes a small segment of his experiences in central Arkansas.

Long after sunset on the 9th of February, *1838*, I arrived on the Arkansas River; the lights of Little Rock shone from the opposite bank, but a strange fantastic scene presented itself on this side of the river. . . . an Indian tribe had pitched their tents close to the banks of the river. A number of large crackling fires, formed of whole trunks of dry fallen trees, which lay about in abundance, offering good shelter against the wind; over the fires were kettles with large pieces of venison, bear, spuirrels, raccoons, o'possoms, wild-cats, and whatever else the fortune of the chase had given them. Here young men were occupied securing the horses to some of the fallen trees, and supplying them with fodder; there lay others, overcome by firewater, singing their national songs with a mournful and heavy tongue. I stood for a long time watching the animated scene.

A tall powerful Indian, decked out with glass beads and silver ornaments, came staggering towards me, with an empty bottle in his left hand and a handsome rifle in his right, and, holding them both towards me, gave me to understand that he would give me the rifle if I would fill his bottle. The dealers in spirituous liquors are subject to a heavy fine if they sell to soldiers, Indians, or Negroes. The poor Indians have fallen so low, and become so degraded by the base speculations of the pale faces, that they will give all they most value, to procure the body and soul-destroying spirits. Though I had but little money left, only twelve cents, I declined the exchange; he turned sorrowfully away, probably to offer the advantageous bargain to someone else, in which case I thought it best to indulge the poor savage, and save him his handsome rifle; I took the bottle out of his hand, filled it, and gave it back to him. On my refusing to accept his rifle, he laid hold of me, and dragged me almost forcibly to his fire, obliged me to drink with him, to smoke out of his pipe, and eat a large slice of venison, while his wife and three children sat in the tent staring with surprise at the stranger. He then stood up, and in his harmonious language related a long history to me and to some sons of the forest who had assembled around us, and of which I did not understand a word. At last as the noise became annoying, I stole away quietly to seek a berth for the night.

When I came again to the ferry on the following morning, the encampment had broken up, and the Indians had embarked on board a steamer, which was to carry them further west. I crossed by the ferry, and had now no longer any cause to be anxious about spending too much money, having paid away my last twelve cents. Rarely had a traveler entered a strange town with so light a purse. My situation in such a place was not at all enviable. The soles of my boots had disappeared, and then the feet of my stockings, so that literally I had gone barefoot on the frozen ground. Yet my self-confidence and courage did not fail me. . . . I found board and lodging at a German wheelwright's, named Spranger, for three dollars a week, and although with all my searching I could not find three cents in my pockets, I agreed to the bargain, giving my gun in pawn; then taking my hunting knife I hastened to a shoemaker's who asked me two and half dollars to re-sole my boots, and accepted my knife as a pledge, lending me a pair of shoes to wear till the boots should be finished. When this was all arranged, I looked about for work, and took many a walk in vain. . . .

In Little Rock many had referred me to a Mr. Fisher, who was well known among the Germans. . . . He had just finished a large frame house, and wanted to make some additions to it. I went to every door in the building to seek some one who could tell me where to find him, but all was as quiet as the grave I then went to another smaller building, and knocked. As no one answered, after knocking three times, I pushed open the door, and entered. In one corner of a miserable room I found an empty bedstead, with broken legs; carpenter's tools lay on the table and floor, and a coffin stood in another corner. At the foot of the bed, on the bare earth, lay a man, with his head on one of the broken legs of the bedstead; his right arm was under his head, and the left lay across his face, so that I could only see the dark hair; the hands were spotted red and black, I thought from the paint of the coffin. I asked him if he knew where Mr. Fisher was. He gave no answer: I supposed him to be asleep, and he appeared to be ill. I went out again quite quietly, and tried some other doors; but they were all locked, and not a soul to be seen. I went back again to the sleeper, and although I called loudly, and shook him by the shoulder, I could get no answer, and came away much vexed. At length, after a great deal of trouble, I found Mr. Fisher, and had my trouble for my pains, for he had no work to give me. In the course of the conversation I enquired about the man in the hut and was told that he had died the day before of the smallpox; my blood ran cold at the words. The doctor had stated the nature of his disease, and desired that nobody should go near him; and as the man was poor, without a cent in the world, he had shut the door, and never been near him again. The poor fellow had been left to himself for three days, without even a drink of water, and at last had died miserably on the floor. Little Rock is a vile, detestable place in this respect, and the boatmen on the Mississippi have good reson when they sing–"Little Rock in Arkansas, the d—-dest place I ever saw." Yet several Germans inhabit the town and neighborhood.

As nothing in the way of work was to be found in the town, I went to the river to try and get something to do on board a steamer. . . . I went first on board the "Fox" and was engaged as a fireman, at thirty dollars a month. In an hour the boat started. I was quite contented. . . . We ran down the Arkansas to its mouth, then up the Mississippi to Memphis, and back again to Little Rock. The work of a fireman is as hard as any in the world; though he has only four hours in the day and four in the night to keep up the fires, yet the heat of the boilers, the exposure to the cutting cold night air when in deep perspiration, the quantity of brandy he drinks to prevent falling sick, the icy water poured into the burning throat, must sooner or later, destroy the soundest and strongest constitution. How I, unaccustomed to such work, managed to stand it, has often surprised me.

In addition, there was the dangerous work of carrying wood, particularly in the dark and wet nights. One had to carry logs of four or five feet in length, six or seven at a time, down a steep, slippery bank, sometimes fifteen or twenty feet in height when the water is low, and then to cross a narrow tottering plank, frequently covered with ice, when a single false step would precipitate the unfortunate fireman into the rapid deep stream, an accident which indeed happened to me another time in the Mississippi. It is altogether a miserable life, offering, moreover, a prospect of being blown up, no uncommon misfortune, thanks to the rashness of the American engineers.

I carried on this work for some time, until the desertation of the cook at Memphis caused a vacancy in that department. Just as the boat was about to start, I offered myself for the place, and was accepted, although I knew nothing more than how to boil the kittle; yet I soon learned as much as was necessary.

When I returned to Little Rock I released my gun and hunting-knife. The next voyage was to the mouth of the Arkansas and back. The rude coarse life among the lowest class of people soon digusted me, and, in addition to this, I had incurred the enmity of the captain, who disliked me, probably only because I was a German. Yet he could not do without me; but as I could not find a substitute, I was obliged to make another voyage, and this time up the river. I already had an idea how my service would terminate, and having my game-bag packed, and my gun, hunting-knife, and a tomahawk that I had purchased, all at hand, I was prepared for anything that might happen.

Two days after our departure, the captain came down to me as I was in the act of giving the remains of a meal to a poor old woman, who was on her way to join her children, but had not wherewithal to pay her passage. An old Pennsylvanian had informed me that the captain had been abusing me. This and the question, "Who gave me permission to give away the provisions?" put me in a rage, and I asked him, rudely, in return, "If he would rather that I should throw them overboard?" The "yes" was hardly out of his mouth, when plate and food were floating in the Arkansas. He gave vent to his rage by springing on me, and seizing me by the breast; in return I sent him sprawling against the opposite side. he was quickly up again, and snatching up a piece of broken handspike, made a desperate blow at me, which I luckily avoided. My fury now knew no bounds; I grasped his throat, and was dragging him to the side to throw him overboard, when his cries brought the engineer and boatswain to his rescue. One of them pulled the captain away by his legs, while the other took me by the shoulders and then both carried the captain, whose head was bleeding severely, into the cabin. I was ordered to go directly to the book-keeper, received my pay, the steamer stopped, I was landed on the bank, the boat returned on board, and I found myself in quite a new and extraordinary position.

All around me was a solitary wilderness,—the river behind me, the ground frozen hard, and covered with a thin sheet of snow—a cold north wind blowing through the leafless braches. I felt in my pocket for my fire apparatus—it was all wet; not a single grain of powder in my powder-horn, and only one barrel loaded. I thought it would never do to discharge my gun for the sake of lighting a fire, and remain unarmed in the wilderness. I cleared away the snow from under a tree, lay down, and tried to sleep; but the wind was too sharp, the cold insupportable, and I was afraid of being frozen. Driven to extremity, I discharged my gun against the root of a tree, lighted a match by the burning wadding, collected dry grass and wood, and in a minute or two had a glorious fire.

Although I heard the howls of several wolves, I did not mind them, but enjoyed a sound sleep. Certainly, on the following morning, I trudged on rather out of spirits, with no powder, and a very hungry stomach.

Fourth of July Celebration in Little Rock

Gerstoecker arrived in the U.S. in the spring of 1837 and left in the fall of 1843. In this time he made several trips to Little Rock. The last time was in July, 1842.

The Fourth of July was to be celebrated as usual in Little Rock by a grand barbecue, a banquet, at the public expense. I went to the appointed place out of curiosity, and found a dozen black cooks, busily preparing for the grand affair. Two trenches about two yards long and four wide, were dug in the garden near the town, the bottom of each was filled with red hot charcoal, the supply being kept up from a large fire near at hand. Pieces of wood were laid across the trenches, and on the wood immense quanities of meat; two halves of an ox, a number of pigs, calves, deer, bears, sheep, etc. were roasting and stewing while people with bottles or jugs of whiskey went about offering it to all present. The meat itself was not particularily inviting, everybody going up and cutting off what he wanted, and holding it in his hands to eat, some standing, some walking to and fro. At a campfire this is all very well, but with such a multitude with greasy hands and mouths is not very attractive.

While Gerstoecker never liked Little Rock, his delight in the rest of the state was apparent, as he wrote:

Of all I had seen in America it was the place which pleased me most; I may never see it again, but I shall never forget the happy days I spent there, where many a true heart beats under a coarse frock or leather hunting shirt.

Gerstaecker, Frederick. Wild Sports in the Far West, *London: George Routledge & Co., 1855.*

The West Family of Pope County

In his search for better opportunities of supporting a large family, David Porter West came to Arkansas in 1839. He landed at Old St. Martin, near Scotia, in Pope County in May of that year. The following letter was addressed to his son Warren and was postmarked "Dardanelle, Arkansas, May 30." In it he summons his family from Tennessee and submits a rather lengthy list of "needs."

The second item from the Wests is a letter from Thomas B. West in Fort Smith to his father at Fort Gibson, dated August 10th 1846.

The last item is a contract made with David Porter West, another son of Major West, for conducting a school at Danville. The contract is dated 1853 and provides a glimpse of what education was at the time.

Dear Son:–

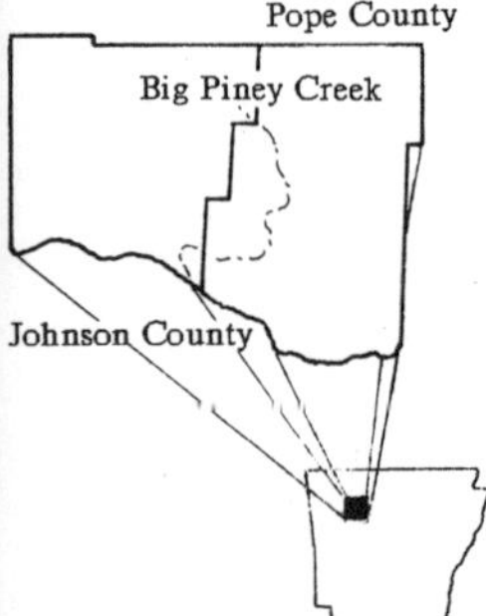

I have purchased me a place–the best quarter section of land you ever saw. Just like such a one as I have often described to you and the other children.

My place lies on the north side of a large creek, Piney. There is a range of mountains for a great extent, abounding in all kinds of game. I have killed some of the largest deer and turkeys you say.

I have about 13 acres to put in corn, about three acres of new ground, but I had to make rails to fence it and my hand is getting hard and my knee failed me yesterday for the first time since I left home.

Tell your mother I have a right smart little cabin with a plank floor. Tell her I have a garden and if I keep my health I can make a plenty to feed my horse and make bread for you all if you can only come without me. . . .

I have not got money to bring me back, therfore, try and come. Start as soon as you can. Bring with you tools of every kind. Get Isaac Hutt to put steel in my hand axe. Tell I. Williams to make chisels, planes and a foot adz. I have been badly pestered to stock my plough. Bring, in fact, all the tools you can get. Bring a keg of chewing tobacco. Get it from Jackson Berry.

Tell your mother to box up and bring everything she cannot wear. Tinware, nails and cans, if you get them to the river they will bring all such things for nothing. Swap your smoothe bored gun to Mulloy for a rifle to run about 60 balls. Tell Mulley to send me the leads and saws that fit my gun. Tell Tom to bring all them old big fish hooks.

I am almost naked for pants. Try and get a bolt of coarse cheap stuff and bring. I do need a home spun shirt.

Go down to Charles Yates and tell him to send me all the leather I have there. Get me a good strong pair of shoes for I am barefooted. But I will tan a buckskin and make moccasins.

I am about 40 miles west of the Killgores, Ragsdales, Griffins, McCartys, etc. They were all well a few days since. Tell I. Williams Elisha is well and is working with Hawkins Gregory. . . .

If you write again, direct your letters to Scotia postoffice, Pope county, Arkansas, where I want you to land in place of Spadra bluff, for Scotia, or St. Martin's, being all one, is only 12 miles from me. If you land there, inquire for Dr. Martin, with whom I will make arrangements. I shall write no more until I hear from you. If I have to come after you, I shall lose my crop.

~~~~

Fort Gibson, Aug. 10th 1846

Dear Father:

I forward you a few lines by the Reverend Mr. McManus. I am now at the post office and he informed me that he was a going to Fort Gibson and I borrowed some ink and paper and write you these few lines. Father I have mended ever since you left and all the boys are agog about except Heufsteadler and Brigance. . . . Once the doctor tole me yesterday morning that as soon as the boys got able to walk he would furnish me with a wagon and give me charge of what was left of the boys and have everything hauled and all we would have to do would be to take our foot in hand as the old saying is and go ahead. They all appear very kind to me and Capt. Felter and his Lieut. came to see me very often, and wanted to send a man to wait on me. W. Duval came up to see me the other day and said anything I wanted I could have it and he insisted that I should go out and see him, and as we have to stay some time, I believe I will accept his offer. I stated to you in the other letter that A. P. was dead. Pa you must write to me as soon as you can.

Give my respects to all the boys.

No more, but remain your son.
~~~~

Thos. B. West.
Fort Smith, Arkansas.

Danville School

The undersigned takes this means of informing the citizens of Danville that he will commence teaching school in this place on Monday the 25th of July [1853] and hopes by strict attention to business to receive a liberal portion of the patronage of said town and the surrounding neighborhood. The first term will continue five months, during which there will no time nor pains be spared to make the school both interesting and profitable to the students in the cultivation of their minds and morals. He proposes to teach spelling reading, writing, Arithmatic, English Grammar and Georgraphy. Tuition fees per month Spelling, reading, writing one dollar, Arithmatic, English Grammar and Geography one dollar and twenty five cents to be paid at the close of the term.
The subscribers furnished a house, benches, etc. David P. West.

Sisk, Sue Catherine West. "The David West Family," Arkansas Valley Historical Papers, *Number 18, September 1958.*

The Paschal Letters (1840-1847)

George W. Paschal was a Van Buren attorney in the early 1840's and later served as a Supreme Court jurist. He came to Arkansas in the Cherokee Removal. His wife, Sarah, was a daughter of Major Ridge, one of the Cherokee leaders. The following letters are addressed to Mrs. Sarah Bird Northrup Ridge, the widow of John Ridge, another of the Cherokee leaders, and a sister-in-law of Paschal, who was assisting her in the settling of her estate.

Van Buren Arks. 14 April 1840
To Mrs. S. B. N. Ridge

My dear Madam:

I have no hope that you could have given relief—but you might have prevented Sarah [his wife] from a relapse more dangerous than any yet, which want of coercion, has coused her to fall to. . . . Her disease, you are aware, is of the mind. The continual lurking of a vengeful spirit which, I neither can comprehend, nor know how to cure.

Sarah Paschal had suffered the loss of her father, Major Ridge, her brother John Ridge, and her uncle Elias Boudinot. All were assassinated for their part in signing the Treaty of Removal which brought the Cherokees to the West.

I do not think we shall be up for travelling will only make the matter worse and bring our troubles on others. Emily [his daughter] is improving but has chills. I only have one chill a day and [as] soon as the fever is off, I go on plunging through rain and rivers returning home with more notes and less money. Please remember us kindly to your children.

Yours truly
Geo. W. Paschal

~~~~

Van Buren
To Sarah Ridge

My Dear madam:

My wife has long had in contemplation to make a visit to yourself and her Mother, but her health, as you have doubtless heard, is so very poor that she has despaired of making the journey on horseback. She is now about writing to her mother to request her to send her Coach down for her, in order that she may go up about the first of July. . . . My object now in writing you is to request that you will send some word to McWilliams to allow your mules to bring down the carriage in case they can get no other horses. . . . Your compliance will therefore much oblige me.

R. McWilliams lived at Honey Creek.

I have not time to begin now to write you any news from Washington. I have only to say that our government manifests a degree of interest and commisseration in your misfortunes worthy of sentiment of good hearts and feelings. They are anxious to do you every justice and they are now in possession of correct information. I am again lanquid—Sarah makes our daughter fat—Thanks—Give my love to your children. I am repectfully yours—

Paschal was, at this time, assisting Mrs. Ridge in the settlement of the Ridge estate.

Geo W. Paschal
~~~~

Major Ridge

A Cherokee Chief

Van Buren, Arks. 29th Aug. 1840
to Mrs. Sarah B. N. Ridge

My Dear Madam:

Capt. Armstrong arrived here yesterday. He has the order in regard to the debts due your late lamented husband. It becomes necessary to put the account in exact form and annex the affidavits of Childers and John Watie.

Capt. William Armstrong was Superintendent of Indian Affairs.

I have this day sent up to Col. Anderson to bring them both and all the books and papers here. Capt. Armstrong says it will be necessary to have Childers and Watie both at Fort Gibson. As the cheapest way of getting Childers I think you had best send one of your fellows to work in his place until he returns. By doing this and furnishing him a horse you can probably satisfy him. I would go up myself but my court convenes in a few days. I have written to Col. Anderson to go for Childers and Jno. Watie but I have not mentioned the propriety of furnishing a hand in the place of Childers. You had best therefore enter him in the subject yourself.

We expect you down at our meeting on the 11th September. Bring a hymn book with you. Sarah and Emily are in tolerable health. I have had slight fevers for several days. I keep moving however through the day. I fear I shall not be able to keep up. Remember us kindly to your family–

Wm. Childers was John Ridge's agent when he came to the Cherokee Nation, West. John Watie, who became head of the Treaty Party after the 1839 assassinations, was a brother of Stand Watie.

I am yours truly
Geo. W. Paschal

Van Buren, Arks. 23 Oct. 1840
To Mrs. S. B. N. Ridge

My Dear Madam

Since my hasty note to you dated 14 Sept. (by mistake) I have been so much engaged that I have not had time to write. . . . We have all much improved in health since that time and can now eat against any [of] them individuals great or small in the State. I am also in some better spirits than when I wrote before. I think that if we were away from hearing of the ill-fated Indians we should be better satisfied. Several things have conspired to make me believe that we shall soon hear of serious difficulties in the Nation.

John Ross opposed the Cherokee emigration to the West and was the tribal chief.

Should the opposition succeed in the presidential election, I am induced to believe that Ross will go to every length. The great encouragement which he has everywhere received from the Whig Party will embolden him to any course. Even in this state they flocked around him, as though he had been some distinguished foreigner—I must confess my patience is well nigh exhausted with a party who seems to know no moral rule in their contest.

. . .

If court should be held in your county in Nov. I will try to bring our family up.

In haste
Geo. W. Paschal

Paschal's letters after 1847 indicate a deterioration of the relationship with Mrs. Ridge, caused by the lack of payment of fees.

29th January 1847
Mrs. Sarah B. N. Ridge
Bentonville, Ark.

My Dear Madam:

Mrs. Ridge was awarded $5,000 by the Treaty of 1846.

Below please find copy of a letter from the Secretary of the Board of Commissioners at Washington on your "Ferry claim. . . ." I have been anxious to see you in regard to this and other matters about which I wrote you. Feel, allowing for all exaggerations which have been brought me, it seems to me impossible that I should have suffered so much injustice from those, for whom I have labored so long and at so heavy an expense to myself. Much less can I believe that your notions of right and wrong could have undergone so great a change as to dismiss those [illegible] on the payment of debts honestly and fairly owed by your deceased husband. My unexpected return renders me unable to pay these debts out of my own pocket were it right that I should do so. I wish you and Col. Anderson to appoint a time for coming to a fair adjustment of the whole matter.

I remain very respectfully yours

Geo. W. Paschal

The two letters which follow reveal the extent of the breach between Paschal and the Ridges.

Washington City, D. C.
18th May 1847
to Honorable Willliam Medil
Commissioner of Indian Affairs

Sir:

I have to request that the residue of the money due to the heirs and legal representatives of John Ridge and to the heirs and Representatives of Major Ridge, may be immediately forwarded to Capt. Wm. Armstrong, Superintendent of Indian Affairs, with instructions to pay the amount decided to be due to the widows of Ridges to themselves or to their proper attornies in fact, if unable to attend in persons, you are already aware that Walter Ridge, son of Major Ridge, is an idiot and will of course have to act by guardian. And I think it proper to suggest that instructions be given that due guardian be appointed by the proper security than the courts of the Cherokee nation, whose proceeding are of course crude, if they require any security at all. The same caution should be observed in regard to John Ridge's children, all of whom are infants and one of whom is also unfortuately an idiot. They reside in Arkansas. I find upon a careful examination of the law that to enforce payment here the guardian should be appointed here. This would be attended with inconvenience and expense. I mention Capt. Armstrong because I think that the money would be more advantageously disbursed than if in the hands of the Cherokee Agent.

As to the notion of Mr. J. W. Washburn [Washbourne] respecting the amount due to the infant heirs of John Ridge I have to remark that the same difficulties would arise about drawing the interest as about the principal at present. Mr. Washburn is a young man who, when he started to Washington, had been married into the family of the Ridges one day. He is not perhaps as competent to judge of the wants and necessities of that family as those who have sustained them for years and to whom they are indebted for the liberality of the Government for an appropriation for the children of men too honorable I hope to be influenced by sordidness. I have felt it due myself to make this remark because of the persecution you informed me he was pleased to give you in regard to myself. The world is too well acquainted with the interest with which I have sustained this family for any honorable

J. W. Wasbourne married Mrs. Ridge's daughter, Sarah.

man to suppose that I could wish to do them a wrong.

I remain vey respectfully your humble and obt. svt.

Geo. W. Pashcal

~~~~

Bentonville, Benton Co. Post Office
Osage Prarie, Arks. May 27th, 1847
Hon Wm Medill
Com. Ind. Affairs

Dear Sir:

I have been at home some time but in consequence of indisposition, I have as yet been unable to continue the business of taking evidence of the heirships of Major and John Ridge's children so that some choosing may be paid their claim and others have it invested. I will have it done very soon and transmit it to you.

Judge G. W. Paschal has sued the heirs of John Ridge for everything they have on earth on the grounds that Mrs. Sarah B. N. Ridge, "being a white lady and having no clan" her children are not the heirs of their father, but that himself and wife are, because the latter was John Ridge's sister. He is now gone, I understand, to procure the whole of the $10,000 allowed by Treaty to the Ridges and will no doubt set before you much false evidence of his rights. I most solemnly declare him to be a swindler and a scoundrel in his attempts thus to defraud the heirs of John Ridge.

We rely entirely upon your promise that the children of John Ridge shall receive their shares of both the $5,000.00 allowed the heirs and representatives of Major Ridge and John Ridge. They need it–much.

Will you be so good as to notify me of Paschal's demands:

Very respectfully
Your Obt. Servt.
In behalf of the widow and children of John Ridge
J. W. Washbourne

Flashback, *Vol. 23 N0. 1, February, 1973.*
~~~~

The following letter is one of several found which were addressed to "Friend Lucas" in St. Louis from several citizens of Arkansas Post. Although all of the letters were interesting, this one reveals the most varied events and is also the only one which could be transcribed with any degree of certainty.

Arks. Post, March 15th 1840

Friend Lucas,

I did not receive your letter of 28th Jany. till a few days ago–as it was contained in a package that was droped at the Wm Noterby [?] farm and as he was absent Mr. N suposing the whole to be for him he retained them until some days after his return. I had received and planted the (unintelligible words) some weeks before. I knew to whom I was indebted for so generous a favour, for which you will please accept my sincere thanks. They are puting out firmly–The interest you manifest for my welfare I assure you is highly gratifying, having embarked into an entirely new business, with very small capital and many obsticles to encounter, and not a voice here to urge me onward any kind remarks is always acceptable, but such kind suggestions, as is contained in yours, coming from an old friend affords me encouragement & delight. for believe me no one feels with more sensativeness than I do the suggestions & kindness of a friend.

You talk of the severity of the winter at St. Louis, with how much pleasure would I welcome you back to Old Arkansas–we have sufferd here a little with cold & wet, but it has been a memoreable[?] healthy winter. A great number of cattle have died but I believe principaly from poverty, the winter range here abouts is pretty much exhausted, I hear of more than 20 head of mine dieing this winter. The grass in the Praririe is springing forth luxuriantly. I shall in a few days drive all my cattle from the bottoms then I shall ascertain the extent of my loss–my hogs are doing well but I have not the real grit and Farrelly has been so unfortunate with the increase of those he purchased of you. I have not been enabled to procure of that stock. Pertins has been equally unsuccessful with those you gave him his fine boar was drowned last week and the sow had 6 pigs 5 of which have died. The sow is a very beautiful & large hog. would weigh I think not less than 250 pounds & is fat–over 300 lbs. I hope you may meet with an oportunity of procuring me some of the best breed of hogs in that country, I shall anxiously expect them. Your suggestions about cattle I shall endeavour to improve from by disposing of my most indifferent & purchasing the best I can find in this country & when I get properly fixed with good pasturage &

houses to winter them, If I think it better, will procure the best English cattle. It is my design to send a boat load of cattle to N. Orleans this spring or in the summer–by way of making collections will take some, & with what I shall have on hand make up a load–It appears impossible to make collections in money altho I have more money due me than at any previous time since I came to this county I cannot obtain enough to meet my obligations. Col. Farrelly holds a note against me in your favour, which I expected to have been enabled to pay long ere this but am yet without the money. If it will be no inconvenience to you to wait with me a while, an indulgence at this time will be highly favourable & acceptable.

I am pleased to learn of the flattering prospects for the success of Genl. Harrison in your state. I fear there is no hope for Arkansas yet. The Whigs are active and meetings have been held in the diferent counties or most of them and delegates appointed to the Whigs state convention to meet at L. Rock the 3 Monday of this month. We held a meeting here last week. H. Stilwell presided & your humble svt. as Secretary. A B. K. Whitford & Richd. Young were elected deligates from this county. We are Whig here to the back bone. We hear that a mighty change is taking place in old Washington County as well as throughout the state a desperate strugle will be made by the Whigs to obtain the ascendency in the next legislature which I think very probable. I learn a mighty strange occurance took place at L. Rock a few days ago in a trial of some man before the circuit court of Pulasky Co. Ashley was on one side & Fowler on the other. The argument became warm & hotter. Ashley became personal. Violent words passed between them. Fowler threw an inkstand at Ashley, struck him on the temple & wounded him badly. Old Caldwell ordered them into the custody of the sheriff & both Ash. & F. wer suspended for the present term of court. It is said that great excitement prevailed on the occasion & some were trying to give it a political hearing. Robt. Johnson said he would beat or have Fowler beaten at the next election & that F. attacked Ashley because he knew he would not fight and much talk by the friends of both parties of rathur a pugnacious tendency was used, Tom Newton said if fighting was what they wanted Fowler & his friends were ready & willing to go at it then & could flog their enemies any & every way. It will be a hot time with the Little Rock folks until after the next election & I expect some fighting of course, we are as peaceable here as lambs. My best compliments to your family. Your friend sincerely,

B. W. Lee

Arkansas History Commission: Small Manuscripts Collection.

Sarah A. Nelson's Letter to Friends

The letter which follows is addressed to two friends in North Carolina and reflects the impressions of a young girl in her new home. Sarah A. Nelson settled with her family in Saline County in 1849. All we know of Sarah is what is revealed in this letter, but the chatty style is that of any young girl of any age.

Arkansas Saline County, February 15th, 1849

Dear Meneci and Emily

I take my seat this evening to drop you a few lines to let you know that we are well. We have all enjoyed very good health ever since we left North Carolina. I like Arkansas very well so far—the people all seem very friendly. We have plenty of neighbors. There is three families lives in a half mile of us. We live on the publicest road I ever saw. There is hardly an hour in the day but what some person is passing. I must tell you something about our journey out here. We had fine weather the most of the time and we saw a great many curiositys on the way. The blue ridge and the mountains was a curiosity to us when we first saw them, but we was glad when we left them—we crossed the blue ridge at the Neddis [?] river gap it was five miles up and eight down.

We came over some very bad road along in the mountains but the Mississippi swamps was as good a road as I would wish to travel except about four or five miles but when we came to the White river bottoms, there was five miles of the worst road I ever saw but they say it is past traveling between Memphis and Little Rock now there has been so much rain. This has been a very rainy winter here but we have not had much cold weather this winter and but one little snow.

There was a fine company of us on the road and a very merry crowd indeed we fell in company with Mr. William Russell and George Johnson and John Johnson and one Mr. Edwards and they all had a family and that made a large crowd and we enjoyed ourselves very well. There was no grown girls in the crowd but Jane and myself and Betsy Johnson and when we got our cooking done at nights we would sing notes for an hour or two—we saw a great deal of pleasure dipping snuff on the road I would be glad if you and Emily was here to take a dip with us this evening—Betsy Johnson did not come to Arkansas she stopt in Tennessee with her two brothers. I was very sorry when she stopt—Mr. Russell lives about one mile from us and they seem like near connexions to us in this strange country. Mrs. Russell is so kind to us that she reminds me of your mother–we have very good society here but there is no old Presbyterians here. They are mostly Baptist and Methodist and some few Cumberland Presbyterians. There is a Methodist campground about a quarter of a mile from us and we live about two miles from a Baptist church–There is a school going on at this time two miles from us–the country is about as much broken here as it is in the Hawfields. We have good spring water here plenty and the people all look very well and I am in hopes that we will enjoy good health here–Father has not bought land yet. He has rented a place this year and expects to buy it when it comes in market. The owner of it died last spring. It has a large double house on it and good chimneys in each end and a kitchen and all other out houses–we have been invited to one quilting but did not go as we had not got acquainted with the people–they do not have many frolics like they do in most new countrys. There is hardly every a ball in this neighborhood and but very few persons that dances–I must tell you what have been doing We have quilted our spreads since we came here and have been kniting socks to sell and get 5 cents a pair. we have got a wheel and are spining and feel as at home as we did in North Carolina but I think of you all very often and would be glad [to see] you but I have not felt discontented yet nor wished myself back– Meneci Jane says you and Mr. Jones must hurra and make up the match and come out here and not think of setting in that old country Tell Emily if she will come here I will give her a beau Tell Cornelia Linen that Calvin Chick came out here with us and living in Little Rock but he says he intends to [go back to] N.C. after his girl–We live twenty miles southwest of Little Rock and it is a flourishing and beautiful town–you must write soon as you get this and tell me all about Hawfield. Give our best respects to Aunt Polly and Betsy and all the neighbors. When you write direct your letter to Benton P.O. Saline County. Jane sends her love to you all. Give my love to your Father and mother and all the family and accept a full portion yourself.

Sarah A. Nelson

Arkansas History Commission: Small Manuscript Collection

From "Bally" to *The Spirit of the Times*

Amusing incidents of life in Hot Springs are related in this letter from one "Bally" to a New York City paper, The Spirit of the Times. *It appeared in the*

October 20, 1849 issue.

Dear Sir: I have lately returned from the Hot Springs in Arkansas, and for the first two weeks saw but little to interest or amuse me. But fortunately after this delay, the "fun" commenced. First, being Friday at 12 o'clock, M, a foot race was on the *tapis*. Distance sixty yards. The favorite resided here, and all the "knowing ones" supposed him invincible. His opponent is, or was, a stranger from the Indian nation, and destitute of backers, or nearly so, but he was well prepared to back himself. A short time before the hour of starting, the ladies began to show themselves on the course; the stranger had two good friends among them, and they backed him manfully. Betting soon began to be pretty brisk among them, and the last bet I saw made, was a bonnet against a pair of shoes and a handkerchief. I held the stakes, as I was one of the judges. To the astonishment of a large majority of the spectators, the stranger won the race with ease, and I learn that he had beaten all the Indians in the nation. It was no slow race, for they went by me like quarter horses. I stood at the out-coming.

At early candle light a wedding came off at the lower end of the valley, distant from our hotel or cabin, about half a mile. This portion of the valley is called Texas, and a lordly set of inhabitants live here. This was a match made in a hurry, the day previous being the first time this worthy couple had ever spoken. The marriage ceremony over, the whiskey and sugar (brown) was passed around; the "Squire" drank freely, and with the "load" he had on at the start, he soon retired. In about thirty minutes there was another couple ready to be joined in holy wedlock, but on inquiry for the "Squire", he was found too drunk to read the ceremony, and this couple were compelled to wait until some future period. At 8 1/2 o'clock, we all started for a ball hard by. On arriving there, I soon found it "one of 'em." First, we all took a chance on a "reel"; then all set down to a sumptuous supper. Among the many dishes, we had "roast beef", "chicken pie", "ham and eggs", "pumpkin pie", etc. etc. I took a cup of tea, and the servant directly handed me a tumbler of milk (as I thought) to drink, but it was to put in my tea. I drank the milk and soon discovered I had made a great blunder, and a number of the ladies were laughing at me. Supper over, we commenced dancing again in good earnest. About 11 o'clock, some gentleman asked the question, "Who's the best dancer among the gals?" One said "Miss Fillopha McD."; another said "Miss Diana P." Soon a trial dance was set. Then a little dispute arose as to what tune they should dance. Miss P. wanted "Roaring River" or the "Arkansaw (Arkansas) Traveller", and Miss McD. Wanted the "Prettiest Gal in the County, Oh!" or "Where did you come from". It was soon agreed that they should dance the four tunes, then each would have a fair shake. They led off with "Roaring River". After about ten minutes, Miss Fillopha stopped all of a sudden, and sang out "Stop that ar music." The music stopped. She then turned to her brother, took her shoes off, and said, "Bub, hold them ar shoes." She then faced Diana, and gave the order, "musicianer, go ahead." The time required to finish the match was 45 minutes. It was a close match, but Diana was pronounced the best at the double shuffle. Mr. McD. (brother of Fillopha) looked on in silence; but when it was over, he stepped into the middle of the floor, and "Gentlemen, I'll be d–d if there is any use in talking! If I had given Fillopha a whiskey cocktail before she started, she would have beat that gal so bad she would not have been seen here again in six months, and Fill han't done with her yet."

Since writing the above, I learn that two or three waggish fellows have been this morning to the bridegroom, and informed him that his wife had a twin sister, and they were so much alike, it was difficult for the neighbors to tell them apart, and last night he married the wrong one; he intended to marry Catura, but he married Nancy. The poor fellow, without saying a word to his wife on the subject, went direct to the Squire, and wished him to undo what had been done, and marry him to the right gal. The worthy Squire told him if he had known this the evening previous, he could have "fixed" it all right, but as one night had elapsed it was too late. . . !

Our landlord is a descendant of that old and celebrated tribe called Israelites, or Jews, and his maker has put his mark on him so plain, that there is no mistaking him, and a "way faring man, tho' a fool, need not err." He is often called Doctor. This title he is proud of. He prescribes sometimes in Homoeopathy, at other times in Hydropathy. His favorite prescription is *Bearsfoot* (a root that is found near here.) He gives it in cases of rheumatism, newralgia, fits, etc.

The Postmaster is a man of some consequence. Besides being postmaster, he is Justice of the Peace, Stage Agent, keeps livery stable, bar-room and billiard room; in fact, he is the smash man of the place; and manager of all the balls in this section of the country. At the ball last night, he paid the fiddler five dollars for the night's playing. He then stumped the fiddler to play poker; at it they went as soon as the ball was over, and the fiddler lost his money; and got in debt five dollars, for which he is to play another night.

Strange things not only happen here in the way of matrimony, but in other portions of this State. Judge J., one of the circuit judges of this State, related to me a fact the other day, and I use his own words.

At a late term of one of my courts, I granted a decree of divorce upon the petition of a lady of one of the back counties in my circuit. On the same day upon which the lady was divorced, she found another husband, and I was called upon to marry them, which I did in short order. Thus did the lady occupy three different positions in society in one day, as the records of the county attest. . . .

The following Sunday I visited the chapel of this worthy divine. The place of worship was well ventilated, being a new and well built log house, minus the "chinking" windows and doors. It being rather a blustering day, the pastor labored under considerable difficulty in keeping his text before him, the leaves of the book blowing to and fro, as the breeze changed. To obviate this he drew his "Bowie" from the back of his neck and deposited it on one side of the text book. But this would not suffice; the opposite side required "holding down" likewise, and he was compelled to search for his "Durringer" and lay that down also. Here was a spectacle, truly! But as all was well now, the pastor went on with the "sarmint."

Bally

The Record, *Vol. XV, 1974. Submitted by Russell P. Baker, Archivist, Arkansas History Commission.*

From Arkansas to Ireland

An exciting discovery of research was this letter from John Keet in Napoleon, Arkansas, to his uncle in Antrim, Ireland. We learn something of the opportunities, wages, and even education in early Arkansas. We are also introduced to a young man who more than likely exemplifies the character of some who helped make Arkansas what she is.

Mr. James Graham,
Newfelk [?]
Antrim
Ireland

Napoleon,
State of Arkansas.
May 25th, 1851

Dear Uncle,

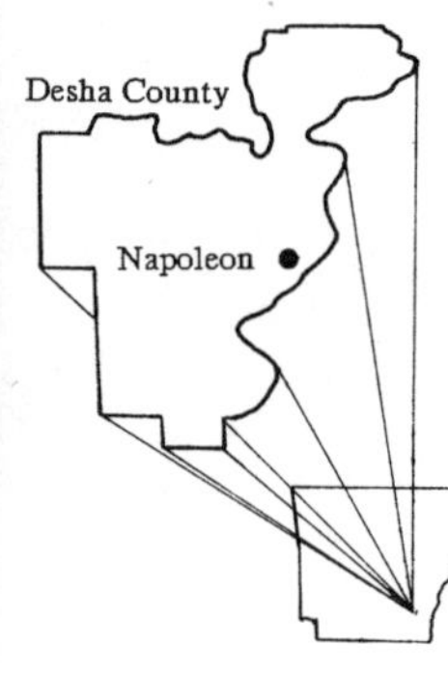

It is now a good while since I wrote you—perhaps too long—but I depended on Wm. or David to write, altho' I think they have not done so. Tom arrived safe and well in New Orleans about the 1st of March and went up to Cincinnati in a few days after. He has concluded to learn the carpenter trade & has gone to work—has been to work for some time. He gets $30 for the first year, $40 for the second & $50 the third, & is found besides in everything but clothing. . . . I came to this place, "Napoleon', in the beginning of April. I was not doing well at New Orleans, & got an offer of better wages to come here. It is a small village, situated at the mouth of the Arkansas river, 640 miles above New Orleans. A merchant of N. O., & one of this state established a house here, to do a general business, grocery, Dry goods, etc, & also for the purpose of re-shipping goods left here by Cincinnati & New Orleans boats intended for the interior of this state. The concern is a new one, but is doing pretty well. I keep the books & attend to things in general. I get $50 per month & found in board etc., which is equal to $80 in New Orleans without board, which is considered good wages there. There are other advantages, however, which make the situation worth more, that is by forming acquaintance & learning something of the country. I probably can, before long, get into business on my own account. A new country presents a much better prospect for that than a city or an old country. I wish I had come here—to this state rather—instead of going to Pennsylvania & killing myself teaching school for nearly nothing & studying what has been of no pecuniary advantage to me. Why, the best wages in Pennsylvania for teaching was $20, in one or two places $25 without board. The other day, a planter across the river (Mississippi) offered me $250 for 10 months to teach his family about 4 children, & give board, washing etc. besides. That would be $25 per month clear. How James K. could get that if he was here just now. Anyhow, if he is getting better or thinks & has any reason to believe he will get better I would advise him to come out here. I can get him plenty of situations to teach—the schools will be small, perhaps only a family or two & he can do it well. People are anxious to get teachers, many, I might say most of the planters have to send their children from home 4 or 500 miles & they would much rather employ a teacher at home. If Jas. can stand another voyage across the "big pond" & if he desires, let him bundle up his "duds" & make for New Orleans; then strike for "Napoleon" & he can get employment in a short time. When tired of teaching, he can go home again if he feels unwell—he will have money—or he can get into a store, I think, after a while. This is a fine healthy state, when you get back from the Mississippi. There are many flourishing towns in it & it is settling fast. I expect to settle in some healthy little town on the Arkansas river, bye & bye, & have a share in a store. I have one or two places in view where a store will do well, & when I have about $2,000 capital, I can commence for myself. I do wish I had come to Arkansas 10 years ago.

This place "Napoleon" is but very small, containing about 100 inhabitants. It is not a pleasant place to live. The Mississippi overflows it every year, sometimes twice; this tenders it unhealthy. They are going to make a "levee" (embankment) this year to keep out the water. It has good facilities for trade & many say that in 10 years, it will be a large place. The *people* of the place are not like those of the North. In fact, the Southern Americans are different from the northern a great deal. They are far inferior in intelligence & morality. They have not the same steady, sober, peaceable, persevering & enterprising character possessed by their northern brethren. . . . Drinking is their principal, I might say their only enjoyment. And O! how strong drink degrades a people—turns them from men to imbeciles & demons, by turns. . . . The intemperate habits of the people here, form my principal objection to the place. This *county* consumes a vast quantity of "liquor" & it presents a greater amount of mortality, taken from the statistics of the state, than any other county in it. . . .

This half of the United States is almost exclusively a cotton growing country & it is considered the best for that article of any other in the country. Farming is done altogether by negroes; planters owning from 10 to 100 of these. The land is very rich & planters have done well the last 2 or 3 years, cotton having been high for three seasons. An acre produces, I think, if I remember right, about 500 pounds cotton, which sells for about $50—I believe they raise sometimes 800 pounds. The plant is coming up now; I have not seen it in the field in any other shape. I can tell you what it is like & how raised etc again October. I frequently visit at a planters across the river—— he shows me his farm, etc, & I will learn how planting & raising cotton is performed. . . .

David wants Jas. to send him a newspaper—he says he has seen no Belfast paper since he came to this country. Jas. promised to send him some. I hope you are all in good health & trust that Elizabeth still continues well. In my opinion she should take plenty of exercise in the *open air*. *Avoid close rooms*. Bathe or wash the whole body *frequently* with *cold* water: and with proper precautions in regard to food, she need not fear consumption. I am convinced people bring almost every disease upon themselves, & this among the rest. Close rooms, with the windows always down, & 3 or 4 sleeping in a room, perhaps 2 in a bed, is quite sufficient to create disease. . . . The draft Sam brought was paid in New York. I sent it to a merchant there who got it cashed. If I had known not merchant or responsible person there, it would not have been worth a cent. Crawford is a fool if he said that anyone in N. Orleans would pay it. My health is middling. I am troubled with Dyspepsia a little. . . .

Yours as of Old,

John Keet

Arkansas History Commission: Small Manuscripts Collection.

Business dealings in Van Buren.

From the following letter we learn that as early as 1851 Van Buren was a source of trade and financial assistance to merchants in the Indian Country. Mr. Corder was obviously one such merchant who desired trade with Van Buren enterpises.

(Private and Confidential)
Lukfahtah C.N. April 8th 1851

Major John Henry
Van Buren
Arks.

Dear Sir:

Per last mail, I received a letter from Moses Greenwood Esq. of New Orleans, in answer to one that I had written him for advice. He says that he has "councilled" with you, and *you both* think that if I will ship my cotton in your name, and for your acct. that you can buy up all my paper at a great discount, and get me out of all my "troubles." That if I think best to purchase goods that I had best purchase of you at Van Buren, that if I have a successful season I can then pay my debts in N. O. and N. York. Now sir I wish you to inform me at what price you think you can buy up all my paper, what you will charge for your trouble, and what percent on your invoice prices you will charge me for goods, should I follow his advice.

Please deal plainly with me—Be as explicit as possible; and give me an answer at your earliest possible convenience; for the time is fast approaching when I must *act*.

In regard to quitting merchandizing, I have this to say; I cannot support my family by hard labor, I am too honest to steal, and too proud to beg. I can do it, by merchandizing if I can continue to get supplies of suitable goods, and more, I can finally pay all my debts, and make money. With the advanitage that I now possess here, of extensive acquaintance, confidence of the people, etc. etc. I am bound to succeed, I will succeed if God will let me. *Men* shan't hinder me. I wrote long since to Mr. Oga [?] and Mr. Green for the precise amts. of the judgements vs me and Price. Never got an answer. I suppose they think that a man who is guilty of the *crime of being poor*, that never has been rich, and is not now able to pay all his debts—is not worth that much attention from their honorable selves. I expect to live to command their respect through influence of the "*Almighty Dollar*" Believing you to possess kind feelings toward, and a disposition to aid me, although I am satisfied that your estimate of my business capacity is *small* I remain your friend and

Very Obt. Servant

E. G. Corder

P.S. If Maj. Henry be absent, Mr. D. C. Williams, will so inform me, at the same give me what information may be in his reach, in relation to the contents hereof, and oblige his friend E. Grandison, Corder

Arkansas History Commission: Small Manuscripts Collection.

A Visitor to Hot Springs from Mississippi

In 1852 Hot Springs had already earned a "celebrated" reputation for travellers seeking better health, as we discover in these letters from A. P. Rodney to his wife at Fort Adams, Mississippi.

Hot Springs, Arkansas
Friday July 2nd, 1852

My dear Wife

According to promise I sit down to write you a few lines. Hoping they may find you and my two lettle boys enjoying good health and also your Father, Brother and Sisters. I will now try and give you a full detail of my journey since I left home. Commencing at New Orleans I shipped on the Pawnee for Napolean accompanied by Cross and Addy and I suppose a slower meaner boat never turned a wheel on the Western Waters than she had. We were crowded to some extent with passengers, the principal part of them was Californians, all down sick with the Chagres Fever, many of whom I feel confident will never reach their homes. And then our state rooms were more than crowded with bed bugs (an article I despise) which made the Boat very disagreeable to us, and as to the eating department it was in proportion to everything else. I really felt sorry for Addy and would have quit the Boat on her account but I was too anxious to proceed on my journey. So on the fourth day out, being Saturday night, we made our landing at Napolean, bidding Addy and Cross adieu. I took my belongings on the wharf Boat Chanciller hoping to escape the bed bugs and get one nights rest but alas I was disappointed in both, as I found the Bugs (assisted by the moskets) equally as numerous as on the Pawnee. However I soon fell into a dose of sleep but soon awakened from my slumber by the wild piercing screams of my next door neighbor. I went to his assistance and found the poor fellow in the last stages of the Cholera. Two physicians was called immediately and they both pronounced him beyond the reach of medicine. This news he received with much distress and spoke of his wife and child and wept that he was thus doomed to die among strangers without the consoling presence of his wife and little child. He gave his money $500 to the owner of the Wharf Boat with the instructions to have the same forewarded to his wife in Little Prarie County, Arkansas with the full particulars of his death. To hear the poor fellow pleading with God to spare his life until he could reach home and then he would die in peace, was enough to make Angels weep, much less strangers like myself. Just after daylight he died and I ascertained that he like myself was waiting for a boat to go up the Arkansas River.

Mosquitoes?

I soon learned that I could not get a boat until Monday at 2 o'clock P.M. and I felt more like retracing my steps than proceeding on my journey. Sometime during the day the Harry Hill landed. I saw John Penney and Harry Filbrien and learned that the cholera had found its way to Jackson and that it had killed some fifty persons, which did not add comfort to my feeling or condition but made me more anxious to leave my present location. Monday at 2 o'clock came at last and I shipped on board the Mail Packet

Emily, bound for Little Rock, a sweet name but alas she was anything but a sweet boat. She was not only small and slow but she actually got along as though she was tired. . . . As for Beef, Mutton, Pork, Chickens, or Turkies, they were strangers to the Emily. Consequently I had but little comfort in the eating line while I was on board her.

At last on Wednesday evening we arrived to my great satisfaction at Little Rock, where I took my lodging at the Anthony House, to wait the arrival of the Mail Coach, which was hourly expected and would leave for Hot Springs at one o'clock A.M.

Feeling somewhat hungary and dinner being over at the hotel, I asked the Land Lord to have dinner prepared for me, which in due time was ready. Shortly after I took my seat at the table (There being several vacant seats) an Indian and his two squaws came in and took their respected seats along my side. I thought I was in a strange land where the White and Red man eat together at a publik house in the Capital of the State. However I enjoyed my meal as I had plenty, and that of what was good. One o'clock A.M. arrived, I paid off my Bill and had my name entered on the way Bill and took my seat (alone) in the Mail Coach bound for Hot Springs, but before I journey further I would tell you that Little Rock is the Capital of the State and is a beautiful little city situated on the left Banks of the Arkansas River, containing a population of 4000 or 5000 inhabitants from which place I traveled a South West Course. At the 13 mile point from Little Rock we stopped and took our breakfast, and it was a real Country Breakfast, just such a one as I like. Here the Post Chaise changed horses and left a mail.

The hour of departure came and we proceeded on our journey through one unbroken forest of Pine. Over, perhaps the Hillyest Rockyest and Roughest Road you ever heard tell of. We finally arrived at a little village called Benton, the County Seat of Saline County, it is one of those obscure poverty stricken, unknown little villages nestled in the Rocky Hills of Arkansas. . . . Here we again changed horses and left a mail and journeyed on our way ever and anon meeting some new traveler bound for Texas, who would hail us to know the distance to Little Rock, the probability of meeting a boat there etc. etc. At one o'clock we stopped and got our dinner, changed horses and mail at 6 P.M. we arrived at the Hot Springs very much fatigued from the jolting of the stage etc.

Thus you see I have caught up with the end of my journey and that I have at last arrived at the celebrated Hot Springs where I have taken lodgings at the Stedham House at 35$ board or 10$ per week for a less time than a month. The Hot Springs somewhat resembles a C. [camp] Meeting. The houses are situated about the same & are all little frame or log cabins, situated in a valley between two mountains, both of which is covered with rock, pine and cedar.

The Hot Springs, eighty in number, comes out of the side of every one of those mountains, besides many cold water springs come close to many of the hot ones and the water is so very hot that it would cook anything. It is as clear as the dew and you can see it boiling for some distance after it comes out of the mountains, and you can feel the heat of one of those springs before you get close enough to dip a cupful. Some Geologist or Scientific man has visited all the Hot Springs in the world, says there will be sometime not far off an awful blowup of this mountain, he says it nearer the surface than any he has ever seen. There is now at this time about two hundred persons here and some of the awfulest cases of rhuematism you ever heard of. Many bad cases have been cured and left for home before I got here. Col. Ginn and Major Jas. L. Trask are here, both of whom was particularily glad to see me. . . . I don't know how long I will remain here, it will depend entirely upon my improvement in health. I am much better than I was when I left home, but I attribute it not to the Springs, as I have been here but one night as yet and have bathed but twice.

I think the rough fare and being confined on a boat has been beneficial, as it has prevented me from taking too much exercise. I left home on the 19th of June and arrived here on th 1st of July making the trip in twelve days precisely. . . . I will now give you a bill of my expenses since I left Home which is more than I anticipated.

Passage from Fort Adams to New Orleans	$ 5.00
Passage from New Orleans to Napolean	$ 10.00
Board on Wharf Boat at	$ 2.00
Passage from Napolean to Little Rock	$ 10.00
Board at the Anthony House	$ 1.50
Washing 8 hrs. at	$ .75
Stage Fare from Little Rock to Hot Springs	$ 5.00
Brakefast and dinner on the way	$ 1.00

Porterage from Boat to Boat	$ 1.00
Bath and hair cutting in New Orleans	$ 1.00
Making a total	$ 37.25

When I left Home I took with me $505 out of which I loaned J.C. Dowty one hundred and fifty dollars and paid Norment Cooper & Co. 35.18 cents for your Pa which gives me a balance on hand here of two hundred and seventy two 57/100 dollars. I did not take Cross's note for what I loaned him. I merely mentiom these matters in case of any accident.

The mail does not leave here for two days yet, therefore for the present I will close. Wishing you and our two little boys a sweet goodnight.

Mrs. E.E. Rodney/Fort Adams/Mi./Politnef of Maj. Trask
Hot Springs, Arkansas, July 8th/52

"Politeness of Maj. Trask" means this letter was hand delivered by Major Trask.

~~~~

My Dear Wife

I wrote you soon after my arrival at this place and for fear it may never reach you, I avail myself of this opportunity of sending you this by Major Trask who leaves tomorrow morning and promises to leave it at Fort Adams, there fore I feel confident you will receive it. I have been here one week and this leaves me much better health than I was, when I left home. However I am broke out with quite a number of very ugly sores besides those two that were on me when I left home, which are much worse and give me some uneasiness as well as pain. I am able to walk without giving me any pain from my rhuematism, but I am very nervous. I bath morning and evening in the warm water. I then go into a vapor bath, which weakens me very much. I have taken boarding for one month, at the expiration of which time I will leave here for the Sulpher Springs forty miles further in the mountains and will remain there two weeks and then if well enough will start for home which will be about the midal of August.

I spent the 4th of July at the Colrbiate Springs 3 miles from here where we had a fine dinner prepared for us.

There was quite a number of persons there and the young men and ladies
~~~~

danced all day. The natives of Arkansas did not attend the barbacue from some cause or other. We had plenty of Champaigne and many fine toasts drank. I did not indulge in either, as I was fearful of a back set, and to be down sick away from home, would be very disagreeable.

Col. Ginn will accompany me to the Sulpher Springs and says he will return to Fort Adams with me and appears to be very fond of my company, his health is greatly improved.

Governor Quitman arrived here in the Stage day before yesterday and took up boarding at the Stedham House where I am stopping. We have about 35 ladys here, all of whom are more or less afflicted with Rheumatism, Dropsay, Paulsey, etc. Some get well, others leave without any improvement. . . . I am greatly in hopes I will get well much sooner as my case is not of long standing. I can feel them now in my back but not in my knee, the swelling has all left my knee. I have an ugly sore broke out on the back of my right hand, they appear very red and much inflamed and pain me when I am in a perspiration. Give my love to your Pa & the family. Kiss Willie for me & Anthony Smith for me and don't whip them much while I am away. Be sure and write, I am very anxious to hear from you & how health is in the neighborhood. I have heard the Cholera is quite bad on the Mi River, Remember me to the Dr. & family, & accept the love of your husband

Anthony P. Rodney
Don't fail to write soon.

McLane, Gerald B. "Hot Springs, Arkansas of 1852," The Record, *Vol. VI, 1965.*

Recruiting from Lawrence County

Settlement of Arkansas undoubtedly was due largely to such letters as we read from Charles Stuart in 1857. Stuart writes to relatives in Tennessee, describing the region of "Larrence" County and encouraging his friends and family to join him.

Larrence County Arkansas June the 1st 1857

Dear Cousin, I take the opportunity of writeing you a few lines to let you know that we are all well at this time hopeing these lines may find you and family all well. I have settled myself in Larrence County Arkansas on or near Spring River four miles from Black river and five miles from powhattan a flourishing little town on Black river where we have an opportunity of shipping all of our supplies this is a convenient fertile country and I believe a tolerable healthy country This is a fine wheat country and cannot be beat for corn and oats also cotton and tobacco grows fine here. Some sechons great for potatoes and vegitables Excilent for turnips. I see know local cause for sickness her and I see nothing to keep this from being a flourishing country. It is settleing fast though there is many good chances for homes yet I have entered two hundred and fifty three acres of land in one. Buddy and I have a choice spring and a high healthy situation I am well pleased with my move more sow than I could have expected. My family is also well pleased. Tell your son William that he would do well to come to this country in fact I think all persons that is not well settled there would do well to move in to the western country there is a large scope of country here and many good places to be entered at 50 and 25 cents an acre. I give 50 cents an acre for mine but lands are graduated according to the time it has been in market there is some good places taken at 12 cents but it is generally 25 and fifty cents an acre times are tolerable hard here on account of a drouth here last season and the severe cold winter and spring I never have seen as much cold weather in one spring I know we had snow and a severe freeze here in April and may have been cold and disagreeable all the time wheat is very prosperous when the wheat crop comes in which will be soon we will be somewhat releived corn is plenty here for the money at 75 cents per bushel Tell John Marchbanks I want him to move here this fall and tell him to write to me amediately and let me know wheather he will come or not. this is one of the greatest places for fish. Black River and Spring river is alive with fish, and I can get them out of Spring river very handy in the spring when they are on the shoots giging by firelight We have fine mills here convenient and excilent water mill in seven miles of me and there is a great steam mill that will start commerce business amediately in four miles of me which will no doubt do great business.

Mr. [unintelligible] you would do well to move here old fellow. Listen to know foolishness for this is bound to be a good country.

Very respectfully yours,
Charles Stuart

Mr. Burrell Utley

Camden Tennessee

Arkansas History Commission: Small Manuscripts Collection.

The Henry M. Stanley Journal

Sir Henry Morton Stanley, noted journalist, famed explorer and locater of Dr. David Livingston in Africa, resided in Arkansas for a few months in 1860 & 1861. Stanley was born in Wales, the illegimate son of John Rowlands, and was registered at birth as John Rowlands. His mother abandoned him to the care of a reluctant grandfather and other relatives. He spent much of his early boyhood in a workhouse where the treatment was harsh and indifferent. At the age of 15, Stanley ran away from the workhouse to his relatives, at whose hands he received the same harsh and indifferent treatment. Finally, he secured a position as cabin boy on a steamer and sailed to America, landing in New Orleans in 1858. There he met a kind and successful merchant named Henry Morton Stanley, who gave him his own name and declared that he would provide for the boy. This short-lived relationship was warm and generous and gave a new direction to the boy's life. It was also this relationship which brought the young Stanley to Arkansas. In the portion of his autobiography which immediately precedes the following excerpt, Stanley writes of the love and respect he held for the New Orleans merchant, whom he frequently refers to as "my father." He relates the circumstances surrounding his sojourn in Arkansas in what is now Bradley County not far from Warren. Mr. Stanley and his protege made the acquaintance of Major Ingham, an Arkansas planter, on a steamer bound for New Orleans from South Carolina. There was talk of both Stanleys going on to Arkansas with the Major, for the elder Stanley had for some time been desirous of opening a business on the Arkansas River. Upon their arrival in New Orleans, the elder Stanley received word that his brother had been injured in Havana and their joint business ventures in Cuba needed his attention. It was then decided that young Stanley would accompany the major to Arkansas and would learn the mercantile business from a friend of the major's. The plan was that as soon as the elder Stanley returned from Cuba, he would join the boy and they would establish a store to be operated by the boy. Unfortunately, the elder Stanley was killed on the trip. Had fate not intervened, Arkansas would have become the home of the man who charted the Congo and relieved Dr. Livingston. In 1861 Stanley enlisted in the Arkansas Volunteers in Pine Bluff. He was sworn in and outfitted at the

Arsenal in Little Rock with the "Dixie Greys" and attached to the 6th Arkansas Regiment of Volunteers. He marched off with the Volunteers and never returned to Arkansas. The chapter in which the following excerpts are found is entitled "Adrift Again," and in it are observations about Arkansas which are revealing and which clearly indicate the talents that made Stanley an accomplished journalist.

Stanley at age 20

"With military clothes, we instinctively assumed the military pose: our heads rose stiff and erect above our shoulders, our chests bulged out, and our shoulder-blades were drawn in. We found ourselves cunningly peeping from the corners of our eyes, to observe if any admired our marital style. The Little Rock 'gals,' crowding about the Arsenal grounds, were largely responsible for the impressive airs we took. The prettiest among them drew into her circle a score or more heroic admirers, whose looks pictured their admiration; and how envied were they who obtained a smile from the fair!"

On, or about, the seventh day from New Orleans, the steamer entered the Saline, and a few miles above Long View we landed on the right bank, and, mounting into a well-worn buggy, were driven a few miles inland to Ingham's plantation.

I am as unaware of the real status of my host among his neighbours, as I am of the size of his domain. It then appeared in my eyes immense, but was mostly a pine forest, in the midst of which some few score of black men had cleared a large space for planting. The house was of solid pine logs, roughly squared, and but slightly stained by weather, and neatly chinked without with plaster, and lined within with planed boards, new and unpainted–it had an air of domestic comfort.

My welcome from Mrs. Ingham left nothing to be desired. . . . The supper which had been got ready was something of a banquet, for it was to celebrate the return of the planter, and was calculated to prove to him that, though New Orleans hotels might furnish more variety, home, after all, had its attractions in pure, clean, well-cooked viands. When the hearth-logs began to crackle, and the firelight danced joyfully on the family circle, I began to feel the influence of the charm, and was ready to view my stay in the western woods with interest and content.

But there was one person in the family that caused a doubt in my mind, and that was the overseer. He joined us after supper, and, almost immediately, I contracted a dislike for him. His vulgarity and coarseness revived recollections of levee men. His garb was offensive; the pantaloons stuffed into his boots, the big hat, the slouch of his carriage, his rough boisterousness, were all objectionable, and more than all his accents and the manner of his half-patronising familiarity. . . . Something in me, perhaps my offishness, may probably have struck him with equal repulsion. Under the pretence of weariness I sought my bed, for the circle had lost its charm.

The next day the diet was not so sumptuous. The breakfast at seven, the dinner at noon, and the supper at six, consisted of pretty much the same kind of dishes, except that there was good coffee at the first meal, and plenty of good milk for the last. The rest mainly consisted of boiled, or fried, pork and beans, and corn scones. . . . I was never very particular as to my diet, but as day after day followed, the want of variety caused it to pall on the palate.

With such society and fare, I could not help feeling depressed, but the tall pine forest, with its mysterious lights and shades, had its compensations. As, in process of time, the planter intended to extend his clearing and raise more cotton, every tree felled assisted in widening the cultivable land. On learning this, I asked and obtained permission to cut down as many trees as I liked, and, like a ruthless youth with latent destructive propensities, I found an extraordinary pleasure in laying low with a keen axe the broad pines. . . . After about a score of the pine monarchs had been levelled, the negroes at work presented new features of interest. On the outskirts of the clearing they were chopping up timber into portable or rollable logs, some were 'toting' logs to the blazing piles, others rolled them hand over hand to the fires, and each gang chanted heartily as it toiled. As they appeared to enjoy it, I became infected with their spirit and assisted at the log-rolling, or lent a hand at the toting, and championed my side against the opposite. . . . For a week, I rose with the darkies at the sound of the overseer's horn, greeted the revivifying sunrise with anticipating spirits, sat down to breakfast with a glow which made the Major and his wife cheerier, and then strode off to join in the war against the pines with a springy pace.

How long this toil would have retained its sportive aspect for me I know not, but I owed it to the overseer that I ceased to love it. He was a compound of a Legree and Nelson, with an admixture of mannerism peculiarly his own. It was his duty to oversee all the gangs, the hoers, wood-cutters, fire-attendants, log-rollers, and toters. . . . One day, however, he was in a worse humour than usual. His face was longer, and malice gleamed in his eyes. . . . A young fellow named Jim was the first victim of his ire, and, as he was carrying a heavy log with myself and others, he could not answer him so politely as he expected. He flicked at his naked shoulders with his whip, and the lash, flying unexpectedly near me, caused us both to drop our spikes. Unassisted by us, the weight of the log was too great for the others, and it fell to the ground crushing the foot of one of them. Meantime, furious at the indignity, I had engaged him in a wordy contest: hot words, even threats, were exchanged, and had it not been for the cries of the wounded man who was held fast by the log, we should probably have fought. The end of it was, I retired from the field, burning with indignation, and disgusted with his abominable brutality.

I sought Major Ingham, whom I found reclining his length in an easy-chair on the verandah. Not hearing the righteous condemnation I had hoped he would express, and surprised at his want of feeling, I hotly protested against the cruelty of the overseer in attacking a man while all his strength was needed to preserve others from peril, and declaimed against him for using a whip in proximity to my ears, which made the Major smile compassionately at my inexperience in such matters. This was too much for my patience, and I then and there announced my intention to seek the hospitality of Mr. Waring, his neighbour, as I could not be any longer the guest of a man who received my complaint so unsympathetically. On hearing me say this, Mrs. Ingham came out of the house, and expressed so much concern at this sudden rupture of our relations that I regretted having been so hasty, and the Major tried to explain how planters were compelled to leave field work in charge of their overseer; but it was too late. . . In another quarter of an hour I had left the plantation with a small bundle of letters and papers, and was trudging through the woods to Mr. Waring's plantation. . . .

Strange to say, in proportion to the period spent at Major Ingham's, I possess a more vivid recollection of the night I passed at Mr. Waring's, and my thoughts have more often reverted to the more ancient house and its snugness and pleasant details, than to the other. As I did not mention anything about the causes of my departure from his neighbour's plantation, it was tacitly understood that I was only resting for the night, previous to resuming my journey next morning, and they did not press me to stay. I begged, however, Mr. Waring to do me the favour to send a buggy for my trunk the next morning. When it arrived, I repacked it; and, leaving it in his charge, I set off on a tramp across country to the Arkansas, rejecting many an offer of aid up to the last minute.

The road wound up and down pine-clothed hills, and, being a sandy loam, was dry and tolerably smooth. In the hollows I generally found a stream where I quenched my thirst, but I remember to have travelled a considerable distance for a young pedestrian without meeting any water, and to have reflected a little upon what the pains of dying from thirst would be like. I rested at a small farm-house that night; and, next morning, at an early hour, was once more footing it bravely, more elated, perhaps, than my condition justified. . . . I saw myself the hero of many a thrilling surprise, and looked dreamily through the shades, as though in some places like them I would meet the preying beasts whom it would be my fortune to strike dead with my staff. But invariably, on being brought to a proper sense of the scenes, and my real condition, I recognized how helpless I was against a snarling catamount, or couchant panther; I was devoutly thankful that Arkansas was so civilised that my courage was in no fear of being tested.

Just at dusk I reached the Arkansas River at Cypress Bend, having travelled about forty miles across country, without having met a single adventure.

Mr. Altschul's store, at which I was to devote myself to acquiring the arts and details of a country merchant's business, was situate about fifty miles S. E. of Little Rock, and halfway between Richmond and South Bend. I found no difficulty at all in entering the establishment, for I had no sooner introduced myself than I was accepted by his family with all cordiality. The store was, in reality, a country house of business. It stood isolated in a small clearing in the midst of Cypress Grove, and was removed from the dwelling-house of the family by a quarter of a mile. It was a long one-storied building of solid logs, divided into four apartments, three of which contained all manner of things that ironmongers, gunners, grocers, drapers, stationers, are supposed to sell; the fourth room, at the back, was used as an office during the day, and as a bedroom at night, by the clerks in charge. I commenced my duties in November, 1860, being warmly hailed as a fellow-clerk by Mr. Cronin, the salesman, and Mr. Waldron, the assistant-salesman. . . .

Mr. Cronin was indeed an artist, but Mr. Altschul did not appreciate him as his genius deserved. The proprietor laid too much stress upon his propensity to drink, which was certainly incurabale, and too little upon the profits accruing to him through his agency. . . . Therefore, though he was invaluable to me as a model salesman, poor Cronin was obliged to leave after a while.

Waldron in a short time found counter-work too irksome and frivolous for his nature, and he also left; then two young men very proud and high-stomached, and not over-genial to customers, were engaged instead.

But by this time I had become sufficiently acquainted with the tone of the planter community to be able to do very well, with a few instructions from Mr. Altschul. I had learned that in the fat cypress lands there was a humanity which was very different from that complaisant kind dwelling in cities. It had been drawn from many States, especially from the South. The Douglasses were from Virginia, the Crawfords from 'Old Georgia,' the Joneses and Smiths from Tennessee, the Gorees from Alabama. The poorer sort were from the Carolinas, Mississippi, Missouri, and Tennessee, the professional men and white employers from a wider area — which included Europe. Several of the richer men owned domains of from six to ten square miles. . . . Though genially sociable to each other, to landless people like myself they conducted themselves as though they were under no obligations. . . . their bearing seemed to say that they yielded to us every privilege belonging to free whites, but reserved to themselves the right to behave as they deemed fitting to their state, and of airing any peculiarity unquestioned, and unremarked by the commonalty. They were as exclusive as the proud county families of Wales. . . .

In time, of course, I became used to it; and, considering their anxieties, the malarial climate, and the irritating 'ague-cake,' they behaved well, on the whole. Their general attitude was, however, stiff and constrained. Each slightly raised his hat as he came in, and their 'Sirs' were more formal and punctilious than, as neighbours or fellow-citizens, they ought to have been.

My proud fellow-clerks were disposed to think it was the dread of the pistol which made them so guarded in speech and action, but I thought that it was the fear of compromising the personal dignity by a disgraceful squabble with men untaught in the forms of good society. Arkansas is sometimes known as the Bear State, and many of its people at that time were singularly bearish and rude. The self-estimate of such men was sometimes colossal, and their vanities as sensitive as hair-triggers. None of them could boast of the piety of saints, but nearly all had been influenced by the religion of their mothers . . . just as much as might enable them to be distinguished from barbarians. It is wonderful what trivial causes were sufficient to irritate them. A little preoccupation in one's own personal affairs, a monosyllabic word, a look of doubt, or a hesitating answer, made them flare up hotly. The true reason for this excessive sensitiveness was that they had lived too much within their own fences, and the taciturnity engendered by exclusiveness had affected their habits. However amiable they might originally have been, their isolation had promoted the growth of egotism and self-importance. This is the essence of 'Provincialism,' wherever it is met with, in country or in city life.

Few visited our store who did not bear some sign of the pernicious disease which afflicted old and young in the bottom-lands of the Arkansas. I had not been a week at the store before I was delirious from the fever which accompanies ague, and, for the first time in my life, was dieted on calomel and quinine. The young physician of our neighbourhood, who boarded with Mr. Altschul, communicated to me many particulars regarding the nature of this plague. . . . Nothing availed to prevent an attack. The most abstemious, temperate, prudent habits no more prevented it than selfish indulgence or intemperance. So, what with isolation on their wide estates, their life amongst obsequious slaves, indigestion, and inflamed livers, their surroundings were not well adapted to make our wealthy customers very amiable or sociable.

Though I had a bowing acquaintance with scores, only half-a-dozen or so people condescended to hold speech with me. The mention of these reminds me that one day one of my friends, named Newton Story, and myself were weighed in the scales, and while Story, a fine manly fellow, weighed one hundred and eighty-five pounds, I was only ninety-five pounds. . . . The frequency of ague attacks had reduced me to skin and bone. It was a strange disease, preceded by a violent shaking, and a congealed feeling as though the blood was suddenly iced, during which I had to be half-smothered in blankets, and surrounded by hot-water bottles. After a couple of hours' shivering, a hot fit followed, accompanied by delirium, which, about the twelfth hour, was relieved by exhausting perspiration. When, about six hours later, I became cool and sane, my appetite was almost ravenous from quinine and emptiness. . . . during the few months I remained at Cypress Bend, I suffered from them three times a month.

The population of the State in that year [1861] was about 440,000; and I find, to my astonishment, that now [1895] it is over a million and a quarter, of whom only about 10,000 are foreign-born. Neither the dreadful ague, which exceeds in virulence the African type, nor the Civil War, has been able to check the population. . . .

Every new immigrant soon became infected with the proud and sensitive spirit prevailing in Arkansas. The poor American settler, the Irish employee, the German-Jew storekeeper, in a brief time grew as liable to bursts of deadly passion, or fits of cold-blooded malignity, as the Virginian aristocrat. . . .

The Autobiography of Sir Henry Morton Stanley. *Edited by his wife, Dorothy Stanley. Boston and New York: Houghton Mifflin Company, The Riverside Press Cambridge, 1937.*

Report from Helena, 1859

Although the following letter is brief, Rev. Otis Hacket gives a clear yet succinct account of conditions in Helena.

~~~~

Mar. 15, 1859. This day resigned again my charge of this parish.

Arkansas
Helena—Rev. Otis Hacket

I find myself obliged to resign my post. I anticipate a few days in the dating of this, and give you my report to the first of April, at which time I wish my resignation of this station to take effect.

I designed to take my family back here again this spring, but finding it impossible to obtain a roof to shelter us, I have no choice but to leave.

Whether I shall give up Old-River Lake, I am not yet certain. It is an interesting field, and if I remain in the South, I shall very likely settle here. Though but little more than six months old as a parish, they are already both more able and willing to STAND ALONE than many congregations that have been established and ministered to for years. If I go there, I am in hopes they will undertake my entire support.

Helena will need still more of nursing. There are difficulties to contend with here that render it anything but an easy field to work. Our members are scattered, most of them living in the country, and the planters look askance upon the town, feel no pride in its growth, and take no interest in building it up. It is little, therefore, and in some instances nothing that
~~~~

they will give toward the building of a church in Helena. Besides, both town and country are now suffering severely from the effects of last year's overflow, and at this present writing we are greatly threatened with another. It is only our levee that keeps the Mississippi out of town and from some of the richest plantations in the country now, and, as the river is still rising, whether this artificial barrier will continue to protect us, is, with many, a question of absorbing interest.

But notwithstanding all drawbacks, Helena grows; and I am still of opinion that it is destined to be an important town, and doubt not but it is the policy of the Church to sustain a missionary here. If the Craig will is sustained—as seems likely to be the case—bequeathing more than half a million of money to the founding of a University here, this, of itself, will do much for the place.

Phillips County Historical Society Bulletin *Vol. 1, Summer 1962.*

The William S. Fulton Letters

William S. Fulton was appointed by the first Arkansas State Legislature to serve as one of its two United States Senators in Congress. Fulton served from 1836 to 1844. For a year, 1835 to 1836, he was appointed by the President of the United States to serve as Governor of the Arkansas Territory, succeeding John Pope. The following four letters from members of his family provide much insight to what life was in the earliest days of statehood. These letters have been placed together as a unit, rather than following the chronological order of previous items.

The following letter is from Lucella Howton [?], Fulton's sister-in-law, to Elizabeth, Fulton's daughter, who was attending school in Washington while her father served in Congress.

Fort Gibson Sep. 25th 1838

My dearest Niece,

Your most acceptable letter in answer to last, came to hand by, the Post-mail, and I reply to it at once. . . . I have nothing in the way of news, either to communicate—The Seventh Regement you know is ordered to florida, & will leave this post, as parts of the fourth redgement takes their place, of which their is no arrival as yet. I dred the comeing of more Cherokees amongst us, full as they are of unfriendly dissatisfied feelings. I try not to think of them, but I find that I cannot help, in spite of my efforts, but fear the savage wretches, I am miserable all the time, and shall continue to be, until I get clear of the Indian country. I am sorry that I cannot aggree with your Ma, in thinking that their is no place like Arkansas, to us all.—on the contrary I regret every day of my life, that any of us ever thought of makeing it our place of residence. for I would like to be where I could enjoy life, whilst I did live, and not to have it constantly harassed by allarms, & horrid fears of massacre all the time. as it is here. on the contrary I would not give one months residence where you are, for a, I can almost say—life time in Arkansas, and when I move again, I shall want to go as far that way as possible. but alas it is not as I please, situated as I am, but if I was independant, Arkansas would not I can assure you retain me long, but enough of this. . . .

I was more than grattified my dear Elizabeth, as you may suppose, to hear from your Ma, that you had acquitted yourself so well at your examination. I sincerely hope my dear girl, that you will continue your industrious habits, and endeavour by all your strength of honor, to excell in all your studies, by a perfect comprehension of each branch. The mear going ones, and committing to memory is of no consequence, without the understanding of it. which is the important matter. do not be affraid of showing ignorance by asking questions, you can never be too old for that, and it is what your teacher expects of you, to ask her for information about everything, that you wish to be informed of, & at the same time determine to impress deeply on your mind, & memory all that she tells you, you will find every word of it usefull to you in afterlife. I wish you to pay particular attention to all those matters, because I hear history, geography, grammar, deffinition & spelling, brought into conversation every day of my life. . . . I consider it necessary that you should be well informed of it all that you may be able to join in conversation, when such subjects are introduced. when you come out, as a young lady in society and having just returned from one of the best boarding schools in the United States, much will of course be expected of you, and of all things, be particular about your spelling. So much laugh, and fun, is made of bad spelling in letter writeing. do not be governed by my letters, as you find much bad spelling in them, but as I am not a young lady on my first footing, it makes no material difference. and your french too, I would advise you to pay particular attention to, we meet with it so often in the fashionable novels of the present day, and it will afford you pleasure to be able to read it. I know, for I am often vexed myself, at not being able to read it, when I meet with it, in an interesting book of any kind. . . .

With much sincere love to all, including Minnerva, I am your aunt

L. C. Howton [?]

Arkansas History Commission: The William S. Fulton Papers.

~~~~

Matilda to William

This letter is from Fulton's wife Matilda, who was at Rosewood the family home in Little Rock. Fulton was preparing to return to Arkansas after the current session of Congress adjourned and his wife was giving him a list of items to purchase and bring home—a long distance shopping list, so to speak.

Rosewood March 1 1840

My dearest Husband

I rec'd last Thursday yours of the 12 by Mrs. Lofton, also our presents. I assure you we were all highly pleased with them, all suited exactly except my shoes. they were all too small. I put them by for Elizabeth. I will send you our measures. I would like you to get winter—as well as summer shoes for us all. Indeed my dear husband, I think it would be a saving of much money if you could bring everything we require for our family for the year in the way of wearing apparel. However I hope we will not require much for myself nor children. The servants stand more in need than we do. I have not made them new cloth this winter. I could not get the men any kind of coats for less than 10 dollars. I told them we could not afford that. they have made out with their old ones. I think as you will be sending your books by sea you could put up such articles as would suit them in summer and winter. Let them be strong and cheap. Do not forget your stockings. we can not get them here for love nor money. I would like to have several pieces of cheap white cotton such as I gave 12 cents for. it is always usefull in the family. I do not wish you to bring me any kind of finery. I have more now than I can use for some years to come. All I want is a cheap plain black silk dress and some dark calico for next winter and white and colored cotton stockings.
~~~~

I know our dear Elizabeth will require everything when she is coming. Indeed I wish you would supply her with all necessaries. Things for parties and all companies. I know we never can stand prices here, for the most trifling thing they ask six prices. I am shure I do not see how the ladies stand it, dress as they all do. our nieces not excepted. I often [say or think] our daughter will never be able to keep way with them, and I sincerely hope she will never wish to do so. I hope she will have her dress maid fashionable and handsome. If you have my dress maid I beleave Miss Halady has my patterns. you must request her to make it larger I have gotten so fat. You must know it is good solid fat. I wish my dear husband if you have the money to spare you would make Sophia a present of a handsome, fashionable dress. She is very much in want of one, also shoes. She thanks you very much for the present you sent her. I am delighted that you have defeated Mr. Armstrong efforts. it was well for Edward you were there. he no doubt would of been entirely thrown out of his situation. I can rejoice two officers were both your friends. I think the folks will see that you have some influence at Washington. I expect poor Edward has had his character nicely scandalized at Gibson and every where else. It is indeed hard that we can not do as others do but we must not complain. I am shure any situation would be proper if we have to be separated in this way. If it was not that our enemys would assist so much in our downfall, but if you should be thrown out of the Senate I have not the least fear but that we can always make a genteel support. I assure you my dearest husband if a willing and ambitious disposition will do it I am more than ready and willing to do my part. You know my dear husband I never was afraid of work. We commenced this world without anything we can shurely begin again, indeed my dear I think we have great cause to be thankful for the many comforts and blessings we have had. If I only can always have my beloved husband and children with me it is all I ask in this world. I have been working out all this week and have had a good deal done. I assure you I make all hands move from the cook down to Julia. I have [?] laying out my yard. I hope we will have everything looking very pretty by the time you and Elizabeth get home. I am delighted to tell you all the shrubbery we got from Mabel is putting out beautifully. The peach trees are in bloom. The weather is delightful; it is as warm as May. I am going all the time I scarcely sit down five minutes in the day. I feare you will hardly know me when you get home I shall be so black and ugly. I threaten to make a foulface to keep the sun off. I hope we will have our garden and yards finished this month. Mr. Lofton did not get my clover seed says he could not get it for less than 15 dollars a bushel. [I said] that was too high, indeed I am glad he did not get it as I think it will be best

Edward was Sophia's (Matilda's sister) husband who had run into some political difficulties at Fort Gibson.

to plant corn. Father gave me the 10 dollars. I wish very much to have the back part of Mr. Harris' house white washed if John can spare the time. I think he is an excellent garderner–does everything neat. Oh how much I wish you were here to give me some of your ideas about things, oh my dearest husband must it be five more months before we have you with us. Is there no hopes of Congress adjourning before July. Give my love to my friend Mrs. Sevier. I feel very sorry for her. I hope Mrs. Cross [?] is pleased with Washington. Give my love to her, and indeed to all my friends. I enclose you a letter to Elizabeth, little Sophia expects your answer to hers, Margaret has a fine daughter a week old tomorrow. I have not seen it yet. Father's family are well. He brought me some [orchard] grass seed last evening to sow in the yard. I feare this letter will not be acceptable as it has so many wants. Allow me my dear husband to add one or two more–churn [?] soda for washing, soda for baking, caraway and sesame seed and hand ground cloves. You will think it is time to stop. Sophia & the children & servants send bushels of love to you & dear Elizabeth and accept my dear husband the sincerest love of your devoted wife

Matilda Fulton

~~~~

The following letter was written by David Fulton to his son the Senator regarding the establishment of a national banking system. David was urging William not to support such a move, though he never actually makes such a statement.

~~~~

Little Rock Jan 31st 1841

Dear William.

It is truly unfortunate for us that there is still no reliance to be placed on the time or certainty of receipt of our communications to the coast. I regret to learn that you had not on the 10th instant received any letter from me. . . . I think it was about 1st Dec. I first wrote and perhaps in ten days or two weeks after a long letter.

All matters in relation our pecuniary affairs present the most gloomy and indeed appaling prospect. the ruinous scheme of loaning money to the people for their relief and prosperity has proved as I feared & often said it would, to be the ruin of the country. And the active and intelegent part of this community have labored under the fatal mistake of most others in this case. that of plunging themselves in debt without consideration. If the eyes of statesmen cannot be opened to the evils of banking, the eyes of the whole community cannot be much longer shut, to the wide spread ruin that has inevitably overtaken our devoted country, from that cause and no other. Everyone who has collections [to] make say there is no money to be had. I find it so as well on my own as your accountant. . . .

The idea of a sweeping change under the new administration is still held out here. I presume that is to be the course adopted. If carried out it will (with the distress of the time) assimulate or realise the close of a war of conquest and subjugation. I am now square with the government and trust when called to settlement shall be prepared at a moments learning. Those however who cry out change and desire to see its worst consequence may be disappointed and perhaps the new administration will not be found so indiscriminate and proscriptive.

Is not the history of the presidential election most astounding. must not the knowledge of such a result through such means have a deep and powerful effect on the public mind. and must not the successful part feel the danger of their position and the most mortifying sensations under such an [undecipherable word] . . . I was told yesterday that specie was rated at 40 percent advance here. and we can make no calculation as to what state it may arrive. This is the effect of banking on credit capital without commercial advantages with exports to meet our imports, or at least a considerable portion of them. I question if our circulation at the present moment could be reduced but few debtors are able to reduce the principal by even a light curtail and the interest will be found more than the speculation which saddled them with the debt (in most instants) was worth. If with the light of experience and elucidation of the subject for the last ten years and the proof of the evils of a paper currency established by law with its fearful power Congress should now establish a National Bank, there is nothing in the whole catalogue of national evils from which the people have any assurance of remaining free and in safety. I trust in God there never will be a Congress so insane and regardless of their own and the public welfare as to inflict such ruin on our country.

We have had some snow and very changeable weather. both families are all in health.

Your affectionate father

David Fulton

This letter from Matilda's sister describes the difficulties and uncertainties of river travel between Fort Smith and Little Rock in 1846.

Fort Gibson July 5th 1846

My dear Matilda

The steam boat departs this afternoon and although much hurried and fatigued, I must endeavor to inform you of our safe arrival at home on the fourth day of July about three oclock in the morning. Only to think two weeks the afternoon before getting from Little Rock to this place, and the most fatiguing journey you can imagine indeed it will be difficult to discribe its horrors.

We only got about fifty miles above the Rock in the Mount Pleasant where we remained several days on board and finding no prospect of a rise in the river. Mr. Wilson concluded that it was no use to wait longer, and was so fortunate or unfortunate rather as it turned out as to meet with a man near, who had five excelent [?] horses two for the barouch in which he drove Harriet--the children, sister & myself. Mr. Wilson, Mrs [?] Davis of Louezia [?] rode the other three. And also a man with a wagon and four oxen to take the baggage. We were all very much opposed to leaving the boat as the propsect for rain was so very great, but Mr. Wilson became impatient and felt convinced that there would be no rise so off we moved and had not got twenty yards when the most violent rain came up, that I ever saw fall. We however got to a house about a mile distant and waited until the rain was pretty well over–and was compeled to start again in our wet clothing in order to make our stand for the night in time. And so continued on from that to Cap. Armstrongs [?] at the Agency through the hardest rains every day and mud up to our necks every step, and the worst of it was we had no clothes to change with on the way, the lode being so grate in the carage we could only take a few things in bundles and they being in the bottom of the carriage got as wet as we did. The wagon was of course behind us all the way except at one house where we had to stop to get the carriage mended. it then overtook us and our banbasces [?] was in a most awful condishion as you may suppose. We covered [?] them up at the boat in the thickest cloths we had not withstanding they got ringing wet. Mine containing my fancy bonnet black one and the little black hat beside some other articles were so much injured that I was compeled to give them to the servants at the house. The others were not opened but I fear by the time we get them that they will be as much injured. Harriet is in grate trouble about her elegant bonnets and finery. We stayed a day and night with Mrs Armstrong and then took the steamboat to this place. The baggage waggon had not got to Fort Coffee so we had to come off without it. We will get it I suppose by the next boat. Or our baggage at least. We found everyone well and delighted to see us. We had visiters immediately and ever since. So that I have scarcely time to write and the boat starting so guess at what you can't read. I will write again very soon. Edward is as fat as can be and all well and sends a great deal of love to all I have not time to say half what I wish so must bid you farewell. Kiss the children most affectionately for me. I want to see them most anxiously already. Your sincerely

Sophia C. Nowland

William S. Fulton

CHAPTER

6

Politics

A Fatal Fight in the Legislature

In the earliest days of the Arkansas Legislature, tempers flared and arguments turned into physical altercations, as evidenced from this letter of James Snell to his father in 1837.

Little Rock, Dec. 5 1837

Dear Father

Col. Wilson is John Wilson, representative from Clark County and the speaker of the House.

Major Anthony is J.J. Anthony, representative from Randolph County.

A most awful and melancholy encounter took place yesterday morning in the House of Representatives between Col. Wilson and Major Anthony, which resulted in the instant death of the latter. It appears from the best evidence we can reach of the matter, that the quarrel originated, while the House was discussing the merits of old Amos Kuykendal's wolf bill. The bill had just past the Senate, and had been sent to the House for concurrence, whereupon the bill was taken up and read, and on motion of Noland, it was suggested that the Certificate of the Justice accompany the account of all persons having wolf scalps; Mr. Anthony then moved to amend the amendment of Noland by saying that the signatures of the President of the Real Estate Bank be attached to it. Col. Wilson who was then occupying the chair, ask him if he intended an insult, to which Anthony made no reply, but got up to address the chair, the Speaker ordered him to take his seat. Anthony observed that he would not. Wilson again told [him] to resume his seat, Anthony still persisted that he had a right to the floor and would keep it. The Speaker then left his seat, placed his hand in his bosom and drew an Arkansaw knife. Anthony seeing this movement drew his also. They then closed in each other. Wilson made a pass at Anthony, but failed. Anthony then made two passes, but Wilson received the blows on his arms. Wilson then made another pass, which ended the affair. He stuck Anthony in the center of the breast, made a wound four inches wide and cut two of the

breast bones in twain and then penetrated to the heart. Anthony expired in an instant. Wilson fainted having his left rist nearly cut in two, and his right arm badly mutalated. I never have witnessed such a seen of confusion and horror. It is awful on account of the two houses being in session. It will go very hard with Wilson. I shall write you more fully next week. You will notice that I am in great haste, I hope however you will be able to make out the contents of this.
Nothing new, all well–

Your Af. son,
James Snell

The House will reorganize itself today, that is assign a new Speaker. Wilson will resign, if not he will be expelled.

Arkansas History Commission: Small Manuscripts Collection.

~~~~

Governor Conway's Message to the Special Session of the Legislature, 1837.

That many and diverse political problems faced the governing bodies of Arkansas in its first year as a state is evident from the following address delivered by Governor James S. Conway to the joint houses of the State Legislature in November of 1837. The message is quite long and deals with a large number of problems; we, however, have selected only portions of the message which reveal those issues of more interest: the starting terms of office for the state's United States Senators, the construction of the Memphis to Little Rock Road, the Seminaries of Learning, and the trespassing of the Republic of Texas within Arkansas' borders.

Governor's Message

Fellow Citizens of the Senate and House of Representatives:
~~~~

By the Constitution of the State of Arkansas, the Governor is authorised on extraordinary occasions to convene the General Assembly. I believed such an occasion had arisen, and caused Proclamation to issue for your convocation. You have assembled, and as the general interests seem to require your attention, I shall without restrictions to the particular causes of your convention proceed to give you information of the state of the government and recommend to your consideration such measures as are deemed expedient.

Our constitution directs that no other or greater amount of revenue shall at any time be levied than is required for the necessary expenses of the government, unless by a concurrence of two thirds of both houses of the General Assembly. The act to provide for a permanent system of revenue for the state, does not appear to have passed both houses of the General Assembly by a concurrence of two thirds, and yet, by it, a greater amount of revenue is levied than seems required for the necessary expenses of the government. It will be percieved from the Auditor's report that at the present rate of taxation, the surplus produced up to the 1st Inst. is upwards of $18000. The fact that our Treasury is full to overflowing is truly gratifying; it is a pleasing, a cheering event. It indicates a provident legislation, and a prosperous people. But the Constitution prudently restricts onerous assesments upon the people. Taxation beyond what is necessary for the legitimate wants of government is oppressive and odious, and should never be imposed. . . . I therefore recommend to your wise consideration the propriety of reducing the taxes to the economical and legitimate demands of the government.

. . . It will be recollected that the General Assembly at the last session elected two senators to represent Arkansas in the Senate of the United States. The regular senatorial term is six years, but under the Federal Constitution the body is divided into three classes and the seats of one third of the senators are vacated every two years. The term of two years is called a Congress. Each Congress is composed usualy of two sessions. In legal contemplation a Congress begins the fourth of March biennially, computed from the termination of the first Congress. When a new state therefore appoints her senators, the duration of their terms is necesarily decided and regulated by these rules of classification. . . . By this political lottery one of our senators was thrown into that class whose term will expire on the third March eighteen hundred and forty one, the other in that whose term closed on the third of March eighteen hundred and thirty seven. You will percieve a vacancy was thus produced in our Federal representation. The Constitution of the United States says, "if vacancies happen by resignation or otherwise during the recess of the Legislature of any state, the Executive thereof may make temporary appointments until the next meeting of the Legislature, which shall then fill such vacancies. . . ." I thought proper to exercise the prerogative granted by the Constitution, and accordingly appointed Ambrose H. Sevier to supply said vacancy, and he now holds his seat by virtue of executive authority. It is therefore incumbent on you at your present session to elect a United States senator for the term of six years from the third of March, eighteen hundred and thirty seven.

~~~~

There follows discussion of judgeship appointments, allocation of land for Seminaries of Learning, the legality of land procured for building the State House, the building of jails and a state penitentiary, the design for the State Seal and the acquisition of salt springs in the Red River bottoms. Governor Conway also reports on the progress of the National Road from Memphis to Little Rock and the funding which will be necessary for building various state roads within the boundaries of Arkansas. The establishment of the State Bank of Arkansas is discussed along with the current rate of interest to be charged on loans.

The General Assembly at its last session adopted a resolution, instructing our Senators and requesting our representative in Congress to procure if practicable the passage of an act to authorize the Governor of Arkansas to change any that he might deem proper of the locations made of the seventy two sections granted by Congress to the Territory of Arkansas for a Seminary of Learning. Congress have not passed such an act, and I of course have not changed any of the locations. If this benevolent grant be judiciously expended, its good effects will be long happily felt by our country. It is a deplorable fact that we have not a single public institution of learning in our state, and are almost destitute of good common schools. The subject of education is one of deep interest and vital importance to our state; it should engage the serious consideration and wise action of the General Assembly. Let it not be postponed, the time is at hand when a public seminary should be commenced. Why delay it? We have the means, and the best interests of the people demand its establishment. I recommend to the Legislature the adoption of such measures on the subject as will ensure the speedy erection of a much needed seminary.

In May last I recieved information that the Republic of Texas had by legislative enactment created a land district, including all that section of the state lying between the main Red river and the sulphur forks, thus
~~~~

embracing the entire county of Miller and about half of the county of Lafayette. Apprehending serious collisions from this unwarrantable assumption by Texas, I caused the Secretary of State of the United States to be promptly apprised of this trespass upon our rights. He gave the [untelligible words] and specified that the National "government will suffer no encroachment upon its occupied territory by the government of Texas." As the general government has thus pledged itself it is presumed all proper and necessary means have been resorted to, to arrest the intrusions complained of, and to prevent their occurrence. It is earnestly hoped however that the United States government will percieve, and duly appreciate the importance of a speedy establishment and emphatic designation of the line between her territory and that of Texas. The government of the United States has purchased a site for an arsenal adjacent to the city of Little Rock, and preparations are now being made to commence the erection of the necessary buildings. The Secretary at War in a communication received from him on the subject asks that the General Assembly be requested to grant to the United States jurisdiction over the land purchased for this depot of arms. I recommend the subject to your consideration, and suggest the propriety of your granting to the Federal Government this usual and necessary jurisdiction. It is the duty, and should be the policy of every government to extend to her citizens in all quarters ample protection. But upon the National Government besides the claim which Arkansas has in common with the other states of the Union, many peculiar circumstances connected with her geographical situation, and resulting from the policy of the United States government, demand in an especial manner that protecting care.

The unsettled and much disturbed Republic of Texas adjoins our state. That she and the government of Mexico will be warring for years to come is most probable. In what manner or to what extent Arkansas would be affected by a protracted warfare between these two powers, it is impossible to foretell. The government of the United States is at peace with both, but neither seems satisfied with the policy adopted towards them, and we are left to conjecture how this seeming dissatisfaction may result. The National government in opposition to our repeated remonstrances, has crowded upon the immediate border of our state numerous tribes of warlike Indians, many of whom were brought in irons and thus forced to become our unwelcome neighbors, with all their vengeful feeling aroused against the whites from being conquored, chained and driven from their homes and the graves of their ancestors. With a sparse population and limited resources, we have undertaken the burdens of self-government, and we are weak in the number of our soldiers, and almost destitute of munitions of war. Wise policy would seem to indicate that a people, so exposed, young and helpless should be on the alert with their applications to the proper source for means of protection and safety. The great importance of the establishment in our state of an arsenal on a large and respectable scale well stored with munitions of war, will be conceded by all who understand our situation. . . . I cannot too strongly press upon your consideration the vast importance to Arkansas of having this repository for munitions of war commensurate with the demands and necessities of our people. I hope the National government may yet take a proper view of this subject, and I recommend that the General Assembly ask of the Congress of the United States an additional appropriation for this object, of at least $150,000, that the plan may be enlarged and the arsenal constructed upon a respectable and suitable scale.

From documents in the office of the Surveyor General of Arkansas, it appears that the public surveys of eight hundred and sixty six townships of land are complete, one hundred and twenty three in progress, and six hundred and seventy five not commenced, forming in the agregate sixteen hundred and sixty four townships. . . . Each of these townships contains thirty six sections, one mile square. It will thus be percieved that the state of Arkansas comprises the extensive territory of near sixty thousand square miles. . . .

Few states in the union possess more local advantages than Arkansas; her climate is mild and healthful, her territory large and fertile and abounds with valuable salt and medicinal springs. . . . Arkansas has likewise peculiar facilities of navigation. . . . Besides these physical, agricultural and commercial advantages, she presents a wide field to the man of science. . . . These are facts that speak for themselves and promise us flattering things. . . . The geographer and explorer have not rendered our state justice. The one tacitly passes over her felicitous position and rich resources, and the other too often gives her a disreputable name, or sanctions and endorses gross misrepresentations of the country and slanders on the people. Notwithstanding the defamatory imputations heaped upon her, Arkansas is fast advancing to that wealth and importance to which her geographical locations and rich resources entitle her. . . . Her citizens have enjoyed good health during the seasons and had a tide of prosperity in their affairs. Her husbandman has abundant crops and reaps this year an extraordinary harvest. . . . In a word, our honest, industrious citizens in every avocation are succeeding well and surrounding themselves with the conveniences and comforts of life. . . . When I view the pregnant subjects that must necisarily claim your attention and require your actions, I feel an anxiety for happy issues, only equaled by the confidence reposed in your intelligence, wisdom and patriotism. . . . Rest assured gentlemen that you shall have my zealous cooperation for the success of any constitutional measure calculated to promote the interests of our constituents and the welfare of our country.

Little Rock, November 6th 1837.

J. S. Conway.

Arkansas History Commission: L. C. Gulley Collection.

~~~~

Feuding in Marion County

Growing up is a temptuous experience for individuals and states alike. Certainly the growing up of Marion County was heated by a feud between two factions of leadership. The following letters offer a view of the magnitude of the feud, if not the percipitating reason.

The first letter comes from a private citizen, serving in the Militia, to Governor Roan.

Crooked Creek Carroll Co. Oct. 15th [18]49

Dear Sir

Yet but seldom I have troubled you in the way of writing and at the same time beleaving you would like to hear from these *diggins*, I have just returned from Marion County, and the excitement is truly great. Genl Wood and his men has taken Jesse Everett, Alex Cowen, Robert Adams, and _____ Stratten, and true bills was found, by the Grand Jurors, of Marion County, for the murder of the three Kings, The Tutt party wants the law executed, and I do think if it was not for Genl. Wood and command, the Tutt Party would shear the same fate of the Kings. I am truly sorry to see such excitement. it extends in Searcy and Marion Co—there is none in this. Our citizens wishes the law executed—our friend J. D. Shaw is strongly implicated with the Everetts. I have thought proper to write to you and wish it considered by you as confidential. My family is in good health and your friend who you will see before this reaches you, who doubtless will tell you all the perticulars, please write me a line to Yellville, I am Capt. of the Carroll Company Headquarters at Yellville.
~~~~

I am yours respectfully,

Wm. C. Mitchell

Confidential

The second letter is a personal, though not official, report from Adjutant General Wood of the Arkansas Militia to Governor Roan.

Headquarters Yellville Marion County, Arkansas
Oct. 13 AD 1849

To His Excellency John Seldon Roan Gov of the state of Arkansas

Sir:

The circuit court at this place adjourned this evening untill court in course: And I learn from Mr. John H. Byers the attorney for the state that the prisoners who, I informed you I had arrested, were indicted for the murder of the kings–the prisoners are Nelson Stratton, Jessee N. Everett, Robert Adams, and Alexander Cowin. They are all indicted for the murder of William L. King Sen., William L. King Jr., and Loomis L. King–seperate indictments for each individual murdered. This evening I received a written request from John Hargrave the sherriff of this county requesting me to assist him in aiding the civil authorities in supporting the laws and maintaining the peace in the county: the sherriff also represents to me, that he does not believe he can find twentyfive men in this county who is not highly prejudiced on one side or the other–and that it will be utterly impossible for him to keep the prisoners himself in this county; and also that he does not believe that he could safely take them out of this county–

Now sir, I am of opinion that nothing but my arrival at this point, with my command saved the county from one of the bloodiest scenes witnessed in a civilized land. The members of the bar have expressed their opinion that had I not arrived at Lebanon, no court would have been holden at that point–nor at this place and it appears a general impression that a general battle would have ensued between the parties–It is very dificult to inform you fully the state of excitement here–And there are many persons here who I think are in danger of being shot down. The excitement reaches all classes, and conditions of life, and the fire of a gun is noticed by all with apparent anxiety–I am clearly of opinion that bloody deeds will be perpetrated here if I remove my troops from here–The company consisted originally, and does now consist of seventy five men, a Captain one Lieutenant–Maj Cox is my aid, and also serjant in case of sickness amongst the troops. I have given express orders to Captain Mitchell, to be as saving and prudent in the disbursement of money as possible–and I am of opinion that he will act with much prudence in the matter.

Now with respect to my position here I have this to say: . . . my presence here is gauling to the friends of the prisoners. It is true many of the friends of the prisoners appear to be quite friendly and express themselves in favors of my remaining here; but it is evident that but few of them are sincere–and it will take a strong guard to keep them all in check. Place the prisoners in the hands or under the controll of one party, and it is litterly setting them at liberty– place them under the controll of the other party and a war must ensue –such, sir, is as near as I can represent to you the condition of affairs here–and I am sorry to say that if there is any difference as to the peace of Searcy or Marion County, it is in favor of Marion –I think I will send some of the troops into Searcy in a few days– The prisoners have many friends there, and they appear to be resolved in takeing the law into their own hands and go in armed parties threatening and ordering whomsoever they please to leave the country There are six others whose names and personal descriptions I give you below, who are equally guilty with the prisoners and were present aiding and abetting in the murder of the Kings, but who have not been arrested. . . . I recommend for your consideration, the propriety of offering such a reward as will induce persons to bring these desperadoes to justice–Now sir I will remain at this point untill further orders from you–and I wish you to give me immediately on the receipt of this such orders as may appear to your Excellency best in this office–

You will be careful to send all communications to me at this point by Batesville.

The Everett party are useing all and every means in the reach of a mad and infuriated party to pison the minds of the people and strangers against the oposite party . . . I learn that some of the Everett party will be down to see you, and no doubt will make many statements contradictory to my communications–but sir, I have been careful in noticing how matters are arranged and have given you a statement from facts.–

I write you this for your own special information and not by way of report–I have kept copies of all orders and communications, and as soon as I can leave here, I will make you a full and detailed report

Yours respectfully

A. Wood
Adj. General of Arkansas

Arkansas History Commission: Small Manuscripts Collection.

The Chester Ashley Letters

Chester Ashley was elected to the United States Senate from Arkansas in 1844, where he served until 1848, when he returned to Arkansas to become actively engaged in state politics. He pursued a business career in land speculation and railroads. With the exception of two personal letters, all of the correspondence reproduced here is of a political nature addressed to Ashley while in the Senate. The two exceptions are from a New York friend who was reporting to Ashley on the conditions of his father and sister, who still resided in New York. While these two letters are of an extremely personal nature, we reprint them for their revelations on coping with mental illness during the time. Unlike other items in this section, the Ashley letters are placed together rather than in chronological order with the other items.

The senator hears from a constituent in the Arkansas Senate on the question of annexing the Republic of Texas to the United States.

Senate Chamber Dec 28th Little Rock 1844

[Hon] Chester Ashley

My dear Sir,

We are still in session and some of the most important business is yet unfinished. . . . Your Letter accompanying the Bills introduced by Mr. Benton of Missouri has been laid before the legislature by an extra from the *Banner* office, and so far as I have been able to ascertain views expressed in your letter in relation to that subject meets with the universal approbation of this general assembly–Whether there will be any action upon this subject by the this General Assembly is some what uncertain as we have such a press of matter before us and all are anxious to get home. While we believe that the views expressed by you will be carried out by you and your colleagues,

Banner office, and so far as I have been able to ascertain views expressed in your letter in relation to that subject meets with the universal approbation of this general assembly—Whether there will be any action upon this subject by the this General Assembly is some what uncertain as we have such a press of matter before us and all are anxious to get home. While we believe that the views expressed by you will be carried out by you and your colleagues, therefore if we should not take any action on the subject we hope our delegates in Congress will not construe it to a want of interest in the views expressed by you on the subject of Mr Bentons Bill for the annexation of Texas—we believe that the subject of slavery either in the States or the Territories of the united states is not one over which Congress can exercise any Control and to concede the provisions of Bentons Bill with regard to the Territory proposed to be annexed; in my Conception to concede a direct interference with the rights of the people who may here after inhabit those regions to establish their own domestic institutions as sovreign and independant states or Sovreignty. The part of Bentons Bills which make it indispensable that Mexico shall agree too the annexation of Texas—is virtually denying the independance of Texas and disavowing her right to act only under the sanction and permission of Mexico—This at once places that great American measure (alike Vital to the well being of all the Governments concerned in it) Beyond the reach of hope, for Mexico will never give her sanction peacibly and it would be Repugnant to our policy to concede that Texas was the property of Mexico, and their attempt to get it by conquest—The fact that Texas has maintained her independance of Mexico for 7 or 8 years and has been Recognized as an Independant Government by the most enlightened and powerful nations of the earth, are the best arguments that her present inhabitants now enjoy the right consistent with their own Constitution and laws to make treaties for their common good. The United states should not then if it is desired to annex her, make the assent of Mexico neccessary in order to affect that object. And that assent will not be given, and when the great and paramount interest of our country shall demand that annexation and we shall be forced to reclaim that Country by force, that Mexico shall then have it in her power to bring up such an admission on our part in judgement against us and hold us up to the Ballance of the world as invading her rights and trampling on that Justice for which we as a nation so far have maintained a good name and of which we are so tenacious be pleased to try to have our Mail Routes established to. Having every confidence in your ability and discretion as well as the Ballance of our delegation to perform to our entire satisfaction your legislative duties: be pleased to permit me to subscribe myself your obd servant

P. F. Gaines

The senator is approached by William Woodruff, Editor of the Arkansas Gazette *about an appointment to West Point for his son.*

Dr Sir,

My eldest son, Alden Mills Woodruff, is desirous of being admitted, as a student, in the U.S. Military Academy, at West Point, and you will greatly oblige him, as well as myself, by endeavoring to accomplishing that object, by making application to the Secretary of War, for his admission on the first occurence of a vacancy in that institution.

Alden was 16 years of age on the 27th August last, is large and well-proportioned for his age, has contracted no exceptional habits, and is, I believe, sufficiently advanced in all the branches of education required, by the regulations of that institution, to entitle a student to admission.

By making early application to the Sec. of War, for the admission of my son, you will confer a lasting favor, on

Yr. friend and obt. servant
Wm. Woodruff

Hon. Chester Ashley,
U.S. Senate,
Washington City,

P.S.— I have addressed a letter to Hon. E. Cross requesting the use of his influence in accomplishing the same object.

The senator is asked to help war veterans obtain their certificates for land.

Residence Near Helena Arks.
Dec. 21 1847

Honbl. C Ashley

Dear Sir

My son Wm. E. Moore together [with] my neighbors John A Gilbert Phillip A. Gilbert John W [Fleenes] and Matt S Finch who served twelve Months as volunteers in the war of the U.S. against Mexico under Captain John Preston Company K. Arkansas mounted gunmen desirous of obtaining *immediately* their land certificates for bounty has requested me to ask the favour of you to use your influence with the proper department to procure them and foreward the sum to *me* or to their address at *Helena*. One of the above young men to wit Matt S Finch. Sold his claim on his return Home from the army whilst in New Orleans for Sixty Dollars on which sale he informs me he drew from the purchaser fifty dollars the balance to be paid him when the Script issues he has understood the [U. S.] would not regard those sales and desires his sent to me or him and that he will refund the amount advanced him as above mentioned The Other Young men has not incumbered their claims in any way. These Soldiers was under the command of Capts Pike and Preston and strange to say those Capts mustered or had these men mustered out of the service without giving any of them certificates of discharge Relying on the vouchers sent by them to the War Department on being altogether sufficient. All of the before mentioned men have made the necessary affidavits as directed (except French) and they presume are on file You would not only confer a favor not to be forgot on the names I have given you above by attending to their request but to the men in Company K to urge the forewarding to this address each of their claims to Helena Please give special attention to the names I have given you.

I am very Respectfully
your obt srt
Wm H Moon

The senator is asked to help the Little Rock Postmaster avoid paying a fine for delayed mail delivery caused by a stalled dray and skittish horses.

Little Rock Arkansas
December the 7th 1846

Hon. C. Ashley
US Senator

Dear Sir, we are reported by the postmaster Little Rock. On route for not delivering all of the mail on the 2nd instant. This matter did occur. there was a large mail a part in the front and a part in the hind boot and both did not contain it all. a dray was stalled just by the office and the horses to the mail coach were much frightend. so that the Deputy post man was kind enough to take the mail out of the hind boot himself and the bags inside the coach were overlooked and not delivered until morning. this driver is Thomas Gillum, who has been driving for us the last four years, and one of the best in the state and most trustyst I expect. You know him. I think very well. he is a very sober young man and him nor the Deputy through the frighte of the coach horses and hurry of the moment neglected the mail some how in the coach. Mr. Reardon tells me the first I saw of him that he had reported the case without comment and since finding out how the occurence all took place he will state it to the department. I have written to the department stateing the matter about as I have to you. Now if you will please give a little attention to this matter and save us from fine it will be a favor that shall be appreciated. Nothing strange here people generally well here a Legistlature yet in session and not the first act of importance enacted so they themselves tell me themselves.

Very respectfully yours,

Howel [Snapp]

~~~~

The following letters are from Ashley's friend in New York, concerning the conditions of Ashley's sister and father. Both letters are of a sensitive nature which should perhaps be kept private, but because they were included with his papers and because they offer some enlightenment on the mentally ill of the day, they are included. No aspersions on Senator Ashley or his family are intended.

Hudson 1st Feb 1839

Dear Friend Ashley

I have been thinking of writing to you for some weeks past, and have only procrastinated hoping to be able to say your sister [Lauraetta] was well.--Your Father wrote, giving you information of her insanity at the commencement–

It is now more that two months, since she has been a Lunatic, without
~~~~

one single interval, not even for a single moment—It is true she is not at all times equally boisterous, still, it is only when exhausted nature compels a little repose, that she is any thing but a wild and raving Maniac. . . .

I am satisfied, that this has been progressing upon her for sometime, even before your visit here.

When I reflect back, I can recollect many interviews with her that seemed strange, and yet I must say, I had no anticipation of a result like this. She is like many other unfortunate beings afflicted as she is, void of every consideration of delicacy, which was once her peculiar trait.

She has destroyed almost every thing she could lay her hands upon—Time after time she has been in a state of perfect nudity, until finally I believe that propensity was broken by the use of a straight Jacket.

Your father has made a lattice not a cage in one corner of the room, and there she is confined most of the time.—

My motive for writing is not to afflict, but to enquire what is to be done with this matter—I freely acknowledge that I think she is badly, very badly managed, although there is no want of parental feeling on the part of your Father; indeed I have never witnessed to any event that unman'd him like this—Never have I seen him weep like a child before—But he is an old Man, and not calculated for such a change and his Wife less We have thought of taking her to Doct Whites Asylum. . . and perhaps it would be best—The ole Gentleman hesitates. I suppose on act of the expense, which would be $ 60. per quarter—

My own opinion is, that the very best thing that can be done for her good, will be to take her either to Worcester or Hartford, and place her in the Asylum—My reasons for preferring these institutions are, that it will be taking her away from all her present associations—She will be amongst strangers and subject to that discipline which is neccessary for her restoration—

I have given this hasty detail, that you may form some idea of your Family's situation here—

And now what is your Father to do? His expenses are neccessarily increased by this affliction, and he has been without a Dollar, except what he has had from a few Friends—I have advanced him a trifle, and must more, for it is impossible for him to get along without. . . .

There is a small balance due your Father, but not enough to pay his present liabilities,—I think it likely that farm of yours has gone principally to pay old debts—

I have troubled you with a long hasty resume, and hope you will appreciate my feelings in so doing, and make all reasonable allowance. . . .

Remember my Family and self to Mrs. Ashley as well as to your Brother and his.
From your old Friend
[Name indecipherable]

~~~~

Hudson 8th April /48

Hon C Asley–
Dear Friend–

Having heard nothing from you since the death of your Father, I have made up my mind to trouble you again about his affairs–

The money you sent to me for his benefit at three different times, he has had whenever his neccessities required it, to the last cent, and he died in my debt something more than $100.–

I would not name this thing to you, if my circumstances were as good as when we last me–The truth is I have been unfortunate, through the bad treatment of one, that I supposed would never injure me–

When you was here you mentioned to me that any advances made for your Father by me should be repaid–Could I realize $100 at this time, it will be all I shall ever ask of any one–I have his watch in my possession which I shall give to any one you direct. It is worth probably about $40. So our Watch makers say–

There are debts due, to other Individuals to the amount of some $200.–

The real estate is claimed by Mrs Van Alstyne, and most of the personal property, but she says she is willing to give her claim to the Furniture etc, for the general benefit of the Creditors–Very little can be realized from this service–

You must pardon me for troubling you, as I should not have done it, had it not been for the conversation had with you, on the eve of your departure from Hudson. . . .

My professional services rendered the Family I have little to say about–

Will you be kind enough, to let me hear from you soon!
Very truly your Friend [indec]

Lauraette is trying to get a school in this City–I fear her mood is not sufficiently balanced to engage in an undertaking of this kind–She seems so desirous to do something herself, that when she talks with me about it, I did
~~~~

not like to discourage her on account of her excitement in the matter—

Arkansas History Commission: The Chester Ashley Papers.

Chester Ashley

CHAPTER

8

Slave Narratives

In 1937 and 1938 a project was instituted under the Federal Writer's Project of the WPA to collect as many accounts of life among the slaves of the South as could be collected. What follows is a portion of that project. Interviewers were sent out with questionnaires to locate and interview any former slaves still living and those people whose mother and/or father had been slaves and who knew anything of the slave condition. The interviewers worked in Arkansas, Alabama, North Carolina and South Carolina. While the results of the interviews are fragmentary, vague and perhaps unreliable in every instance, they do provide us with some idea of slave living just prior to the Emancipation Proclamation, and we feel they are worthy of having a place in these first-hand accounts.

Arkansas History Commission: WPA Slave Narratives

J. F. BOONE

My father's old master was Henry Boone. My mother came from Virginia–north Virginia–and my father came from North Carolina. the Boones bought them. I have heard that my father, Arthur Boone, was bought by the Boones. They wasn't his first masters. I have heard my father say that it was more than a thousand dollars they paid for him.

He said that they used to put up niggers on the block and auction them off. They auctioned off niggers accordin' to the breed of them. Like they auction off dogs and horses. The better the breed, the more they'd pay. My father was in the firstclass rating as a good healthy Negro and those kind sold for good money. I have heard him say that niggers sometimes brought as high as five thousand dollars. . . .

My father don't know much about his first boss man. But the Boones were very good to them. They got biscuits once a week. The overseer was pretty cruel to them in a way. My father has seen them whipped till they couldn't stand up and then salt and things that hurt poured in their wounds. My father said that he seen that done; I don't know whether it was his boss man or the overseer that done it. . . .

My father said they breeded good niggers—stud 'em like horses and cattle.

. . .

My father was whipped by the pateroles several times. They run him and whipped him. My daddy slipped out many a time. But they never caught him when he slipped out. They never whipped him for slippin' out. That was during the time he was a slave. The slaves wasn't allowed to go from one master to another without a pass. My father said that sometimes, his young master would play a joke on him. My father couldn't read, His young master would give him a pass and the pass would say, "Whip Arthur Boone's — and pass him out. When he comes back, whip his — again and pass him back." His young master called hisself playin' a joke on him. They wouldn't hit him more than half a dozen licks, but they would make him take his pants down and they would give them to him jus' where the pass said. they would't hurt him much. It was more devilment than anything else. He would say, "Whut you hittin' me for whin I got a pass?" and they would say, "Yes, you got a pass, but it says whip your —." And they would show it to him, and then they would say, "You'll git the res' when you come back." My father couldn't read nothin' else, but that's one word he learnt to read right well.

ELLEN BRASS

Father Free Raised

My father was free raised, The white folks raised him. I don't know how he became free. All that I know is that he was raised right in the house with the white folks and was free. His mother and father were both slaves. I was quite small at the time and didn't know much. They bought us like cattle and carried us from place to place.

Slave Houses

The slaves lived in log cabins with one room. I don't know what kind of house the white folks lived in. They, the colored folks, ate corn bread, wheat bread (they raised wheat in those times), pickled pork. They made the flour right on the plantation. George Harris, a white man, was the one who brought me out of Louisiana into this State. We traveled in wagons in those days. George Harris owned us in Louisiana.

Slave Sales

We were sold from George Harris to Ben Hickinbottom. . . . I don't know whether it was a auction sale of a private sale. I am telling it as near as I know it, and I am telling the truth. Hickinbottom brought us to Catahoula Parish in Louisiana. Did I say Harris brought us? Well, Hickinbottom brought us to Louisiana. . . .

Random Opinions

The white folks ain't got no reason to mistreat the colored people. They need us all the time. They don't want no food unless a nigger cooks it. They want niggers to do all their washing and ironing. They want niggers to do their sweeping and cleaning and everything around their houses. The niggers handle everything they wears and hands them everything they eat and drink. Ain't nobody can get closer to a white person than a colored person. If we's a wanted to kill 'em, they'd a all done been dead. They ain't no reason for white people mistreating colored people.

FRANK BRILES

I was born right here in Arkansas. My father's name was Moses Briles. My mother's name was Judy Briles. . . . They belonged to the Briles. . . .

My father was under slavery. He chopped cotton and plowed and scraped cotton. . . .

I have heard them tell about the pateroles. . . . Them and the Ku Klux was about the same thing. Neither one of them never did bother my folks. It was just like we now, nobody was 'round us and there wasn't no one to bother you at all at Briles' plantation. . . . It was way down in the west part of Arkansas. . . . My father and mother came from Virginia, they said. My father used to drive cattle there, my mother said. I don't know nothin' except what they told me. . . .

The woman that bossed me, she died. . . . she made clothes for me, She kipt me in the house all the time. She was a white woman. I know when they was setting them free. I was goin' down to get a drink of water. My father said, "Stop, you'll be drowned." And I said, "What must I do." And he said, "Go back and set down till I come back." I don't know what my father was doing or where he was going. There was a man—I don't know who–he come 'round and said, "You're all free." My mama said, "Thank God for that. Thank God for that." That is all I know about that.

ADELINE BLAKELEY

Honey, look in the bible to get the date when I was born. We want to have it just right. Yes, here's the place, read it to me. July 10, 1850? Yes, I remember now, that's what they've always told me. I wanted to be sure, though. I was born in Hicknem county, Tenn. and was about a year when they brought me to Arkansas. My mother and her people had been bought by Mr. John P. Parks when they were just children–John and Leanna and Martha. I was the first little negro in the Parks kitchen. From the first thay made a pet out of me. I was little like a doll and they treated me like a plaything–spoiled me–rotten. . . .

After Mr. Parks came to Arkansas he lived near what is now Prarie Grove, but what do you think it was called then–Hog Eye. . . .

It was the custom to give a girl a slave when she was married. When Miss Parks became Mrs. Blakeley she moved to Fayetteville and chose me to take with her. She said since I was only 5 she could raise me as she wanted me to be. But I must have been a lot of trouble and after she had her baby she had to send me back to her father to grow up a little. For you might say she had two babies to take care of since I was too little to take care of hers. They sent a woman in my place.

Honey, when I got back, I was awful: I had been with the negroes down in the country and said 'Hit' and 'Hain't' and words like that. Of course all the children in the house took it up from me. Mrs. Blakeley had to teach me to talk right. . . .

Mrs. Blakeley taught her children at home. Her teaching was almost all they had before they entered the University. When I was little I wanted to learn, learn all I could, but there was a law against teaching a slave to read and write. One woman–she was from the North–did it anyway. But when folks can read and write its going to be found out. It was made pretty hard for that woman.

JOSEPH SAMUEL BADGETT

My mother had Indian in her. She would fight. She was the pet of the people. When she was out, the pateroles would whip her because she didn't have a pass. She has showed me scars that were on her even till the day that she died. She was whipped because she was out without a pass. She could have had a pass any time for the asking, but she was too proud to ask. She never wanted to do things by permission. . . .

Father and Master

My mother's master was named Badgett—Captain John Badgett. He was a Methodist preacher. Some of the Badgetts still own property on Main Street. My mother's master's father was my daddy. . . .

Patrollers, Jayhawkers, Ku Klux, and Ku Klux Klan

Pateroles, jayhawkers, and Ku Klux came before the war. The Ku Klux in slavery times were men who would catch Negroes out and keep them if they did not collect from their masters. The pateroles would catch Negroes out and return them if they did not have a pass. They whipped them sometimes if they did not have a pass. The jayhawkers were highway men or robbers who stole slaves among other things. . . . The jayhawkers stole and pillaged, while the Ku Klux stole those Negroes they caught out. The word 'Klan' was never included in their name. . . .

CAMPBELL ARMSTRONG

I couldn't tell you when I was born. I was born a good while before freedom. I was a boy about ten years old in the time of the Civil War. that would make me about eighty-five or six year old. . . .

House and Furniture

I used to live in an old log house. Take dirt and dob the cracks. The floors were these here planks. We had two windows and one door. That was in Georgia, in Houston County, on old Dempsey Brown's place. I know him—know who dug his grave.

They had beds nailed up to the side of the house. People had a terrible time you know. White foks had it all. When I come along they had it and they had it ever since I been here. You didn't have no chance like folks have nowadays. Just made benches and stools to sit on. Made tables out of planks. I never saw any cupboards and things like that. Them things wasn't thought about then. The house was like a stable then. But them log houses was better than these 'cause the wind couldn't get through them.

Free Negroes

You better not stop on this side of the Mason Dixie Line either. You better stop on the other side. Whenever a nigger got so he couldn't mind, they'd take him down and whip him. They'd whip the free niggers just the same as they did the slaves.

Marriage

You see that broom there? They just lay that broom down and step over it. That was all the marriage they knowed about.

Rations

They's weigh the stuff out and give it to you and you better not go back. They'd give you three pounds of meat and a quart of meal and molasses when they's make it. Sometimes they would take a notion to give you something like flour. But you had to take what they give you. They give out the rations every Saturday. That was to last you a week.

Selling and Buying Slaves

They'd put you up on the block and sell you. That is just what they'd do--sell you. These white folks will do anything,–anything they want to do. They'd take your clothes off just like you was some kind of a beast.

You used to be worth a thousain dollars then, but you're not worth two bits now. You ain't worth nothin' when you're free.

Self-Support and Support of Aged Slaves in Slave Times

I ain't able to do no work now. I ain't able to tote that wood hardly. I don't git as much consideration as they give the slaves back yonder. They didn't make his rice. When he died, he had a whole lot of rice. They stopped putting all the slaves out at hard labor when they got old. That's one thing.

CORA ARMSTRONG

Ex-Slave and Riddles

I was born in the Junction city community and belonged to the Cooks. . . . When ever I do something and I knew I was going to get a whipping I said make it to old Miss. She would keep me from getting that whipping I was a [devilish] boy. . . . I never went to school a day in my life. Old Miss would carry me to church sometimes when it was hot so we could fan for her. We had palmeter fan leaves for fans. We ate pretty good in slavery time, but we did not have all of this late stuff. Some of our dishes was possum stew, vegetables, persimmon pie and tato bread. Ma did not allow us to sit around grown folks. When they were talking she always made us get under the bed. Our bed was made from pine poles. We children slept on pallets on the floor. The way slaves married in slavery time they jumped over the broom and when they separated they jumped backward over the broom. they were better in slavery time to my notion than they are now because they did not go hungry, neither necked. They ate common and wore one kind of clothes.

CYRUS BELLUS

My father's master was David Hunt. My father and mother both belonged to him. They had the same master. I don't know the names of my grandfather and mother. I think they were Jordans. No, I know my grandmother's name was Annie Hall, and my grandfather's name was Stephen Hall. Those were my mother's grandparents. My father's father was named John Major and his mother was named Dinah Major. They belonged to the Hunts. I don't know why the names was different. I guess he wasn't their first master.

Slave Sales, Whipping, Work

I have heard my folks talk about how they were traded off and how they used to have to work. Their master wouldn't allow them to whip his hands. No, it was the mistress that wouldn't allow them to be whipped. They had hot words about that sometimes.

The slaves had to weave cotton and knit sox. Sometimes they would work all night, weaving cloth, and spinning thread. The spinning would be done first. They would make cloth for all the hands on the place.

They used to have tanning vats to make shoes with too. Old master didn't know what it was to buy shoes. Had a man there to make them.

My father and mother were both field hands. They didn't weave or spin. My grandmother on my mother's side did that. They were supposed to pick–

the man, four hundred pounds of cotton, and the woman three hundred. And that was gittin' some cotton. If they didn't come up to the task, they was took out and give a whipping. The overseer would do the thrashing. The old mistress and master wouldn't agree on the whipping.

Fun

The slaves were allowed to get out and have their fun and play and 'musement for so many hours. Outside of those hours, they had to be found in their house. They had to use fiddles. They had dancing just like the boys do now. They had knockin' and rasslin' and all such like now.

Church

So far as serving God was concerned, they had to take a kettle and turn it down bottom upward and then old master couldn't hear the singing and prayin'. I don't know just how they turned the kettle to keep the noise from goin' out. Bit I heard my father and mother say they did it. The kettle would be on the inside of the cabin, not on the outside.

BOB BENFORD

Slavery-time folks? Here's one of em. Near as I can get at it, I'se seventy-nine. I was born in Alabama. My white folks said I come from Perry County, Alabama, but I come here to this Arkansas country when I was small.

My old master was Jim Ad Benford. He was good to us. I'm goin' to tell you we was better off then than now. Yes ma'am. They treated us right. We didn't have to worry bout payin' the doctor and had plenty to eat.

I recollect the shoemaker come and measured my feet and directly he'd bring me old red russet shoes. I thought they was the prettiest things I ever was in my life.

Old mistress would say, "Once on here, you little niggers" and she'd sprinkle sugar on the meat block and we'd just lick sugar.

JEFF BAILEY

I was born in Monticello. I was raised there. . . . I been a hostler all my life. I am the best hostler in this State. . . .

I gits ten dollars a month. The check comes right up to the house. I used to work with all them money men. Used to handle all them horses at the post office. They ought to give me sixty-five dollars but they don't. But I gits along. . . .

I father's name was Jeff Wells. My mother's name was Tilda Bailey. She was married twice. I took her master's name. . . .

My father's master was Stanley–Jeff Stanley. . . .

My father's master was a good man. . . . I was a little baby settin' in the basket 'round in the yard and they would put the cotton all 'round me. They carried me out where they worked and put me in the basket. . . . When they got through they would put me in that big old wagon and carry me home. There wasn't no trucks then. . . . when they got through pickin' the cotton, he would say, "Put them children in the wagon; pick up and put 'em in the wagon. . . ."

Tilda Bailey, that was my mother. She and my father belonged to different masters. Bailey was her master's name. She always called herself Bailey and I call myself Bailey. . . . My father and mother had about eight children.

UNCLE WILLIAM BALTIMORE

I was borned on the Dr. Waters place about twelve miles out of Pine Bluff on the east side of Noble Lake. My gran'mammy and gran'pappy and my mamma and my pappy were slaves on de Walder plantation. I was not bought or sold–just lived on de old plantation. I wasn't whipped neither but once I mighty near got a beatin'. . . .

Dr. Waters had a good heart. He didn't call us 'slaves'. He call us 'servants'. He didn't want none of his niggers whipped 'ceptin when there wasn't no other way. . . . Dr. Waters liked me cause I could make wagons and show mules. Once when he was going away to be gone all day, he tole me what to do while he was gone. The overseer wasn't no such good man as old master. He wated to be boss and told me what to do. I tole him de big boss had tole me what to do and I was goin' to do it. He got mad and said if I didn't do what he said I'd take a beating. I was a big nigger and powerful stout. I tole the overseer fore he whipped me he'd show himsilf a better man than I was. When he found he was to have a fight he didn't say no more about the whipping.

I worked on de plantation till de war broke. Then I went into the army with them what called themselves secesh's. I didn't fight none, never give me a gun nor sword. I was a servant. I cooked and toted things. In 1863 I was captured by the Yankees and marched to Little Rock and sworn in as a

Union Soldier. I was sure enough soldier now. I never did any fighting but I marched with the soldiers and worked for them whatever they said.

KATIE ARBERY
815 W. Thirteenth, Pine Bluff, Arkansas

The boss man—that was what they called our master—his name was Paul McCall. He was married twice. His oldest son was Jim McCall. He was in the War. Yes ma'am, the Civil War.

Paul McCall raised me up with his chillun and I never did call him master, just called him pappy, and Jim McCall, I called him brother Jim. Just raised us all up there in the yard. My grandmother was the cook. . . .

Old buckwheat cakes and good strong butter
to make your lips go flip, flip, flutter,
Look away, look away, look away, Dixie land.

Pappy used to play that on his fiddle and have us chillun tryin' to dance. Used to call us chillun and say, "You little devils, come up here and dance" and have us marchin.

My cousin used to be a quill blower. Brother Jim would out fishin' canes and plat 'em together—they called 'em a pack—five in a row, just like my fingers. Anybody that knowed how could sure make music on 'em. Tom Rollins, that was my baby uncle, he was a banjo picker.

I can remember a heap a things that happened, but 'bout slavery, I didn't know one day from another. They treated us so nice that when they said freedom come, I thought I was always free.

I heerd my grandmother talk about sellin' 'em, but I was just a little kid and I didn't know what they was talkin' about. I heered 'em say, "Did you know they sold Aunt Sally away from her baby?" I heered 'em talkin', I know that much. . . .

I never went to school but three months, but I never will forget that old blue back McGuffey's. Sam Porter was our teacher and I was scared of him.

. . .

Ain't none of the white folks ever mistreated me. . . .

Lord, we had plenty to eat in slavery days—and freedom days too.

AUNT ADELINE
101 Rock Street, Fayetteville, Arkansas

"I was born a slave about 1848, in Hickmon County, Tennessee," said Aunt Adeline who lives as care taker in a house at 101 Rock Street, Fayetteville, Arkansas, which is owned by the Blakely-Rudgens estate.

Aunt Adeline has been a slave and a servant in five generations of the Parks family. Her mother, Liza, with a group of five Negroes, was sold into slavery to John P. A. Parks, in Tennessee, about 1840.

"When my mother's master came to Arkansas about 1849, looking for a country residence, he bought what was known as the old Kidd place on the Old Wire Road, which was one of the Stage Coach stops. I was about one year old when we came. We had a big house and many times passengers would stay several days and wait for the next stage to come by. It was then that I earned my first money. I must have been about six or seven years old. One of Mr. Parks' daughters was about one and a half years older than I was. We had a play house back of the fireplace chimney. We didn't have many toys; maybe a doll made of a corn cob, with a dress made from scraps and a head made from a roll of scraps. We were playing church. Miss Fannie was the preacher and I was the audience. We were singing "Jesus my all to heaven is gone." When we were half way through with our song we discovered that the passengers from the stage coach had stopped to listen. We were so frightened at our audience that we both ran. But we were coaxed to come back for a dime and sing our song over. I remember that Miss Fannie used a big leaf for a book.

"I had always been told from the time I was a small child that I was a Negro of African stock. That it was no disgrace to be a Negro and had it not been for the white folks who brought us over here from Africa as slaves, we would never have been here and would have been much better off.

"We colored folks were not allowed to be taught to read or write. It was against the law. My master's folks always treated me well. I had good clothes. Sometimes I was whipped for things I should not have done just as the white children were.

"When a young girl was married her parents would always give her a slave. I was given by my master to his daughter, Miss Elizabeth, who married Mr. Blakely. I was just five years old. She moved into a new home at Fayetteville and I was taken along but she soon sent me back home to my master telling him that I was too little and not enough help to her. So I went back to the Parks home and stayed until I was over seven years old. My master made a bill of sale for me to his daughter, in order to keep account of all settlements, so when he died and the estate settled each child would know how he stood. . . .

"My mother seemed to have a gift of telling fortunes. She had a brass ring about the size of a dollar with a handwoven knotted string that she used. I remember that she told many of the young people in the neighborhood many strange things. They would come to her with their premonitions.

"Yes, we were afraid of the patyroles. All colored folks were. They said that any Negroes that were caught away from their master's premises without a a permit would be whipped by the patyroles. They used to sing a song:

Run nigger run,
the patyroles
Will get you."

LUCRETIA ALEXANDER
1708 High Street, Little Rock, Arkansas

I been married three times and my last name was Lucretia Alexander. I was twelve years old when the War began. . . . My mother and her children were their property. Her first master was Toliver. . . .

The first overseer I remember was named Kurt Johnson. The next was named Mack McKenzie. The next one was named Pink Womack. And the next was named Tom Phipps. Mean! Liked meanness! Mean a man as he could be. I've seen him take them down and whip them till the blood run out of them. . . .

My mother was treated well in slavery times. My father was sold five times. Wouldn't take nothin'. So they sold him. They beat him and knocked him about. They put him on the block and they sold him 'bout beatin' up his master. He was a native of Virginia. The last time they sold him they sold him down in Claiborne County, Mississippi. Just below where I was born at. I was born in Copiah County near Hazlehurst, about fifteen miles from Hazlehurst. My mother was born in Washinton county, Virginia. Her first master was Qualls Tolliver. Qualls moved to Mississippi and married a woman down there and he had one son, Peachy Toliver. After he died, he willed her to Peachy. Then Peachy went to the Rebel army and got killed.

My mother's father was a free Indian named Washinton. Her mother was a slave. I don't know my father's father. He moved about so much and was sold so many times he never did tell me his father. He got his name from the white folks. When you're a slave you have to go by your owner's name.

My master's mother took me to the house after my mother died. And the first thing I remember doing was cleaning up. Bringing water, putting up mosquito-bars, cooking. My master's mother was Susan Reed. I have done everything but saw. I never sawed in my life. The hardest work I did was after slavery. I never did no hard work during slavery. I used to pack water for the plow hands and all such as that. But when my mother died, my mistress took me to the house.

But Lawd! I've seen such brutish doin's—runnin' niggers with hounds and whippin' them till they was bloody. They used to put 'em in stocks. When they didn't put 'em in stocks, used to be two people would whip 'em—the overseer and the driver. The overseer would be a man named Elijah at our house. He was just a poor white man. He had a whip they called the BLACK SNAKE.

I remember one time they caught a man named George Tinsley. They put the dogs on him and they bit 'im and tore all his clothes off of 'im. Then they put 'im in the stocks. The stocks was a big piece of timber with hinges in it. It had a hole in it for your head. They would lift it up and put your head in it. There was holes for your head, hands and feet in it. Then they would shut it up and they would lay that whip on you and you couldn't do nothin' but wiggle and holler, "Pray, master, pray!" But when they'd let that man out, he'd run away again.

They would make the slaves work till twelve O'clock on Sunday, and then they would let them go to church. The first time I was sprinkled, a white preacher did it; I think his name was Williams.

The preacher would preach to the white folks in the forenoon and to the colored folks in the evening. The white folks had them hired. One of them preachers was named Hackett; another, Williams; and another, Gowan. There was five of them but I just remember them three. One man used to hold the slaves so late that they had to go to the church dirty from their work. They would be sweaty and smelly. So the preacher 'buked him 'bout it. That was old man Bill Rose.

The niggers didn't go to the church building; the preacher came and preached to them in their quarters. He'd just say, "Serve your master. Don't steal your master's turkey. Don' steal your master's chickens. Don't steal your master's hawgs. Don't steal your master's meat. Do whatsomever your master tells you to do." Same old thing all the time.

My father would have church in dwelling houses and they had to whisper. . . . Sometimes they would have church at his house. That would be when they would want a real meetin' with some real preachin'. It would be during the week nights. You couldn't tell the difference between Baptists and Methodists then. They was all Christians. I never saw them turn nobody down at the communion, but I have heard of it. I never saw them turn no pots down neither; but I have heard of that. They used to sing their songs in a whisper and pray in a whisper. That was a prayer-meeting from house to house once or twice—once or twice a week.

Old Phipps whipped me once. He aimed to kill me but I got loose. He whipped me about a colored girl of his'n that he had by a colored woman. Phipps went with a colored woman before he married his wife. He had a girl named Martha Ann Phipps. I beat Martha 'bout a pair of stockings. My mistress bought me a nice pair of stockings from the store. You see, they used to knit the stockings. I wore the stockings once; then I washed them and put them on the fence to dry. Martha stole them and put them on. I beat her and took them off of her. She ran and told her father and he ran me home. He couldn't catch me, and he told me he'd get me. I didn't run to my father, I run to my mistress, and he knew he'd better not do nothin' then. He said, "I'll get you, you little old black somethin." Only he didn't say "somethin." He didn't get me then.

But one day he caught me out by his house. . . . He had two girls hold me. they was Angeline and Nancy. They didn't much want to hold me anyhow. Some niggers would catch you and kill you for the white folks and then there was some that wouldn't. I got loose from them. He tried to hold me hisself but he couldn't. I got away and went back to my old mistress and she wrote him a note never to lay his dirty hands on me again. A little later her brother, Johnson Chatman, came there and ran him off the place. My old mistress' name was Susan Chatman before she married. Then she married Toliver. Then she married Reed. She married Reed last—after Toliver died.

One old lady named Emily Moorehead runned in and held my mother once for Phipps to whip her. And my mother was down with consumption too. I aimed to git old Phipps for that. But then I got religion and I couldn't do it. Religion makes you forgit a heap of things.

Susan Reed, my old mistress, bought my father and paid fifteen hundred dollars for him and she hadn't never seen 'im. Advertising. He had run away so much that they had to advertise and sell 'im. He never would run away from Miss Susan. She was good to him till she got that old nigger beater—Phipps. Her husband, Reed, was called a nigger spoiler. My father was an old man when Phipps was an overseer and wasn't able to fight much then.

Phipps sure was a bad man. He wasn't so bad neither; but the niggers was scared of him. You know in slave times, sometimes when a master would git too bad, the niggers would kill him—tote him off out in the woods somewheres and git rid of him. Two or three of them would git together and schemes it out, and then two or three of them would git him way out and kill 'im. But they didn't nobody ever pull nothin' like that on Phipps. They was scared of him.

We came to Arkansas in slavery times. They brought me from Copiah County when I was six or eight years old. When Mrs. Toliver married she came up here and brought my mother. My mother belonged to her son and she said, "Agnes (that was my mother's name), will you follow me if I buy your husband?" Her husband's name was John Beasley. She said, "Yes." Then her old mistress bought Beasley and paid fifteen hundred dollars to get my mother to come with her. . . .

Interviewer's Comment:

I'll bet the grandest moment in the life of sister Alexander's mother was when her mistress said, "Agnes, will you follow me if I buy your husband?" Fifteen hundred dollars to buy a rebellious slave in order to unite a slave couple. It's epic.

can be adopted I would be in favour of having the principa
building or head of the institution located near one of o
main roads, within from 7 to 20 miles of Little Rock.
Thereby in a great measure superceding the necessary
expense of making a good road to the establishment.
guarding against the evil tendencies of the young students
participate in the immorality and dissipation, common
in all cities of any magnitude, which are calculated
divert their minds from their studies and prove injurio
to them in many other respects.

With one fourth of
proceeds of the seventy two sections, five preparatory schools
might be established, subject to the supervision of the princi
teachers located at the head of the institution. — Three of
primary schools might be located at proper points to suit
people in the North Eastern, Northern, and North Western parts
the State; and the other two at points most convenient f
the people in the Southern part of the State.

I repeat that I should deem it unwise to draw from t
head of the institution more than one fourth of the procee
of the seventy two sections; and should think it impolitic a
injurious to authorize at most more than five primary sc
of the institution to be erected out of the fund.

I submi
these suggestions to the Senate, and hope if this plan is not
adopted, that the General Assembly, in its wisdom, will de
and adopt some other, which will insure to the people of
Arkansas, both rich and poor, as far as practicable, a
the benefits of a Seminary of Learning ~~and to secure to~~ of
the first class. Any legislative action upon the subject calcu
to cause the speedy erection of a Seminary of Learning, and to secu
to the State the greatest good, and its inhabitants the perpetual benefi
therefrom, will meet my hearty cooperation.

Little Rock Ar.
20th. Nov. 1838.

J. S. Conway.

James Conway

CHAPTER

9

Education

Governor Conway Addresses the Arkansas Senate on the Establishment of Schools

The establishment of public education in Arkansas was a slow and undoubtedly frustrating process. There was confusion on alloting the lands for schools as established in an act of Congress; possibly other matters of more pressing nature interfered, and even possibly some local politics hindered the process for establishing public schools. Certainly the War Between the States slowed the process some, but consideration for such schools was in the minds of the Arkansas Senate in 1838, as evidenced by the following letter from Governor James S. Conway, dated November 20, 1838.

Gentlemen of the Senate

I have received a resolution of the Senate, in the words following, to wit

Resolved

That the governor be requested to submit any plan or suggestion to the two houses of the General Assembly in a special message, that may be in his possession, in relation to the erection of a Seminary of Learning from the proceeds arising from the seventy two sections of land donated by Congress to the State of Arkansas.

Having no plan or suggestions in my possession except such as occur to my own mind, the earnest desire I feel for the Legislature to adopt measures which will insure the speedy erection of a Seminary of Learning, and the flattering propect of having immediate legislation upon the subject, prompt me, in responding to your resolution, to make such suggestions to the Senate, as have recently occurred to my mind, with a hope that, should they not accord with the views of a majority of the members of the General

Assembly, they will at least be found to be, such as are favorable to the convenience of the people of many counties remote from the interior of our state.

I do not believe that we could legally appropriate the proceeds of the seventy two sections to the establishment of separate and independent institutions under the law making the grant. But the idea has occurred to me that, perhaps, a Seminary of Learning might, under the law, be legally established with primary or preparatory schools located at points to suit the convenience of the people at a distance from the main Building or head of the institution. That preparatory schools being under the management or supervision of the principal teachers of the Seminary according to prescribed rules and regulations adopted and pointed out by law, might perhaps be considered parts of a Seminary of Learning although not located at the same point.

If under the law making the grant of the seventy two sections an institution could be legally established upon this plan, (and it seems probable to me that it might) it would certainly be more convenient to the people, and would enable many of our citizens who could not well afford to send their children to the head of the institution to have the benefit of the primary schools located near them and managed by assistant teachers according to the directions of the principal teachers of the Seminary.

I should think it unwise to draw from the main part of the institution more than one fourth of the proceeds arising from the seventy two sections and the adoption of any policy which would have such a tendency could not in my opinion but injure the institution by lessening the head in character and usefulness.

If this plan can be adopted I would be in favour of having the principal building or head of the institution located near one of our main roads, within from 7 to 20 miles of Little Rock.

Thereby in a great measure superceeding the necessary expense of making a good road to the establishment and guarding against the evil tendencies of the young students to participate in the immorality and dissipation, common in all cities of any magnitude, which are calculated to divert their minds from their studies and prove injurious to them in many other respects.

With one fourth of the proceeds of the seventy two sections, five preparatory schools might be established, subject to the supervision of the principal teacher located at the head of the institution.—Three of these primary schools might be located at proper points to suit the people in the North Eastern, Northern, and North Western parts of the state; and the other two at points most convenient for the people in the Southern part of the state.

I repeat that I should deem it unwise to draw from the head of the institution more than one fourth of the proceeds of the seventy two sections; and should think it impolitic and injurious to authorize at most more than five primary schools of the institution to be erected out of the fund.

I submit these suggestions to the Senate, and hope if this plan is not adopted, that the General Assembly, in its wisdom, will devise and adopt some other, which will insure to the people of Arkansas, both rich and poor, as far as practicable, all the benefits of a Seminary of Learning of the first class. Any legislative action upon the subject calculated to cause the speedy erection of a Seminary of Learning, and to secure to the state the greatest good, and its inhabitants the perpetual benefit therefrom, will meet my heavy cooperation.

Little Rock, Ar J. S. Conway
20th Nov. 1838

Arkansas History Commission: L. C. Gulley Collection

Miss Sophia Sawyer's School

Sophia Sawyer was a teacher-missionary among the Cherokees in their original home in Georgia. She was a part of the mission at Brainerd when the Cherokee Removal began in the 1820's. She objected so strenuously to the Removal that in 1836 she left the missionary field. Her friendship with the John Ridge family brought her to Fayetteville, where she opened a school for young ladies to teach the Cherokee girls still remaining after the Nation was removed to Oklahoma. Her dissociation with the Missions had caused her to lose favor with the Missionary Board and only after considerable effort was she able to gain the support of the Board of Foreign Missions for her seminary in Fayetteville. The following letters, some from her and some from her students, are addressed to Rev. David Greene of the Mission House in Boston and record a great deal about the school and something of Miss Sawyer's personal fortitude in establishing her seminary.

Honey Creek, C. N. Dec. 27, 1838

Rev. D. Green
Dear Sir,

After having been tossed upon a sea of difficulties, I have found a haven of rest in this island of hope, the house which I now occupy. We entered it last Tuesday as a place of residence and instruction. The first year in Arkansas has been to me a year of the greatest suffering that I have ever experienced. Not from the climate merely or chiefly; but from the moral and intellectual condition of the country, & from those influences, which I could not escape, & in which I must live & move without doing good. . . . My life, my health, my reason, & all that is valuable in existence, depend on objects about which I think, feel, & act. O to be able to turn the current of my thoughts & feelings, & stand where,

"My joys, my griefs, my passions, & my powers
Make me a stranger."

Mr. [John] Ridge has built & furnished a small house for instruction, just in the edge of a beautiful prairie; here I live altogether, except taking my meals with the family at the house, that is, for me, eight minutes walk from this place. A few girls are to occupy the house with me, & board at Mr. Ridge's. These with Mr. R.'s children & what Cherokee pupils can be gathered from families, who we hope will settle around us, will constitute my field of labor. Discouraging as circumstances are I know the Saviour can make me useful even here. Mr. Huss who you know is one of the best men in the world, has the care of the Church seven or eight miles from here. . . . He is a great favorite of Mr. Ridge. . . . Mrs. Ridge has more influence & moral courage; she has also a brother & sister, with their companions, here in Mr. Ridge's employ. Her sister, & sister's husband are professors of religion. Mr. Ball, her sister's husband, who is clerk in the store, is decidedly pious, & a good English scholar–seems a man of firm principle & good judgment. I hope much from him, when I wish to see the whys & wherefores in Arith. Other questions in science & theology I can note down & wait for explanations from Mr. Worcester & Mr. Wasburn. I never wanted instruction more than at the present. I fear I love the Bible, & desire heaven, for intellectual pleasure more than for Holiness.

Mr. Ridge has taken a stand in morals, & in favoring the Christian religion, that it will be difficult for a man of his habits & temperament to retain. He cannot hear truth without uneasiness. He cannot escape it in the position in which he has placed himself. He has tampered with the cause of temperance, by selling wine, until he had become disgusted with wine drunkards, & says he will sell no more. He has a most interesting family of sons. (John Rollin, Herman Aeneas and Andrew J.) who, if they follow the instructions he is causing them daily to receive, will shun the path of the destroyer, & loath the vices of their people. The only daughter (Susan), who is capable of sufficient age to receive instruction, is almost constantly with me–sprightly lovely child, full of budding fine. . . & if we are faithful, these germs of character will open into full grown flower & finished beauty of mature age.

I have received for attending Court in the old nation eighteen dollars & half. This is gone, I hardly know where, some in presents to those who waited on me during the paroxysms of fever at the different missionary stations, & some for shoes for myself, & to restore a blanket stolen from under my care, etc. The house which I occupy, and the furniture, cost from four to five hundred dollars–probably will exceed five hundred when it is completed. Such presents as Mr. & Mrs. Ridge make in clothing I receive & continue my labours in their family & among their people in the character of benevolence sustained by the patronage of the Board. . . . My health, from irregularity, & a want of compliance with directions given me in N. York had been miserable. Without positive pain, it was hard to conceive how I could suffer as I did during paroxysms of fever. During the first attack of fever I was at Dwight, with Miss Stetson, to whom I am under great obligation for what she has done for me, a stranger in this country. . . . I hear Mr. Wor.'s constitution will prematurely fail under the difficulties with which he is daily struggling. Though patient, cheerful, & contented, he is certainly flesh & blood, & must feel the complicated, perplexing, & overwhelming labours, that hourly press upon him. I do hope Mr. Vail will come to his relief.

Yours in Christ
S. Sawyer.

P.S. May I have the Annals of Education & the [Missionary] Herald sent to me by the way of Park Hill? Mr. Huss will go there often, I have seventeen dollars yet of the money of the Board–will try to do the best I can. Do try to sustain district schools.–The Indians can do more than they have done,–make then do it.

Fayetteville, Female Seminary,
July 26, 1841

Rev. David Greene
Mission House

Dear Sir

As I have a letter to write for the approaching examination, I have at the request of Miss Sawyer, taken the liberty of addressing it to you, presuming from all I have learned of you, that you would take a lively interest in the advancement of the course of education in this remote region.

I will give you a brief description of our seminary, its locality, etc.

It is in the southwestern part of town, on an eminence overlooking a widely extended and fertile valley, with numerous ranges of mountains in the distance, presenting the most beautiful and picturesque landscape that can be conceived of, the building is a frame, two stories high, twenty by twenty-eight feet, with a piazza above and below stair ten feet wide running the whole length of the building, with an enclosed yard one hundred feet square.

I will now present you with some of the rules of the school. We assemble at the Seminary at, or before, sunrise in the morning and receive lessons in writing until the ringing of the bells for breakfast (I think early rising has been of great advantage to the young ladies, and has enabled them to accomplish more through the day than they could otherwise have done) at eight attend prayers and reading the scripture, after that the various lessons of the day are attended to until twelve. The small children are at school only six hours in the day and have much time given them for recreation in the back ground.

Miss Sawyer has forty-eight scholars including twelve Cherokees. The examination will take place the first Tuesday and Wednesday in August next, which closes the present session. I think all the scholars now here intend returning the next session except Miss Adair, a young lady who wrote to you last summer and some two or three others.

The Seminary was dedicated on the fourteenth inst. By the Rev. Mr. Washburn, Presbyterian minister, who laboured at Dwight twenty years for the benefit of the Indians, besides preaching a great deal, he taught a school several years during his stay there and succeeded in doing much good, he has now left the Nation and is living about twenty-five miles from this place in the adjoining county of Benton. I do not think he will return to the nation again.

Miss Stetson, another of our teachers has left Dwight, I was truly sorry to hear of her having left, and hope the Lady that succeeds her, may prove to be as faithful as she has been.

Miss Sawyer wishes to be remembered to you, and requests me to say that she intends writing to you as soon as the session is out.

With sentiments of high regard, dear sir, permit me to subscribe myself your young Cherokee friend.

Nancy Drew

The following post script from Miss Sawyer was added to Nancy Drew's letter.

The house and ground about which you are perhaps tired of hearing is estimated by some at $2,000, by others $1,500, is now paid for except $500 which sum I have been advised, by a friend, a clerk in the bank, to draw from the bank rather than to give my note on interest as should the bank fail, as they expect it will, it would receive its one [own] notes and I be no loser, whereas should I give my note to creditors, in the failure of the bank, silver would be demanded. . . . Should health continue two sessions longer, with less success than has hitherto attended my school in a pecuniary view, I shall be able to pay all contracts and call the house my own so far as we can be said to own anything. Hitherto I have felt and acted as if the house belonged to creditors though it was made sure to me by deed, for should sickness or death prevent payment and the house be sold in this time of pressure for money I must nearly sacrifice what I have paid by selling for much less than its value. . . .

[Midst] all my collision with opposite characters, my sex has protected me not only from the pistol and bowie knife, but from insult and profanity. In one instance only I was told that I was out of a woman's place in transacting business. I replied that I had the responsibilities of a man to sustain and if he did not do justice I would no longer pain my feelings by acting myself, but yield it to an attorney and left him abruptly. This man has since become one of my best friends and has since told me that he neither understood my motives or character. . . . Old Mrs. Ridge is now on a visit here. She and her daughter, Mrs. Paschal, desire a respectful and grateful remembrance to you.

More than ever yours, S. S.

P. S. Jan. 5: Pardon this scrawl and I will never send another such while I am able to do better. Am reading Channing's Works and can scarcely take time to eat or sleep, such is the delight and sympathy I feel in his writing on slavery. Jan. 8: Is it possible he is not a Christian? I wish I could see him and tell him more of the poor slave.

Miss Sophia Sawyer

Fayetteville Fem. Seminar
June 1842

Rev. David Greene, Mission House
Boston, Mass.
Dear Sir:

We all have a composition to write for the examinations and Miss Sawyer told me, although I was a very young girl, perhaps you might be interested with the few lines that I have to write. . . . Miss Sawyer has been in very bad health this spring, she has had two or three spells of sickness though she has never left her school a single day, her friend sent her suitable food, the young ladies also were very kind to her; the sudden changes of the climate effected her constitution very unfavorably. . . . Brother Combs . . . is now writing in the Clerk's Office, he sends his best regards to you; we expect he will start to Princeton, to go to school soon, under the direction of Mr. Walker who is going to educate him at his own expense. Mr. Walker gave Miss Sawyer the land on which her house was built. She has a very fine framed house, situated in the southwest part of the town; her school house is twenty-eight feet by twenty. The upper piazza commands a beautiful prospect of the hills and prairies of the south; the room above is plastered and the lower room is ceiled and painted a dark slate color as high as the windows. She is very comfortably situated; her yard is 100 feet square, it is all sown with bluegrass and she has twenty-five different trees in it; she has some flowering shrubs. I will now give you the rules of the school, the first three days of the week we study our various studies; on Thursday and Friday we study Arithmetic, every morning Miss Sawyer opens the school with prayers and reading in the Bible. When the girls study Geography she uses the globes. Miss Sawyer has Sabbath school every Sabbath morning for the small children, in the afternoon the young ladies attend Bible Class which has sixteen scholars in it. I am studying Grammar, Geography, Polite Learning, Arithmetic, History of the United States, Natural History, definitions, etc. Every Friday and Thursday in the afternoon we recite six lines in the Definition book but sometimes we recite less than that. Thursday afternoon three o'clock, if you were to look in here you would see some ciphering on the Blackboard, groups of young ladies in each corner of the room. The small children also are scattered over the yard working on their slates. As you walk down the back street you will see the school house, you will then open the front gate and front door also. The first thing that will come to your view will be the Death of Napoleon, Pocahantas saving the life of Captain John Smith, and Bonaparte encamped; on the right hand you will observe the large map of the World; opposite to it, behind the stove, is the large map of the United Staes, also in the southeastern part of the room is George Washington, the first President of the United States also Lafayette standing at Washington's grave; and the Solar Sistem [sic]. In the northeastern corner are the Prodigal son in misery, and the map of the Indian Territory. I do a great many sums on the Blackboard; I am well pleased with it. Miss Sawyer has seventeen pictures down stairs; and seven maps also; she has thirty-three scholars. The two young ladies, Miss Obryant and Miss Hildegrand, that sleep at the school house, eat at Mrs. Shepperd's. As I said before I am studying Arithmetic although I am not very far advanced in it. I am also studying Natural History it tells of the Quadrapeds, Birds, Fishes, Serpents, Reptiles and Insects, it tells of the Whale, it is the largest animal of which we can give any certain account. The Greenland Whale measures from fifty to eighty feet in length; some of those found in the South Seas measure sometimes one hundred and fifty. Their tongue is capable of yielding five or six barrels of oil. I think the best of all my studies, I like Polite Learning, it tells of Arts and sciences, Theology, Religion, Philosophy, Physics, Mechanics, Hydrostatics, Pneumatics of Lightning and Thunder. The reason that thunder is not heard for some time after the lightning is seen is that the sound is much longer at arriving at our ears, than light is at our eyes for light moves almost instantaneously; but sound moves at the rate of 1,142 feet in a second; where the lightning acts in an extraordinary violence, it breaks or shatters whatever lies in its way. When the explosion is high in the air it will do no mischief; but when near the earth it may kill animals, destroy trees, burn houses, etc.

From your young friend
Martha C. Trimble

~~~~

Fayetteville, Dec. 7, 1839
Rev. David Greene,
Missionary Rooms, Boston

Dear Friend,

We came to Fayetteville on account of my father's death. When he was killed my mother was so disturped [sic] that some of us were fearful that she would not live under it. . . . Two Physicians attended on her, & she is now getting better. I think she will soon be well. I do not know much about the nation but I think it is in a confused state. Gen. Arbuckle the commander at Fort Gibson is trying to take the murderers but I do not think he will make out because it needs a more energetic man than he is to perform it.

Miss Sawyer has a school in this town. She has about thirty scholars, the most of whom are boys. My sister, brothers & myself are going to her school. I have gone through Ancient Geography & the Ancient History of Greece. I am now going over Modern Geography again, & I am studying Arithmetic & definition & we have paid some attention to grammar. I am learning to play on the flute. My sister studies Modern Geography, Arithmetic & definitions. Miss Sawyer will close the 20th of this month & will begin again the third Monday in January. Mr. Rettig the man who is teaching me to play on the flute is from the higher class in Germany, & a very learned man. His wife is from the higher class in Switzerland, & is a fine painter. . . . Mrs. Rettig has the promise of twenty two scholars in learning to paint. There is another school in this town; but it is for girls. The lady who teaches is from Europe. Her name is Mrs. Dixon. She has a good many scholars.

In this towm there are three groceries & the people sometimes fight with knives & pistols, & some men have been killed here, but the people do not seem to mind it much. In this town there are two saddler shops, two tailor shops–three blacksmith shops–one silversmith, one gunsmith, eight stores, & two taverns & a good many other houses. There are also several lawyers & they have a good deal of business. This town is a county seat.

The climate is various in this country. It is sometimes cold one day & the next warm. In the Summer it is very warm, in the Winter very cold.
~~~~

There are a great many animals in this state. The principal of which are deer, wolves, wild cats, foxes, rabbits, opossoms, rakkoons [sic], squirrels, pole cats & a great many other small animals. There are some panthers, a few bears, a great many wild turkeys, wild chickens, patridges [sic], & a great many other fowls. In the Nation there are a good many animals, but very wild on account of the indians hunting them so much. I have seen some animals in the nation, which the white people call gophers, but I have never heard the Cherokees call their names, & I do not think they have any name for them. . . . They live under the ground in winding holes in which they keep their provisions. They stay under ground all winter & make their appearance in the spring again. Their food is corn, & the stocks in vegetabeles. There are a great number in the prairies. Where they make their habitations there is a large pile of dirt, which they root up. Sometimes I see so many habitations near together that they look like a little village. Some panthers have been killed in town, & great many have been killed in the state. Some panthers have passed through this town.

Thursday, 19, 1839

There is a church in this town, which I forgot to name when I told about the houses. There is also a post & stage office.

Please to write to Miss Sawyer & the scholars & encourage us in the pursuit of useful knowledge, & please to tell me of the faults in my letter. Give my love to David Greene & tell him that I should be very glad to receive a letter from him.

From your young friend,
John Rollin Ridge

Fayetteville, April 3rd, 1840

Rev. David Greene
Missionary Rooms, Boston

Dear Friend,

Miss Sawyer says that you would be interested to hear from the school. She has, at this time, 47 scholars. I am studying fractions of Oral Arithmetic, Grammar, Definitions of words; and I expect to study Mattebrun's Geography, besides reading and writing, I have just finished my ancient geography. Miss Sawyer still keeps sabbath school, and has a great many scholars, she has upwards of 15 in the Bible class, she has four Cherokee girls, who came up from the nation a few days ago, and I expect they will attend the sabbath school, they are now studying Mattebrun's Geography, Grammar, reading and writing, one of them, grammar, and Parley's Little Geography. The school will be out about the 1st day of July, that is if we can keep the house in which Miss Sawyer is teaching until that time. There is another school in this town, but it is a female school, the lady that teaches has not near as many scholars as Miss Sawyer, her name is Mrs. C. Dixon, she came from Tennessee. . . . My father and mother live in this town, I have one sister who goes to school to that lady which I was telling you taught a female school. She is studying Geography, Dictionary, grammar and arithmetic, besides reading and writing. She reads very well, and can write almost as good a hand as I can, she has been going to school to Mrs. Dixon all the time she has been here. . . .

This evening the class in grammar tried to form three nouns in the possessive case, one in the singular number and two plural nouns, one forming its plural by the addition of S and the other without the addition of S. Now I'll try to write three in the possessive case such as bird's nest—women's clocks—girls' bonnets.

~~~~

April 21st 1840

Last Friday evening two more Cherokee girls came up from the nation and their uncle was trying to get board for them. Today our class in geography had to recite a long lesson about the state of Connecticut, and none of us knew it perfectly but one of the Cherokee girls who is in the class, and I was very much ashamed and I determined I would get it before I went at anything else. There are thirteen scholars in the grammar class and twenty three in the definition class and seven in geography class and twenty four writers, eight who read in Natural history, all boys, eleven young ladies who read in the first book of history.

From your young friend
~~~~

Enis Combs Trimble

Sat. May 1, 1840
Rev. David Greene

Dear Sir,

Here I am with 51 pupils of every age and character in this land of crime and outlaw where I am met at every turn "such and such" things are popular among the people let their private character or rather notorious vices, be what they may. They wish me to pass over and allow the female pupils to associate with such characters. What is highly esteemed among men is an abomination in the sight of God; I reply, I must decide respecting the company the pupils keep in the absence of their parents. Just in the trying hours of preparation to go where even the females of the family were of a doubtful character the fathers came and referred it entirely to me so this lady, where they board will have no more power to take these dear girls into improper company. Pardon me, dear sir, for this detail, the pupils are Cherokees. You must sympathize and pray for me. I often inquire why a poor, weak, sensitive female is thus left to stem the current alone. Where, again I enquire, are our talented preachers? That this ground is left unoccupied until vice shall have become so deep rooted that years of labor will be necessary to do what months could effect now. O for one enlightened intelligent Christian to come and aid in our monthy review, on the Sabbath. I have sometimes invited criticisms and referred doubtful questions to clergymen present until I became alarmed that the pupils would be led into error. . . . Mrs. Ridge has purchased a home in this town and I am aiding her in training her children. The changing weather affects me very unfavorably but I cannot yield to disease with so much in my hands. We have a kind physician next who is my friend and his counsel does good like a medicine. Do not cease to feel with me because I came here. The world is the field.

S. Sawyer

Flashback. *Vol. V, 1973.*

Female Sem. July 10th, 1842

Dear Sir,

Released from the cares and labors of school, I am sitting in the upper piazza, enjoying the scenery which is spread out in endless beauty before me. I am happier in the possession of the house and grounds we occupy than I anticipated any earthly possession could give. And I suspect much of the pleasure arrives from gratified pride that I have accomplished what I have undertaken. I shall not only be able to sustain myself in independence, but have to give to my patrons in the great cause for which I long since professedly gave myself. This, however, is only in prospect, I may be sick and call for aid tomorrow but should my health continue even as imperfect as it has been for the past year I shall in one term more have all contracts paid and something left to do good with. Faithful and devoted friends have sustained me the past season amidst the trials of illness and the efforts of enemies to destroy my character and school. My health is now very precarious, a few months since Mr. Washburn told me that I could not expect to live long; and I only asked for strength to finish this session. My cough and fever left me however by degrees and by the unwearied kindness of friends and pupils; I have been able to finish the term and settle business with a prospect of keeping one more session.

The Fayetteville Female Seminary, 1852

July 11th

The above was copied by a pupil. I have just to say the horses and drivers are waiting. I am going to the Nation to visit friends–Should I live to return and open school the seventeenth (Aug) you will hear from me.

Yours sincerely
S. Sawyer

Miss Sawyer's dire prediction that she might not live to start another session did not materialize and she describes her visit to the Nation. She is looking forward to a debt-free period following this session and also notes that Rollin Ridge is in the East pursuing his studies.

INDEX